SOULS FOR SALE

Souls for Sale is published as part

of the Max Kade German-American

Research Institute Series. This series

provides an outlet for books that reflect the

mission of the Penn State Kade Institute:

to integrate the history and culture of

German-speakers in the Americas with

the major themes of early modern scholarship

from the sixteenth to the early

nineteenth century.

SOULS FOR SALE

Two German Redemptioners Come to Revolutionary America

The Life Stories of
John Frederick Whitehead
and Johann Carl Büttner

Edited with Introductions and Notes by
Susan E. Klepp
Farley Grubb
and
Anne Pfaelzer de Ortiz

with the assistance of
Matthew Muehlbauer and Uta Kresse Raina

The Pennsylvania State University Press
University Park, Pennsylvania

LIBRARY OF CONGRESS
CATALOGING-IN-PUBLICATION DATA

Souls for sale: two German redemptioners come to revolutionary America :
the life stories of John Frederick Whitehead and Johann Carl Büttner / edited by Susan E. Klepp,
Farley Grubb, and Anne Pfaelzer de Ortiz ; with the assistance of
Matthew Muehlbauer and Uta Kresse Raina.
p.   cm. — (Max Kade German-American Research Institute series)
Includes bibliographical references and index.
ISBN 0-271-02881-5 (cloth : alk. paper)
ISBN 0-271-02882-3 (pbk. : alk. paper)
1. German Americans—Pennsylvania—Philadelphia Region—Biography.
2. Whitehead, John Frederick. 3. Büttner, Johann Carl, b. 1754.
4. German Americans—Pennsylvania—Philadephia Region—History—18th century.
5. Redemptioners—Biography. 6. Redemptioners—History—18th century.
7. Immigrants—Pennsylvania—Philadelphia Region—Biography.
8. Immigrants—Pennsylvania—Philadelphia Region—History—18th century.
9. Philadelphia Region (Pa.)—Biography. 10. Philadelphia Region (Pa.)—History—18th century.
I. Whitehead, John Frederick. II. Büttner, Johann Carl, b. 1754. III. Klepp, Susan E.
IV. Grubb, Farley Ward, 1954– . V. De Ortiz, Anne Pfaelzer.
VI. Series

F158.9.G3S68 2006
973′.04310748′11—dc22
2006003631

The Pennsylvania State University Press
is a member of the Association of
American University Presses.

It is the policy of
The Pennsylvania State University Press
to use acid-free paper. This book is printed on
Natures Natural, containing 50% post-consumer waste,
and meets the minimum requirements of
American National Standard for Information
Sciences—Permanence of Paper
for Printed Library Materials,
ANSI Z39.48–1992.

Contents

List of Illustrations and Map

Preface

The German-speaking people who arrived in the New World in the eighteenth century often had little in common. They came from different regions ruled by various forms of government; they were poor, comfortable, or moderately wealthy; they were urban and rural, they were skilled and unskilled, literate and illiterate; they were pietists, Lutherans, Calvinists, or Roman Catholics, if they were religious at all. They even spoke different dialects. Once in the New World, they scattered. Some assimilated quickly into English ways, some slowly; some settled in communities that remained German speaking into the twentieth century.

This diverse and diffused population has generally been considered too unwieldy to study as a whole, even if their English-speaking neighbors often lumped these varied individuals and groups together as Germans. Scholars have tended to study subsets of these Germanic immigrants, some by place of origin or place of settlement, but most often by religious affiliation.[1] One consequence is that more secular Germans have been largely ignored or studied as singular individuals—a few are widely known among specialists, more

---

1. Aaron Fogelman, *Hopeful Journeys: German Immigration, Settlement, and Political Culture in Colonial America, 1717–1775* (Philadelphia: University of Pennsylvania Press, 1996), esp. 39–42, focuses on emigrants from the northern Kraichgau region. Stephanie Grauman Wolf, *Urban Village: Population, Community, and Family Structure in Germantown, Pennsylvania, 1683–1800* (Princeton: Princeton University Press, 1976), looks at one small town with a predominantly German population. Numerous studies have used the voluminous records of churches and their pastors as the basis for study. A very few examples are the essays in Harmut T. Lehmann, Hermann Wellenreuther, and Renate Wilson, eds., *In Search of Peace and Prosperity: New German Settlements in Eighteenth-Century Europe and America* (University Park: Pennsylvania State University Press, 2000); Beverly Prior Smaby, *The Transformation of Moravian Bethlehem: From Communal Mission to Family Economy* (Philadelphia: University of Pennsylvania Press, 1988); Renate Wilson, *Pious Traders in Medicine: A German Pharmaceutical Network in Eighteenth-Century North America* (University Park: Pennsylvania State University Press, 2000); Dietmar Rothermund, *The Layman's Progress: Religious and Political Experience in Colonial Pennsylvania, 1740–1770* (Philadelphia: University of Pennsylvania Press, 1961); A. G. Roeber, *Palatines, Liberty, and Property: German Lutherans in Colonial British America* (Baltimore: Johns Hopkins University Press, 1993); and Jeff Bach, *Voices of the Turtledoves: The Sacred World of Ephrata* (University Park: Pennsylvania State University Press, 2003).

remain obscure—but not as important components of the experiences and varied worldviews of German-speaking migrants and their descendants.[2]

The descriptive and introspective autobiographies of indentured servants Johann Carl Büttner and John Frederick Whitehead, who were nominally Lutheran in religion, are as unique as their personalities, but they are also representative of the little-studied migrants who neither left Europe for religious purposes nor became active members of a sect or congregation on arrival in the New World. Their accounts also document the recruitment process for indentured servants in unusual detail and reveal the fates of two young men once they had served their terms. Whitehead's and Büttner's ideas and values, their economic and personal motivations, their encounters, successes, and failures, help to open up new directions for the study of German identity and culture in the Atlantic world.

Narratives of immigration to the American colonies are not particularly rare. Letters, journals, diaries, pamphlets, and memoirs have survived and have been extensively mined by historians to make the story of this country's origins more accessible. But the majority of the surviving documents were written by well-to-do or middle-class immigrants, who constituted only the wealthier half of those who emigrated from Europe.[3] Such immigrants did

2. Some of the well-known German migrants and travelers who wrote from an essentially secular point of view include Gottlieb Mittelberger, *Journey to Pennsylvania,* trans. and ed. Oscar Handlin and John Clive (Cambridge: Harvard University Press, 1960); Friederike Charlotte Louise von Riedesel, *Baroness von Riedesel and the American Revolution: Journal and Correspondence of a Tour of Duty, 1776–1783* (Chapel Hill: University of North Carolina Press, 1965); Johann David Schoepf, *Travels in the Confederation, 1783–1784* (New York: Arno, 1968). Less well known are Dieter Pesch, ed., *Brave New World: Rhinelanders Conquer America; The Journal of Johannes Herbergs* (Kommern: Martina Galunder-Verlag, 2001); George S. MacManus, ed., *Memoirs of Charles N. Buck: Interspersed with Private Anecdotes and Events of the Times from 1791 to 1841* (Philadelphia: Walnut House, 1941); W. T. Stauffer, trans., "Hans Stauffer Note-Books," *Perkiomen Region* 10, no. 3 (1932): 95–114; Anon., ed., "George Erion, The Ragman," *Der Raggeboge: The Rainbow* 11, nos. 3–4 (1977): 3–17. Unpublished is "Ein Kortzer Bericht von Caspar Wistar," trans. Rosalind J. Beiler (typescript); see Rosalind J. Beiler, "Caspar Wistar: German-American Entrepreneur and Cultural Broker," in *The Human Tradition in Colonial America,* ed. Ian K. Steele and Nancy L. Rhoden (Wilmington, Del.: Scholarly Resources, 1999), 161–79.

3. For instance, many clergymen wrote journals, letters, and narratives of their immigration experiences, as did merchants and landholders. See Nehemiah Curnock, ed., *The Journal of the Rev. John Wesley, A.M., Sometime Fellow of Lincoln College, Oxford, Enlarged from Original Mss., with Notes from Unpublished Diaries, Annotations, Maps, and Illustrations,* vol. 1 (London: Robert Culley, 1833); R. W. Kelsey, "An Early Description of Pennsylvania. Letter of Christopher Sower, Written in 1724, Describing Conditions in Philadelphia and Vicinity, and the Sea Voyage from Europe," *Pennsylvania Magazine of History and Biography* 45 (1921): 243–54; John W. Kleiner and Helmut T. Lehmann, eds. and trans., *The Correspondence of Heinrich Melchior Muhlenberg,* vol. 1, 1740–1747, and vol. 2, 1748–1752 (Camden, Maine: Picton Press, 1993, 1997); Gottlieb Mittelberger, *Journey to Pennsylvania in the Year 1750 and Return to Germany in the Year 1754,* trans. Carl Theo. Eben (Philadelphia: Joseph Y. Jeanes, 1898); Henry Melchior Muhlenberg, *The Journals of Henry Melchior Muhlenberg,* 3 vols., trans. Theodore G. Tappert and John W. Doberstein (Philadelphia: Muhlenberg Press, 1942); Julius F. Sachse, "A Missive from Pennsylvania in the Year

not share the experience of the poorer half, who arrived in the New World penniless and who, like Whitehead and Büttner, paid for their passage by selling themselves into servitude. While the wealthier travelers observed and recorded the conditions of the servant class, their perceptions, arising from their own privileged lives, are necessarily different.

Few of those who came as servants to the American colonies seem to have been inclined to write narratives or memoirs of their experiences as immigrants. Whether this was because they were only marginally literate or because they had no time or little interest in documenting their experiences cannot be said. In a world where literacy was measured by the ability to sign one's name, many of the immigrant servants who were considered literate may have been able to read only enough to make out passages from the Bible or a story in the newspaper.[4] Literary pursuits, however, were probably low on the list of daily tasks. In addition, nineteenth-century historical societies and archives were most interested in preserving the papers of prominent men, religious leaders, and elite families, so that many of the documents of the lower classes have not survived.

As a result, while a great deal is known about migration to the American colonies and about indentured servitude in general, we have little firsthand evidence of the conditions under which these immigrants traveled and served out their contracts. Why did they leave their homes and extended families? Why did they choose the American colonies as a destination? How were indentured servants treated? Where did they live? How were they fed and clothed? Were they given any freedoms at all? What happened at the end of their indenture? One can imagine that the servants' own answers to these questions would differ radically from the answers provided by the literary evidence of the middle class.

A few narratives by servants do exist, most by immigrants from the English-speaking world.[5] These autobiographical sketches have given us a more

---

of Grace 1728," *Publications of the Pennsylvania German Society* 28 (1909): 5–25; and Hermann Wellenreuther and Kurt Alands, eds., *Die Korrespondenz Heinrich Melchior Muhlenbergs: Aus der Anfangszeit des Deutschen Luthertums in Nordamerika, 1777–1787* (Berlin: Walter De Gruyter, 2003), for just a few examples. See also the story of Caspar Wistar in Rosalind J. Beiler, "The Transatlantic World of Caspar Wistar: From Germany to America in the Eighteenth Century" (Ph.D. diss., University of Pennsylvania, 1994).

4. Farley Grubb, "German Immigration to Pennsylvania, 1790 to 1820," *Journal of Interdisciplinary History* 20 (winter 1990): 428–31. See also Whitehead's initial, but partially conventional, apologies regarding his literary abilities.

5. See, for example, J. Stevens Cox, ed., *The Felon's Account of His Transportation at Virginia in America, by John Lauson* (St. Peters Port, Guernsey: Toucan Press, 1969); Daniel Kent, *Letters and Other Papers of Daniel Kent, Emigrant and Redemptioner, to which have been added a few interesting Hawley and Spackman Papers*, comp. Ella K. Barnard (Baltimore, 1904); Susan E. Klepp and Billy G. Smith, eds., *The Infortunate: The Voyage and Adventures of William Moraley, an*

complete and accurate picture of immigrant indentured servant life in colonial North America. But the institution of immigrant indentured servitude in colonial America and the early United States spanned two centuries and included the Welsh, Irish, Scots, French, and German in addition to the English.[6] Thus any additions to this body of literature are of great value. Narratives by servants who immigrated to British America from countries other than Britain are even more valuable because, until now, only one was known to have survived.[7] Not only do such narratives add to the fund of personal stories from which we can learn how individuals lived and fared; they broaden our ability to generalize about the conditions and treatment of the entire group of servants, and to determine whether significant differences exist across time and nationality, and between the experiences of native and nonnative speakers of English.

Precisely because there are so few of these accounts, authentication is of great importance. Since all writing is influenced to a greater or lesser degree by status, education, personality, and motivation, the information contained in any personal narrative cannot be taken as unmediated fact. Autobiographers may exaggerate their accomplishments or minimize their failings. Their memories of dates and events, and even their own intentions and reactions, can be faulty. They can omit significant details.

Substantiating such accounts can be difficult. Most immigrant indentured servants were engaged in agricultural labor.[8] Their masters took them to

---

Indentured Servant (University Park: Pennsylvania State University Press, 1992; rev. ed. 2005); Edward M. Riley, ed., *The Journal of John Harrower, an Indentured Servant in the Colony of Virginia, 1773 to 1776* (New York: Holt, Rinehart & Winston, 1963).

6. See Nicholas Canny, ed., *Europeans on the Move: Studies on European Migration, 1500–1800* (New York: Oxford University Press, 1994); P. C. Emmer, ed., *Colonialism and Migration: Indentured Labour Before and After Slavery* (Boston: Martinus Nijhoff, 1986); David W. Galenson, *White Servitude in Colonial America* (New York: Cambridge University Press, 1981); Farley Grubb, "The Long-Run Trend in the Value of European Immigrant Servants, 1654–1831: New Measurements and Interpretations," *Research in Economic History* 14 (1992): 167–240.

7. Johann Carl Büttner, *Büttner, der Amerikaner. Eine Selbstbiographie Johann Carl Büttners, jeßigen Amts-Chirurgus in Senftenberg und ehemaligen nord-amerikanigen Kriegers, Mit dem Bildniße des Versaffers* (Camenz: E. S. Krausche, 1828). This is a relatively rare book in America. Only five libraries in the United States list it in their catalogue, namely, Brown University's Military Library, the Cleveland Public Library, Johns Hopkins University Library, the Library of Congress, and the New York City Public Library. The editors also found an uncatalogued copy in the University of Illinois Graduate Library (now catalogued). See also Charles Frederick Heartman, trans., *Narrative of Johann Carl Buettner in the American Revolution* (New York: Heartman, 1915). Only 320 copies of this translation were printed, and only 116 libraries in the United States list this book in their catalogue—copy no. 306 is held by the University of Delaware Morris Library.

8. Frank R. Diffenderffer, "The German Immigration into Pennsylvania Through the Port of Philadelphia from 1700 to 1775. Part II. The Redemptioners" (part 7 of "The Narrative and Critical History"), *Publications of the Pennsylvania German Society* 10 (1899): 1–328; Farley Grubb, "Immigrant Servant Labor: Their Occupational and Geographic Distribution in the Late

relatively isolated farms, where they had few opportunities to engage in public activities. Their narratives may contain few references to people, places,
and events that can be independently traced through surviving records. When
we can verify portions of a narrative, there is no assurance that the entire
work is a truthful or typical recounting of the servant experience, but such
partial verification does lend credibility to the work as a whole. In most cases,
piecemeal verification has to suffice.[9] Yet the individual voice of the narrator
provides the information that cannot be gleaned from official documents and
general surveys of the importance of bound labor in the development of the
British Empire and the early American Republic.

Coincidence, serendipity—call it what you will—we have here a remarkable
opportunity. Two narratives by German immigrant servants in the American
colonies and early United States have survived and have become available for
examination. It is more than remarkable that the two authors were thrown
together by circumstance prior to their voyage to America, and that they
made their journey together on the same ship, the *Sally*, in 1773. They appear
not to have been friends, although they must have known each other. They
did not keep in touch with each other after their arrival in the colonies—one
was sent to New Jersey east of Philadelphia, the other to a rural county in
Pennsylvania northwest of Philadelphia—and they wrote their life stories
independently of each other, at different times, on different continents. John
Frederick Whitehead's account was taken down by a friend around 1795 in
the United States; Johann Carl Büttner presumably wrote his account during
the 1820s in Germany. While Büttner's story was first published in Camenz
(Kamenz) in 1828, Whitehead's was carefully preserved in a box, passed down
from father to son, and is seeing publication only now. The existence of two
independent narratives allows us to verify those portions that cover the same
events. At the same time, they provide two very different views of the same
situation. The extent to which each manuscript authenticates the other lends
extraordinary credibility to the rest of the stories; the differences allow us to
see how the rest of each man's story might be colored by his personal biases.

The two narratives enhance our knowledge of German indentured servitude and German secular tradition in colonial America. Büttner's and
Whitehead's memoirs would be of great value if this were all they did. But
they do far more: they inform us of three phenomena about which even less

---

Eighteenth-Century Mid-Atlantic Economy," *Social Science History* 9 (summer 1985): 249–75;
and Grubb, "German Immigration to Pennsylvania," 431–34.

9. Variations in the spelling of family and personal names as well as place names make this
sort of verification more difficult. For instance, Büttner's own name has numerous variants,
among them Buettner, Butner, Botner, Böttner, Bittner, and Pittner.

is known. The first of these is the role of agents in the process of recruiting employees to work overseas, mostly in the Far East, for the Dutch East India companies, the largest of which was the United Netherlands Chartered East India Company (*Verenigde Nederlandse Geotroyeerde Oöstindische Compaigne,* or VOC) which monopolized the spice trade in Southeast Asia. Büttner's and Whitehead's narratives both describe recruitment by VOC agents. A great many rumors circulated about the kidnapping of German emigrants and their forced servitude in America via the transatlantic redemptioner servant system.[10] Büttner's and Whitehead's stories allow us to compare what is known about the transatlantic redemptioner system to the process of recruitment by VOC agents, or soul sellers, as they were labeled by those who feared them. It becomes apparent that the tales of kidnappers may well have been confused references to VOC recruiters rather than to shippers involved in the transatlantic redemptioner system.

Second, these narratives inform us that there was a category of immigrant to the colonies of which we were previously unaware. We know that both the well-to-do and the poor immigrated intentionally. While they came under radically different circumstances, both groups purposely chose to immigrate. We also recognize a second category of immigrants, those who came because they were under a sentence of penal servitude—mostly English convicts.[11] But Whitehead and Büttner appear to represent a third category: those who were, for lack of a better term, accidental emigrants, people for whom migration to the American colonies was the unintended result of plans gone awry.

Finally, little is known about how European immigrant servants to America fared after their initial labor contracts were completed, particularly in the late colonial period, and we are especially short of firsthand accounts in this area. Did independence lead to success or disappointment? The postservitude careers portrayed by Whitehead and Büttner are as unexpected, complex, and informative as can be. Success as an outcome of migration to America was not automatic. Whitehead, who stayed in America, appears to have experienced more economic hardship after being freed than did Büttner, who took advantage of wartime opportunities to pursue a military career (albeit a checkered one) and finally returned home to Germany. This is interesting in what it tells us about the role of chance, circumstance, individual choice and initiative, and family connections in Europe—as opposed to a simple choice of New World versus Old World location—in determining postservitude success.

10. See, for instance, Diffenderffer, "German Immigration into Pennsylvania."

11. Farley Grubb, "The Transatlantic Market for British Convict Labor," *Journal of Economic History* 60 (March 2000): 94–122; Abbot Emerson Smith, *Colonists in Bondage* (New York: W. W. Norton, 1947).

Acknowledgments

We incurred many debts in the course of our research on this project, too many to fully and adequately acknowledge here. But, first and foremost, we wish to thank the Whitehead family for recognizing the historical value of John Frederick Whitehead's memoir. John Frederick Whitehead IV donated the original manuscript to the Pennsylvania State Library and Archives so that future scholars could learn from his remarkable ancestor's autobiography. John's appreciation of and respect for the manuscript, along with that of his son Dennis, had been cultivated by John's grandfather, Ethan Edwin Whitehead, and father, Stanley Whitehead. Dennis Whitehead also worked on the manuscript for many years, struggling to make an accurate transcription of a sometimes indecipherable document. We thank all of these generations of the Whitehead family for their contribution to scholarship. We want to thank Peter Potter at Penn State Press for introducing us to John Frederick Whitehead and then enthusiastically supporting this book. We also wish to thank Rosalind J. Beiler and Hermann Wellenreuther for their helpful comments on the manuscript.

Part of this research was done by Farley Grubb while on sabbatical leave at Harvard University. He gratefully acknowledges resource support provided by the Harvard University Economics Department and financial support provided by a 2003–4 American Philosophical Society Sabbatical Fellowship Grant. Farley Grubb and Anne Pfaelzer de Ortiz wish to thank Tracy L. Deliberty and Linda Waughtal Parrish for providing invaluable assistance with GIS mapping programs, and Linda Waughtal Parrish for doing much of the actual programming. In addition, they wish to acknowledge research fund support from the Economics Department of the University of Delaware.

Anne Pfaelzer de Ortiz wishes to thank Henry Retzer for providing access to and translation of a 1782 letter written by Johann Carl Büttner, Per Koeltz for translation of German texts, C. C. Stirk for assistance with map reproductions, and the libraries and staff at the University of Delaware Morris Library, the University of Illinois Graduate Library, the Urbana (Illinois) Free Library, and the Delaware State Bureau of Archives and Record Management, Hall of Records, Dover, Delaware.

Susan E. Klepp, Matthew Muehlbauer, and Uta Kresse Raina wish to thank Christian and Uta Kresse for their invaluable research at the Stralsund City Archives. We also want to thank the staff at the Stadtarchiv der Hansestadt Stralsund for patiently answering many e-mailed questions, as well as the staffs at the Historical Society of Berks County, the Historical Society of Pennsylvania, and Craig Horle and Joseph Foster at the Biographical Dictionary of Pennsylvania Legislators, Temple University. Klaas Kresse, Regina Gramer, and Emily Rush provided valuable assistance in deciphering the text. Farley Grubb helped immensely in validating Whitehead's arrival and sale.

Susan Klepp also thanks Richard Immerman, chair of the History Department at Temple University, for providing a research assistant at a crucial stage in this project; Matt Muehlbauer, for going well above and beyond the requirements of a research assistant to continue working on this project through summers and additional semesters; and Uta Kresse Raina, for volunteering to work on this project simply out of fascination with Whitehead's story. Many colleagues have informed my understanding of freedom and servitude in early America, among them Billy G. Smith, Leslie Patrick, Susan Branson, Simon Newman, Tom Humphrey, Ruth Wallis Herndon, David Waldstreicher, and Karin Wulf.

General Introduction
German Immigration to Early America

I n 1773, while still in their teens, John Frederick Whitehead and Johann Carl Büttner independently migrated alone out of Germany and sailed to Philadelphia, where they worked as bound servant laborers in the nearby countryside for a number of years.[1] By chance they traveled to America on the same ship. There is no indication that they knew about, met, or corresponded with each other before or after the voyage. Their fates after servitude diverged significantly. Later in life, both set down their memoirs. Despite experiencing the same voyage to America and similar working conditions as servants there, their personal perspectives on and interpretations of those experiences are vastly different. Their narratives, Whitehead's published here for the first time, provide a rare glimpse into the transatlantic migration process and servant labor experience of Germans immigrating to colonial America. At present, theirs are the only known firsthand accounts by Germans who migrated as servants.

This introduction presents the broad contexts within which Whitehead's and Büttner's experiences are set, including the quantitative dimensions of German transatlantic emigration, the nexus of contractual relationships in the transatlantic passenger and servant business, and the use of autobiography as a communicative device. We also assess how representative their experiences

1. The term "Germany" is used throughout to refer to German-speaking areas of central Europe. In this period the area that is now called Germany was a patchwork of smaller autonomous and semiautonomous principalities, duchies, electorates, city-states, etc., such as Saxony, Bavaria, Württemberg-Baden, Hanover, Hamburg, and so on. Consult any historical atlas for details. In America, Germans seldom referred to themselves or to other Germans by their political unit of origin, e.g., as Wüerttembergerians, but typically only as Germans. The same was true for English-speaking colonists when referring to Germans in America. When Americans occasionally used specific political-unit names, such as "Hessian" soldiers or "Palatine" and "Dutch" immigrants, the names were often used generically and inaccurately.

were. Separate introductions, dealing specifically with Whitehead and Büttner as individuals, precede each narrative.

Quantitative Dimensions

John Frederick Whitehead (1757–1815) and Johann Carl Büttner (1754–182?) were part of a substantial German exodus to eighteenth-century America. German-speaking migrants were the largest segment of non-British European arrivals to British North America. About 108,000 Germans arrived between 1720 and 1775, approximately 80,000 of them landing in Philadelphia. In comparison, the export of British convicts to all of colonial America between 1718 and 1775—roughly half of all English arrivals—numbered only 50,000, and Irish migration to the Delaware Valley between 1730 and 1774 was only 52,000. From the end of the Revolution to 1820 another 21,000 to 25,000 Germans crossed the Atlantic and landed in Philadelphia.[2]

The typical German migrant to colonial America followed the Rhine into the Netherlands, embarked at Rotterdam, cleared English customs at Cowes on the Isle of Wight, debarked at Philadelphia, and settled in Pennsylvania or New Jersey. Between 1727 and 1775 about 90 percent of the Germans debarking in Philadelphia had embarked at Rotterdam. Between 1763 and 1775 roughly 67 percent of ships from Rotterdam cleared English customs at Cowes, and 28 percent cleared English customs at Portsmouth. The volume of migration, however, fluctuated over time. Between 1727 and 1748 about twelve hundred Germans landed in Philadelphia each year. This migration peaked between 1749 and 1755, with an average of just over 6,500 landing in Philadelphia each year. By 1760 slightly less than half of Pennsylvania's

---

2. Aaron S. Fogelman, *Hopeful Journeys: German Immigration, Settlement, and Political Culture in Colonial America, 1717–1775* (Philadelphia: University of Pennsylvania Press, 1996), 1–12; Aaron S. Fogelman, "From Slaves, Convicts, and Servants to Free Passengers: The Transformation of Immigration in the Era of the American Revolution," *Journal of American History* 85 (June 1998): 43–74; Hans-Jurgen Grabbe, "European Immigration to the United States in the Early National Period, 1783–1820," *Proceedings of the American Philosophical Society* 133 (June 1989): 192; Farley Grubb, "The End of European Immigrant Servitude in the United States: An Economic Analysis of Market Collapse, 1772–1835," *Journal of Economic History* 54 (December 1994): 818–19; Farley Grubb, "The Transatlantic Market for British Convict Labor," *Journal of Economic History* 60 (March 2000): 94; Guenter Moltmann, "Three Hundred Years of German Emigration to North America," in *Germans to America: Three Hundred Years of Immigration, 1683–1983,* ed. Guenter Moltmann (Stuttgart: Foreign Cultural Relations, in cooperation with Inter Nations, Bonn-Bad Godesberg, 1982), 8–15; Ralph B. Strassburger, *Pennsylvania German Pioneers: A Publication of the Original Lists of Arrivals in the Port of Philadelphia from 1727 to 1808,* vols. 1–3 (Norristown, Pa.: Pennsylvania German Society, 1934); Marianna S. Wokeck, *Trade in Strangers: The Beginnings of Mass Migration to North America* (University Park: Pennsylvania State University Press, 1999), 45–46, 172–73.

population was thought to be of German ethnicity. German immigration fell off sharply during the Seven Years' War (1756–63) and then resumed at roughly a thousand landing in Philadelphia each year through 1774. German migration to America between 1765 and 1775 peaked in 1773—the year White-head and Büttner arrived in Philadelphia—with about eighteen hundred landing in Philadelphia that year. Immigration ceased during the Revolution and then continued at a slower pace thereafter—an average of 650 landing in Philadelphia each year between 1785 and 1808. By the time of the 1790 census, a third of Pennsylvania's population was reported to be of German ethnicity. Between 1809 and 1815 German immigration to America again dropped off to almost nothing, but another spurt, averaging just over two thousand per year to Philadelphia, occurred between 1816 and 1819.[3]

The volume of ships arriving with German passengers and the voyage conditions experienced by Germans crossing the Atlantic also varied over the colonial era. From 1727 through 1749 and from 1763 through 1769 an average of five to eight ships arrived in Philadelphia each year carrying around 180 German passengers each. From 1750 through 1754 these yearly averages rose to eighteen ships carrying 300 passengers each, declining from 1770 through 1774 to nine ships carrying 98 passengers each. German passenger ships carried on average about one passenger per measured ton of shipping, except during peak migration years such as 1750–54, when the number of passengers per ton was higher. Most ship captains who participated in the German passenger trade did so only once. Out of 317 voyages between 1727 and 1775, with 190 captains known to have ferried German passengers to Philadelphia, only ten made more than five voyages with German passengers. The typical length of time at sea from Rotterdam to Philadelphia was eight to ten weeks, though on rare and unlucky occasions a ship could be more than six months at sea. Finally, while there was considerable variation by voyage and ship, on average 3.6 percent of the adult male German passengers died during the voyage. Another 3.5 percent arrived too sick to walk off the boat in Philadelphia. By contrast, the British transatlantic slave trade to Virginia in this period averaged 1.44 enslaved individuals per measured ton of shipping, and the voyage mortality for slaves was between 10 and 15 percent.[4]

3. Frank R. Diffenderffer, "The German Immigration into Pennsylvania Through the Port of Philadelphia from 1700 to 1775. Part II. The Redemptioners" (part 7 of "The Narrative and Critical History"), *Publications of the Pennsylvania German Society* 10 (1899): 97–106; *Historical Statistics of the United States: Colonial Times to 1970* (Washington D.C.: U.S. Bureau of the Census, 1975), 1168; Fogelman, *Hopeful Journeys*; Grubb, "End of European Immigrant Servitude," 818–19; Moltmann, "Three Hundred Years of German Immigration," 8–15; Strassburger, *Pennsylvania German Pioneers*; Wokeck, *Trade in Strangers*, 45–46, 113–65.

4. Farley Grubb, "Redemptioner Immigration to Pennsylvania: Evidence on Contract Choice and Profitability," *Journal of Economic History* 46 (June 1986): 417; Farley Grubb, "Morbidity

Whitehead and Büttner's voyage from Rotterdam to Philadelphia (clearing English customs at Portsmouth) on the *Sally* was typical in some respects but atypical in others, which should be kept in mind when assessing their narratives of the journey. Approximately 210 of the *Sally*'s passengers landed in Philadelphia. The ship was rated at about 213 measured tons (150 registered tons), thus yielding a (landed) passenger-per-measured-ton ratio of 0.99 on their voyage. The ship's captain, John Osmand, was experienced in the trade, having made at least five prior voyages from Rotterdam to Philadelphia on the *Sally* with German passengers—one of them, in 1767, with even more passengers. Whitehead's and Büttner's narratives indicate that the time they spent at sea, estimated to be at least seventeen weeks, and the mortality on their ship, estimated to be as high as 15 to 25 percent, were both well above the average experienced in this trade.[5]

The key demographic difference between German and British immigration to colonial America was the relatively high proportion of families among the Germans. Fewer than 10 percent of English migrants to Pennsylvania were married persons or dependent children, whereas between 51 and 72 percent of German migrants to Pennsylvania were either married persons or dependent children. Surviving passenger ship lists for the years 1730 to 1750 also indicate a high degree of kinship or coincidence of last names among German passengers on a typical voyage, with about 17 percent of the men sharing a last name with at least one other man, listed next to theirs, on their ship's passenger list. Finally, German immigrants were relatively educated and literate—roughly 80 percent of the adult males after 1750 could sign their

---

and Mortality on the North Atlantic Passage: Eighteenth-Century German Immigration to Pennsylvania," *Journal of Interdisciplinary History* 17 (winter 1987): 567–74; Farley Grubb, "The Market Structure of Shipping German Immigrants to Colonial America," *Pennsylvania Magazine of History and Biography* 111 (January 1987): 41, 47; Wokeck, *Trade in Strangers,* 78–79, 115–16, 240–76.

5. Grubb, "Redemptioner Immigration to Pennsylvania," 417; "Ships Registered for the Port of Philadelphia, 1727–1775," *Pennsylvania Magazine of History and Biography* 26 (1903): 487; Strassburger, *Pennsylvania German Pioneers,* 1:713–17 [LIST 264C], 748–49 [LIST 306C]; Wokeck, *Trade in Strangers,* 240–48. The *Sally* was registered in Philadelphia on October 22, 1766, as being 150 registered tons, built in Philadelphia, captained by John Osmand, and owned by Samuel Howell. "Measured" tons is a better measure of relative cargo capacity across ship sizes than is registered tons. For an explanation of the conversion algorithm of registered tons into measured tons and what the conceptual differences are, see Grubb "Redemptioner Immigration to Pennsylvania," 417, note b to table 4 and the sources cited therein. The estimated mortality on Whitehead's and Büttner's voyage is only a conjectural guess based on the difference between the number of passenger signatures actually on the debarkation oath and the reported number that should have been on the oath, and on the difference between the number of passengers landed compared with the maximum landed by Captain Osmand on previous voyages. If Büttner's claim that there were three hundred passengers on the ship is correct, then the voyage mortality may have been as high as 30 percent.

names in German. Whitehead and Büttner were typical German immigrants in that they were educated and literate in German, but their narratives and the passenger list from their voyage indicate that they were atypical in that neither man was related to anyone else on the ship. The voyage itself was atypical in the relatively small number of family or kinship groups among the German passengers.[6]

When German immigrants debarked in Philadelphia, the principal port of arrival in America, they entered not only one of the largest English-speaking cities in the Atlantic world (though still small compared with London) but also a deadlier disease environment (for them) than they had left in Europe. Immigrants were especially at risk during the first year after their arrival, both because the arduous transatlantic voyage compromised the health of many new arrivals and because immigrants had not yet built up immunities to the particular strains of diseases they would face in the New World—a process called seasoning. As we have seen, between 1727 and 1754 3.5 percent of German adult male passengers arrived too sick to walk off the ship in Philadelphia. In 1727, 1735, and 1743, this rate was higher—between 8.5 and 11 percent. The crude death rate (deaths per thousand individuals per year) between 1738 and 1762 for German immigrants during their first year in Philadelphia has been estimated at around 61.4. In 1738, 1741, and 1754 it was much higher, 105, 182, and 105, respectively. By contrast, the crude death rate for the resident population in Philadelphia for these years averaged 37, the rate rising above 60 only in 1759.[7]

While Whitehead's and Büttner's narratives indicate that they suffered and saw others suffer illness during the voyage, neither mentions illness-related health problems at debarkation, and Büttner mentions nothing about illness-related health problems after debarkation. Whitehead describes suffering from significant health problems during his first year or so after arrival—serious enough impairments that his master lost a substantial amount of Whitehead's labor as a result. Whitehead's and Büttner's narratives seem typical in their depiction of what German immigrants were likely to experience healthwise upon and soon after debarkation.

6. Bernard Bailyn, *Voyagers to the West: A Passage in the Peopling of America on the Eve of the Revolution* (New York: Knopf, 1986), 210–11; Farley Grubb, "Colonial Immigrant Literacy: An Economic Analysis of Pennsylvania-German Evidence, 1727–1775," *Explorations in Economic History* 24 (January 1987): 63–76; Farley Grubb, "German Immigration to Pennsylvania, 1790 to 1820," *Journal of Interdisciplinary History* 20 (winter 1990): 421–31; Strassburger, *Pennsylvania German Pioneers*, 1:748–49 [LIST 306C]; Wokeck, *Trade in Strangers*, 51.

7. Grubb, "Morbidity and Mortality," 573–85; Susan E. Klepp, *Philadelphia in Transition: A Demographic History of the City and Its Occupational Groups, 1720–1830* (New York: Garland, 1989), 225–306; Billy G. Smith, "Death and Life in a Colonial Immigrant City: A Demographic Analysis of Philadelphia," *Journal of Economic History* 37 (December 1977): 863–89.

The Context of Emigration from Germany

John Frederick Whitehead's and Johann Carl Büttner's immigration to British North America came at a time when migration seemed to be a leitmotif in German-speaking principalities, duchies, and kingdoms. Many indigenous factors are thought to have contributed to emigration out of central Germany. In general, German lands were poorer than other central European regions, and many people still suffered religious persecution. Poverty was the consequence of the persistent aftereffects of the Thirty Years' War, intrusive bureaucracies and high taxes, rapid population increase, poor harvests caused by drought, and incessant wars that led to death, disease, and the destruction of property and crops. Inheritance laws in some Germanic areas that prohibited the division of property and favored the eldest son also contributed to creating a steady flow of emigrants from German lands in the eighteenth century. Urbanization, which was proceeding more quickly than the natural rate of increase, meant that internal migration from countryside to city was also increasing. This in turn may have made the next step—emigration—psychologically easier. Finally, religious freedom, while a minor theme by the eighteenth century, was still significant. The major Christian denominations—Roman Catholic, Lutheran, and Reformed—were mutually intolerant. Minority faiths—Mennonite, Amish, Moravian, and other pietist sects—had little or no protection under the laws of any European state. Both religious persecution and persistent poverty led thousands of people to emigrate.[8]

Interestingly, Whitehead's and Büttner's narratives say little about these larger issues. The circumstances leading to their decisions to emigrate appear

---

8. Rosalind J. Beiler, "Distributing Aid to Believers in Need: The Religious Foundations of Transatlantic Migration," in *Empire, Society, and Labor: Essays in Honor of Richard S. Dunn*, supplement to *Pennsylvania History: A Journal of Mid-Atlantic Studies* (summer 1997): 73–87; Lutz K. Berkner, "Inheritance, Land Tenure, and Peasant Family Structure: A German Regional Comparison," in *Family and Inheritance: Rural Society in Western Europe, 1200–1800*, ed. Jack Goody, Joan Thirsk, and E. P. Thompson (New York: Cambridge University Press, 1976), 71–95; Georg Fertig, "Transatlantic Migration from German-Speaking Parts of Central Europe, 1600–1800: Proportions, Structures, and Explanations," in *Europeans on the Move: Studies on European Migration, 1500–1800*, ed. Nicholas Canny (New York: Oxford University Press, 1994), 192–235; Fogelman, *Hopeful Journeys*, 15–65; Robert Jütte, "Poor and Poverty Relief," in *Germany: A New Social and Economic History*, vol. 2, 1630–1800, ed. Sheilagh Ogilvie (New York: Arnold, 1996), 377–85; William O'Reilly, "Conceptualizing America in Early Modern Central Europe," *Explorations in Early American Culture*, supplement to *Pennsylvania History: A Journal of Mid-Atlantic Studies* 65 (1998): 101–21; Jan de Vries, *European Urbanization 1500–1800* (Cambridge: Harvard University Press, 1984), 272–73; Hermann Wellenreuther, "Contexts for Migration in the Early Modern World: Public Policy, European Migrating Experiences, Transatlantic Migration, and the Genesis of American Culture," in *In Search of Peace and Prosperity: New German Settlements in Eighteenth-Century Europe and America*, ed. Hartmut T. Lehmann, Hermann Wellenreuther, and Renate Wilson (University Park: Pennsylvania State University Press, 2000), 3–35; Wokeck, *Trade in Strangers*, 1–17.

far more haphazard, accidental, and idiosyncratic than the influence of these larger forces would suggest. Apparently wanderlust, personal family issues, and the accident of circumstance were also important determinants of who emigrated overseas, where they went, and who stayed behind in Germany.

In eighteenth-century Germanic states, patriarchal family structures predominated both by law and by custom. Men ruled over their wives and children. The urge to migrate was often affected by family considerations.[9] But Büttner's and Whitehead's family backgrounds and the role they played in their decisions to leave Germany could not be more dissimilar. Büttner came from an intact nuclear family and had many siblings. His father appeared to be loving and indulgent—disapproving but tolerant of his son's wanderlust. Whitehead, by contrast, came from a broken home with a violent and overbearing stepfather who not only abused Whitehead but allowed others to abuse him as well. While Whitehead's desire to migrate can be viewed as having a strong "push component"—a desire to escape his family circumstances—Büttner's desire to migrate can be viewed as having a strong "pull component"—the lure of riches and adventure just over the horizon trumping his comfortable family circumstances, although his connections to family eventually pulled him back to Saxony. These differences in family background may also partly explain the two men's rather dissimilar interpretations of their experience and postservitude outcomes. But, as these two narratives illustrate, while family background was important to migration, its importance was complex and varied. Family circumstances were not a uniform determinant or causal force in the decision to migrate.

The attraction of America to German emigrants was fairly insignificant—more of a sideshow than a definite lure. Internal migration within Germany, seasonal and permanent labor migration to the Netherlands, recruitment by the Dutch East India Company (*Verenigde Nederlandse Geotroyeerde Oöstindische Compaigne,* or VOC), and migration to lands in eastern Europe and Russia involved substantially more German emigrants than did emigration to America.[10] David Eltis has concluded that for "every German that moved to the Americas, nine migrated in the opposite direction."[11]

9. See also Berkner, "Inheritance, Land Tenure, and Peasant Family Structure"; David Sabean, "Aspects of Kinship Behavior and Property in Rural Western Europe Before 1800," in Goody, Thirsk, and Thompson, *Family and Inheritance,* 96–111; David Sabean, *Property, Production, and Family in Neckarhausen, 1700–1870* (New York: Cambridge University Press, 1990).

10. See the separate introduction to Büttner's narrative in this volume for more details on the VOC and its recruitment of Germans.

11. David Eltis, "Introduction," in *Coerced and Free Migration: Global Perspectives,* ed. David Eltis (Stanford: Stanford University Press, 2002), 17.

German emigration to America in the eighteenth century was about a fifth or even less of emigration to eastern Europe. One of the most significant population shifts in eighteenth-century Germany was migration southeast to the Balkans, east to Hungary, Poland, and the Crimea, but predominantly north and east into Russia, where Germans made up the majority of new settlers. Attracted by Catherine II's lenient immigration policy for Germans and her promise to grant religious tolerance, German settlers went by the thousands to Russia. Empress Catherine the Great intended to increase the population and tax revenues in her empire and promote her own ethnic stock by giving settlement priority to the allegedly hard-working Germans. Thus between 1764 and 1774 more than a hundred German colonies were founded in the middle and lower Volga region. These were in addition to the hundred thousand Germans who already lived in the Russian empire by the mid-eighteenth century.[12]

The VOC, using recruiting agents who scoured Germany, sent many Germans to work in the East Indies. The numbers they recruited at times rivaled those migrating to eastern Europe, as in the decade surrounding Whitehead and Büttner's emigration out of Germany. The likelihood of running into a recruiter for the VOC in Germany was far greater than running into a recruiter for emigrant shippers headed to America. Finally, the volume of internal and seasonal labor migration within Germany and into the Netherlands appears to have been at least several multiples of the number of Germans migrating to the East or being recruited by the VOC.[13]

In this historical context, Whitehead's and Büttner's narratives illustrate the larger issues involved in German emigration. Both men came from areas experiencing economic decline. Both engaged in substantial internal migration within greater Germany before being lured by the fabled riches of the East Indies. They both ended up in northern Germany, where VOC agents recruited them. While in Germany, emigration to America was not their overriding intention. Even while in Amsterdam seeking a position with the VOC, they did not mention America. Only at the very end of their European

12. Ernest Benz, "Population Change and the Economy," in Ogilvie, *Germany: A New Social and Economic History*, 47; Fertig, "Transatlantic Migration," 203; Andreas Gestrich, "German Religious Emigration to Russia in the Eighteenth and Early Nineteenth Centuries," in Lehmann, Wellenreuther, and Wilson, *In Search of Peace and Prosperity*, 77; Richard Hellie, "Migration in Early Modern Russia," in Eltis, *Coerced and Free Migration*, 317–18; William O'Reilly, "To the East or to the West? German Migration in the Eighteenth Century: A Comparative Perspective," paper delivered at the Philadelphia [now McNeil] Center for Early American Studies, March 21, 1997; Wellenreuther, "Contexts for Migration," 3–35.

13. J. R. Bruijn, F. S. Gaastra, and I. Schöffer, *Dutch-Asiatic Shipping in the Seventeenth and Eighteenth Centuries*, vols. 1 and 2 (The Hague: Nijhoff, 1979, 1987); Fertig, "Transatlantic Migration," 203; Jan Lucassen, "The Netherlands, the Dutch, and Long-Distance Migration in the Late Sixteenth to Early Nineteenth Centuries," in Canny, *Europeans on the Move*, 153–91.

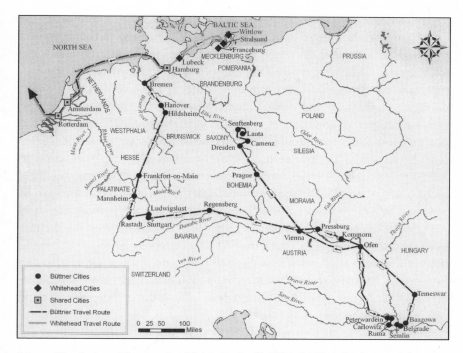

Map 1 Wanderlust: The travels of John Frederick Whitehead and Johann Carl Büttner in Europe prior to their emigration to America.

Notes: Whitehead's travels took place entirely in northern Germanic areas prior to his signing on with VOC recruiters, while Büttner's took him not only through Germanic areas but also through portions of eastern Europe into Polish, Moravian, Austrian, and Hungarian areas. Countries and their boundaries have changed since the 1770s, which is the period represented by this map. The Germany that we know today did not exist and the Germanic areas were divided into principalities and kingdoms too numerous to show on this map, although a few of these political divisions have been included. The city names used in the map are spelled as they were by the two men in their memoirs. Whitehead's Franceburg is today known as Franzburg, and Wittlow is on the Island of Witts. Büttner's Camenz is Kamenz, Pressburg is now known as Bratislava, Kommorn is Komorno, Ofen is now called Budapest, Peterwarden is Petrovaradin, Carlowitz is Sr. Karlovici, Semlin is Zemun, Belgrade is Beograd or Belgrad, Banzowa is Pancevo, and Temeswar is now Timisoara.

adventure, when employment by the VOC did not materialize, does America seriously enter the picture. America appears as a minor sideshow with little inherent attraction, a last-minute outlet for dashed hopes, a hazily conceptualized place of which the two men had only a vague consciousness. As such, their narratives are a corrective to the literature on German emigration to America, a literature that perhaps too often presents America as the obvious and even the only choice for emigrants who ended up there.

The literature on German emigration to America also emphasizes the extent and significance of migration networks—religious, commercial, and personal—and the role that such networks played in the migration process to America. Chain migration was a by-product of information networks, especially personal and local community contacts, and a substantial amount of such information and advice about America—about commercial and personal migration contacts, and about how the migration process worked (the do's and don'ts of migrating)—flowed across the Atlantic. This has been seen as an important component of the story of German emigration to America.[14] Whitehead's and Büttner's narratives, however, indicate that they had no migration network connections, whether religious, commercial, or personal, to America throughout the process of migration and settlement in America. Whitehead and Büttner were not directly part of an existing chain of migrants, nor did they directly foster a new chain of migrants. Whitehead did not maintain contact with family in Europe and Büttner did not remain in America. Whether this makes their migration experience atypical depends on two other factors, namely, the socioeconomic status of the emigrants and where they originated in Germany.

Roughly half of all Germans migrating to America between the 1740s and the 1820s could not pay their travel expenses before sailing and ended up paying part or all of these costs by selling their labor as indentured servants (bound contract laborers) upon arriving in America.[15] The evidence on the extent and significance of migration networks for Germans migrating to America comes primarily from the wealthier half of the German emigrant stream—from those who did not have to sell themselves as servants to pay

14. Beiler, "Distributing Aid to Believers in Need"; Rosalind J. Beiler, "From the Rhine to the Delaware Valley: The Eighteenth-Century Transatlantic Trading Channels of Caspar Wistar," Mark Haberlein, "Communication and Group Interaction Among German Migrants to Colonial Pennsylvania: The Case of Baden-Durlach," Hartmut T. Lehmann, "Transatlantic Migration, Transatlantic Networks, Transatlantic Transfer," and Hermann Wellenreuther, "Recent Research on Migration," all four in Lehmann, Wellenreuther, and Wilson, In Search of Peace and Prosperity, 172–88, 156–71, 307–30, and 265–306, respectively; Fogelman, Hopeful Journeys; Otto Langguth, "Pennsylvania German Pioneers from the County of Wertheim," trans. and ed. Don Yoder, Pennsylvania German Folklore Society 12 (1947): 149–289; Wellenreuther, "Contexts for Migration," 3–35; Wokeck, Trade in Strangers, 18–165.
15. Farley Grubb, "The Incidence of Servitude in Trans-Atlantic Migration, 1771–1804," Explorations in Economic History 22 (July 1985): 316–39; Grubb, "End of European Immigrant Servitude," 794–824; Farley Grubb, "The Auction of Redemptioner Servants, Philadelphia, 1771–1804: An Economic Analysis," Journal of Economic History 48 (September 1988): 583–603; Farley Grubb, "Servant Auction Records and Immigration into the Delaware Valley, 1745–1831: The Proportion of Females Among Immigrant Servants," Proceedings of the American Philosophical Society 133 (June 1989): 154–69; Guenter Moltmann, "The Migration of German Redemptioners to North America," in Colonialism and Migration: Indentured Labour Before and After Slavery, ed. P. C. Emmer (Boston: Martinus Nijhoff, 1986), 105–22; Abbot Emerson Smith, Colonists in Bondage (New York: W. W. Norton, 1947), 3–4, 20–25.

for their passage—and primarily from sources on emigration originating in the upper Rhine region, thought to be the source of most German emigrants to America in this period.[16] We know much less about the migration network experience of the poorer half of the German emigration stream—those who sold themselves as servants—and of those Germans who originated from regions outside the upper Rhine region.

Both Whitehead and Büttner fall into the latter two categories. If their narratives reflect the experience of the poorer half of the German emigration stream to America—the bound servant class—and of German emigrants from outside the upper Rhine region, then this portion of the German emigration stream was likely to have had far fewer migration network contacts to and in America than wealthier emigrants from the upper Rhine. In this sense, they were more likely to be accidental emigrants.

The Process and Contractual Mechanics of German Immigration to America

In other ways, Whitehead and Büttner's transatlantic journey conforms to recent analyses of the process that transported tens of thousands of Germans to America in the eighteenth century. Merchants and ship owners based in Rotterdam, London, and Philadelphia formed business networks that provided regular transatlantic transport for migrants from the continent. These entrepreneurs developed a system that financed transportation by relying on the high demand for labor in the Philadelphia region. Shippers allowed passengers to travel on credit and pay after arrival in Philadelphia. While this market appears to have been competitive and operated fairly in theory, and often in practice, there was ample opportunity for fraud: recruiters lied about options, ship captains padded bills, and passengers smuggled contraband goods or ran away upon arrival.[17] Migrants also faced a web of contractual and legally binding relationships that circumscribed the migration process.

Either before crossing the border into the Netherlands or shortly after arriving in a Dutch port, a prospective German emigrant to America entered into a shipping contract for transportation overseas from a Dutch port. This

---

16. See the sources cited in note 14 above.

17. Diffenderffer, "German Immigration into Pennsylvania"; Karl Frederick Geiser, *Redemptioners and Indentured Servants in the Colony and Commonwealth of Pennsylvania* (New Haven: Tuttle, Morehouse & Taylor, 1901), 5–76; Grubb, "Market Structure of Shipping German Immigrants," 27–48; Grubb, "Auction of Redemptioner Servants"; Farley Grubb, *German Immigrant Servant Contracts Registered at the Port of Philadelphia, 1817–1831* (Baltimore: Genealogical Publishing Co., 1994); Moltmann, "Migration of German Redemptioners"; Smith, *Colonists in Bondage*, 3–66; Wellenreuther, "Contexts for Migration," 3–35; Wokeck, *Trade in Strangers*.

contract specified the port of debarkation, the fare for passage, including cash versus credit options, and the food and other conveniences to be provided on the voyage. The following is a typical immigrant shipping contract in the German transatlantic passenger trade:

We, the undersigned, I, Nathan Ray, Captain of the Ship Commerce, on the one part, and we passengers on the other part, accept and obligate ourselves hereby as persons of honor.

On the first part, We passengers, in order to undertake our voyage hence to Philadelphia in North America with the above-mentioned Captain Nathaniel Ray, are obligated to behave ourselves quietly and as good passengers during the voyage, and to be fully satisfied with the food below specified, agreed upon between the Captain and ourselves, and as regard water and further provisions, to comply with regulations the Captain shall find necessary, in view of contrary winds and the requirements of a long voyage.

In the second place we agree to pay our passage with the following stipulations:

Those who are in position to settle (for the passage money) in Amsterdam, to pay for one person whether man or women,

(Children under 4 years old being free)

From 4 to under 14 years six and one-half guineas;

From 14 years and older thirteen guineas.

Those who cannot settle here but will settle in America, to pay

(Children under 4 years being free)

From 4 to under 14 years seven and one-half guineas;

From 14 years and older fifteen guineas.

Those who pay their passage in America shall be bound to produce it within 10 days. No passenger shall be allowed to leave the ship in America without knowledge of the Captain, especially such as have not yet settled for their passage. If one of the passengers dies on the voyage, the family of such a person shall be obligated to settle for his passage, if he dies beyond the middle point of the voyage hence. But if he dies on this side of the middle point the loss shall be to the account of the Captain.

On the other part, I, Captain Nath. Ray, obligate myself to convey faithfully the undersigned passengers to Philadelphia in North America, if God grants a prosperous voyage, to furnish them with the necessary conveniences on the ship, and further to provide the food hereinbelow specified. For this conveyance the above-mentioned passage money must be paid to me. Distribution shall be made daily among these passengers, to wit, to one full passage, (a half passage in proportion, and for children nothing):

Sunday. A pound of beef with barley.

Monday. A pound of flour, and a pound of butter good
 for the whole week.

Tuesday. A half-pound of bacon, cooked with peas.

Wednesday. A pound of flour.

Thursday. A pound of beef with potatoes.

Friday. One half-pound of rice.

Saturday. Peas, a pound of cheese and six pounds of bread
 for the whole week, and one half-pound of bacon.

A quart of beer and a quart of water per day. Vinegar also is to be taken along on the ship, not only to keep the same clean, in order to insure good and fresh air, but also for the refreshment of the passengers.

Since beers sours during the voyage and is very harmful to the health of passengers, only enough beer for a part of the voyage will be taken along, and when this is gone a double portion of water will be given. Half of the water will be supplied for cooking. Each morning a small glass of Holland gin and each week now and then some vinegar.

We promise to fulfill all the above-mentioned and to this end bind our persons and property as of right.

Done at Amsterdam . . . [passenger signatures follow].[18]

Adult passage fares from Dutch ports to Philadelphia in the eighteenth century ranged between five and fourteen pounds sterling (£13.65 for the contract cited above). Fares were lower in peacetime and higher in wartime. This sum might easily exceed the value of a year's income for a typical German immigrant. Thus a substantial proportion of German immigrants used the credit option in the shipping contract that allowed them to borrow the passage fare from the shipper and repay it upon debarkation in America. Scholars have called this method "redemption," and those who used it, "redemptioners." The credit fare was roughly 15 percent above that for passengers who paid cash in advance. This 15 percent markup just barely covered

18. From the ship *Commerce*, Captain Nathaniel Ray, who landed 235 Germans from Amsterdam in Philadelphia on October 9, 1803, in Strassburger, *Pennsylvania German Pioneers*, 3:131–32. See also the ship (voyage) contracts in Langguth, "Pennsylvania German Pioneers," 259–62; Strassburger, *Pennsylvania German Pioneers*, 3:112–14, 137–38; Michael Tepper, ed., *Emigrants to Pennsylvania, 1641–1819* (Baltimore: Genealogical Publishing Co., 1978), 257–60. Few actual ship (voyage) contracts have survived, including those from the voyage Whitehead and Büttner undertook.

the interest cost of capital, the cost of debt collection upon arrival, and re-demptioner default due to death, illness, and escape. Thus shippers earned, on average, no excess profits on redemptioners compared with what they earned on passengers who paid cash in advance.[19]

How redemptioners repaid their loans upon landing in America was up to them. Some migrants had friends or relatives who would be summoned once the ship arrived to pay the migrants' fares, using familiar, religious, or other networks to help facilitate this outcome. Passengers also brought over household goods to sell in order to pay off their fares—but this option was unavailable to poorer passengers, who could not afford the guns, teakettles, bolts of cloth, and other valuable items that could be sold profitably in the New World. New arrivals without friends, kin, cash, or commodities had to sell themselves into servitude to repay their debts. If they refused to pay, the shipper could have them put in debtors' prison or sell them into servitude to recover his loans. While ship contracts frequently stated that payment had to be made within ten to fourteen days of arrival, Pennsylvania law (after 1765) allowed redemptioners a full thirty days after arrival to render payment to the shipper and prohibited additional charges for their provisions while living on the ship during that period. Most redemptioners ended up negotiating their own labor contracts with American employers, who in exchange paid the shipper the sum required within the thirty days allotted by law. Redemption-ers had to agree to sell just enough of their future labor, via alienable fixed-term servant contracts, to close the deal. Thus, per transportation debt, the length of the servant contract depended on the redemptioner's health, skill, age, education, perceived labor productivity, family circumstances, and the local labor market conditions at the time of arrival in America.[20]

In 1769 the Reverend Henry Melchior Muehlenberg, head of the Lutheran Church in Pennsylvania, described the arrival and debt-repayment process for Germans landing in Philadelphia as follows:

> Before the ship is allowed to cast anchor at the harbor front, the pas-sengers are all examined, according to the law in force, by a physi-cian, as to whether any contagious disease exists among them. Then the new arrivals are led in procession to the City Hall and there they must render the oath of allegiance to the king of Great Britain. After

19. Grubb, "Market Structure of Shipping German Immigrants," 46; Grubb, "Redemptioner Immigration to Pennsylvania," 411–15.

20. Grubb, "Auction of Redemptioner Servants," 585–86; Farley Grubb, "The Disappearance of Organized Markets for European Indentured Servants in the United States: Five Popular Explanations Reexamined," *Social Science History* 18 (spring 1994): 5–9; Frederic Trautmann, "Pennsylvania Through a German's Eyes: The Travels of Ludwig Gall, 1819–1820," *Pennsylvania Magazine of History and Biography* 105 (January 1981): 40–41.

that they are brought back to the ship. Then announcements are printed in the newspapers, stating how many of the new arrivals are to be sold. Those who have money are released. Whoever has well-to-do friends seeks a loan from them to pay the passage, but there are only a few who succeed. The ship becomes the market-place. The buyers make their choice among the arrivals and bargain with them for a certain number of years and days. They then take them to the merchant, pay their passage and their other debts and receive from the government authorities a written document, which makes the newcomers their property for a definite period.[21]

Roughly half of all British and German immigrants entered servitude to pay for their passage to the New World. Given the differing demographic characteristics cited above, there were almost no British or Irish immigrant servants who were married persons or dependent children, whereas a substantial number of German immigrant servants fell into one or the other of these categories. Between 1785 and 1804, where records are complete enough to identify the family status of all German immigrants who entered servitude, parents and dependent children made up 51 percent of all German immigrants and 44 percent of German immigrants sold as servants. Among these German immigrants, slightly more than half the single adults entered servitude, and they made up 55 percent of all German immigrants entering servitude. Despite the large involvement of families, the typical servant among German immigrants, as among British immigrants, was still a young, single adult male, like Büttner and Whitehead.[22]

An example of a typical servant labor contract signed by German immigrants upon arrival in Philadelphia to pay their passage from Holland follows:

Printed and sold by ANDREW STEUART, in Second-street [Philadelphia]

This Indenture

Witnesseth, That   *Mary Elizabeth Bauer with the consent of her father &* *in Consideration of Twenty seven pounds [Pennsylvania currency] paid by* *her master Samuel Pliasants for her passage from Holland* as also for other Causes, *she* the said *Mary* hath bound and put *her* self, and by those Presents doth bind and put *her* self Servant to the said *Samuel* to serve *Him his* Executors and Assigns, from the Day of the Date hereof, for

21. Quoted in Strassburger, *Pennsylvania German Pioneers,* 1:xxxvii.

22. Grubb, "Incidence of Servitude in Trans-Atlantic Migration," 320–27; John J. McCusker and Russell R. Menard, *The Economy of British America, 1607–1789* (Chapel Hill: University of North Carolina Press, 1985), 243; Smith, *Colonists in Bondage,* 20–22.

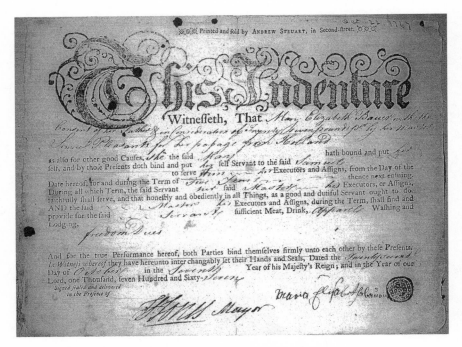

Fig. 1 Example of a German redemptioner immigrant servant contract. Unfortunately, Büttner's and Whitehead's contracts have not survived, but this one is probably very close to what they would have signed. See pp. 15–16, for transcript. Courtesy of the Historical Society of Pennsylvania, Philadelphia.

and during the Term of *Five Years* thence next ensuing. During all which Term, the said Servant *her* said *Master his* Executors, or Assigns, faithfully shall serve, and that honestly and obediently in all Things, as a good dutiful Servant ought to do. AND the said *Master his* Executors and Assigns, during the Term, shall find and provide for the said *servant* sufficient Meat, Drink, *Apparel* Washing and Lodging, *freedom dues* And for the true Performance hereof, both Parties bind themselves firmly unto each other by these Presents. In witness whereof they have hereunto interchangeably set their Hands and Seals, Dated the *Twenty second* Day of *October* in the *Seventh* Year of his Majesty's Reign; and in the Year of our Lord, one Thousand, seven Hundred and Sixty-*seven* Signed sealed and delivered in the Presence of [signatures of the Mayor of Philadelphia and of Mary Elizabeth Bauer][23]

23. Miscellaneous Collection, Box 9c, White Servitude Folder f. 1, Historical Society of Pennsylvania, Philadelphia. Italics indicate that information was handwritten by the contracting parties in the blank spaces on this one-page preprinted contract form. Few actual contracts have survived, including those of Whitehead and Büttner.

German immigrants who entered servitude in America did so exclusively via the redemption method for financing migration. This method differed from that typically used by British and Irish immigrants—what scholars have called indentured servitude. This method involved signing fixed-length servant labor contracts before embarkation that shippers then sold in America to employers who bid the highest amount. By contrast, the German redemption method entailed signing a fixed-debt contract at embarkation. The redemptioner then negotiated directly with American employers upon debarkation for the shortest servant contract that would settle the contracted debt to the shipper.

For Germans migrating to North America, the redemption method was used for at least a century, from 1720 to 1820. The typical contract length negotiated by adult German redemptioners was between three and five years—similar to that of adult British and Irish immigrant indentured servants.[24] How much reliable information American masters could glean from prospective German servants, and how much German servants could glean about prospective American masters, in the face-to-face contract negotiation process that took place on board the ships that had just arrived at Philadelphia from Rotterdam is hard to tell. One purchaser of German redemptioners complained, "Whether they will be worth anything is a lottery, for the choice of strangers in this way is truly a leap in the dark."[25] Likewise, servants probably knew little about local working conditions or about the reputations of particular masters. Competitive market forces, however, had an impact. Servant contract compensation received by redemptioners landing in Philadelphia per year of labor ended up being comparable on average with what free laborers earned in Philadelphia.[26]

The origins of the redemption method and why Germans used it exclusively, while the British stuck to the indentured method, is still a matter of speculation. The incidence of risk differed between the two methods. Under redemption, shippers fixed the payment they were to receive in America before embarkation. The emigrant could anticipate the typical contract length

24. Geiser, *Redemptioners and Indentured Servants*, 5–76; Grubb, "Redemptioner Immigration to Pennsylvania," 408; Grubb, "End of European Immigrant Servitude," 794–824; Grubb, "Auction of Redemptioner Servants," 583–603; Farley Grubb, "The Long-Run Trend in the Value of European Immigrant Servants, 1654–1831: New Measurements and Interpretations," *Research in Economic History* 14 (1992): 167–240; Grubb, *German Immigrant Servant Contracts*; Farley Grubb, "Labor, Markets, and Opportunity: Indentured Servitude in Early America, a Rejoinder to Salinger," *Labor History* 39 (May 1998): 235–41; McCusker and Menard, *Economy of British America*, 243; Smith, *Colonists in Bondage*, 20–22; Strassburger, *Pennsylvania German Pioneers*, 3:112–14, 131–32, 137–38; Tepper, *Emigrants to Pennsylvania*, 257–60.

25. Nicholas B. Wainwright, ed., "The Diary of Samuel Breck, 1814–1822," *Pennsylvania Magazine of History and Biography* 102 (October 1978): 490.

26. Grubb, "Auction of Redemptioner Servants," 586–92.

for such a debt under average circumstances. But the emigrant didn't know exactly how much labor it would take to repay this debt until after debarkation. Thus the risk that the emigrant's labor value might depend on unexpected changes in American market conditions or on the emigrant's physical health after embarkation—and thus that servant contract length might also be affected—fell on the emigrant, not the shipper. This risk position was reversed under the indentured method. In exchange for assuming this risk, the redemptioner was able to choose and negotiate directly with his American employer—something not allowed the indentured servant.[27]

The ability to negotiate directly with prospective American employers may have been more important to German immigrants than to British because of the high proportion of families among German immigrants. The redemption method allowed German parents the flexibility to observe the servant market in America and decide after arrival how best to redistribute the family's total passage debt among its individual members. In particular, some children might take on the passage debt of a parent or of other children in the family and so serve in their place, or a parent might take over the passage debts of some children, thus saving these children from servitude. The redemption method also allowed parents more oversight regarding the servant contracts entered into by their children. For example, some parents were able to negotiate specific, tailor-made education clauses for their children. Finally, redemption allowed servants opportunistically to choose specialty contract clauses, such as job-specific work restrictions, that would have been too costly to negotiate on a contingency basis before embarkation. More than half of the German immigrant servants, however, did not migrate in family groups, nor did they negotiate any specialty clauses into their contracts, as was the case for Büttner and Whitehead. They appear to have assumed the redemption risk for no benefit. Why did they not opt for the indentured method?[28]

The answer appears to lie in the fact that most German immigrants to America incurred substantial migration debts before embarking on the transatlantic journey. The cost of migrating to and subsisting in Dutch seaports before booking passage overseas was high, and many German migrants had to resort to borrowing money from recruiters, hostel keepers, and middlemen to cover these costs. This was something that their British and Irish counterparts typically did not experience. The Dutch holders of these pre-embarkation

27. David W. Galenson, *White Servitude in Colonial America* (New York: Cambridge University Press, 1981), 14; Grubb, "Redemptioner Immigration to Pennsylvania," 407–11.
28. Grubb, "Labor, Markets, and Opportunity," 240; Grubb, "Redemptioner Immigration to Pennsylvania," 410–11; "Munstering [Mustering] Book for the *Britannia* Capt. James Peters from Rotterdam 3rd July 1773" (manuscript, AM 209, Historical Society of Pennsylvania, Philadelphia).

debts wanted them liquidated before the emigrant sailed. Shippers purchased (liquidated) these debts and added them to the debts owed by the immigrants for passage. Thus many German redemptioners, including both Büttner and Whitehead, sold themselves into servitude in America for sums well in excess of the shipping cost of passage because they had incurred substantial debts before embarking. The size of these debts varied substantially, from almost nothing to as much as 35 percent, and even in a few cases as high as 50 percent or more, of the initial passage fare.[29]

The sale and liquidation of pre-embarkation recruitment and migration debts incurred by prospective overseas migrants in the Netherlands was a long-standing feature of the labor recruitment process used by the VOC. The VOC had the largest recruitment operation for overseas labor in the Netherlands, with extensive recruitment efforts reaching deep into Germany.[30] The redemption method used by German immigrants to America may have simply been an adaptation of methods the VOC used for debt repayment that allowed a given prospective emigrant to consolidate and sell the debts he owed to different agents in the labor recruitment process. While scholars have not noted this before, the experiences of both Büttner and Whitehead lend credence to this possibility.[31]

Regardless of the origins of the redemption method, the fact that passage debts (as opposed to passage fares) varied far more for German immigrants than for British and Irish immigrants to America made the redemption method preferable for German immigrants. Signing fixed-length servant contracts before embarkation, as British immigrants did under the indentured method, would have created what economists call a "lemons" problem for German immigrants.[32] Because of the variable pre-embarkation debts added to the cost of passage, German contract lengths could vary because of differences in both servant labor productivity and passage debts. If contract lengths were fixed before embarkation, buyers in America would not know what factor or factors caused a given servant's contract length to be shorter or longer. Risk-averse buyers would interpret a longer contract as a

---

29. Farley Grubb, "Babes in Bondage—Parental Selling of Children to Finance Family Migration: The Case of German Migration to America, 1720–1820," *Journal of Interdisciplinary History* 37 (Summer 2006); "Munstering [Mustering] Book for the *Britannia*."

30. Bruijn, Gaastra, and Schöffer, *Dutch-Asiatic Shipping;* Lucassen, "Netherlands, the Dutch, and Long-Distance Migration," 153–91.

31. For an exception, see Anne M. Pfaelzer de Ortiz, "German Redemptioners of the Lower Sort: Apolitical Soldiers in the American Revolution?" *Journal of American Studies* 33 (August 1999): 280–82.

32. See George Akerlof, "The Market for Lemons," *Quarterly Journal of Economics* 84 (August 1970): 488–500; "Adverse Selection" and "Asymmetric Information," in John Eatwell, Murray Milgate, and Peter Newman, eds., *The New Palgrave: A Dictionary of Economics*, vol. 1 (New York: Stockman Press, 1987), 32–34, 133–35.

sign of an immigrant worker's low productivity (a lemon) rather than a sign of higher debt, and would thus offer a low price per contract length. The redemption method solved this "lemons" problem by revealing both the debt and the physical condition of the redemptioner to potential buyers.

While the quantitative dimensions, legal aspects, and contractual mechanics of German immigration to and servitude in colonial America are known, we have until now had no detailed firsthand accounts by German redemptioners of why they decided to emigrate, what the recruitment process was like, and how the actual master-servant relationship functioned. Most of our descriptions of the trade have come from well-to-do German travelers who were at best only tangentially involved with the poorer half of the German migration stream. The Büttner and Whitehead narratives go a long way to filling the gaps in our knowledge of this aspect of early American history.[33]

Autobiography as Literature and History

Autobiography was still a new literary genre when John Frederick Whitehead and Johann Carl Büttner were constructing themselves through their life stories (and through their adopted names). Autobiography developed in tandem with the novel, both literary forms emerging early in the eighteenth century. Because autobiography inscribes on the subject a unified purpose, a literary imagining of life's trajectory, it is more likely than other genres of self-writing (diaries, correspondence) to seek causation, explanation, and meaning in the subject's life. The recounting of life in an autobiography is like the plotting of a novel: through the process of writing the subject or hero exhibits her or his moral character. The difference is that autobiographical accounts are presumed to be factual, even if the author must be selective and artful in recounting experience, while fiction is clearly invention masquerading as fact.

Büttner does not mention or demonstrate clearly his literary influences or role models. By contrast, Whitehead, while he does not spell out his models

---

33. See the assessment in McCusker and Menard, *Economy of British America*, 242–43. For the known descriptions of the German servant trade provided by German immigrants or English travelers who were not themselves redemptioners or servants, i.e., by Henry Bradshaw Fearon, Ludwig Gall, Gottlieb Mittelberger, Henry Melchior Muehlenberg, Elder Johannes Naas, and Christopher Saur, see the quotations in Diffendeffer, "German Immigration into Pennsylvania," 191–93, 239–45, 300–303; Donald F. Durnbaugh, "Two Early Letters from Germantown," *Pennsylvania Magazine of History and Biography* 84 (April 1959): 231–33; Grubb, *German Immigrant Servant Contracts*, vi–vii; Gottlieb Mittelberger, *Journey to Pennsylvania in the Year 1750 and Return to Germany in the Year 1754*, trans. Carl Theo. Eben (Philadelphia: Joseph Y. Jeanes, 1898), 26–28; Strassburger, *Pennsylvania German Pioneers*, 1:xxxvii; Trautmann, "Pennsylvania Through a German's Eyes," 40–41. See also Rosalind J. Beiler, "The Transatlantic World of Caspar Wistar: From Germany to America in the Eighteenth Century" (Ph.D. diss., University of Pennsylvania, 1994).

or influences, at least demonstrates that he has some knowledge of and interest in the works of particular poets and classical texts. Both young men
were literate and had received regular schooling in Germany, and at least
Whitehead had had access to a fairly large library in the noble household in
which he was employed before emigrating. Thus both men probably had
been exposed to and influenced by the German and English literary trends of
the eighteenth century.

The earliest autobiographies were typically written by the famous—nobles,
generals, politicians, diplomats, courtiers, and clergy—and by the infamous,
especially actors, actresses, criminals, and the mistresses of the rich and
famous. But commoners were also drawn to autobiography, initially narrat-
ing their paths to conversion as part of the religious revivals and awaken-
ings sweeping across Europe and the colonies in the middle decades of the
eighteenth century. In America, the first slave narratives found a small but
growing audience of educated northerners horrified by the trade in human
beings. Captivity narratives, the popular accounts of colonials forcibly adopted
by "Indians," by contrast, usually cast Euro-Americans as victims of Native
American barbarity. Benjamin Franklin worked on his autobiography, the
story of his determined rise from runaway servant to world-famous scientist
and diplomat, until shortly before his death in 1790. In Germany, Johann
Wolfgang von Goethe began his autobiography in the first decade of the
nineteenth century.[34]

Autobiography assumes a unique individuality and a coherent life course.[35]
The autobiographer is self-aware and traces the development of a distinctive
personality by emphasizing his or her formative experiences and the emotional and psychological responses to those experiences. It is a form that
became available not only to the politically influential or scandalous individual, as were earlier memoirs, but to all. As Ann Fabian has written, it was

34. Benjamin Franklin, *Memoirs*, ed. Max Farrand (Berkeley and Los Angeles: University of
California Press, 1949); Johann Wolfgang von Goethe, *Memoirs of Goethe: Written by Himself* (*Aus
Meinem Leben, Dichtung und Wahrheit*) (London: Henry Colburn, 1824); Gregor Sebba, "Intro-
duction: Goethe's Autobiography, Truth or Fiction?" in *The Autobiography of Johann Wolfgang
Von Goethe*, trans. John Oxenford (New York: Horizon Press, 1969); Wellenreuther, "Contexts
for Migration," 22; David Waldstreicher, *Runaway America: Benjamin Franklin, Slavery, and the
American Revolution* (New York: Hill and Wang, 2004).

35. Stephen Carl Arch, in an otherwise very useful series of analyses of particular texts,
argues that there was no true autobiography until the word came into widespread use circa 1810.
Most literature on the subject describes a gradual evolution of the form. See his *After Franklin:
The Emergence of Autobiography in Post-Revolutionary America, 1780–1830* (Hanover: University
of New Hampshire Press, 2001); Felicity Nussbaum, *The Autobiographical Subject: Gender and
Ideology in Eighteenth-Century England* (Baltimore: Johns Hopkins University Press, 1989); Patricia Meyer Spacks, *Imagining a Self: Autobiography and Novel in Eighteenth-Century England* (Cambridge: Harvard University Press, 1976); Cathy N. Davidson, *Revolution and the Word: The Rise
of the Novel in America* (New York: Oxford University Press, 1986).

the late eighteenth and early nineteenth centuries' combination of "Enlightenment faith in the rational capacity of all human beings and a Romantic interest in individual lives [that brought about] the impulse to discern and articulate an order in the apparent chaos of a life"—even the life of an obscure person.[36]

Novels also highlighted individual experience. Those involving adventures to strange lands were an important literary influence in the eighteenth century. Daniel Defoe's *Robinson Crusoe,* first published in 1719, recounted the adventure of an otherwise unremarkable person, and enjoyed a resurgence of popularity in America around 1800, judging by its numerous reprintings by various publishers, as well as on the European continent, as illustrated by the retelling of the *Robinson Crusoe* story for children by Joachim Heinrich Campe.[37]

Novels explored the emotions for didactic reasons and not only titillated the reader with tales of mad, headlong passion, unrequited love, seduction, elopement, illicit sex, dishonor, sorrow, longing, and lingering pathetic death, but also upheld, often through contrast, the ideals of true love, social respectability, and personal fulfillment in marriage. The recounting of individual experience, whether in fact or in fiction, should, according to the conventions of the time, guide the reader to virtue. Both Whitehead and Büttner cast their autobiographies as moral lessons for the next generation; this was a commonplace stance designed to turn self-revelation into useful knowledge and avoid the self-centeredness inherent in the autobiographical form.[38] The reader could find his or her own moral compass by learning from another's trials.

In both autobiographies and novels, youth was depicted as the crucial stage in life. Most eighteenth- and nineteenth-century novels focused on the perils of courtship. The choices made during these crucial negotiations of passion and respectability would presumably shape the lives of the heroes and heroines forever. In autobiographies, too, the emphasis was often on the experiences of youth, though not usually on courtship. Youthful experiences

36. Ann Fabian, *The Unvarnished Truth: Personal Narratives in Nineteenth-Century America* (Berkeley and Los Angeles: University of California Press, 2000), 2. See also Joyce Appleby, *Inheriting the Revolution: The First Generation of Americans* (Cambridge: Harvard University Press, 2000).

37. Joachim Heinrich Campe, *The New Robinson Crusoe; An Instructive and Entertaining History, for the Use of Children of Both Sexes* (London: John Stockdale, 1788; reprint, New York: Garland, 1976); Daniel Defoe, *Robinson Crusoe* (1719; reprint, New York: W. W. Norton, 1975); Pat Rogers, *Robinson Crusoe* (London: Allen & Unwin, 1979).

38. Laura Rigal, *The American Manufactory: Art, Labor, and the World of Things in the Early Republic* (Princeton: Princeton University Press, 1998), 56. For an earlier example, see also J. Stevens Cox, ed., *The Felon's Account of His Transportation at Virginia in America, by John Lauson* (St. Peters Port, Guernsey: Toucan Press, 1969).

formed the individual personality, opening some options and foreclosing others. The experiences of adulthood were generally depicted as the culmination or fruition of choices already made in youth, and were of less interest to the autobiographer. This was the case for both Whitehead and Büttner, who sketched their courtships, marriages, and adult careers only briefly, after giving lengthy accounts of their youthful adventures.[39]

Both Whitehead's and Büttner's accounts of the self are transitional documents incorporating several of the literary genres that contributed to the development of autobiography: the picaresque tale or travel account, the conversion narrative, the scandalous memoir, the crime story, the romance, the didactic morality tale, the captivity tale, and, particularly for Büttner, the eyewitness history of political or military figures and events. Whitehead also employed poetic, pastoral, melodramatic, and gothic genres in telling his life story. His focus on his emotions and individual perceptions differs significantly from Büttner's relatively sober narrative approach. Detailed descriptions of places, incidents, historically significant battles and people, and his own actions and adventures make up the bulk of Büttner's memoir; he offers little introspection or reflection upon the events he describes, though he does at times offer an assessment of his behavior as a cautionary moral lesson for his readers. There is no overarching "plot" in Büttner's account of himself. It is primarily a picaresque tale of travel and adventure organized chronologically around dramatic events. Even though Büttner wrote some thirty years after Whitehead and called his publication a *Selbstbiographie* (autobiography), his account is far less deeply influenced by contemporary literary tropes than is Whitehead's. Even his early twentieth-century translator did not consider his work an autobiography, but chose to call it a narrative, "an interesting medley of serious incidents and accidental exploits." The sequence of episodes Büttner recounts lacks the thematic unity of Whitehead's presentation of his life story.[40]

In marked contrast to Büttner's, Whitehead's manuscript is pensive and emotive, or perhaps self-indulgent. How much of this was due to the lingering effects of abuse in childhood or to the influence of the new masculine ideal of the emotive man, as illustrated by Goethe's enormously popular romantic novel *The Sorrows of Young Werther* (1774 and scores of other editions in English and German) is hard to say. In any case, Whitehead's manuscript is certainly influenced by novels, poetry, and contemporary autobiographies. He uses various devices to describe his anguished feelings of isolation and

39. See Camilla Stivers, "Reflections on the Role of Personal Narrative in Social Science," *Signs: Journal of Women in Culture and Society* 18 (winter 1993): 408–25.

40. Charles Frederick Heartman, trans., *Narrative of Johann Carl Buettner in the American Revolution* (New York: Heartman, 1915), introduction, no page numbers.

homesickness upon leaving Stralsund and Hamburg and his despair during his incarceration in Amsterdam by the "soul sellers" who sought to place him and other migrant inmates on outbound vessels. At various points Whitehead's prose also employs language that may strike modern readers as highly melodramatic and maudlin, especially in contrast to Büttner's rather sober journalistic tone, but that highlights his reflections and intense emotional responses to crucial turning points in his youth.

Considering that Büttner and Whitehead traveled on the same ship to America under similar recruitment circumstances, their interpretations of their experiences, including those they had in common, could not be more dissimilar. Together, therefore, these two autobiographies provide an uncommon breadth of insight into the range of understandings that poor eighteenth-century migrants to America had of themselves and their world.

Part I: John Frederick Whitehead

Introduction
Understanding the Worlds of John Frederick Whitehead

John Frederick Whitehead (also known as Johann Friedrich Kukuck) composed his autobiography in 1795. He was not a typical writer. He was neither famous nor infamous, just a thirty-eight-year-old man, married with small children, a poor, rural Pennsylvania tenant and weaver, an immigrant from the German-speaking states of northern Europe. He was, at least on the surface, typical of many other recent arrivals in late eighteenth-century America. Born in Pomerania in 1757, he migrated to the colonies in his midteens. He was different from others of his time primarily because in the early years of the Republic, at the height of the French Revolution, he decided to dictate his life story to more affluent friends and neighbors. After his death in 1815, his descendants carefully preserved the manuscript of his life and adventures as they migrated from Pennsylvania to Ohio, Indiana, Illinois, and, finally, California.

Whitehead was a servant in Europe in his youth, an indentured servant in America for six and a half years in late adolescence, and a landless weaver in early adulthood. His autobiography offers intriguing details on the labor recruitment process that transported thousands of poor single men and women from Germany and nearby parts of northern and central Europe to the New World. Whitehead's narrative also provides fascinating vignettes of life in the various communities in which he lived, including the Swedish-controlled city of Stralsund in Pomerania on the coast of the Baltic Sea; the Free and Hanseatic City of Hamburg among the northern Germanic states; Amsterdam and Rotterdam, in the United Netherlands; and Berks County in Pennsylvania. Perhaps most significantly, his is an introspective personal account of the feelings and hopes and fears of a young man growing up under difficult circumstances. This fascinating memoir has only recently been made available to the public by his descendants. It is a welcome addition to the personal accounts of travel and settlement written by ordinary colonists, the impoverished, anonymous, and usually bound immigrants who were the majority of arrivals in American ports in the eighteenth century.[1]

Pomerania

Whitehead grew up in the state of Pomerania in and around the city of Stralsund. Pomerania was a German-speaking region, although under the rule of the King of Sweden, Gustav IV. Major social and political changes in Pomerania began in the fourteenth century, when thousands of German subjects immigrated into the region and formed separate German settlements among the native Slavs. The result was that the local Slavic population became a minority that had to adjust to the customs and language of the German immigrants. The region of Pomerania was highly disputed among the central and northern European powers of Prussia, Denmark, Sweden, and Russia beginning with the Thirty Years' War (1618–48), when the territory was first divided between Sweden and Brandenburg (later Prussia). With the Peace of Osnabrück in 1701, Pomerania was joined to other German states, since the Swedish king also served as an elector within the Holy Roman Empire, although that "empire" had little authority. During the First Nordic War, King Charles XII of Sweden capitulated in Stralsund in 1715, when the province came under Danish control. The Peace of Frederiksborg

1. Otto Pollak offers brief insights in "German Immigrant Problems in Eighteenth-Century Pennsylvania as Reflected in Trouble Advertisements," *American Sociological Review* 8 (December 1943): 674–84. The journal of a paying passenger, Johannes Herbergs, is translated in Dieter Pesch, ed., *Brave New World: Rhinelanders Conquer America: The Journal of Johannes Herbergs* (Kommern: Martina Galunder-Verlag, 2001). Our thanks to Marianne Wokeck for this citation. The few other accounts concern British migrants, including James Annesley, *Memoirs of an Unfortunate Young Nobleman, Returned from Thirteen Years' Slavery in America: A Story Founded on Truth and Addressed Equally to the Head and the Heart* (London: Freeman, 1763); Peter Williamson, *The Life and Curious Adventures of Peter Williamson, Who Was Carried Off from Aberdeen and Sold for a Slave* (Aberdeen, 1804); Olaudah Equiano, *The Interesting Narrative and Other Writings*, ed. Vincent Carretta (New York: Penguin, 1995); and Susan E. Klepp and Billy G. Smith, *The Infortunate: The Voyage and Adventures of William Moraley, An Indentured Servant* (University Park: Pennsylvania State University Press, 1992, rev. ed. 2005). A rare account by a woman is Elizabeth Ashbridge, "Some Account of the Fore Part of the Life of Elizabeth Ashbridge," in *Journeys in New Worlds: Early American Women's Narratives*, ed. William L. Andrews et al. (Madison: University of Wisconsin Press, 1990), 117–80. There are very few other firsthand accounts.

of 1720 returned Pomerania to Sweden and at the same time gave Prussia some Pomeranian territory. During the Seven Years' War (1756–63), Pomerania again became the battleground between Swedish and Prussian troops. Prussia continued to expand in the area as a result of the French-Dutch War of 1772.[2]

Whitehead's childhood was shaped in the aftermath of these wars, which further complicated the already unstable finances of his stepfather, burdened his grandparents with quartered troops, and, through a postwar accident in an ammunition storage facility, destroyed much of his hometown. While the Prussian part of Pomerania benefited from an economic boost, because the Prussian government protected the rights of the small farmers, the Swedish part was neglected because of Sweden's own declining economic and political position in the eighteenth century. Whitehead's determination to seek opportunity elsewhere may have stemmed, at least in part, from the grim economic realities of a declining Swedish empire and a partially destroyed city. His decision to leave may not have been as foolish or rash as he later suggested.

Stralsund, as one of the major port cities on the Baltic Sea, had played an important role in the Hanseatic League, a mercantile alliance founded in medieval times of the most powerful northern European port cities that controlled the Baltic and North Atlantic sea trade. Starting in the twelfth century, the most powerful northern German mercantile cities began to ally in order to encourage trade in luxury goods and achieve special trade privileges for their members. The cities of Lübeck, Bremen, and Hamburg were leaders of the organization, which expanded its trade networks north and east.[3] In the absence of governmental protection of the North Sea, the league itself protected its commerce and its trade routes, granted its members exclusive trading rights, and tried to achieve trade monopolies. The constituent cities were allied against possible enemies and maintained, at the peak of their power, highly profitable trade networks in luxury goods between the more than one hundred Hanseatic cities.[4] The decline of the Hanseatic League began gradually in the fifteenth century, but the trade networks it had established remained largely intact and were used and protected by private entrepreneurs.

2. Robert Nisbet Bain, *Charles XII and the Collapse of the Swedish Empire, 1682–1719* (New York: G. P. Putnam's Sons, 1914), 266–67; Johannes Hinz, *Pommern: Wegweiser Durch ein Unvergessenes Land* (Augsburg: Bechtermuenz Verlag, 1997), 366–67.

3. Philippe Dollinger, *The German Hansa* (Stanford: Stanford University Press, 1970), 26–30; Helen Zimmern, *The Hansa Towns* (London: T. Fisher Unwin, 1889).

4. While the exact numbers are still being debated among scholars, Dollinger mentions that there were about seventy full-member towns of the league, which were called "Towns of the Hansa" and about another hundred partial members referred to as "Hanseatic Towns." Dollinger, *German Hansa*, 85–88.

Whitehead's journey from Stralsund to Hamburg and Amsterdam shows that even long after the political and economic power of the Hanseatic League had declined, the major cities were still vitally connected through the Hanseatic infrastructure, and the cities still allowed relatively unrestricted trade and travel between former members of the league. One item of trade was human labor. Johann Carl Büttner, recruited, like Whitehead, in Hamburg, notes that the Hansa cities were full of "soul venders" tied to the international market in bound and waged labor based in Amsterdam.[5]

Family

Patriarchal relations prevailed in much of Europe and its colonies in the mid-eighteenth century. As can be seen in Whitehead's case, fathers ruled over their wives and children by law and custom. Their authority included the right to punish their wives and children physically. A husband's "right to correct behavior physically [was] tied to implicit or explicit assumptions about the foundations of household unity. Power had to be located at one point in the house [and]. . . . [v]iolence was integral to state ideology" concerning the family's role in the preservation of property, according to David Warren Sabean.[6] Whitehead's mother and grandmother may have been appalled by the severity of Whitehead's beatings by his stepfather, but they had no authority to stop the abuse and could only try to pacify Whitehead's stepfather or wait until he was in a better mood and ask that young Johann Friedrich be sent away to his grandmother's house.[7]

Marriages were in large measure economic alliances, a means to raise social status or insurance against economic hardship. Distinct gender roles meant that the labor and skills of both an adult man and an adult woman were necessary to maintain a household. In the eighteenth century it was quite common, especially in the countryside, for widowers and widows to remarry very quickly because of the difficult economic conditions faced by single adults, especially those with small children. Thus families consisting of many children who might not be related, as spouses became widowed multiple times, were common in eighteenth-century German lands. As the literature on this subject indicates, stepchildren were part of the family, but

5. Büttner, Büttner, der Amerikaner, 7.

6. David Sabean, Property, Production, and Family in Neckarhausen, 1700–1870 (New York: Cambridge University Press, 1990), 133.

7. It was possible for women to assert themselves, but the social and legal costs were great. See Steven Ozment, The Bürgermeister's Daughter: Scandal in a Sixteenth-Century German Town (New York: St. Martin's Press, 1996).

because they were related only by law they were often not treated equally.[8] In addition, divergent attitudes on illegitimacy may have played a part in family culture. Premarital pregnancy was common, particularly in the countryside, but was ideally to be followed by marriage.[9]

This context may shed some light on Whitehead's case. His mother, Ann Gristow, married or remarried within a year of her presumed husband's death. And although a blood relationship does not necessarily indicate the status and treatment of particular family members, it seems that Whitehead's relationship with his stepfather was influenced by the fact that his stepson was not his biological heir and may have been illegitimate. Custom dictated that the stepchild be provided for, but in a patriarchal society this was considered a net loss, since a stepson was not part of the lineage. Whitehead's stepfather was obviously concerned about making his stepson as productive as possible as soon as possible, having him serve as his valet and putting him to work herding geese. Whitehead's stepfather used his position as head of the household as well as his physical superiority to intimidate Whitehead as a child and to take money from him when he was older, but he did not use what little authority he possessed to protect the child from his superior's abuse. Ideally, heads of household were honor bound to protect all their subordinates; in reality relationships might more closely resemble the story of Hansel and Gretel or one of the other cautionary folktales recorded by the brothers Grimm. It was therefore not surprising, as Farley Grubb has discovered, that fatherless boys were particularly prone to emigrate and did so without regard for changing economic cycles or religious factors.[10]

The frequently harsh realities of patriarchal family life were being challenged in the eighteenth century by sentimental, romantic, and egalitarian ideas that saw affection as the only appropriate foundation of marriage. Whitehead includes several stories of relationships based on deeply felt love that challenged the familial authority of fathers, ran contrary to familial economic interests or status considerations, and even occurred outside the strictures of law and religion. New ideas about emotional fulfillment through marriage promised a revolution in family relations by giving both women and men more power as individuals to determine the course of their lives and to seek their own interests. In liberating the young from paternal authority, these new standards also left the young and naïve with less protection than before against fortune hunters and other predators. Whitehead, writing in the 1790s,

8. Michael Mitterauer and Reinhard Sieder, *The European Family: Patriarchy to Partnership from the Middle Ages to the Present* (Oxford: Basil Blackwell, 1982), 16.

9. Ibid., 125–29.

10. Farley Grubb, "Fatherless and Friendless: Factors Influencing the Flow of English Emigrant Servants," *Journal of Economic History* 52 (March 1992): 85–108.

approved of these new relations. He thought young men and women should be free to choose their marriage partners. But as the parent of several small children, Whitehead also sought a balance between the rights of individuals and the careful counsel of parents.[11]

The conflict between parental authority grounded in social and economic prudence and individual choice based on romantic desire and emotional fulfillment existed in the New World as well as in Europe. The Quakers with whom Whitehead lived as a servant, and with whom he chose to stay when a free man, tended more than other groups to rein in the authority of parents over their children's marriages. Eighteenth-century Quakers emphasized love and companionship between husband and wife and as the appropriate basis for childrearing, but also gave the local meeting considerable supervisory powers over courtship.[12] The tensions between the claims of the individual and those of the family and community, between love and fiscal prudence, between independence and obedience, between emotion and respectability, were expressed somewhat differently in Pennsylvania than in Europe, but balancing these competing values was difficult in both settings. Both economic and status considerations and love seem to have played roles in Whitehead's own marriage. Whitehead's poverty undoubtedly limited his prospective partners to women of little wealth, even if his choice became "his dear companion," while back in Europe Büttner was able to draw on family connections in making his more advantageous match.[13]

A Question of Names and Texts

Verifying John Frederick Whitehead's text as authentic was not difficult. The provenance of the volume can be traced through his male descendents. Whitehead's autobiography was given first to Whitehead's eldest son, John, who gave it in turn to his son Michael, who was married in Vermillion, Illinois, to Ann Showalter in 1846. Michael and Ann Whitehead's second son, Ethan Edwin Whitehead, was born in Lawrenceville, Indiana, and later

11. See G. J. Barker-Benfield, *The Culture of Sensibility: Sex and Society in Eighteenth-Century Britain* (Chicago: University of Chicago Press, 1992); Jan Lewis, "The Republican Wife: Virtue and Seduction in the Early Republic," *William and Mary Quarterly*, 3d ser., 44 (October 1987): 689–721; Lawrence Stone, *The Family, Sex, and Marriage in England, 1500–1800* (New York: Harper, 1977).

12. J. William Frost, *The Quaker Family in Colonial America* (New York: St. Martin's Press, 1973); Barry Levy, *Quakers and the American Family: British Settlement in the Delaware Valley* (New York: Oxford University Press, 1988); Susan E. Klepp and Karin A. Wulf, *A Novel Life: The Diary of Hannah Callender Sansom, 1757–1787* (University Park: Pennsylvania State University Press, forthcoming).

13. Whitehead memoir, 155; Büttner, *Büttner, der Amerikaner*, 124–25.

moved to California, where the manuscript remained in the family's possession in Los Angeles until being donated to the Pennsylvania State University
Library in 2003.[14] The arrival and indenture of Johann Friedrich Kukuck and
the tax and census records for Frederick Whitehead validate Whitehead's
account, but only the autobiography links the person named Kukuck, who
can be traced back to Amsterdam but who has, insofar as the public records
show, no future after landing in Philadelphia, with the person named Whitehead, who, according to public records, has a future in Pennsylvania and
Ohio, but no past. Only Whitehead's life story provides the connections that
link and make sense of the public records.

Whitehead's American career proved much easier to validate than his early
life. The primary problem is his surname; Whitehead, the name he used
in America, is an English, not a Germanic, surname. Berks County records
usually list him simply as Frederick Whitehead, and this is also how he
signed his poem advertising a reward for lost sheep at the end of the 1790s.
The name that Whitehead was given at birth is a matter of conjecture.
"John Frederick" translates easily into German as Johann Friedrich. German
equivalents of "Whitehead" include "Wittkopf" or "Wittkoff" in the local
dialect, "Blondkopf" and "Weisskopf" (Weißkopf) in standard German. But
he bore his stepfather's surname in childhood and adolescence, signing his
name "Johann Friedrich Kukuck" upon his arrival in Philadelphia.[15] He had
undoubtedly been given that name in infancy, when his mother married
Joachim Kuckuck, since by law he then came under the authority of his
mother's husband.

Wittkopf was a common name in the city of Stralsund. Most Wittkopfs
were tailors, merchants, or shippers and were thus bourgeois in social class.
Efforts at finding a birth or baptism record for a Johann Friedrich under
any of the German variants of Whitehead or Kuckuck/Kukuck, or Gristo, his
mother's maiden name, in the Stralsund Stadt Archiv have proved fruitless.
Whitehead states that his father's parents died young and that his father's
friends (that is, in the language of the day, his family or guardians) had
helped set him up in business. He notes that his paternal grandfather was a

14. It is interesting that the family history of the Whiteheads was intertwined for several generations with the kin of Whitehead's former master, John Starr. There were Starrs living in
Hamilton County, Ohio, where Frederick Whitehead lived at the end of his life. According to the
1830 census, Jeremiah Starr lived in Vermillion, Illinois, along with several other Starrs, and
Jeremiah Starr published A California Adventure and Vision: Prose and Poetry in Cincinnati in
1864. For the Whitehead genealogy, see e-mail message from Dennis Whitehead to Peter Potter,
editor-in-chief, Pennsylvania State University Press, March 28, 2003, copy in the possession of
Susan E. Klepp.

15. See Ralph B. Strassburger, Pennsylvania German Pioneers: A Publication of the Original
Lists of Arrivals in the Port of Philadelphia from 1727 to 1808, vols. 1–3, ed. William John Hinke
(Norristown, Pa.: Pennsylvania German Society, 1934), 2:867–68.

merchant, and there is a record of a trader named Johann Wittkopff who declared bankruptcy in 1739. But while the surname is common, there is only one other Johan Wittkopf in the local records. A master tailor, Johan Christian Wittkopf is listed as marrying Maria Elisabeth Hensch in 1756, the year before Johann Friedrich's birth.[16] No other Johann or Friedrich Wittkopf appears in the Stralsund records. Whitehead asserts that a status differential between his mother and father created a permanent rift between Whitehead's parents, on the one side, and his father's friends, on the other. Since the father was supposedly buried in 1757 in St. Jacob's churchyard (Sankt Jacobi Kirche, still standing), when Whitehead was three months old, church records should record both events. The records of St. Jacob's Church survive, but there is no baptism that can be linked to the author either under Wittkopf or under his mother's name, nor is there a burial recorded for the father under one of the varied spellings of Wittkopf or Weisskopf. Unfortunately, all local records are recorded on separate alphabetized cards, and it is not possible to access the fragile originals and search by date.

This failure to recover Whitehead's father's name may indicate that John Frederick's original surname was not one of the Germanic versions of Whitehead. The differences in social status between his birth parents may hint that they never married—perhaps the father did not die but abandoned Whitehead's pregnant mother and married Hensch. If so, Whitehead would have been illegitimate. Whitehead may not have been baptized, or his mother may have given birth in a distant town. This might help explain both his interest in tales of illicit love and illegitimacy as well as his stepfather's anger at his very existence.

But it is also possible that his American surname had origins outside Pomerania, rather than being a translation of his biological father's. Whitehead did have a neighbor in Pennsylvania named George Whitehead Jr., a Quaker who died in 1780 without male heirs. It is just possible that the young servant considered this neighbor a surrogate father and, when stripping himself of his hated stepfather's surname, adopted the name Whitehead.[17] That he did not mention this Whitehead in his autobiography may be another instance of his focus on authority figures rather than on his peers and closest friends. Another possibility is that "Whitehead" might simply describe Kukuck's hair color. When Whitehead "began to strip off [his] old tattered European Skin . . . and exchanged it for a good sound American Buckskin,"

16. Birth, Marriage, and Death Records, Stadtarchiv der Hansestadt Stralsund, hereafter SHS. We are deeply indebted to Christian and Uta Kresse for their research in these archives and for the assistance of the local archivists.

17. "Whitehead," Exeter Monthly Meeting Records, Historical Society of Pennsylvania, Philadelphia (hereafter HSP).

he may have stripped off his European identity as well.[18] In any case, White-head's origins remain a mystery.

Although documents verifying his presence in Stralsund between 1757 and 1772 have yet to be found, Whitehead's manuscript offers evidence of his detailed knowledge of the place, of contemporary events, and of prominent people that supports the overall authenticity of his memoir. Whitehead's experiences in Hamburg have yet to be verified, but the city was both an important port and a sugar-refining center in the mid-eighteenth century, which lends credence to his account. His arrival in Pennsylvania is much better documented. About five weeks after swearing the oath of loyalty to George III, Whitehead entered into an indenture with Mordecai Lee and James Starr. He was the next to last of the redemptioners to be sold.[19] Lee and Starr transferred ownership to John Starr, James's brother and Mordecai's brother-in-law. All three lived in Maidencreek Township in Berks County, Pennsylvania, northwest of Philadelphia.

Maidencreek Township, Berks County

Maidencreek (or Maiden Creek) is a translation of Ontelaunee, a word of Susquehannock or Shawnee origin, and now the name of a reservoir that engulfs the original site of the local Quaker meetinghouse and the school-house. The Blue or Endless Mountain forms the northwestern edge of the township. The land is well watered, gently rolling, and fertile, and the inhabitants' occupations are given in the tax lists of 1794 as farmers, artisans, and operators of a local forge, several tanneries, and grist and sawmills. It remained a rural district until quite recently but is currently becoming a suburb of Reading, the county seat.

Whitehead mentions the poor roads in his account; the area did not attract contemporary travelers who might have written descriptions. However, an 1841 diary entry by Eliza John describes a landscape and some Quaker families that would have been familiar to Whitehead.

> May, 1841—we traveled on to Maiden Creek. Arrived at our kind friends James and Sarah Starss about one oclock . . . [we] passed Maiden Creek Meeting House and some excellent buildings and delightful farms. . . . The buildings are chiefly stone, verry neatly finished off. Limestone houses look better than common stone. We

18. Whitehead memoir, 142.
19. Our thanks to Farley Grubb for this analysis of the records.

traveled over the Oley hills, verry rough indeed. Most distressing bad roads. We passed a beautiful little town called Freedensburgh. Chiefly stone the houses were, small and neat. Stores, taverns, and so forth. Next we came to Exetre and passed their meeting house, then on to Emily [and] John Lees, near Monoquscy Creek. We had traveled sixteen miles from Stars, awful roads, and arrived at Lees just before dark.[20]

The township was a rarity in the county for having a substantial number of English-speaking Quakers, most of them from Ireland. Still, a large portion of the township was German. The surnames in the 1794 tax list suggest that more than 60 percent of heads of household were of German origin.[21]

Berks County was overwhelmingly pro-American during the Revolutionary War, and even local Quakers were neutral rather than pro-British, as many wealthy Philadelphia Quakers were in private. The Revolution brought refugees from British-occupied Philadelphia into Reading; prisoners of war were housed there as well. Rents soared. A large ammunition dump was located in Reading after 1777 that caused considerable concern about the possibility of a disastrous explosion; the Germans in particular must have known of the Stralsund explosion of 1770. Edicts issued by the revolutionary county government and enforced by the militia commandeered wool, flax, thread, and cloth for the American army and clothing became scarce. Roving army units seized animals, fodder, and food. Troops were quartered in private houses and, as Whitehead notes, these men were frequently drunk and disruptive on payday. What united the vast majority of residents behind revolution and war was a long-standing complaint about the underrepresentation of the county in the provincial assembly, a fierce devotion to property rights—not only did the German Lutherans and Reformed oppose the gradual abolition of slavery but so did local Quakers—and the memory of "great oppression" in Europe.[22]

The Revolution produced lasting changes. The county gained the representation in the assembly that it wanted, but it was the Germans rather than the English who now dominated local politics. Owen Ireland has shown that the Germans voted for German candidates in 1788, no matter what their party affiliation, while by 1798 most Berks County Germans supported the Democratic Republicans. Most Quakers were Federalists and were outvoted

20. See http://freepage.genealogy.rootsweb.com/~nungesser/John/ElizaDiary/.

21. Maidencreek Tax Lists, microfilm of the originals, Historical Society of Pennsylvania.

22. Laura L. Becker, "The American Revolution as a Community Experience: A Case Study of Reading, Pennsylvania," paper delivered at the Conference on the Founding of Pennsylvania, University of Pennsylvania, Philadelphia, October 16, 1982, 9; Karen Guenther, "Berks County," in *Beyond Philadelphia: The American Revolution in the Pennsylvania Hinterland*, ed. John B. Frantz and William Pencak (University Park: Pennsylvania State University Press, 1998), 67–84.

in the county four to one.[23] This political shift and the lingering resentment of Quaker neutrality may be among the reasons for the migration of so many Quakers to Roaring Creek and Catawissa Townships in the postwar period.

Maidencreek Township had an unusual economic and social structure.✓ Instead of a pyramid—a broad base of poor folks, a sizable number of middling sorts, and a few individuals of extreme wealth—or a bell curve—a few desperately poor, a large segment of the comfortable, and a small elite—the township was divided into two distinct groups: the propertyless and those farmers and manufacturers with a hundred acres or more. There was almost no one in between. Of the heads of household listed in the 1794 tax list, forty-eight owned no land; twelve had between 1 and 99 acres (most had 50 acres or more); fifty had 100 to 250 acres; and seven had more than 250 acres. The same pattern prevailed in the tax assessments. The assessed value of the largest group (fifty-three individuals) was less than £100, and the vast majority of these poorest householders had less than £40 in taxable wealth. Only twelve households possessed real and personal estates worth £100–399, while forty-three had between £400 and £799 and nine had taxable property valued at more than £800.[24] This bimodal distribution suggests that it was not economically feasible to move gradually from propertylessness to sustainable farming by purchasing a few acres now and again. The aspiring poor would somehow have to make a leap from tenant to owner of one hundred acres or more, a difficult if not impossible maneuver.

Poverty in Berks County and elsewhere in southeastern Pennsylvania was in part a consequence of the shortage of land. Berks County was well settled by the time Whitehead arrived, and land prices were high; "only the wealthy could buy [land] behind the line of settlement."[25] In addition, war—the American Revolutionary War, the wars of the French Revolution, and the conflicts leading to the War of 1812—played havoc with markets and prices. Productivity was low even in the best of times and was always labor intensive. Bad weather could disrupt production. The ever-present possibility of sickness, injury, and death among craftsmen, tenant farmers, and wage earners might destroy a family's economic independence, and John Frederick Whitehead was neither strong nor robust. The changes associated with the early stages

23. Owen Ireland, *Religion, Ethnicity, and Politics: Ratifying the Constitution in Pennsylvania* (University Park: Pennsylvania State University Press, 1995), 283–84; Morton L. Montgomery, *Political Hand Book of Berks County* (Reading, Pa.: B.F. Owen, 1883), 61.

24. Maidencreek Tax Lists, 1794, in Berks County Tax Lists (microfilm of originals, HSP). For an overview of Pennsylvania in this period, see Susan E. Klepp, "Encounter and Experiment: The Colonial Period," in *Pennsylvania: A History of the Commonwealth*, ed. Randall M. Miller and William Pencak (University Park: Pennsylvania State University Press, 2002), 47–100.

25. James T. Lemon, *"The Best Poor Man's Country": A Geographical Study of Early Southeastern Pennsylvania* (Baltimore: Johns Hopkins Press, 1972), 70.

of industrialization rewarded some craftsmen but marginalized others, including many weavers.[26]

John Frederick Whitehead finished his indenture and became a landless weaver and a cottager. He chose one of the most common trades in rural Pennsylvania. In 1800, about 4 percent of all heads of household, and about 12 percent of all artisans, were weavers.[27] This occupation did not promise a lucrative future. When Whitehead wrote his autobiography in 1795, he was quite aware that to remain in Maidencreek as a propertyless weaver was to remain poor. When he walked out the front door each day, everything he saw belonged to someone else.

A Weaver and a Cottager

Marianne Wokeck has found that most German bound laborers were purchased by Germans, but Whitehead's master was a Quaker, as was Büttner's. Whitehead suggests that it was the coincidence of the annual meeting of the Friends being held in Philadelphia that brought so many Quaker buyers to the *Sally* in 1773. The majority of Berks County residents were German, but Maidencreek Township contained one of the few English-speaking and Quaker communities in the county.[28] After he obtained his freedom Whitehead chose to remain in Maidencreek rather than move away and settle in a community of ethnic Germans. With one unhappy exception, he lived among Quakers. After six and a half years of service, he had established significant relationships with the close-knit community of Starrs and Lightfoots and their kin. He was able to use his connections and the ties among his former master's kin and neighbors to secure employment and housing. Whitehead's decision to adopt English ways was typical. Most German immigrants recognized that they were moving to an alien culture and would have to adjust. And, as Wokeck has pointed out, "the less stake emigrants had in the community they left behind [in Germany], the more likely they were to be open to the ways of their adoptive country."[29] Whitehead had no fondness for his

26. Billy G. Smith, "Introduction: 'The Best Poor Man's Country'?" in *Down and Out in Early America*, ed. Billy G. Smith (University Park: Pennsylvania State University Press, 2004), xi–xx; and Gary B. Nash, "Poverty and Politics in Early American History," ibid., 9–14.

27. Farley Grubb, "German Immigration to Pennsylvania, 1790–1820," *Journal of Interdisciplinary History* 20 (winter 1990): 432; Lee Soltow and Kenneth W. Keller, "Rural Pennsylvania in 1800: A Portrait from the Septennial Census," *Pennsylvania History* 49 (January 1982): 36.

28. Wokeck, *Trade in Strangers: The Beginnings of Mass Migration to North America* (University Park: Pennsylvania State University Press, 1999), 141ff.

29. Marianne S. Wokeck, "German Settlements in the British North American Colonies: A Patchwork of Cultural Assimilation and Persistence," in *In Search of Peace and Prosperity: New German Settlements in Eighteenth-Century Europe and America*, ed. Helmut T. Lehmann,

stepfather, was embarrassed by the prospect of returning to his former master, and, as far as is known, never attempted to contact his mother once he
settled in Pennsylvania. He had come alone, with no familial or strong insti-
tutional religious ties to the local German community. So it is not unusual
that he, like many others, assimilated among the British as quickly as possible. Whitehead moved and lived among Quakers for at least twenty years
after his arrival in Philadelphia, and various aspects of his life and beliefs suggest the impact of Quaker ideas on his outlook. Yet Whitehead never seems
to have become a Quaker himself. He was married in 1786 in the faith in
which he had been raised, though not in church. The Lutheran minister came
to his father-in-law's house to sanctify the union. His bride, Ann Thomson (or
Thompson), however, had an English surname, and her religious background
is unknown. His marriage was simply another step in becoming American.
Büttner, on the other hand, had a supportive family and good prospects back
in Germany and he returned there as quickly as possible.

After obtaining his freedom early in 1780, Whitehead tried to acquire a
trade, alternating between working as a day laborer and pursuing several
unsuccessful attempts to adopt a new vocation. His experiments with different trades show how he used local networks of families and neighbors. One
neighbor, Thomas Lightfoot, recommended him to a tanner in Philadelphia.
George Worrall, a local shoemaker who married one of John Starr's nieces,
took Whitehead on as an apprentice for a brief time. Finally, Whitehead
apprenticed himself to a local weaver, Thomas Pearson, who was brother-in-
law to John Starr twice over. Whitehead's efforts to secure adequate housing
for his family also demonstrate his networking efforts. Of the family's various
domiciles described in the manuscript, two were owned by Quaker neighbors, Thomas Lightfoot and John Hutton. A third was owned by John Parvin,
brother of another of neighbor, Francis Parvin, also Quakers. In addition,
at one point Whitehead and George Worrall's families shared living space
(apparently happily).[30]

He finally settled on becoming a weaver. The normal apprenticeship for
this trade lasted seven years. Whitehead learned the craft quickly, he asserts,
but it was several years before he could support a family. Once he had mastered the necessary skills, he had to purchase or make the tools of the trade.
Ideally, he needed three looms, one for linen, one for wool, and one for figured work. Each loom cost about £2. Since each loom required a space of five

---

Hermann Wellenreuther, and Renate Wilson (University Park: Pennsylvania State University
Press, 2000), 195.

30. Ibid., 108, 117, 118, 119–20, 121–22; *Friends' Meeting Records of Berks County*, compiled
from the original by John E. Eshelman (bound volume of photocopied originals), Historical
Society of Berks County, Reading, Pennsylvania, 250–51, 258–59, 313, 386–87.

and a half by four and a half feet, Whitehead needed a substantial workspace, or help dismantling and erecting the appropriate looms. Preferably the weaving area should have been away from living quarters since weaving is a dusty, dirty process. But looms and space were only the beginning. Spinning wheels, reels, swifts, spooling wheels, spool winders, spool racks, a warping board or warping mill, a bobbin winder, shuttles, bobbins, a raddle (warp regulator), reeds (for regulating thickness), brushes, shears, needles, papers for drafting designs, and a temple (width regulator) were required. Linen cloth had to be washed and bleached. If he (or more probably his wife, Ann Thomson Whitehead) also dyed cloth, he needed large and small iron pots for the purpose. He needed access to a fulling mill for the last stages of woolen production.[31] Weaving required a heavy investment, and not surprisingly it took Whitehead several years between learning the trade and setting up as a head of household to accumulate the basic equipment. Even then, suitable housing for his workshop and home remained a problem.

Weaving was not only a complex craft requiring heavy investments in tools and equipment, it was a financially precarious occupation. Weather could affect the flax harvest and sheep and wool production. The weaver had to depend on local farm laborers to hackle the flax and comb and card the wool, and on at least six (and more commonly twelve) outside women spinning at their wheels at home to produce linen and woolen thread for the loom. He needed the labor of his wife and his children to operate efficiently, setting up the looms, repairing threads, winding spools, bleaching, washing, and performing countless other tasks. Most cloth was "bespoken"—produced on order for specific customers—so the weaver was dependent on the individual orders of local customers. Locally woven cloth was always in competition with imported cloth, so the vagaries of international trade could affect his business. In addition, the cotton gin was patented in 1794 and the mechanized weaving of cheap cotton cloth soon eliminated linen production. The simultaneous introduction of Marino sheep was changing woolen weaving as well. It is not surprising, then, that successful hand weavers did not expand production but left the trade as quickly as they could to take up the easier and more profitable business of farming. Whitehead's later moves, to Windsor Township and Catawissa Township in Pennsylvania, and to Hamilton County in Ohio, were signs that he had abandoned weaving and was seeking cheap land to farm. "It may seem strange," Adrienne D. Hood has argued, "that after working so hard to acquire a skill an individual abandoned it. For many, however, the remuneration from weaving was a means to the end of acquiring

31. Adrienne D. Hood, *The Weaver's Craft: Cloth, Commerce, and Industry in Early Pennsylvania* (Philadelphia: University of Pennsylvania Press, 2003), 87–97, 107.

property. . . . Farming, not the labor-intensive craft of weaving, was the route to wealth in this region."[32] By 1810 Whitehead would be listed in the federal census as a farmer.[33]

Whitehead's experience as a weaver was fairly typical for a cottager, or landless worker. Lucy Simler and Paul Clemens have studied the careers of cottagers in late eighteenth- and early nineteenth-century Chester County, Pennsylvania. Cottagers or inmates were renters. Signing one-year contracts with landowners, they received a house and sufficient land for a garden and for grazing a single cow. Most cottagers rented an extra acre or two and took on additional debt for the use of horses and wagons, store purchases, and services. Cottagers paid landowners for rent, use of equipment, and livestock with agricultural labor, especially at harvest, and, if the cottager had a craft, with goods and services. Wives and older children also provided labor. This was not a barter system, as all transactions were calculated in cash and balances due were paid at the end of every year.[34] It was the labor requirement that distinguished cottagers from renters or simple tenants. The system provided farmers with the seasonal labor needed in flax and wheat cultivation—the primary staple crops of southeastern Pennsylvania. They could not efficiently employ extra labor year round because there was too little for a hired hand to do in the winter and midsummer. Most of the slaves in the county worked at the forges, not on farms.[35] The southern system of heavy investment in bound labor did not fit the seasonably variable demands of northern staple crops. Having cottagers living nearby and obliged by contract to work at peak periods fit local conditions better. Cottagers, especially those with a trade, received the benefit of full-time work and access to the resources owned by the landlord.

Whitehead's memoir confirms Simler's finding that cottagers were mobile, changing their residence every few years. One reason for this was the difficulty of finding affordable and adequate housing. Whitehead had great difficulty in this respect, perhaps because the high rents of the war years persisted through the 1780s. He describes the first home he shared with his wife as having no glass in the windows, no chimney, and a leaky roof. His description matches the archaeological reconstruction of a contemporary

32. Ibid., 103–4.

33. Manuscript Census Returns, Catawissa Township, Pennsylvania, under Whitehall.

34. Lucy Simler, "The Landless Worker: An Index of Economic and Social Change in Chester County, Pennsylvania, 1750–1820," *Pennsylvania Magazine of History and Biography* 114 (April 1990): 167–99; Paul G. E. Clemens and Lucy Simler, "Rural Labor and the Farm Household in Chester County, Pennsylvania, 1750–1820," in *Work and Labor in Early America*, ed. Stephen Innes (Chapel Hill: University of North Carolina Press, 1988), 106–43; Lucy Simler, "She Came to Work: The Female Labor Force in Chester County," paper given at the Seminar of the Transformation of Philadelphia and the Delaware Valley Project, Philadelphia, May 11, 1987.

35. Guenther, "Berks County," 83.

tenant cabin in Delaware.[36] He did not complain about other places he lived, but his memoir records that he moved five times in the first nine years of his marriage. Whitehead spent only a year or two in each location, though he may have stayed longer at the last one. Simler found similar mobility among workers listed in the tax roles in East Bradford, Chester County, between 1810 and 1821: one-third of cottagers moved after a year's residence and half after two years.[37] Cottagers shopped for lower rents, better housing, and higher wages. Landlords anticipated the coming year's needs and might prefer strong young laborers, tenants with many children, craftsmen who were carpenters, weavers, tailors, or shoemakers, or women skilled in spinning, knitting, nursing, cheese making, or other fields, depending on projected circumstances.

Once Whitehead mastered a trade that would gain him a place in the cottager labor and housing market, he was able to marry and became the head of a household. Heading a household meant paying taxes. Tax lists verify that he was a resident of Maidencreek from 1789 to 1794 (there are no extant records after 1794). They also indicate that he held no land but owned a cow and other unnamed assets, probably a rented house and an acre or two, assessed at values between £20 and £30 local currency, the lowest assessments possible. After 1795 records indicate that the Whiteheads moved at least three times, a greater distance each time. Census records reveal that by 1800 he had moved his family to Windsor, a township near Maidencreek and still within Berks County. Here his herd of eight sheep was stolen, an indication that he had acquired substantially more livestock and, undoubtedly, more land on which to graze these animals. But whether he owned or rented his place in Windsor is unknown. By 1810 he and his family had moved to Catawissa Township in what was then Northumberland County, Pennsylvania (where he was erroneously recorded in the federal census as "Frederick Whitehall") and which is now Columbia County, more mountainous terrain than found in Berks County. Although listed now as a farmer, he did not stay long—perhaps he was still a tenant. Whitehead's will indicates that by 1815, when he died at age fifty-eight, he had moved to Colerain Township in Hamilton County, Ohio, near Cincinnati, a newly settled area founded only in 1794.[38]

36. John Bedell et al., *The Ordinary and the Poor in Eighteenth-Century Delaware: Excavations at the Augustine Creek North and South Sites (7NC-G-144 and 7NC-G-145)* (Cultural Resources Group/Delaware Department of Transportation [Eugene E. Abbott, Series 159], 2001), chapter 6 at http:www.deldot.net/static/projects/archaeology/augustine_creek/chapter_6.html.

37. Whitehead memoir, 156; Simler, "Landless Worker," 177–78.

38. See reels 52–53 of Berks County Tax Lists (microfilm of originals, HSP); *Pennsylvania in 1800: A Computerized Index to the 1800 Federal Population Schedules of the State of Pennsylvania*, ed. John "D" Stemmons (Salt Lake City: Stemmons, 1972), 655, and *Population Schedules of the Third Census of the United States 1810*, roll 53, Pennsylvania (Washington, D.C.: National Archives, 1953), 245, Will of John Frederick Whitehead, 163–64.

Colerain Township was on the Great Miami River, with flat terrain and fertile soil that may have given the family an opportunity to acquire cheaper and
more productive farmland. Hamilton County was also notoriously unhealthy,
plagued by various unspecified fevers that may have hastened Whitehead's
death, his wife's death, and the deaths of two of the children.[39] John Whitehead, the eldest son, remained in Ohio along with his maternal uncle, Michael
Thompson, both now farmers, but the other children apparently had already
moved west.

Whitehead improved his family's socioeconomic circumstances in the
years after he dictated his memoirs by acquiring first livestock and then
the status of farmer. Most cottagers studied by Simler and by Clemens were
owed small amounts of money at the end of the year, and a careful and
healthy cottager might accumulate both cash and goods over the years, especially if he had a large family, since the labor of both boys and girls could add
to the family coffers. By moving toward the frontiers of Pennsylvania and
then Ohio, Whitehead was much more likely to have been able to afford to
purchase land. By 1810, if not before, he was a farmer; there were weavers in
Catawissa Township, but he was no longer one of them.

The only other indication of his later financial situation comes from a
record of an estate sale in 1819, after the death of his widow, Ann Thomson
Whitehead. The total value of this remnant of Whitehead's personal estate
was $162. This sum was approximately six months' income for a typical
laborer of the era, but some possessions had undoubtedly been sold or distributed among the children before the vendue, or estate sale. What remained
for the sale were gardening and cooking utensils, primarily equipment used
by women, and a few luxury items like silver spoons, tea sets, books, and a
mirror. The tools for weaving and farming, the stuff of men's work, may have
been sold or distributed earlier. Had Frederick Whitehead chosen to write
his life in 1815 instead of 1795, he might well have been able to pen a happier
ending that celebrated modest accomplishment in achieving a degree of economic independence and in amply providing for his wife and children, rather
than regret over his youthful indiscretions and servile status.

A Cottager's Autobiography

Frederick Whitehead develops two themes in bringing order to his frequently
uprooted life. Much of his self-evaluation bewails the decisions and attitudes

39. P. S. Connor, "Medical," in *The History of Cincinnati and Hamilton County*, ed. S. B. Nelson and J. M. Runk (Cincinnati: Nelson and Company, 1894), 225. See Appendix C to Whitehead's memoir for Whitehead's children.

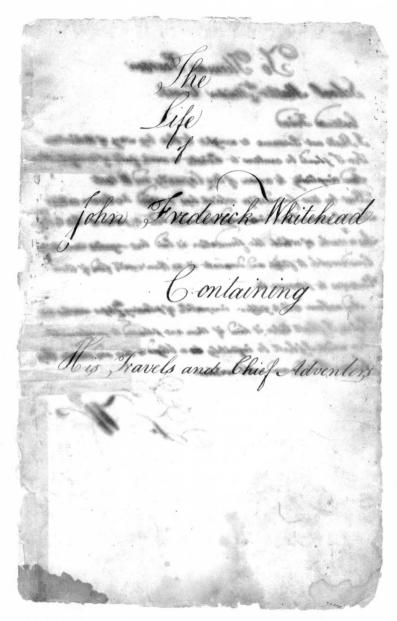

Fig. 2 Title page of John Frederick Whitehead's memoir, written in his own hand. Courtesy of the Pennsylvania State University Libraries, University Park.

of his adolescence. In the depths of his despair, he resorts to well-rehearsed poetic dirges and pastoral tropes of a lost idyllic existence. He uses his personal history and his strong emotional responses to events to tell a morality tale—for the benefit of his children, he explicitly states—one that warns against the recklessness of youth.[40] This purpose is most evident in Whitehead's discussion of those people who sought to dissuade him from his desire to travel, such as his master in Stralsund and his uncle in Hamburg, as well as in his generally negative assessment of his achievements up to 1795.

The danger of impetuous youth, however, competes with another theme in the manuscript, that of the victimization of the innocent or vulnerable by those in authority. The theme of oppression left little room for any account of companionship and friendship, just as his preoccupation with his rash youthful decisions precluded any substantive discussion of his successes. He stresses the negative influence on his life of certain authority figures, particularly his stepfather. As a consequence, he largely ignores his relationships with people who would not have demanded deference and subordination— his siblings, friends, fellow servants, his wife and children, and even the friend to whom he dedicates his work, Thomas Pearson. The manuscript explores this theme of injustice not only through events Whitehead experienced first-hand but also in the stories he relates of events in Stralsund during his childhood and early adolescence, particularly the story of Mary Flinton, a young woman seduced by a local nobleman, to which Whitehead devotes a large portion of his manuscript.[41] While condemning her for the crime for which she was ultimately executed, Whitehead nonetheless sympathizes with Flinton, who was spurned by those who should have helped her, thus creating the circumstances that led to her demise. He admires her virtuous acceptance of guilt and her willingness to face the legal consequences of her actions, and he uses the story to serve as a warning to young women to protect their chastity, very much as Samuel Richardson did with Pamela and Clarissa, the heroines of Richardson's best-selling eighteenth-century novels.[42] Flinton's tragic life is important because it links individual responsibility with an admonition to those in authority to exercise their responsibilities with love and affection, not caprice or harshness.

The primary virtues Whitehead celebrates are fairly commonplace—reason, restraint, and self-awareness, with chastity added to the list for young women. There is also a more radical insistence on the essential equality of masters and subordinates. Whitehead's hatred of deference, dominance, violence, and

---

40. Whitehead memoir, 75, 82–83.
41. Whitehead memoir, 69–74.
42. Samuel Richardson, *Pamela, or Virtue Rewarded* (1741), and *Clarissa; or, The History of a Young Lady; Comprehending the Most Important Concerns of Private Life* (1747–48).

deceit emerges in his telling of his life as both a moral lesson and a stinging social critique. It is this theme that helps explain the timing of Whitehead's decision to write. The year 1795 was the high point of the French Revolution—at least as news of events overseas would have reached remote Berks County. Slavery and nobility had been abolished, the monarchy overthrown, and all French men were being granted equal civil and political rights. It was far more radical than even the Pennsylvania phase of the American Revolution, although in the United States, too, democratic pressures were challenging elitist politics, as sharply contested elections, a developing political party system, and growing nationalism were pulling the Republic in directions that the revolutionaries of 1776 would scarcely have imagined.[43] At this moment in history, Whitehead, formerly a lowly page in an aristocratic household, might have imagined that he could have prospered and won respect had he stayed in Stralsund. It was, however, a fleeting moment. The wars of the first through fourth coalitions and the excesses of Robespierre, the corruption of the Directory, and the dictates of Napoleon would soon dash hopes for the widening revolution that Whitehead predicted in his "Prophecy of the Revolutions and Comotions of the World."[44] Whitehead never added a postscript to his autobiography. The moment of revolutionary promise had passed from Europe and he uprooted himself once more, moving to the frontiers of Pennsylvania and Ohio and looking to the west, not to events abroad, for opportunity and yet another chance at respectability.

Beyond Whitehead's intent to impart moral lessons and his use of contemporary literary forms to express his inner thoughts and feelings, other aspects of the manuscript also reveal him to be a knowledgeable and literate man. He read widely and was interested in the natural world, in history and travel accounts, in medicine, and in theology and the supernatural, among many other topics. Rosalind J. Beiler has noted that Whitehead was able to sign his name in the Latin script used by the British when he arrived in the colonies, whereas most of his fellow passengers, including Büttner, wrote their names in the German script. This, she writes, "suggests a different level of cosmopolitanism or comfort with other forms of writing and perhaps languages. . . . This flexibility in paleography skills is something . . . observed in German

43. Among the many works on the popular politics of the 1790s are Michael Merrill and Sean Wilentz, *The Key of Liberty: The Life and Democratic Writings of William Manning, "A Laborer," 1747–1814* (Cambridge: Harvard University Press, 1993); Susan Branson, *These Fiery Frenchified Dames: Women and Political Culture in Early National Philadelphia* (Philadelphia: University of Pennsylvania Press, 2001); Simon P. Newman, *Parades and the Politics of the Street: Festive Culture in the Early American Republic* (Philadelphia: University of Pennsylvania Press, 1997); David Waldstreicher, *In the Midst of Perpetual Fetes: The Making of American Nationalism, 1776–1820* (Chapel Hill: University of North Carolina Press, 1997).

44. See Appendix A to Whitehead's memoir.

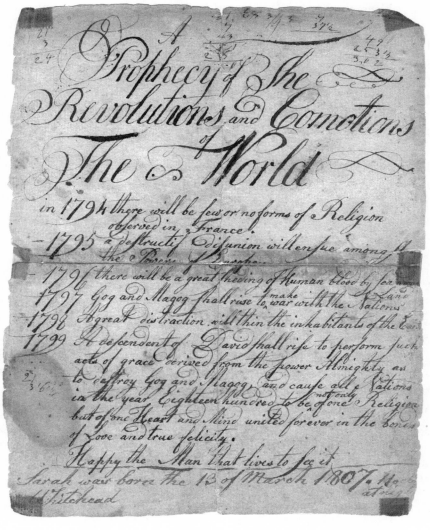

Fig. 3 A page in John Frederick Whitehead's handwriting, apparently written shortly after he completed his memoir. Courtesy of the Pennsylvania State University Libraries, University Park.

records from market towns doing business with the Netherlands but is usually absent in the southwest or even in the eastern parts of the country."[45] He was apparently well educated. Yet for all his experience and knowledge, the preface to his memoirs depicts Whitehead on the defensive in his attempt at autobiography. This attitude toward his literary effort may stem from his remaining awkwardness with English, especially with spelling. The preface begins with an apology for "the many defects and irregularities which are undoubtedly to be found in this Work," which he attributes to his "low circumstance in the World." He explains his imperfect mastery of English as the result of a life spent under the pressure to earn an income; but it is snobbery, the contempt of the urbane for rusticated artisans, that makes him angriest and most defensive about his literary abilities.[46] Given the apologetic introduction, which in part simply reflects the literary conventions of the time, it is ironic that Whitehead's account is more sophisticated in its deployment of contemporary literary forms than is Büttner's unreflective narrative, written by a prosperous burgher in the heart of Europe.

A Note on This Edition

An unusual aspect of the manuscript is that Whitehead did not actually inscribe his memoirs; rather, he dictated his life story to friends, who wrote while he worked at his loom. The only parts that appear to have been written in his own hand are his dedication to Thomas Pearson and the appendices— the "Poems on Severel Occasions," the "Prophecy of the Revolutions and Comotions of the World," and the list of his children's births. These sections tend to have more spelling and grammatical errors than other portions of the manuscript, but they also indicate Whitehead's facility in penmanship, both in English and in German.

Dictation raises issues of transliteration. Most of Whitehead's memoir addresses events and people in Europe (readers may be surprised to discover that, in 126 original pages of manuscript, he does not address his experiences

---

45. Rosalind J. Beiler to Peter Potter, January 21, 2005, 3, copy in the possession of Susan E. Klepp.

46. Whitehead memoir, 52–53. For the place of German culture, primarily political culture, and German identity in the British colonies and early Republic, see Wokeck, "German Settlements," 191–216; Aaron S. Fogelman, *Hopeful Journeys: German Immigration, Settlement, and Political Culture in Colonial America, 1717–1775* (Philadelphia: University of Pennsylvania Press, 1996); A. G. Roeber, *Palatines, Liberty, and Property: German Lutherans in Colonial British America* (Baltimore: Johns Hopkins University Press, 1993); Steven M. Nolt, *Foreigners in Their Own Land: Pennsylvania Germans in the Early Republic* (University Park: Pennsylvania State University Press, 2002).

in America until page 99). The text contains German names and phrases, along with some Dutch words, that were written by friends whose first, and possibly only, language was English. Moreover, at times his transcribers must have misheard Whitehead—in some places this is obvious—or they failed to keep up with the flow of reminiscence and either left words unfinished or omitted them altogether.

The manuscript is idiosyncratic in grammar, syntax, punctuation, and spelling, but it is generally quite legible. It is in remarkably good condition for its age, although there is some fading, occasional missing letters near crumbling margins, and ink blotches and erasures that sometimes obscure letters or whole words. To facilitate the reading of the text, the editors have noted only gross misspellings and have inserted letters and punctuation as needed for easier comprehension. Missing letters have been supplied silently, while square brackets indicate where whole words have been inserted by the editors. Crossed-out words have not been included except in a very few cases where they add information about Whitehead's intentions. The editors have provided corrected German spellings of many names and places. The text has been broken into chapters and a few long passages have been silently divided into shorter paragraphs. The editors have attempted to remain faithful to the original while making this fascinating account readily accessible to modern readers.

The Life of John Frederick Whitehead
Containing His Travels and Chief Adventers

TO THOMAS PEARSON[1]
SCHOOL MASTER AT MAIDEN CREEK[2]

Esteemed Friend,
I Shall not Presume to wright to thee by way of dedication
For I should be cautious to dedicate a work so erregular
Aand cimpli[3] to a man of thy Capacity and taste.

But by that friendship which has resided between us these
Sevirel years I am incouregd and made bold to present this to thy vew
Aas a work of which the foundation is laid but requires some thing
Considerable to finish and decarate it as thou will find if thou
Voutsafes[4] to perruse it.

And as I am all to gether incapable of placing the stops, marks and
Points, I shall take it kind if thou art pleased to perform it
For which I shall be infinitely a bliged to thee and remain thy
Sincisr Friend and well wisher.

JW
JFW

"PREFACE"

Kind Reader,

If by chance this Work should present itself to Thy view thou mayest
perhaps cry out at it, "posh,"[5] this is not worth perusing and so throw it by.
therefore I shall take the Liberty to detain thee with a short Preface by way of
Apology for the many defects and irregularities which are undoubtedly to be
found in this Work. but as it is the performance of a poor ignorant Country
Fellow whose Genius is weak but its Instruments still weaker and alltogether
incapable of displaying itself with Judgment and Regularity, yet is too Ambi-
tious to be Idle, therefore I flatter myself that the Candid Reader will mix his

1. Thomas Pearson was the first full-time schoolmaster in Maidencreek Township. Local
Quakers had established an English school in a log cabin next to the meetinghouse sometime
before 1784, when Pearson took over. He began with twenty-three students and charged forty
shillings (two pounds) per year per student, a substantial tuition. Morton L. Montgomery, *The
History of Berks County, in Pennsylvania* (Philadelphia: Everts, Peck and Richards, 1886), 1024.
2. In the margin here are scribbled "the W" and "themest."
3. Simple.
4. Vouchsafes.
5. I.e., bosh, contemptible nonsense or foolish talk.

Censure with Judgment and Clemency. I further hope that my unskillness will be pardoned if I acquaint the Reader with my Ignorance in the English Tongue for I can justly say that what little I have obtained I alltogether gained by my own Labour without a Moment's Assistance of a Teacher.

and As I am a Man but of low circumstance in the World, being a Weaver by Trade, I have to fling the Shuttle both late and early for the Maintainance of myself and Family so that I have no Time to study Grammar with all its Genders, Syntaxes, Conjunctions, Adjectives, Nouns and Pronouns and I know not what all, nor have I opportunities for to be acquainted with the beauties of Eloquence and Ornaments of Speech. therefore it can not be expected otherwise but that my Stile should be low, irregular and blunt, consisting only of such Words as are commonly used among us Country People in our Discourse which will by no means please the Taste of a high learned Citizens, especially such as have seen the outside of the Academy at Philadelphia or perhaps made a few bows to the Professors of Trenton College.[6] such learned and inconsiderate Critics I greatly fear will say that there are so many Scriblers arising in America, especially among the Rural sort or Country Clowns, so that one might Thattch Houses and Churches with their Volums of Nonsense and that it would be better for them and their Country if they desisted from Scribling and mind their Plough and, such as have Trades, study how to improve them [2][7] than for to undertake a Work of which they are altogether incapable of performing.

But this is only because they fear that the Clowns (as they are pleased to call us) should prove too hard for them as to Natural Wit and Eloquence: for Nature is no respecter of Persons but extends her bounty to whomsoever she pleases from the King that sits on his Throne of Gold and Ivory down to the Peasant that dwelleth in a Cottage, who may equally, as to his Natural Parts, had he but learning, vie with a Tully[8] or a Cicero—witness some of our Indian Speakers who I may venture to say will some Times baffle the greatest professors of Rhetoric in the City of Philadelphia. yet not withstanding Learning in itself is truly excellent and Magnificent, it embellishes the Natural Parts of a truly wise and ingenious Head, and those bright and great Ideas of his Genius he is capable of explaining with Eloquence and Harmony, which is

6. The Academy of Philadelphia, created in 1749, became the University of Pennsylvania in 1791. "Trenton College" is apparently a reference to Princeton College, although it was never situated in Trenton. As the College of New Jersey prior to 1756, it had been located in Elizabeth and Newark.

7. The original manuscript page number is given in square brackets.

8. Tully usually refers to Marcus Tullius Cicero (106–43 BCE), the Roman politician, writer, and orator. Either Whitehead is confused and assumes that Tully is a separate person, or he is referring to Servius Tullius, a legendary king of the very early Roman Republic, who, according to some accounts, was born a slave and rose to be king.

the only Thing the unlearned have to struggle with, as I have felt by experience. for, as I said before, my Genius is but weak, I yet many Times had an
Idea of Things which seemed to be bright and Sensible but for want of
Knowledge to explain myself have frequently [had] to pass them by in Silence
which often makes me think on the ingenious Stephen Duck[9] when he says

> "My fate detains me silent to remain
> For want of learning to improve my strain."

Learning and a great Genius may be compared to both a Man and Mony,
whereas the contrary is only a Man without Mony, but learning without a
Taste may be compared to Mony without a Man and is in reality but of little
or no benefit to Mankind. but as for my Part I think myself happy that I have
obtained as much English so that I am capable of reading a Chapter in the
Bible or Testament but as for the Art of spelling I never was capable of obtaining [it] so am intirely deprived of that useful and necessary Art of writing but
have altogether to [3] depend on one or other of my Friends who sometimes
on a Rainy Day would come and write now and then a little as I related to
them. this at the first appearance seemed to be a very tedious and labourious
Task so that I little expected ever to see half the performance of this Work
and I should have been intirely discouraged had I not been frequently thinking on myself and [the] Shuttle that flinging it through the Webb now a
Thread and Then a Thread till at last I finished a long and tedious Webb, so
now a little and then a little perhaps might also finish my tedious History.

Now if any one should think that it had been fitter for me to study at my
Trade and so improve my Business I must say that there ought to be a relax-
ion of both Body and Mind—Amusements to brighten the one and rest to
restore vigour and activity to the other. for if a Man should be continually
hurried to and fro in his Business without intermission the Statesman would
be hurried out of his Senses and the Merchant would forget to what part of
the World his Commerce extended, the Lawyer should forget his Harangue
at the Bar, and the Priest his Eloquence in the Pulpit; the commonalty would
be spent with fatigue and in short all Things would grow into a universal
Confusion. therefore an Allwise Providence who foresaw the Disorder which
would arise was Graciously pleased to give Man a Time of Recreation, but to
our Shame many of us weak daring Creatures have grossly abused this Time
by strange and abominable inventions as Dice and Cards, the Billiard Tables,

9. Stephen Duck (1705–56) was an English farmhand and self-taught poet who eventually
received a pension from Queen Caroline in recognition of his talent. His most famous poem
is "The Thresher's Labour," which originally appeared in *Poems on Several Occasions* (London:
[S. Richardson], 1736).

hurling the Tenice Ball, playing a Match at Crickets, Bull beating,[10] Horse rac-
ing, Cock fighting, Balls and Mascorades, Operas, Comedies and Tragidies,
and many Things never designed by Heaven for the recreation of Man; but
these are chiefly the Amusements of such as one may call the Vulgar great.
others again are endued[11] by Nature with a different Taste and amuse themselves greatly by reading such Books as befits their Humour, which is sometimes for Poetry or History, Geography, Divinity or Astronomy and many
more too tedious to mention. as for my part I should gladly embrace the
amusements of reading, especially History, but my leisure Hours are so few
that they may be called next to none, except on the Sabath after Church, but
then I am so fatigued with my weeks labour that after stamering over a Page
or two I frequently drop a Sleep. [4]

Now since I had so little Time for reading I had to chuse some thing for
my Amusement which was reflexion and recollection. this the Mind was
capable of performing when my Hands were busy at Work and by reading
a little of the Lives of others it frequently put me in mind of my own and
by frequent reflexion Things [were] kept fresh and lively in my Memory, so
that I at last concluded it would be a pleasing though a tedious Task to have
it wrote down in some form or other for my own amusement and that also
my Children might see what their Father underwent when he was, as it were,
entering in the Strength of his Youth and that they may also learn what it is
to live in the World.

Now, to conclude, I heartily wish that it was in my Power to please the
Taste of the Reader, but I know my in ability of pleasing any Man of learning. therefore I think it best to make it a matter of indifference to me whether
it pleases them or not, whether correct or incorrect, good or bad English. perhaps the unlearned and Ignorant like myself may pick out here and there
a little to be entertaining or Instructive and if so I shall think my self fully
rewarded for all my Toil. [5]

"A SHORT ACCOUNT OF MY FATHER JOHN WHITEHEAD"

My first intention was to begin my History with an Account of my Father[12]
but I found the Task attended with so much difficulty, having no Memoran-
dum or Manuscript except what is in my Head and that is only by hear say

10. Bull baiting.
11. Endowed.
12. There is no record that can be linked to Whitehead's birth, his father's death, or his parents' marriage. Stadtarchiv der Hansestadt Stralsund, hereafter SHS. Our thanks to Christian

when I was but a Child and has chiefly slipped my Memory so that I can give but little account of him who gave me being. but as far as I can recollect he was the Son of Merchant in the City of Stralsund in the Swedish Pommarania.[13] his Parents both were taken off the Stage of Life before he arrived to a State of Maturity. hereupon he was put out by his Friends[14] to a Broker which Business he inclined to follow when arrived to a State of Manhood but it pleased Heaven to take him out of the World in the prime of Life in the Year 1757 and was interred in St. Jacob's Church-Yard and as he left the World almost as soon as he appeared in a State of Business he left but a small Estate and me his Son of about three Months old to my Mother and as he displeased his Friends who thought my Mother to be his Inferior, as being only the Daughter of a Taylor and he the Offspring of a Merchant, they were never reconciled whilst my Father lived so that after his Decease they intirely broke off and look at one another as strangers. [6]

and Uta Kresse for their research in the archives and to the local archivists for their assistance. Perhaps James Whitehead of Maidencreek Township, Berks County, was a father figure to the author of these memoirs. See William J. Buck and Gilbert Cope, comps., "Exeter Monthly Meeting Records" (Philadelphia: Genealogical Society of Pennsylvania/Historical Society of Pennsylvania), an alphabetized scrapbook of notes on meetinghouse records, created in 1871 and 1874, hereafter EMMR. Whitehead was known by his stepfather's surname, Kukuck, until he changed it to Whitehead at some point after arriving in Pennsylvania.

13. Pomerania.

14. Friends, meaning family members, guardians; those who had charge of your interests.

THE LIFE[15] OF
JOHN FREDERICK WHITEHEAD

Chapter 1: Early Childhood[16]

I was born in the Year 1757 in the City Stralsund in Swedish Pommarania. my Parents being Lutherans, I was educated according to the same Doctrine but my Father left the World in the prime of Life and my Mother (Ann Whitehead) who was young and lively married again soon after her Year of mourning was ended to one Joakim Kukuck (and of as ill an Nature as the Bird whose Name he bore).[17] he was the only son of Hance[18] and Margaret[19] Kukuck who lived at the Place named Oldenhagen[20] in Swedish Pommarania. the old Man was universally beloved by all his Friends and Neighbours being a man willing and capable of lending Assistance to all in Time of need especially in setting broken Bones, curing of Wounds and many Things incident to Human Life. his Business was the Care of a Park and Forest belonging to the Family of a Gentleman deceased. his Income per Annum I can not remember but it was sufficient to maintain him and his Family in a decent manner. and after following many Years that [7] Employment he resigned his Post and moved to a Town called Bordt[21] where he took upon him the Care of a Toll-Bridge and a small Fishery [and] where he ended the Cares of his Life leaving his whole Estate to his Wife to do with as she thought fit. for his Son (my Step-Father) had always been so stubborn and disobedient a Child that his Father not only disinherited him but also, when he resigned that important Post at Oldenhagen, he recommended to the Family one who was not related to him but as he thought [this man was] more worthy to be recommended than his ungrateful Son. this however raised my Father's Spirit to that degree that he vowed revenge and swore he would shoot his aged Father who always had been a tender and Affectionate Parent, often entreating him

15. In the space to the right of "Life" and "of" appear the following words, written in the same hand as the bulk of the manuscript: "within a league and"; "within a league"; "within . . . leaguue . . . a league and an half the City."

16. To make the memoir easier to read, the editors have inserted chapter titles.

17. The cuckoo eats the eggs of other birds and then lays its own eggs in the nest, crowding out any surviving nestlings. Joachim Kuckuck, retired artillerist, died August 15, 1796, from "stitches in the side," meaning a pulmonary complaint brought about by excessive consumption of alcohol, at the age of seventy. SHS.

18. Hans.

19. Margret or Maragrete.

20. Either the district of Altenhagen in the town of Behnkenhagen, near Stralsund, or the town in the County of Stralsundland on the route to Rostock.

21. Possibly the town of Barth on the Baltic Sea, not far from Stralsund.

with Tears in his Eyes to refrain from his profligate Life and take upon him the work of reformation.

But, however, he was not quite wicked enough or else was restrained by Divine Providence, for he did not execute his design tho' I believe he fully intended it.

The old Man was by a short visitation of Sickness took off the Stage of Life in the year 1768 and his Wife following him not long after left to her Daughter in law (my Mother) in her Will several Household Goods and Bedding.

They seemed both very affectionate to me so that I could not forbear inserting this short Account of them but now I have to return and to begin with my Step Father who seemed to be weary of the reproofs his Parents gave him [and] resolved to leave them so that he might have a larger swing to licinciousness. he accordingly went to the Island of Gasmont,[22] which is about Six German Miles[23] square, well timbered and fertile. it lies within a League and a half of the City Stralsund in the Baltic Sea and is the Estate of one Graff Brash.[24] here my Father had the good Fortune to enter in the Service of this Nobleman [8] as a Huntsman: he being trained up from his Youth that to[25] Employment was thereby not only become a Dextrous marksman but also skillful and well acquainted with all the niceties of that Art as training the Hounds, the Horse, the Falcon and all Things necessary for that diversion. But here before I enter any further I think it necessary to give a few hints concerning this Earl, who was a favourite to Adulphus Frederick,[26] then King of Sweden, under whose Reign the Government consisted of a King and Council. but this Earl studied how to give his Sovereign an Arbitrary Power and so turn his Government into an absolute Monarchy. but his design was discovered before he was able to put it in Execution for he was betrayed by one whom he little expected: hereupon he was seized and put into confinement and had his Trial in the City of Stockholm where he was found Guilty of high Treason. his Hoary Head was condemned to the Block and he ended Life on the scaffold.[27]

22. Jasmond.

23. The length of a "German mile" varied by locality but was usually between 7,400 and 7,600 meters, or between 23,000 and 24,000 feet. See definition of "mile" in Jan Smits, "Mathematical Data for Bibliographic Descriptions of Cartographic Materials and Spatial Data" at the Koninklijke Bibliotheek website, http://www.kb.nl/kb/resources/frameset_kb.html?/ kb/skd/ skd/mathemat.html.

24. "Graf" is a title of nobility equivalent to the rank of earl. Erik Brahe was the "premier nobleman of Sweden." Michael Roberts, *The Age of Liberty: Sweden, 1719–1772* (Cambridge: Cambridge University Press, 1986), 181.

25. The "to" is inserted in superscript and apparently should have been inserted before "that," not after.

26. Adolf Fredrik reigned 1751–71.

27. Brahe, seven associates, and the queen, Lovisa Ulrika, were offended by partisan struggles in the parliament and formed a court party seeking to stage a coup d'etat in favor of the

Now after the old Man's decease great alterations were made in the Family and my Father, who was no favourite to the young Peer was sometime after discharged. how long he had been in the Service of this Nobleman I can not say but this I know—it suited his inclination, for his Master being chiefly at Court, he found little or nothing to do but to dress and go to Sports and being near the City he commonly visited it once or more a Week. he became acquainted with my Mother in the Year 1758 being a Man as to his outward appearance of a Handsome Shape and Genteel behaviour, well dressed in his Green Attire, Ruffled Shirt, Boots and Spurs, by which he made no inconsiderable Figure in that part of the World. my Mother thought he must be somebody to be Sure, but her Father, who looked for something more than just the outward appearance of a Man, made some sly enquiry into the circumstance of him who was to make him and his Daughter happy but found that he was like a guilded Statue which appears well and lively but by [9] close examination is dead, hard and Senseless and in reality good for nothing but to please the Eye.

But alas my Mother was not to be put off so, for she had that weakness which too many of the Fair Sex possess: he pleased her fancy. this furnished her with many excuses, saying that a bad Character was like a Snow ball on the top of a Mountain[28] and She did not doubt but if he was married and Settled he would become a Sober and Affectionate Husband, for it was certain that a reformed Rake would make the best of Men.[29]

But alas had she only considered that where there is no Religion there can be no reformation, it must be something Supernatural that will turn an old Profligate to be a Saint. but how ever, they were married in the same year 1758 and their Nuptials kept with Joy and Mirth but Oh! the many Hours of Affliction and Days of Trouble which ensued are too many to be mentioned. they were no sooner married then he let her know what he was in reality, but alas! it was too late. my poor Mother wept but as the common Proverb is "what cannot be cured must be endured," there was now nothing left but Patience and resignation with some little hope of reformation which was the only Staff to support her anxiety.

---

monarch. They were discovered in 1756. Brahe and seven others were executed, the queen was lectured, and the king was forced to sign an agreement that he would not attempt such a move again. Franklin D. Scott, *Sweden: The Nation's History* (Carbondale: Southern Illinois University Press, 1988), 248; Roberts, *Age of Liberty*, 181.

28. That is, needing only a slight push to move or change.

29. This sentence suggests that Whitehead and perhaps his mother were familiar with the influential eighteenth-century novels by Samuel Richardson, *Pamela, or Virtue Rewarded* (1741), and *Clarissa; or, The History of a Young Lady; Comprehending the Most Important Concerns of Private Life* (1747–48).

My Father having no Trade and thinking it below him to work at common Labour was for a considerable Time doing nothing to the support of his Family nor did he care much for them or any thing else except Drinking and Gaming. but it happened that one of my Uncles, named Herny Tribsus,[30] who was a Man of Prudence and Conduct, took my Father in Hand and told him that it would never do for to be both a Sluggard and Spendthrift therefore if he had a mind to work, as by all probability he would be obliged to do, he would recommend him to a Gentleman named Ghies who was the chief [10] Superintendant of the Kings Mint and acquainted with my Uncle who was a Stamper at the said Mint.

Here I think it may not be a mess[31] [to] insert a few hints of the making of this necessary evil which all the World Strives for to get as much as possible. the Dollars are cast in Moulds but all other Coin is made thus: first the Silver is melted in black Lead Crusibles which are placed in the Furnace. then they have a Box of about eighteen Feet in length and eight in breadth and nearly three in depth; this is filled with a fine black Sand tempered according to Art. then they take an Iron which is the width and thickness of the Coin which they enter into the Sand. then two Men go after with Ladles full of Metal and fill up every place where the Iron has entered. the Metal being thus cast into Bars it is took to an Instrument called the Roller which makes it even and to an exact thickness and from thence it is taken to an Instrument called the Cutter which by turning round cuts it circular and of an equal bigness and from thence to the Stamp where it receives the impression.

I have sat many an Hour by my Uncle when he was at work and although I was but a Child I seemed to be highly pleased to see so much Mony which I may compare to a Farmer when he has cleaned up his Crop of Wheat and swept [it] together in his Barn Floor.

But to return again to my Story, my Father complied with the Advice of my Uncle and with his Assistance got employ at the Furnace where he staid till the Work ceased, which was as soon as the War ended which was then commenced between Sweden and Prussia.[32]

My Uncle then removed his Family to Hamburgh,[33] [he] being a [11] Cabinet maker followed his Trade but my Father stayed at Home unemployed in any sort of Business. but it happened not long after this that his Father sent him a Letter and told him [the son that] he should remove his Family out of Town and come to him [the father] (knowing the Country would suit

30. Henry (in German, Heinrich), and Treibsus, Tribsis, or Tribsies. The uncle was the husband of a sister of Whitehead's mother. It was a common surname in the region.
31. Amiss.
32. Seven Years' War (1756–63).
33. Hamburg.

him [the son] best not being so near Taverns and Ale houses) and although he [the father] was greatly offended and [the son had] abused his Paternal Care and tenderness he [the father] freely past it by and buried it in oblivion if he [the son] would behave more dutiful and regular for the future and [then] he should not only find a constant and affectionate Father but likewise a constant Benefactor to him and his Family.

Upon this my Father concluded to move and we left the City accordingly in the Year 1764 and moved to the Vilage of Oldenhagen where my Grandfather resided.[34]

Now although the War was ended and open Hostilities ceased there were yet the Dregs and rubbage of War [such] as theft and robbery, for the Armies although [the soldiers were] disbanded [they] are not yet dispersed nor marched off to their respective Quarters and Cities so that the Country was yet crowded with those Domineering Hictors[35] who think where ever they are all is their own and if they meet with the least affront of a Peasant he may soon expect to be grossly abused if not [have] his Habitation set on Fire.

My Grandfather, who was a good liver, had the ill Fortune to be frequently crowded by those disagreeable Guests and I happened one Day to be in the Room where a Number were carousing for the last Time, for it was said they were to march to the City of Stralsund the following day. there happened to be one of them that had lodged [12] at my Grandfathers for a considerable Time who was of an agreeable and familiar Disposition so that considering his station might be called a clever Fellow. this man always had some Diversion with me calling me his Piper or Drummer and being very well acquainted with my discontent of living in the Country and that I was very anxious of going back again to the City, he frequently would tell me that when ever he marched back again to the City I should certainly go along with him to see my Granny. now to complete the Joke he came and told me that it was high Time to get ready for he was going to set off early the next Morning. this he spoke with so much assurancies that I was confident he was in earnest. upon this I went and told my Mother that Christian (which I think was the Soldier's Name) was going the next Morning to which she smilingly said he was only going to play a trick upon me but my Grandfather, who was of a cheerful Disposition and sometimes loved to carry on a Joke, said I should go and that he would charge Christian to take particular care of me and see me safe arrived at my Granny's House and that he himself would provide us with Provision during our Journey. accordingly I got up very early next

34. This move apparently occurred before the incident in which Whitehead's step-grandfather recommended another man for his former position, thereby infuriating Whitehead's stepfather.

35. Hector, a Trojan hero; also a blustering, domineering fellow, a bully.

Morning and fixed myself as I thought for my Journey. the old Man then took a Wallet and went into the Cellar on pretense of putting up my Provision whilst I was getting Breakfast but instead of Bread and Cheese, as they called it, there was a stout lump of a Stone put in each end of the Wallet and my Mother to help on the sport put one of my Shirts and other Things along with my pretended Bread and Cheese. I then took my leave of them all with a Staff in my Hand and Wallet on my Shoulder and off I waddled in full hopes of being soon again in the City but I had gone only a few Perches[36] till I fell behind. upon this the aforesaid Christian told me to pull along and he would assist me in carrying my Wallet. but soon after I had to cross [13] a Ditch on a small Long[37] off which I fell into the Mud and the Wallet being well loaded got round my Neck which made me struggle considerably before I could free myself so as to get up. this made a deal of Sport for the rest, especially the old Man (my Grandfather) who seemed to be highly diverted with the Joke. I now saw that it was only a trick they had played upon me and vexed with it and the disappointment I left my Wallet in the Mud and returned back again crying but the more I cryed the more they laughed till at last I ceased from crying and joined them in laughter and so the Sport ended.

But notwithstanding all this the old Man took a particular fancy for me and called me his Fritz.[38] my Mother finding an opportunity to relate unto him the cruel usage I met with from his Son, my Step Father—which the old Man seemed to take hard—and said he knew well his Son's ill temper but how to have him otherwise was not in his Power to know.

We lived agreeably a little while but the Son soon falling out with his Mother and then with his Father we had again to seperate and moved to a Town called Franceburgh.[39]

But before I go further I think it suitable to insert here a Strange appearance which I thought I beheld in the Skies at the Vilage of Oldenhagen in the eighth Year of my Age. as I was standing at the Window my feeble mind began to contemplate on the beauties of the Skies which appeared to me of a Crimson Colour although the Sun was at a great height being nearly ten O'Clock A.M. but while I thus was gazing at its beauty there appeared—or at least I thought appeared to me—the Visage of a Man which presently grew to the Shoulders, Arms, Breast &c. till it appeared perfectly in the Shape of a naked Man of an Inormous Size in Colour resembling red hot Iron. [14] its

36. A perch was equal to a rod. Although the length varied by locality, a typical measurement was five and a half yards or sixteen and a half feet.

37. Log.

38. Fritz is a shortened version of Friedrich (the author's name), and is here used as a term of endearment.

39. Franzburg, south of Stralsund.

front seemed to be forward ready to march but its Sides and Face were turned towards the Earth of which it seemed to take a view and so strode away but having still his Face turned towards the Earth. my Grandmother saw me thus standing as amazed [and] asked me what I saw but I giving her no answer she came up to me and seeing by my Countenance that I was struck with Admiration and Awe asked again what I saw or what twas the matter, to which I then replyed that I had seen a Man in the Skies who I thought was looking at what we were doing. but as it was by that Time intirely gone out of Sight and none of them had seen any Thing of it, they concluded that it only had been a Cloud which my Childish Fancy or Imagination had formed into the appearance of a Human Being.

Not long after this we were visited by a most Malignant Distemper which raged among the horned Cattle, so that it was generally believed had it held on awhile longer it would have bereaved all Pommararia of the benefit of those useful Animals whereby the Farmer is not only enabled to raise the staff of Life but [cattle are] also capable of supplying the Country with Meat, Milk, Butter and Cheese. but whether this was any Thing relative to what I saw in the Skies I am by no means going to determine for I was too Young in Years and my Understanding [was] not sufficient for to make my Obser-vations so as to say that I am positive it was the real appearance of a Man. yet not withstanding I thought then and think yet I never saw a Man plainer walk on the Face ofthe[40] Earth than I saw that [man] walk in the Skies. it moved not slow and steady along like a Cloud, but it stepped regularly one Foot after the other; nor have I ever seen a Cloud move with the tenth part of that velosity with which that [15] seemed to go, for it was but a few Moments in my Sight when it once began to move, and as far as my Eyes were capable of following, it retained the perfect Shape of a Human Being.

I have wished many a Time since that I had shown it to the rest when it appeared visible to me but my attention was so closely engaged that I never considered or thought the least of showing it them till I was asked.

But to return as I said before, we moved to the Town of Franceburgh where my Father had the good Fortune to enter in the Service of a Gentle-man of great Estate, named Natz, for a Huntsman but he soon fell out with his Master upon which he recieved his discharge. he then came Home and I may venture to say was worse than ever. he scarse was at Home a Day in a Week, but drinking, gaming and running in Debt, as the saying is—"over Head and Ears"[41]—seemed to be all his Employment. he would go out in the Morning and scarse ever return till Eleven or Twelve at Night and poor me

40. The two words are run together in the original.
41. A variation of the German idiom "over both ears," similar to the English expression "in over one's head."

if I had not put in Order his [boot]Jack and Slippers, Night Cap, Candle and Tinder Box, I might expect a severe correction and as I was but a Child I sometimes would neglect some Article or other but my Mother mostly took care that nothing was amiss either by telling me or doing it herself before she went to Bed.

my Mother had raised a parcel of Geese. it was my Employment to Herd them but one day they took a flight in the Corn and as bad Fortune always attended poor me it happened that the Overseer of the aforesaid Gentleman was near and saw them or presently enquired under whose care they were, upon which it was told him they were under mine for I was not present but was in search of them. hereupon he went and found me and my Geese coming out of the [16] of the Corn, upon which he with out many Words fell a beating me to that degree that I was scarsely able to crall[42] Home. my Arms, back and Sides were black and blue and almost in a jelly so that I did not get over it for several Weeks. my Father seemed to be offended at it and threatened to give the overseer a Drubbing of which he undoubtedly was capable had he been in earnest but I believe in reality he cared but little about it. but my Mother happened to see the Overseer shortly after. she reproved him sharply for the abuse he had gaven me. he excused himself saying how us Boys had got to be very careless, that he often had found one or others Geese in the Corn which brought him into his Master's Displeasure, and bieng[43] that Day in an uncommon ill Humour it happened to be my ill Fortune to fall into his Hands. however he seemed to be sorry and promised to be more mild for the future.

It happened not long after this that Sophia Gristo,[44] my Grandmother of my Mother's Side, arrived from the City of Stralsund to pay us a visit. but as soon as she arrived and not seeing me (who always had been her favourite) made her presently enquire after me and my Mother telling her that I was on the Commons guarding a parcel of Geese and I would be Home soon in the Evening. but my Granny impatient of seeing me insisted upon my Mother to take a walk with her into the Commons that so she might see me. upon this they both arrived but my little Step Brother ran before to bring me the joyful Tidings that Granny was arrived from Town to see us and I no sooner received the News I then ran with all my might to meet her. but as ill fortune always attended me, so it happened that in my career[45] I struck a Stone that stuck up above Ground with my right Foot and being [17] with out Shoes it nearly broke my big Toe, for as I fell with great violence (being on the descent

42. Crawl.
43. Being.
44. Gristow.
45. I.e., careening.

of a Hill) I not only recieved some sad bruises but also sprained my Ancle and big Toe. I rolled about on the Ground for some Time in extream Pain but my Granny coming in sight I gathered myself up and went limping and crying to meet her. my Mother lapped up my Toe and my Granny made me a present of a Pair of Slieve Buttons and an Knife at which I was so rejoiced that it added a considerable relief to my Wounds and Bruises. my Mother drove Home the Geese and I limped after them but there was never any Thing more done to my poor Toe, for as I was at that Time [inured] so as not to mind trifles it was neglected by which it grew to a Shape as it pleased and is not only deformed but also often painful to me unto this Day.

At the first arrival of my Grandmother she intended to stay a considerable Time but something happened which made her stay but short which was as follows: my Father was sitting at the Table reading [and] one of his Hounds was lying beneath by him which was my favourite Dog. I often used to fondle on him and called him my Tierras[46] (which was the Dog's Name). but it happened he was at that Time in an ill humour or something the matter which I knew not, for as I went to him in my usual way he growled at me which he never offert before. my Father looked about to see what was the matter with the Dog and seeing poor me he fell a kicking me to that degree that the Blood ran out of my Mouth and Nose so that both my Mother and Grandmother were busily employed to stop the Blood.

Chapter 2: In Service

This unnatural usage of my Father made my Grand mother request of him to let me go with her that she would [18] take care of me and bring me up as a Child of her own but my Father would not comply with her request, not for any regard he had for me, but only to be cross and ill natured both to her and me. she finding that nothing could be done at that Time desisted from further importuneing him and set out for Home the following Day and left me awhile longer to struggle with my hard fortune. but thanks be to Heavin it proved to be but a short Time, for it was about the latter End of June when she was with us and in the Month of August my Grandfather Jacob Gristo came and so took me away and joyfully I went in full expectation to live more comfortably and happy than I had done at Home with so ill natured a Step Father, in which I was not mistaken, for they were both exceeding kind and affectionate to me and allowed me almost more liberty than I wanted and

46. The most likely translation is that *Tier* (animal) has been combined with *Rasse* (thoroughbred) to mean purebred animal; less likely is that *Tier* is combined with *-aas*, to suggest a sly, ingratiating animal.

when I sometimes did amiss the Apology would be I was a poor Fatherless Child. their indulgence was so great that had I naturally been of a wicked disposition it might had proved my ruin but as I was to the contrary of a bashful and quiet disposition it added but little to the Name of a spoiled Boy. I never delighted in playing or ramping[47] like some other Boys of my Age which led some into a belief that I was but of low parts, and indeed my Grandmother herself seemed for some time to be of that opinion—not but that Nature had done her part in giving my[48] sufficient Wit—but she feared that my Step Father had knocked the Sense out of me. but, however, she found her suspicion to be groundless, for my chief diversion was as it is to this Day in reading. and I was chiefly ~~all the Time~~ kept to School to the Age of ten Years but had the ill Fortune of having very cross Masters who would correct me for little or nothing, except the last Master I went to never gave me that I remember a Stroke or an Angry Word. I undertook to read the Bible through but not performing it regularly I began it a second Time. the places I [19] chiefly delighted in were the History of Joseph and his Brethren, of Sampson, of David, Daniel, Tobit, Judith, Esther and some others too tedious to mention. my Grandmother would sometimes say unto me I fear thou wilt study thy Senses away, come put by thy Book and play awhile. sometimes I would go and [spin] my Top awhile in the Street but sometimes I would say that I had no inclination to play and begged of her to let me be at my Book. I also took great delight in Writing, especially large Hand, and what's called German Text, also a writing which we call Flactor[49] which are large letters adorned with my[50] Strokes and sometimes ornamented with little Flowers. had I took as much delight in Arithmetic perhaps it might have been of more service to me.

My Grandmother now became acquainted with an old Gentlewoman which was a Widow. her Husband had been an officer in the Army but whether he was slain in the Field of Battle or expired peaceably on the Bed at Home I can not say. this old Gentlewoman seemed to take aparticular fancy to me, often admiring my accuteness and Sensible Answers which I made to all her enquiries. my Grandmother had an opportunity to give her a full Detail of the hard usage I had recieved from my Step-Father at which she seemed to be affected and moved with compassion towards me, recommended me to a Gentleman of Note in the City named Theodore Fanesson[51]

47. Romping.
48. Me.
49. Fraktur (also called Gothic or Black Letter) is an ornamental and decorative script in common use among Germans into the twentieth century.
50. Many.
51. Theodor von Essen (1737–1824), a member of a very prominent aristocratic family, was a lawyer, *Hofrat* (counsel of the court), and *Worthalter* (speaker of the city council), among other

who was a young Man of about Twenty seven Years of Age, of a great Family and very rich. he was by Profession a Counsellor at Law which occasioned him to have a deal of writing done. this Gentleman sent for me, but I being too bashful to go by myself took my Grandmother along who served instead of [a] Spokesman for me and herself, for I had to say [illegible] little and left all to her. the Gentleman desired that I should write [illegible] copy and take it to him that so he might see how I could write, this I promised to perform and soon after when I found myself in a pretty good humour to write I retired in order to study what subject to chuse and those Lines came into my Mind which were nearly as follows: [20]

As God doth lead me I will go
If he commands I will obey
If he is pleas'd his will to show
I'll follow where he leads the way
Thro' Briers and Thorns or Burning Sand
Ah let it be then far or near
Thro' raging Seas or Hostile Land
If he protects me nought I'll fear.

Those Lines I took to him and the Subject seemed to please him well but the Letters were not sufficient to be of service to him. yet he made no doubt that after sending me a Twelve Month to School I might be a correct writer and able enough to copy off several writings for his private use. I now left my Grandfather's Dwelling and entered into the Service of this Gentleman in the Tenth Year of my Age and lived with him about five Years in an extraordinary manner. for I may venture to say that it was indeed the happiest Time I ever had or have had since in all my Life. it was indeed a Time almost without Trouble, except now and then when I through carelessness neglected my Duty, and when I deserved correction I recieved it from a Hand that had reason and Humanity. I was not buffeted and bruisd, kicked or knocked over with anything that came to Hand but a box on the Ear with a gentle reproof seemed to be my chief correction. only once I was corrected in an unsual way, yet no more than I deserved. the case was this: when I entered into the service of my Master he was Single and lived with his Parents but before a Year was alapsed he joined in a Marriage State and before the Nuptials were consummated I was arrayed in a new attire. but nothing was more remarkable than my Hat which was finely adorned with a Gold lace nearly three [illegible]

things. If his age is given correctly, the year is 1764. Our thanks to Regina Gramer for her assistance in translating these titles.

Inches wide with a large Gold Butten and loop with two Tassels of the same Metal. I thought much of my fine Hat [to] besure and took great care of it by keeping it [21] in a Wooden Box lined with Paper. but after some Time it grew old to me and I began to be more careless about it, so that I left it one Evening hanging in the Entry and not being careful of shutting the Door some thieving Rascal came and Stole it away. I did not miss it till next Morning, when I remembered my Hat and went to put it by but to my surprise it was gone from there, upon which I ran up Stairs and looked in my Box for I was in hopes that some of the Girls had put it by. but to my Sorrow no Hat was there and I soon had good reason to beleive it was Stole and fearing my Master's displeasure, who often had reproved me of leaving it there, I kept it concealed for nearly two Weeks before it was found out.

The things I chiefly misbehaved in were such as telling sometimes an untruth, staying too long when I was sent on Errand, or dressed myself too slovenly. and sometimes when my Master was abroad some of the Gentry would come to pay him a Visit and I not acquainting him with it as soon as he returned Home it was a capital Crime. but as I grew older I grew more careful in my Business.

There was one thing remarkable in my Master and worth inserting here. I often received Mony at the Generosity and disposition of the giver for myself, especially at their Feasts and entertainment. this Mony I had to give to my Master with a little Book which I kept. he received the Mony and so wrote in my Book how much he received and by so doing I might have gathered a handsome Purse which I would have recieved in full at the Time of my departure.

But as it is the business of a faithful Historian to communicate both the good and evil, I have to confess that as I grew older in Years and higher in Stature I also grew prouder and higher in in Mind and although I received very good clothing of my Master I saw many fine things that I thought suited me extraordinary well that I should look smart and the Girls might think me a fine Fellow. upon this I ceased from giving my Master the Mony [22] and so made no further use of my little Book but squandered my Mony away for trifles such as fine Buckles, Buttens, Snuff Boxes, a Cane to walk with and several other trifles too tedious to mention. sometimes I would be greatly mortified by seeing a thing which I eagerly wished for but my Purse not being capable of purchasing it I had to leave it. but at last the old Adversary of Mankind[52] saw a fit Time to seduce me and by his influence I was so far led astray that when I wanted to buy some fine thing and I had not sufficient Mony of my own, I would take of my Master's, who as I said before was very

52. The devil.

rich, and the Mony lying by heaps in his counting Room. but blessed be God who was pleased to strike the Root of this growing evil with the sharp lashes of Conscience so that I was ashamed and confounded within myself to think I should thus abuse the confidence and trust my Master put in me. and I looked upon it with abhorhence to think how I would have felt had my Master been in the Room in some corner or other unknown to me and had seen me taking it and although I had flattered my self thus that it could be no harm to take a little where there was so much and that only for to buy such things as I was going to wear in his service and fancied myself that he ought to have given me such things so as to look smart like other Boys in my circumstance which excuse it is true seemed to me at that Time to be a very good one. but alas I found it to be but a very insignificant one when I came to see truly what I had done and though I had but taken three or four Times and no more at a Time than about eighteen Pence Sterling, it proved great trouble to me afterwards and I promised to myself never to do so more and this I may say was the greatest Crime to my knowledge that I have committed in all my Life.

Nothing very remarkable happened whilst I lived with this worthy Master whom I may call without flattery an extraordinary Man. for it seemed that Nature had poured on him her Graces with profusion and bestowed on him all the good Qualities that can be possessed by Finite Creatures. sometimes it is true at their entertainments he would take a Game or two at Cards but this was more to please the humours [23] of his Friends than for his own diversion. his chief amusement was to play on the Spinnet[53] and Sing to the Notes he played.

Chapter 3: Romance and Crime in Stralsund

Now I said before that nothing very remarkable had happened but this is relating to myself. for there are many things that happened to which I was a Spectator, of which I make no doubt would prove entertaining to some but as we are [all] of a different Taste and humour, it might also prove tedious again to others. therefore I thought it the fittest way to desist from mentioning them except some few which are of the Tragic kind and have made such deep impression on my Heart so that it seemed as if it was not in my Power to forbear inserting them.

the first Actress which appears upon this mournful Stage is a Young Woman named Mary Flinton;[54] she was the only Daughter of an honest

53. Spinet, a musical instrument resembling the harpsichord.
54. Catharina Maria Flindt, age twenty-six, seamstress, was put to death by the sword for the murder of her child on January 4, 1766. Death Register and Document 3, Number 6181, SHS.

Tradesman and worthy Citizen named John Flinton but it pleased Heaven to take him off the the Stage of Life before his Daughter arrived to a State of maturity. and after his departure the Mother thought it fittest to sell their House and several unnecessary Furnature and so put part of the Mony out upon Interest for their support and take the remainder to buy themselves a lodging Room in Saint George's Cloyster which was a large and beautiful Edifice capable of containing nearly one Hundred Families at a convenient rate.

Here she lived for several Years and her Mother, who seemed almost to Idolize her darling Child and thought there was scarcely her equal in the City. she was one that had been favoured by Nature in a good degree and her outward accomplishments seemed to be hieghtened by the accomplishment and beauties of her Mind which by all appearance seemed to be chaste and Virtuous. her carriage seemed to be graceful, accompanied with a modest yet lively chearfulness that sparkled in her Eye. had Nature been less bountiful in the formation of her frame she might by all propability not have arrived to so deplorable an End. her brilient Eyes shot forth such peirceing rays as kindled the fire of Love in many: but what proved her overthrow was that it wounded the Heart of a Man of Quality who seemed to be so deeply affected, although he knew the impossibility of ever joining with her in Marriage, yet resolved to enjoy her if possibly he could as a Mistress. upon this he endeavoured to seek all opportunities that lay in his Power for to obtain her company in which he at last after many fruitless attempts succeeded. [24]

But he no sooner enjoyed her then he found that he had not been mistaken in her Personal Merits and that her Conversation was equally charming and agreeable to the rest of her deportment. this was another Dart which wounded him still the deeper. but he being a Man endowed with that Quality which is too apt to draw the attention of the unguarded, his high Birth and Station, added to his Eloquence and soft persuasions, together with the rest of his allartments[55] in all the misteries of Love, obtained at last his Wishes and became perfectly Master of her Heart. for by the Powerful influence of his Eloquence, together with the thought of having so illustrious a Lover, her Innocence was betrayed and she became a prey to vice which soon led her out of the truly delightful Path of Virtue and the sweet inamolet[56] retreats of Innocence into the sullen and gloomy Melancholy recesses of Misery and Woe

---

Apparently Whitehead was not the only person who sympathized with her plight; all the servants of the "Schopenbrauermeister," or pint brewmaster, were put on trial for refusing to participate in her execution.

55. Allurements.

56. Enameled, that is, beautified with various colors; or perhaps emollient, i.e., softening, soothing.

and at last to an Ignomious Death. for she became by degrees as greatly enamoured and if any thing [she was] more deeply affected than her Lover so that they indulged themselves so far in the pleasures of Love till the bitter fruit of their unhappy embraces began to ripen and she became pregnant by him.

But As soon as he came to be acquainted with her condition, instead of providing a suitable apartment for her and other necessaries, he forsook her and left her entirely to shift for herself as well as she could but, however, he escaped not unpunished for so base and most cruel an action as I shall mention by and by. being thus deserted by her Lover, together with the sad reflection of what she had done, the public Scorn and reproach which was hastening now upace wrought so powerfully upon her that a great alteration visibly appeared unto all such as knew her. that lively chearfulness which once sparkled in her Eyes whilst in a state of Innocence now became clouded with a sad and Melancholy gloom and those Cheeks that once glowed as the dye of Vermillion or vied with the blushes of the Rose now turned pale and withered like that Flower beneath a Northern blast. it further seemed as if all things conspired and contributed to the destruction of this unhappy young Woman. in the first place she was forsaken by her Lover and secondly when her Mother became acquainted with the condition, she was altogether incapable of withstanding so great a blow [25] but grief overcame her so as to break her Heart which was a mighty stroke upon her desolate and forlorn Child which[57] seemed altogether inconsolable [and] which made all that knew her pity her in their Hearts—for yet her shame was undiscovered which she endeavoured to conceal it as much as possible and being a Woman of so fair and excellent a Character none would have believed their own Eyes if even her shape should have betrayed her.

She now concluded to go to an Aunt of hers to acquaint her with the secrecy and likewise ask her advice what she should do in so deplorable a condition. but alas her own natural Aunt instead of comforting, reproached her, saying what an abominable shame she had brought upon herself and all her Relations and that it was a Scandal to her Mother in the Grave and in short bid her be gone:

Now the agonies in which this unhappy creature must have been the reader must judge himself, for I am incapable of finding Words to express my own feelings, and what seemed almost a wonder is that in the height of her agitation she did not lay violent Hands on herself. but the busy Adversary and eternal Enemy now saw a fit Time to whisper those temptations into her Ears, as she confessed that it seemed as clear to her as if it had been uttered vocally, which was that as she was of so fair a Character there was

57. Who.

none that would let such thoughts into their Heart that a Woman so universally esteemed on account of her chastity and Virtue should be guilty of being pregnant in an illegal way—it was therefore but a small matter to cover her shame by dispatching only the produce of her unhappy Love.

This at first seemed to strike her with Horror and she could not yield to it for some Time but at last she proved too weak to withstand the tempter and accordingly when the Time appointed by Nature was expired, the pangs of Child birth came upon her at the dead of Night and she brought forth a charming Daughter which was no sooner born but the weak defenceless Babe was barbarously dispatched by the Hands of its own Mother. and the whole transaction was performed without any assistance except the evil one who without doubt was busy [26] in this barbarous action, which is both abominable and unnatural, exceeding by far the Beasts of the Field or the Fowls of the Air, who would certainly cry shame at Man were they endowed with the excellency of understanding and the knowledge of Speech. but yet let us mix our Censure with the Clemency and not prove too severe on this unhappy young Woman for we are all poor frail Mortals and liable to fall and him that thinks himself the most secure may make the first mistep. for if we rightly consider the whole transaction from first to last we will find that there are two Persons who must certainly bear a great part of the blame. the first must be her Lover and the second her aunt: her Lover for being the greatest and chief sorce of all this Mischief and her Aunt for being too severe and turning her out of Doors, lashing her with a reproachful Tongue when she needed the most to be comforted, but, however, the first escaped not unpunished and the latter not without Censure.

What way the Murder was committed and how it was discovered few knew the certainty of; some had it one way and some another. but that it was committed and discovered was certain and she was seized and put in confinement and on her Trial confessed herself guilty, upon which she was condemmed by the Law of the Land to be beheaded.

Now we must leave her awhile lying in Prison and return to her Lover who now greatly reflected on the evil of which he alone seemed to be Author. the sharp lashes of Conscience and the Agonizing pangs of remorse punished him so that he grew in a sort of phrenzy. the Phisicians who were sent for confessed that it baffled their skill and that it was altogether the agitation of his Mind which occasioned the Disorder, but, however, he began after sometime to recover and, as he afterwards confessed, was greatly releived by a Stratigem that came unexpectedly into his Mind which was this: as it was impossible for him to relieve the poor and distressed Criminal (that once had been his sole delight and object of his Heart) with Mony or by any fair means from the Sword of Justice, there was no other way for him than for to endeavour to do it [but] by force. but this could not be performed [27] except by the force of Arms and how to accomplish this he was altogether at a stand because [of] the impossibility of succeeding without a sufficient Number [of supporters] and how to obtain that Number without exposing himself to great danger of being being discovered and handled by the Law (which was very severe in such cases). it puzzled him most extreamly till the time of her execution grew near at hand so that he had no longer Time to delay if he intended to do anything towards rescuing his fair Criminal. he now concluded to let follow what would if it cost him his whole Estate or even his Life in the pursuit of delivering her out of the Chains of Death.

Accordingly he went and acquainted several of his intimate Associates with his design—who were all young blades full of vigor and activity and promised him their Assistance to the utmost of their Power—and he gathered an illustrious company of nearly twenty six Men who were all of the young Nobility and sons of the foremost Men in the City. they all met at the House of the ringleader where they concluded when to begin the Assault and it was agreed that it should be the Night before her execution. upon this they took an Oath to keep it secret and not to flinch at the appointed Time but in spite of all this caution it was whispered about and it reached the Ears of the Goaler[58] who went to a Magistrate and acquainted him with what he had heard. upon this a strong Guard was appointed at the Door of the Goal[59] but this by no means discouraged the Assailants who at the Time appointed came Armed with Swords and Pistols and dressed in as disagreeable [a] Figure as they possibly could invent and demanded entrance of the Yard which [the Guards] thought it their duty to oppose. hereupon a smart Scrimmage began pretty quickly and the Assailents being by far the strongest Party both in Number and dexterity, especially in handling the Sword, the Guard was soon overpowered: one Man [was] slain and several wounded. upon this they broke open all before them (though some strongly believed that the Goaler had been bribed and that he only demanded a Guard to avoid suspicion—but this could not be proved—yet he was deprived of being Goaler ever after) and as soon as they arrived at the apartment of the fair Criminal, her Lover took her in his Arms and weeping saluted her with a Kiss. but as there was no [28] Time for Conversation or delay in that place, they concluded not to free her from her Chains till they had arrived to a place of more security. accordingly they bore her off into a Boat which was prepared for that purpose, in which they conducted her over a small Lake which lay adjacent to the Goal, then broke off her Irons and put her into a Stage and so hoisted her off to the next

58. Gaoler, or jailer.
59. Gaol, or jail.

Stage where she was conducted by a Servant of her Lover from Stage to Stage till she arrived to the distance of nearly three Hundred Miles from the Sword of Justice where she was left with plenty of Mony for her Sustenance till she could get into a way of business.

Now the City was full of Noise and it seemed to be the subject of almost every one's Discourse but it soon dwendled away and was almost forgotten till, to the astonishment of every one that heard it, after Twelve Months were elapsed she returned again of her own accord and delivered herself up to the Goaler who was struck with admiration at so an extraordinary event and when asked how she came to return, her reply was that the Rod of Conscience had been continually chastising her and had thus drove her back to receive the punishment due to her Crime and so voluntarily entered the Room from whence she had been taken.

Upon this the Goaler went immediately to one of the Burger Masters[60] to acquaint him with what had happened, who bid him to keep it secret till she was examin'd, for by so doing they should not only find out the whole Transaction of her escape but also should have a good opportunity of seizing the Ring leader before he could make his escape. accordingly two Magistrates were chosen for her examination who went and received a satisfactory reply to all their enquiries. now this was a sad stroke and had like to have cost her Lover a World of trouble but as it happened that [since] all was performed by Men of high Birth and Station there was but little done. the Ringleader was confined but soon again set at Liberty upon Parole and after some Time was sentenced to pay a Fine of nearly two hundred Ducats and serve three Years in the Army as a common Trooper. but alas, had this been dun by the common class of Men, the Ringleader would not have escaped with his Life nor the rest of being severely punished.

Now as her Sentence had been passed above a TwelveMonth [before] there was now nothing to do but for to execute her which was performed soon after her arrival and two of the Principal Ministers offered their Service in [29] converting and preparing her for her final change. they visited her alternately for near a Week before her execution and on the last Evening the Sacrament or the Lords Supper was tended to her, which she recieved with all the Devotion in appearance of a true Christian and on the following Day about Nine OClock she was took in a Coach accompanyed by the aforesaid Ministers and a Military Guard of nearly five hundred Men, with an innumerable and promiscuous crowd of Spectators, to the place of Execution where she in full resignation yielded her Neck to the Sword and departed in peace with all Men and I hope also with the Lord.

60. Burgomaster, one of the city mayors or councilors.

Now my chief design in relating this is that perhaps some tender Plants of the fair Sex who yet are adorned with the beauties of sweet smiling Innocence may look into it as into a looking Glass where at once they may behold the happiness of Innocence and Virtue as also the retched[61] reward and deplorable end of Vice in this their once charming Sister who was not inferior to the greatest Number of her Sex in natural accomplishments and perfection while she retained her State of Innocence, but alas, into what an Abyss of Woe and Misery she plunged herself into from that Moment she departed with those precious Jewels—Chastity and Virtue. her Life must have been indeed the most retched when we consider that an Insect will struggle and a worm will bend for their lives but this unhappy Creature, who was to the distance of near three hundred Miles, returned again and for what? only for to be deprived of that which is the most near and dear to all things that exist in the Breast of Life. and what is there that a Man will not do to save his Life, except it proves to be unto him aburden which must have been certainly the case with this unhappy Woman. therefore you dear young Women it is the wishes of my Heart that you may not depend too much upon your own Strength nor rejoice too much in your beauty but remember him that created you and beg for aid of him that is Omnipotent that so you may be enabled to with stand the Powerful persuasion of your pretended Lovers who by their smooth and flattering Eloquence might make you grasp as it were an imaginary Empire [or] at least make you ride in a Coach and six.[62] remember our first Parents[63] who lived in a State of perfect happiness whilst they retained their Innocence but alas, by the voice of the Serpant they not only brought Death and destruction on themselves but also on all their unhappy Offspring. and so it is unto this Day the [30] voice of the Serpent [or] by his influence that the Tongue of pergured[64] Men doth basely flatter and betray and often, Ah! too often, lead to utter Destruction [even] a charming young inoffensive Woman who might have bin considered in her State of Innocence as the Pride and Ornament of her Sex and the perfect workmanship of a Supreme Creator.

Now the second Actor was a Soldier named Kanitz[65] who was a Man beloved by all his Officers and fellow Soldiers, and considering his station, was accounted a sober and well minded Man. but it happened one Day that he got in company with one that was a Carpenter who persuaded him to take a Game at Cards to which he yielded. and they played for a drink by which they both got pretty merry but not so as to be called drunk. the Soldier, being

---

61. Wretched.
62. A coach drawn by six horses.
63. Adam and Eve.
64. Perjured.
65. This individual has not been identified.

weary with the amusement of Cards, desisted and the Carpenter also and deverted themselves with other exercise of which one of them was thus: there was a large Stone lying at the back Door of the Tavern to which the Carpenter said to the said Kanitz that he was incapable of lifting it to which he replyed that he was not only capable of lifting it but was also able to carry it to a certain distance. hereupon they laid a Wager and the Soldier performed the Task upon which he demanded the Wager which his Antagonist refused. upon this a Quarrel arose and Kanitz happened to give him an unlucky blow which at an instant hurled him off the Stage of Life.

Now in some Countries, especially America, this would not have been looked upon as Willful Murder and therefore would not have been punished by Death but in this part of the World the Laws and Statutes are different, for if any Man dies immidiately beneath the blow of an other, whether designedly or not, it is Life for Life. he was confined and had his Trial where he was condemmed to the Sword. he was a Man remarkably tall and well shaped so that he was taken notice of even by the foremost rank of People so that the Lady Hopkin (Wife to the illustrious Hopkin Generalisimo of the King's Forces in Pommarania and Comadore of the City of Stralsund)[66] presented him with a Suit of White Muslin made in the form of [a] Shroud and soon after he was led to the place of execution attended by a Minister and Guard together with a multitude of Spectators. his uncommon tallness made me think on Saul, King of Israel,[67] for his white Thrumcap[68] appeared nearly a foot above the numerous crould.[69] now the heighth of his Stature, his white Dress and the paleness of his Visage, together with the agitation [31] or rather the fervent ajaculation which he poured forth to his Maker with all his might, could not help but strike the beholders with a solemn dread and there were but few but what shed tears of Pity. he seemed not to be afraid to die but like a good Soldier and a Christian he, with an undaunted Courage, yielded his Neck to the Sword which put an end to his Life.

The third Actor[70] was [a] poor miserable Wretch who for some Capital Crime had been condemmed to the Wheelbarrow[71] for Nine Years which

66. Possibly Anders von Höpken (1712–89), one-time Swedish chancellor and powerful political figure, who left the government in 1761.

67. 1 Samuel 9:2, "Saul, a choice young man, and a goodly . . . from his shoulders and upward he was higher than any of the people."

68. A cap made of thrums, or waste threads from a loom.

69. Crowd.

70. Daniel Wilhelm Seefeld, a soldier, was executed in 1771 for the murder of a child in the town of Rügen. His body was treated as Whitehead stipulates here. Urkunde Rep. 3, Number 6186, SHS.

71. Convicts were often assigned hard public labor both to instill shame and to warn others of the consequences of crime. They were hobbled by a ball and chain and pushed a wheelbarrow as they worked.

[handwritten marginalia: but. okay in America for no... whites —]

Time was no sooner expired but he committed a shameful Murder by cutting the Throat of a little Girl about five Years of Age. as this was looked upon by every Body to be nothing else but a notorious wickedness, it was punished with the most Infamous Death that the Law could inflict. he first was whipt for three succeeding Days by the Hangman with thirty lashes each Day and on the fourth Day he was haled[72] out to the Place of execution by the Hangman on the same Cart which he used the[73] drag the Carren[74] out of the City and was besmeared with the Dung of the defunked Carcases. his Eyes were blindfolded and his back [placed] towards the Place of execution where his right Hand was first separated from his Body and then his Head. the Body was next divided into Quarters and thrown upon the Scaffold nearly Eleven feet high. his Head was also erected on a Post of the same heighth with the Hand nailed below.

Chapter 4: The Explosion of 1770

But as these were Malafactors and only suffered the punishment due to their Crimes, it was but a small matter to what I am now going to relate. for there suffered not only two or three but a multitude, as I may say, of Innocent People and worthy Citizens by a most deplorable accident which happened as follows. but to give my reader a more perfect Idea of the dismal Scene I shall first give a short account of the City and its fortification.

There were Eleven Gates which were large Edifices adorned with Turrets and other Ornaments but three of them were distinguished from the rest of the principal Gates and were named Frank Gate, Kniper Gate and Tribsace Gate. there were also raised three Walls for its defence and were distinguished by the out Wall, the middle and the inner Wall which contained nearly four hundred Cannons, the out Wall being lowest and the inner [32] the highest by which means they were capable of playing on the Enemy with all their Cannons. between the outer and middle Walls there was a vacancy of near a Quarter of [a] Mile in width, and between the middle and inner Walls a vacancy of nearly fifteen Perches. these vacancies were filled with Water which was let in from the Sea by [a] Sluce. each Wall was built with Stone below Water and of hard burnt Brick above its hieghth from the foundation. I can not say but the Brick Wall from the Surface of the Water might be near eighteen feet [high] and nearly thirty in Diameter,[75] topped out with

72. Hauled.
73. To.
74. Carrion.
75. Breadth or width.

Earth in the form of a Primarade[76] which raised it near fifteen feet higher.
this was the out Wall and the two others proportionable to this according
to the art of fortification, except the inner Wall which was the highest had a
fine walk on the top near ten feet wide and planted with Trees so close as to
afford a delightfull Shade and by its heighth was always fanned with a cool
breeze for which it was frequently visited in the Sultry Heat of Summer by
the Gentry who had raised many Grassy Seats and Tables to drink a Bottle
of Wine; they also whre[77] entertained with a beautiful prospect into the
Country. these Walls are joined by Bridges made of timber and plank with
strong banisters at the Sides which are kept well tarred and some painted to
save the Planks from wearing. they are first covered with bark of the Birch
Trees and then paved with Stone so wide that two Waggons may go a breast.
those narrow lanes are all the passages that lead to the City beginning at
the out Wall and ending at the inner Gate which proves no inconsiderable
expense to the People.

Now at the inner Wall nearly within ten Perches of Tribsace Gate there
stood a large Magazine[78] filled with Gun Powder but the chief superintendant
of the King's Powder works took a Notion that it was too full although it
was of a considerable bigness, for it was no less than Seventy feet high from
the Surface of the Ground to the beginning of the Roof and no less than thirty
feet in Diameter. it was in the form of Pillar and its Wall nearly Seven feet
thick built of hard burnt Brick except that part under Ground which was
of stone, and it was said that some of them were so large that [33] they might
try the strength of a good Team.[79] they also said it had a vault under Ground
nearly eighteen feet deep which was filled with an imminse quantity of Gun
Powder without being put up into Barrels. the whole structure was without
any Timber, except the Door and shutters, for every Story in it was Arched
and the Roof likewise after the same manner.

Now as I said before that the chief Superintendant thought it too full.
it is agreed by several of the Head Officers to transport some of it into
another Magazine where there was more room and fill the loose Powder into
Barrels.

Accordingly twelve Men and an Engineer were chosen of which unhappy
Number one of my Uncles named Andrew Schwigert[80] happened to be one
to perform this Work but before it was accomplished to the whole Structure
blew up in the Air, as near as I can remember on the 15th Day of June 1770

76. Promenade.
77. Were.
78. The "Pulvermagazin."
79. A team of horses or oxen.
80. German spellings include Andreas and Schweigert, Schwiegert, Schwigert, or Schweigerd.

about one oClock P.M.[81] how it happened none could tell but it seemed most likely it was done by a Candle down in its lowest apartment where there was no light except the light of a Candle. my unhappy Uncle was at Home [at] nearly twelve [o]Clock eating his Dinner but he seemed to be (as my Aunt related) in the greatest agony of Mind that a Man could be. a little Dinner served him and he said that he believed it would bi[82] the last for ever for he was assured in his Mind that some dreadful Disaster would behappen him but what it would be was not for him to know. my Aunt persuaded him with tears in her Eyes to not be too hasty in going back but he by no means would be persuaded to stay but went in haste to receive, as it were, the impending blow for he had been gone but a little while till it blew up with a most tremendious explosion. the whole City felt the Convulsion and trembled beneath its Apalet[83] Inhabitants. some concluded that we were to share the same fate with a Neighbouring City called Oldkuna,[84] which was sunk by an Earthquake and lay covered in the Ocean but they soon were relieved of that fear of [its] being an natural Earthquake for the dreadful tidings soon flew from one Quarter to another of what had happened. it was our good fortune to live quite at the other end of the Town so that we recieved little or no damage. I was immediately sent off with orders to not make too much delay but bring Word back as quick as I could how matters were [34] (by this Time the Smoke was coming into our part of the City like a think[85] Cloud and almost darkened the Sun which was then as it were in its full strength). pursuant to his Orders I went but when I arrived within an hundred Perches or more of the Place of Destruction the Houses began to appear very ragged. the Tiles, Windows and Ceilings all were torn, shivered to pieces; all kind of Crockary Ware, Tumblers, Glasses and China Plates had met the same fate. but this was nothing to what I saw when I arrived within forty Perches for then the Houses appeared no more ragged but leveled to the Ground and not only the Houses but also the City Walls and Gates, Earth and Water, Trees and Cannons, Bridges and drawbriges, all were mixed thus one another so that there appeared to be a perfect Chaos. but still all this seemed to be but trifles in comparison to the many Lives of Innocent People that were lost. the shrieks and lamentations together white[86] the Dolerious groanings of the

81. See the *Pommerschen Zeitung* no. 342, December 11, 1940, reprint of article of December 12, 1770. SHS.

82. Be.

83. Appalled.

84. Probably Cape Arkona, the northernmost point on the island of Ruegen, the white cliffs of which are sometimes unstable. A Pomeranian folktale also describes the sinking into the sea of the mythical city of Vineta; see Selma Lagerlof, "Die Stadt auf dem Meeresgrunde," in *Pommersche Erzaehler: Heiteres und Besinnliches* (Tübingen: Horst Erdmann Verlag, 1973), 65–73.

85. Thick.

86. With.

dying and wounded I am altogether incapable of expressing. it would have even melted a Heart of Stone into Tears to behold so shocking a Scene where a tender Mother would rage, like distracted, thumping her Breast and tearing her Hair with lamentable crys after the loss of four, five, six or more of her tender Offspring with a beloved and affectionate Husband. also, a Father would stand wringing his Hands and deploring the loss of his Children and loving Wife. some were lying without Arms, some without Legs, some were cut in two, some whose Heads were crushed and others lying with pieces of Timber sticking in their Bodies and some that had escaped the danger of being slain were frightened into Convulsions and some into Hysteric Fits. Women that were pregnant parted with the untimely Birth and in short I thought it and think yet it appeared almost as Terrific a Scene as ever the Eyes of Man beheld. for it was agreed that as if an Enemy had thrown in ten thousand Bums[87] it could not have done half the damage. it exceeded by far the Field of Battle for when a Soldier marches forth to encounter his Enemy, the cause he fights for and the Glory of Victory animates his Spirit so as to throw himself voluntarily in danger which he must expect from an enraged Enemy. [35] but this was a different case: there was no visible Enemy and the People were in their peaceable Habitations where they thought themselves secure from all danger of such kind and as it was at that time a[88] Day [when] I make no doubt but that many were resting themselves on their Couches or Beds of ease, little expecting the impending danger that was ready to burst upon them and that Death was looking them in the Face with an uplifted Arm ready to strike the mortal blow.

There happened to be one amongst the unhappy Number whose fortune was particularly singular from the rest, as I have learned, and I fancied myself that it would not be tedious to the reader if I should insert hear the following account. he was the Son of a Wealthy Gentleman in the City of Berlene[89] in the Kingdom of Prussia but it proved to be his ill Fortune to be deeply enamoured with a young Woman of low degree but otherwise endewed with all the beauties and ornaments becoming her Sex. but knowing his Father would by no means be pleased to give his Consent for them to be joined in Marriage, he was at a great loss to know how to act but it happened one Day that the old Gentleman seemed to be in an uncommon chearful Humour. his Son then thought fit not to let slip that opportunity of acquainting his Father with his design, yet he thought it fittest not to begin too rash but first to pry into his Fathers opinion concerning his intended Bride. upon this, he began

87. Bombs.
88. Of.
89. Berlin.

to speak greatly in Praise of the said Girl, alledging how happy he would be if he should have the good fortune ever to be joined in Marriage with a Woman of so amicable a disposition and other good Qualities befitting her Sex. but the old Man soon began to mistrust what his Son was upon and bid him to explain himself which he did with as much Humility and Eloquence as Love and Filial Duty could invent. but the old Man grew in a passion and told him at once his Doom and what he might depend upon in case of disobeying which was that he should not only be disinherited but also be deprived of the liberty of ever entering into his House while he drew the Breath of Life. the young Man now [36] threw himself at his Father's Feet, beseeching him with Tears in his Eyes not to cross him thus in the most important point of Sublunary[90] happiness, telling him further that without the darling object of his Love he desired no Life, for it would only prove a burden to him without her. he further said that he knew in his Heart he always had been an obedient and Dutiful Child but if he should absolutely dissapoint him in this Important [affair,] he greatly feared that he should have to disobey. but his Father, like an old Oak, was too stiff to bend and by no means flexible to the pitiful moving intreaties of his only Son who lay at his Feet in an Attitude of Grief and Dispair, for the old Man was too much settled on his Lees[91] in the pursuit of Wealth and Honour so that in a tone of displeasure he replied that what he had said should be performed. the poor young Man now plainly saw that nothing was to be done in getting the approbation of his Father [and] went unto his Love and acquainted her with all that passed between him and his Father. the poor young Woman, who was equally enamoured and as deeply affected in Love as her illustrious Admirer, was struck with Grief and dispair by hearing the dismal sentence her Lover was to receive on her account if they should join Hand in Hand and Heart in Heart and tie the powerful knot of Marriage. and thinking no Man on Earth that was so rich and of so great a Family as her Lover could possibly forsake all for the sake of a poor and insignificant Woman like her, the reflexition of this melted her Heart and after a solemn silence that lasted a considerable Time she, with a Shower of Tears, broke forth into a loud exclamation against her ill Fate, thinking herself to be for ever deprived of him whom she loved more than her own Life. and being no longer able to support her Grief she sunk motionless into the Arms of her Lover who supported her on his Knees bedewing her Cheeks with the flowing Tears. and as [37] soon as she recovered he addressed her with the most Cordial Speech saying: "my dearest Charmer, be not dismayed, nor let thy Heart be sunk into the Abys of Despair, for be

90. I.e., earthly.
91. I.e., hardened, morally or spiritually indifferent. Cf. Jeremiah 48:11; Zephaniah 1:12.

assured that I am resolved to forsake all I possess in the World rather than be separated from thee, my sole delight and only object of all my Sublunary happiness, and that Power that has been Graciously pleased to join and knit our Hearts so closely in the Bonds of Love will also be pleased to support us even in a Time of the greatest Danger and Difficulty and I also make no doubt but that some Power will also in its own Time soften the Stony Heart of my Father if we but do our part which is Patience and full resignation to the Will of Heaven."

This Speech, which was far beyond what she expected, perfectly satisfied her and she appeared easy and chearful. but how to perform the solemnity of Matrimony was a Task of great difficulty for none are invested with that Power except the Priest and he also is incapable of performing it without the Consent of Parents and the publications for three succeeding Weeks from the Pulpit. hereupon they resolved to forsake their Country for two Reasons: first to escape persecution of his Father and secondly it was generally believed that the Prussian Laws were more severe than the Swedish. therefore they concluded to take Stage for the City of Stralsund where they safely arrived but found as much difficulty in being joined in Marriage as they had found at Home and there was no other way but for him to list[92] into the Army. and then by the assistance of his Captain he was in a capacity to obtain his Wishes. now this was another sad stroke, that one who might possess a large Fortune should be reduced to so low an Ebb as to join the Miserable Life of a common Soldier but as there was no other way for him to do, he, as a true [38] example and patern of pure Love, surmounted all difficulties he Could and they were joined in Marriage. but alas, it happened that their lot was to have their Quarters in that unhappy part of the City where they both perished with many more nearly a Week after their Marriage and as the House wherein they lived was but small their Bodies were not mangled and by the way they were found in the rabbage[93] it was supposed that he had been sitting in a Chair holding his dear Companion on his Knees, supporting her Head with his left Arm and his right round her Waist and as they were loving and their Hearts so Safely united whilst alive they also were not separated in Death: they both were entered in one Coffin and buried in the common Grave.

I wish this might be a warning to all Parents so as to be not too severe on their Children in this important point of Marriage. Parents may propose but their Sons and Daughters must have the liberty of choosing and refusing, for it is them that have to bear all events consistent to a Matrimonyel Life. and I think there is nothing more absurd and ridiculous than for Parents

92. Enlist.
93. I.e., rubble.

to make up a Match between their Children without the least Knowledge
whether they have any regard for one another or not but so that they can
only join their Estates and keep their Coffers filled seems to be the chiefest
care of too many Parents in the World—although there is nothing more certain [than] that Heaven never Instituted the Solemnity of Marriage for the
Gold but [rather] for the Hearts of Men. now therefore if a Parent is sensible
and truly convinced that the Heart of his Son or Daughter is sincerely united
and firmly knitted by Heaven to the Heart of another who is altogether
worthy of being an imbosomed companion he ought not to restrain them, for
if he does it is separating that which Heaven hath united together which
should remain till the Lord of Life himself is pleased to separate them. but I
am by no means intending to blame a Parent for giving his Advice or his
command if good and reasonable. Children must and ought to obey. and further, if a Parent sees his intended Son or Daughter[39]-in-Law is altogether
unworthy of being [a companion,] so as a chearful, Innocent young Woman
[is] to be joined to a selfish, morose, ill natured Curmogen[94] of a Fellow, or
at the other Hand, [if] a Sober, well behaved and Industrious Man [is] to be
joined to a Careless giddy Coquette that is nothing but full of Gallantry—in
such cases a Parent may reasonably endeavour to obstruct such Marriages to
the utmost of their Power. but where there is no obsticle in the way except
an empty insignificant Title or a few bags of Gold, I can not pity such Parents if they should meet with such Trouble and perplexity as often arises
from a Clandistine Marriage.

But to return as they were buried in the common Grave. this was a large
Pit dug on purpose to hold several Coffins for as the Weather then was hot.
it was not likely that each Family could be interred in the usual way, except
some few who for distinction sake were interred separate. for it was com-
puted that between seven or eight hundred were slain and many dying of
their Wounds so that near a Thousand lost their lives in this deplorable
accident besides the entire ruin of their Furniture and Houses which were
no less than three hundred [households] that were intirely ruined besides a
great Number that recieved a considerable damage. it could never rightly [be]
determined what the total Sum of the loss would amount to but by all likelyhood it could not help being an immense Sum. yet had it been in our parts
of the City the loss would have been infinitely greater because of it being
inhabited by most of the considerable Merchants and gentry whose Houses
were for the most part from four to seven Stories high and [were] richly furnished within of [one] curiosity or other. whereas that part of the City where
it happened was only inhabited by the common class of People and their

94. Curmudgeon.

Houses only from to one to three Stories high so that the Disaster chiefly lit on the Heads of the Poor who suffered and the rich were saved [so] that they might reach forth their helping Hands to their truly distressed fellow Citizens. three of the most Wealthy Merchants offered not only a handsome bounty but also went through the City to collect what Mony they [40] could for the relief of the Sufferers. I never could learn how much they gathered but I heard some say they had speeded[95] beyond expectation for every one seemed to contribute to it with all his Heart according to his ability. it also happened that the following Spring our Sovereign Gustavus the third,[96] who had been on his Travels to France and Germany, came on his returning Home through the City where he stayed near two Weeks. with what acclamations of Joy, Illuminations and other Curiosities he was received and entertained [it] would prove too tedious to mention, for every Day seemed to bring forth new inventions and amusements. and one Day he was pleased to take a walk to the place of Desolation and although the Face of things were then greatly altered, he like a Father mourned for the loss of his Children and the reflexion of having lost so many peaceable Subjects melted his Heart into Tears as he not only gave a handsome bounty out of his own private Purse but also obliged the Crown together with the Royal Family to reach their helping Hands, so that when I left the City that part began to appear better than before, for the Houses were again nitty[97] refitted and inhabited.

There is one thing more happened which I can not pass over in silence which was on the following Morning about the dawn of Day after the Magazine blew up, we were alarmed by the most dreadful Lightning accompanied with a clap of Thunder such as I never have heard of in all my Life for the Lightning blazed for near two Minutes and the Thunder came considerably before the Flash was expired and I have heard the Night Watch say a Ball of Fire nearly as big as a Barrel came out of the Air and Struck the Roof of Saint Nicholas's Church where it bursted at the Instant it struck with a report as lound[98] as of a Gun but the Roof being strong and covered with Copper it did no damage but again about ten oClock A.M. it thundered again [41] exceeding hard and struck the Steeples of Saint Nicholas and Saint Mary. Saint Nicholas received not much damage and the Fire was soon extinguished but the Steeple of Saint Mary blazed in the air to the astonishment of the beholders. some of the Devout Spectators fell on their Knees and, in an Attitude of Adoration, poured forth ther Prayers imploring Mercy from god and not to be swept

95. I.e., succeeded.
96. Gustaf III of Sweden reigned 1771–92. He was in the midst of a European tour when he succeeded his father to the throne of Sweden in February 1771. He visited Stralsund in April 1771. SHS.
97. Neatly or fitly.
98. Loud.

away intirely with the Besom[99] of Destruction. and I have no reason to dis-
beleive but [that] their Prayers were answered by a Gracious God, for the Fire
abated and was extinguished without much damage although the Gallary
where it was set on Fire was exceeding high. yet Water being handy—which
is kept in large Tubs aloft in the Steeple after the following manner: there
are placed beneath the Cover of the Steeple, which is of Copper, where there
is fixed a sprout[100] so as to throw the Water in to them when ever it Rains
and, to hinder them from running over, a pipe is fixed level with the top of
the Tub by which means the Waters discharges itself on the Roof when it
is within an Inch of running over and by this method they are always supplied with many Hogsheads of Water without ever fetching any from below.
I have seen the Water in those Tubs covered with a green scum and when
stirred had an offensive smell but this must not be regarded in Time of danger and it is also supposed by Naturalists and Philosophers that old stinking dirty Water is far superior to fresh and clean Water in the extinction of
Fire. the commoner class of People were for having a Day of Thanksgiving
to be observed in every Year as a Memorial for Ages to come of the Mercies
of God—and as [with] the Children of Israel they sung his praise but soon
for got his Works—for the learned Heads and selfwise Philosophers soon
endeavoured to contrive a the way to deprive Divine Providence of all its
Operations whether blessings or chastisements: they said there was nothing
Supernatural on the case, whereas the Magazine was set on Fire by the carelessness of the labourers and the effluvia of the Powder, which was of the
same Nature like the sulpherous exhalations, it could not be cleansed out of
the Air but by the discharge of Electric Fires.[101]

I hope the reader will pardon my length of Time in giving this Narration
because it appears to me not only awful but also instructive. it shows us that
uncertainty of our Lives and all Sublunary things and that we are never safe
[42] from imminent danger, even in a place where we may reasonably expect
to be the most secure. it shows us plainly that this Moment we may call ours
but the next is in the Hands of Providence, for we see here how many of our
fellow mortals are hurled off the Stage of Life, as it were in a Moment, without having as much Time as to say "Lord have Mercy on me." and although I
would willingly hope the best yet I fear that there were many thus unprepared
for so sunden and unexpected change from Time to Eternity. but as it is not
my place [to say] whether they were prepared or not; I went[102] it fittest to leave
them to the Mercy of a Gracious God and turn again to my own Business.

99. I.e., broom.
100. Spout.
101. I.e., lightning.
102. As written. Perhaps Whitehead intended "think" or "find."

Chapter 5: Wanderlust

The following Year [1771] in the beginning of August I was bit by a Mad Dog which came into the House and abused my Mistress's Lap Dog and I to rescue him recieved a Wound in my right Hand. my Master nor me had the least mistrust of the Dog being Mad and I make no doubt but that both of us would have considered it no more than a common Wound and so might have delayed the cure till it had been too late, had it not been my good Fortune that the Hangman whose Business it was to dispatch such Dogs happened to be in the pursuit of him, who overtook and killed him in my sight. my Master, who seemed to be more alarmed than myself, sent me immediately to the executioner of the Malafactors, who was in general allowed to be preferable to any Physician in performing the cure of this dreadful Malady, who gave me a Powder resembling Snuff. this I had to take with a piece of Bread and Butter, which he engraved with many Hyerogliphics and Magical Characters. thend after eating this he took me into the Parlour where he went to a little Closet and fetched his Sword which he drew out of its Sheath and I must confess that the glittering Blade together with the thoughts of [its] having sent so many to Eternity, I was seized with a solemn dread and I bieng but a Boy and not knowing what he was going to perform, it made [me] nearly tremble with awe. but the Officer soon percieving the disorder I was in smilingly told me I had nothing to fear, for he should only give me a small Wound in the end of my Finger just so as to draw Blood, which he did, and said he hoped the cure was performed and so put by [the] Sword which was of so curious workmanship [43] I think it deserves a place in my History. the Blade I think was nearly three Feet in length and about four Inches in width, in the form of a Dagger except it being blunt at the end and both edges exceeding sharp. its burnished Steel may almost be compared to a looking Glass, for near two feet and then for three Inches or more it seemed a perfect White and this same length again of a deep Blue and from that to the Hilt of a Gold colour curiously engraved with Flower de Lerces[103] and other ornaments. the Hilt was also very rich and suitable to the Blade for its materials consisted chiefly of Ebony and the Mother of Pearl which was curiously wrought after the fancy of the Artist and as it is looked upon as the Pride and Ornament of that Office. I have heard of some being so vain as to spend a handsome Estate upon the embellishment or decoration of this Implement of Death. but to return, as soon as I went Home I acquainted my Master with the Operation which appeared to him too much [of] the Nature of Powouring[104] and not

---

103. Fleur-de-lys.
104. Powwowing, i.e., employing magical medicine.

having faith enough to depend altogether on it, I was sent to a Physician, who knew my Master was rich, [and] proved as I thought no way saretan[105] with his Drugs. but whether he or the Marshal performed the cure I cannot determine but thanks be to Heaven I felt no Simtons[106] of that intolerable Disease but kept in a State of perfect Health and Vivacity.

My Master, who was a great lover of Poetry, especially the works of the Immortal Milton[107] but I could not understand it because it being in the Lattin Tongue, only I heard him say many Times that it was an excellent performance. he had also a large Library filled with Books of all kinds which were so many I may venture to say they would load a Waggon with two Horses. my business was every Spring to cleanse them from Dust and Cobwebbs which proved to be my ruin for I found many Books that were very entertaining and having but little else to do I spent a deal of Time in cleaning and reading them. but none seemed to draw my attention more than History and Geography. this was the first Spring that put me in motion to Travel and seek my Fortune in the wide World. the more I read the firmer I grew in my resolution of traveling till at last I acquainted my Master with it who soon found that the Instruments of[108] chief sorce of that notion were only Books. therefore he endeavoured as [44] much as lay in his Power to put me out of that notion by telling me I was too young, I could not consider the danger and difficulty which always accompanied a traveller either by Sea or Land, nor had I sufficient Mony to bear my expenses and should only [lead] to distress, Poverty and want, and perhaps at last be sold a Slave during Life. but if I was sure I could better myself and would and must go, he would prove no obsticle betwixt me and my Fortune. he further said that it [was] impossible for me to feel the pangs of a distressed Traveller, for I could read of People perishing with cold at the Straits of David in Greenland[109] and sit all the time comfortably by a warm Stove. I also could read of People dying with the extream Heat in the Deserts of Lybia whilst I was beneath the cool Shade of his Walnut Tree. I further could read of whole caravans perishing in the Deserts of Arabia for want of Water while I could go the Cellar and drink Beer or Wine. therefore he would have me to consider the matter truly before it was too late and I need think to find it [was not] so easy as I imagined for he could assure me there was a great difference between experience and only reading the matter.

105. Probably "spartan."
106. Symptoms.
107. John Milton (1608–74), the English poet who composed Latin verse in his early career.
108. Or.
109. Davis Strait.

But all this wholesome advice and demonstration waited[110] but little, for go I must to seek my fortune and fancied myself already on the Coast of Brazil gathering Gold and Diamonds by handfuls. my Master, [who] found I was inflexible and by no means brought over by wholesome Advice, gave up the Contest and left me to myself for to force me was not in his Power by the Law of the Land.

But before I proceed in any further I think it necessary to give a few more hints of my Parents, which as I have mentioned before, I left in the Town of Franceburgh where they stayed but a short Time after I left them and moved. the Island of Witts[111] lies between Gasmond [and] Rugan[112] but it being a desolate and barren place, scarce anything growing except Juniper of which there was great plenty, they stayed not long there but removed to the City of Stralsund where my Step Father listed in the first Battalia[113] of the Artilery. he was now almost arrived to the lowest pitch of fortune and he seemed to be somewhat reformed and stayed more at Home than usual. but as the old saying as "why Jack would not eat his Supper, which was because he had it not," so it was now with my [45] Father for his income was three pence per Day and one Bushel of Rye per Month which was by far an insufficient support for his Family, having a Wife and four small Children.

But fortune again shifted his Scene and seemed to smile on him, for it happened that he got acquainted with one with who was a Valet de chamber to [a] Noble Man, Baron Arrenfelt.[114] this Valet recommended my Father to his Master as a fit Hand to Fish and Fowl for him. this Nobleman had a Summer Seat on the Island of Delminhorst,[115] which lies between Rugen and Pommarania within half a Mile of the City. the East end of [the] Island lies high and very convenient for a Campaign in Time of War for which reason it is fortified and [has] Barracks fitted for that purpose. but the West end lies low, is fertile and supports a large drove of Cattle belonging to this Nobleman. hereupon my Father was sent for by the Baron who told him if he had a Mind to desist from the Life of Soldier, he might go and live on the Island, take Care of the fortifications and keep the Ferry and what liesure Hours he had might Fish and Fowl for him. and if he caught more than he needed my Father might have the rest to do with as he thought fit, for hunting and fishing is not allowed on this part of the World but to such as are called Masters of the Game or else such as pay a smart rent for the Liberty. how much

110. Weighed.
111. Wittow is the northern peninsula on the Island of Rügen or Ruegen.
112. Jasmund is the northeastern part of the Island of Rügen.
113. Battalion.
114. In German, von Ahrenfeld or von Ahrenfelt.
115. Perhaps Danholm, on the Island of Rügen, as Delminhorst is an interior town near Bremen, more than a hundred miles from Stralsund.

my Father had per Annum I can not say but it was sufficient to maintain
him and his Family in a decent manner. he gladly embraced the opportunity
and my Mother rejoiced to see them again refitted in a State of decency and
by all appearancs they undoubtedly might again have been well had it not
been for Step Father's Infernal temper and disposition. for not long after
they were well settled some little disturbance arose, the truth of it I could not
learn but it was something my Step Father should have said concerning the
Family of his Master, who reproved him gently, cautioning him to beware of
making disturbance in his Family. upon which my Father with his customary roughness belched forth most execrable curses calling his Master and all
that [he] had said whatever it was by the most Infamous Names he could
invent, in which he was pretty dextrous, and to set his Character in its full
light I can do [no] better than to insert here one of his Sentiments by which
the reader easily may see what sort of a Christian he was. he said that he [46]
was not affraid of any thing living nor dead, neither [Angel] nor Devil, and as
for his Maker he was well assured that he must forgive Sins if he intended
to have any souls. but to return again to my Story, the Baron's Spirit was so
highly exasperated with the rough usage of my Father who was so much inferior to him that he caned [him] with his own hands, and further told him
that he should be sent to the House of correction. but he [Kukuck] soon found
an opportunity to acquaint my Mother with what had happened and also what
was to come [and] he concluded it was the fittest for him to fly while he had
an opportunity. upon this both him and my Mother entered the Boat, he to
fly from correction and she to bring back the Boat.

Now what seemed most remarkable was that at that very juncture when
my Father was taking his flight, I was standing on the other Shore waving a
white Hankerchief which was the signal for the Boat to come and fetch me
over in order to take my last farewell and as Soon [as] they arrived I saw by
their Countenances that something extraordinary was the matter. my Father
jumped out of the Boat and told me in short that he was going away and so
bid me farewell. he went off whit[116] a few Clothes, some Mony and [a] bruised
Back and whether hi[117] ever has returned or not I can not say but I saw him
once more which I shall mention hereafter. my Mother then bid me come
in the Boat, which I did, and both of us worked it back in perfect silince and
remained so till we got to the House. my Mother then began with Tears in
her Eyes to relate to me the whole sad story. now any one that has sympathy
and a Heart that can feet[118] for his fellow mortal may think that one that once
lived well and then be reduced [to] almost to the lowest Ebb of fortune and

116. With.
117. He.
118. Feel.

then to be reenstated again to a comfortable Life and then meet so sunden and hard a change with[119] be enough [to] sink into Despair. but it happened therivin[120] with my Mother who being inured to hardships and disappointments, drop'd a few Tears [and] with a composed chearfulness said that it was only what she was well accustomed to. she had a fine Garden to which she said she could not enjoy the fruit of her Labour but that it would do good to them that came after her for she had to move from that place the following Day and [47] and rented a couple of lodging Rooms in the City with an intention to take in Boarders. and as she was a handy Verdle[121] Woman and particularly skillful at [the] working of Lace for ruffles and Capborders, I flatter myself that she can live [more] comfortably alone that with so ill natured a Companion.

Now the Time of departure drew nigh. it was reduced from Weeks to Days and from Days to Hours, for I had agreed with one named Layswich who was Captain of a Vessel to be ready to set sail from that Time two Weeks [after] for the City of Luback,[122] which Time was now expired and my big Heart began to fail pretty fast. I now found that my departure would not be so light a matter as I had imagined. I was resolved to keep up my Spirits and show as little reluctance as possible but in the after Noon the Boatswain came and told me they would be ready [to] set sail the next Morning if the Wind was fair. it struck me to the Heart and [a] cool chill ran through my Blood and raised me as it were at once from that Visionary Dream that had flattered me [that] it was nothing to leave all in the pursuit of Fortune. the bitter Cup of separation was now to be taken and drained as it were to the very bottom. I now went to my Mother for the last Time and took an everlasting farewell and how my Heart felt none can imagine. for none can know but such as by experience have felt what it is to leave a tender Mother, Brothers and Sisters, and all Friends and Associates without the least expectation of ever seeing [them] again. I could say but little and we both wept. she kissed me and bid me remember her last embraces, being as sure as if she was on the point of expiring that she never should behold my Face again in this World. she recommended me to the protection of Divine Providence and bid me be a good Boy and avoid bad company as much as possible. and as I was intending to go to my Uncle who lived in Hamburgh, she bid me remember her Love to her dear Sister when I arrived there.

I was now drawn as it were between two Cords nearly of an equal strength, the one or the other would give way. for the greatest part of that Night the

119. Will.
120. Therein.
121. Versatile.
122. Lübeck.

one [cord] was to [not] leave my Mother in the situation she was in, being deserted by my Father with four small Children, of which one was at her Breast, and all my near and dear Relations, Friends, and Associates [48] without the least hopes of ever seeing them again. and the other cord was the pursuit of Fortune and being laughed at by my companions if I stayed, for they would frequently tease me and say I could [not] leave them and I had not a Heart stout enough to attempt any such matters as to travel—no more then an old wife—to which I frequently replyed they should see to the contrary and I let them know I had a Heart like a Man which was not of so quamish[123] and effeminate disposition as they would be were they in my case, to which they would say they would see how stout I was. now the reflexion of being laughed at together with the pursuit of fortune proved the strongest cord and the other to my sorrow gave way for my Spirit was too great and could not bear to be teased or laughed at, therefore I concluded to come up to one of our Proverbs "Ick bin dafoehr, aber moeth dadoehr" which is [to say] "I have began it and must go through with it." I got up early in the Morning, dressed myself and got ready. I ate my Breakfast but indeed [only] a little served[124] and about eight oClock in the Morning word came that the Vessel had hoisted Anchor and was under sail. I then called in a Man to carry my Trunk to the Wharf and my Master and Mistress went into the Parlour to bid me farewell. I could say but little but [could] not forbear to weep aloud. my Mistress was almost as deeply affected as myself and wept likewise but my Master with a look of sympathy took his farewell giving me his last and wholesome Advice and bidding me to remember him in my Adversity and reflect on my self as the only cause of it and not forget him in my Prosperity which he wished that Heaven might be pleased to grant me.

Chapter 6: Hamburg

I then left the place of my Nativity in the beginning of May 1772 and took shipping for the City of Luback where I arrived about the middle of the said Month. nothing remarkable behappened us in this Voyage. all went well and the People were chearful except my self, for with what reluctance I left my Native Land none can imagine. as soon as I arrived on Shipboard I fixed my Trunk and sat down upon it with my Eyes fixed steadfast on the City which now grew less every Moment till it disappeared and vanished as it were forever out of my view and I took my last farewell heartly to this effect: "and

123. Squeamish.
124. I.e., he had no appetite.

must I thus leave thee O Stralsund City dear, and I dob of[125] [49] my Heart, fair and pleasing thou hast been to me but yet I must not only leave thee but also my near and dear Relations, Associates and Companions. O then adieu forever, for never shall those sad Eyes behold thee more, Ah never more! Farewell my Native Land, my Natal Air that first inspired my feeble Lungs with Vital Breath and my first Cries were heard in the Arms of the Midwife."

The Steeples which were very high and had diverted my Eyes for a considerable Time after the City disappeared now vanished at once out of view by going round a point of Land to which I said, "O you Torrets[126] whose enormous heights I always beheld with Admiration but never gazed on you with so much attention as this Moment [when] you began to disappear but if your Spires even extended far above the Clouds it would be only sufficient to see you but yet a little while."

I then shed plentiful Tears, and after my Stare was exausted I wiped them away and made the matter as light as I could. the Captain, who perceived that I was in great trouble, came to me in order to chear me up but it was not in my Power to be chearful. he invited me into the Cabben, telling me that there were Passengers who all were chearful and he made no doubt but their company would be agreeable to me. I thanked him for his kindness and told him it suited best my inclination to be alone, therefore if he pleased I would take it kind of him to let me remain in the place I choosed, which was in the forecastle. upon this he went away and soon after one of the Passengers came and treated me with a Glass of Brandy which I tasted for manners sake. but he also riquested me to come into the Cabben which I refused with as much decency as I was capable of and I never entered the Cabben but once and this was on the Sabbath and all of us met together in order to worship. I did eat, drink, and sleep but little for some Days and Nights. but after some Time I began to be weaned by degrees and became again somewhat chearful but it was a considerable Time [50] before I became intirely weaned from the Breast of my Native Mother Earth. I composed a few Verses which I think may not be amiss [to] entertain the Reader with. they are nearly as follow:

> Ah cruel Fortune is it thy command
> That I should thus forsake my Native Land
> Leave all my Friends thy favours to explore
> In unknown Regions and a foreign Shore
> Yes Fortune bids and I her to obey
> Leave all my Friends and mourning go away

125. Doff off.
126. Turrets.

Bear then the Mast the Specious[127] Sail display
And this fair breeze shall waft us on our way
Spread wide the Canvas that the Bark[128] may glide
And its strong Kiel[129] the rolling Waves divide
Stand at the Helm the sturdy Rudder play
While Luna[130] smiles and Phebus[131] guilds[132] the Day
The Compass great Magnetic Needle mind
And watch the motions of the fickle Wind
So may great Neptune[133] Source of Britain's fame
Be pleas'd to smile and hail us on the Main
With his great Trydon[134] smoothe the foaming Tide
That thus our Bark may forth in safety ride
For my dear Country the exchange must be
The rolling Billows of the Baltic Sea
And if great Jove[135] call forth his gloomy Clouds
And bids the Storms to rend our Mast and Shrouds
Sends the feirce tempest bids the Thunder roar
And the dread Lightnings blaze from Shore to Shore
We still will hope that his Almighty Hand
Will lead us safe unto our destined Land.

The wind seemed for the most part unfavourable which made our V Voyage tedious, so that we were the greatest part of two Weeks [51] before we arrived at Luback which was on the eighteenth of the said Month in the After Noon and that Evening lay close in the Harbour where we cast Anchor and the Captain went on Shore but I stayed that Night on Shipboard. but next Morning early I took a walk to see the curiosities of the City and likewise to enquire when the Stage was going for Hamburgh which I was told would set out the next Morning at Seven oClock. I then concluded to spend one Night more on Shipboard, for as I was altogether a Stranger to the place I thought it fittest and safest lodging. and next Morning [I] got ready in good Time, discharged my Passage and one of the Sailers carried my Trunk to [the] Post Office where again I payed for my Journey to Hamburgh and so went off at the afore[said]

127. Spacious.
128. A relatively small sailing vessel.
129. Keel.
130. The moon.
131. Another name for Apollo, the Greek god of the sun.
132. Gilds.
133. God of the sea.
134. Trident.
135. Jove, also Jupiter, god of the sky and lightning, chief of the Roman gods.

Hour and arrived at Six oClock in the Evening at the Post Office at Hamburgh. and as I knew the Name of the Street and place where my Uncle lived I had no difficulty to find him, for there are People that follow for a livelihood to conduct Strangers to their respective Lodgings or Habitations. they also have a little Car in the form of a Wheelbarrow to carry Trunks &c. but as the City is very large and my Uncle's Dwellings a considerable distance from the Post Office, I began [to be] almost alarmed and frequently would ask [the] Guide if he knew the place or if he rightly understood me, to which he always replied that he did understand me and also knew the place very well and that we should be there before long. but it began to be Sundset and we still went on till near Dark. then my Guide stopped at the Door and told me that it was the place I had mentioned. I then joyfully knocked at the Door and my Aunt asking who there was that knocked, I replied "a Stranger who desires to have an Nights lodging," to which she replied "Ah Stranger I know thee" and so bid me come in. she immediately opened the Door and I went in and met with a joyful welcome. I could scarcely forebear shedding a few tears of joy to see once more my favourite Aunt after an absence of nine [52] Years. I then asked for my Uncle and likewise how she knew it was me that knocked, to which she replied that my Step Father had arrived there before me and had acquainted them with my coming and if nothing happened I they might expect me about that Time. and he was gone with my Uncle to the City of Altena[136] which was nearly a Mile distant and she expected them Home pretty soon. this spoiled the Joke which I was intending to have by making myself known to them. soon after they arrived Home my Father smiled and said that he was there arrived before me, to [which] I replied that it was a surprize to me to see him there, to which he said that it was more than he himself expected and that his stay would be but short. and I thought it appeared very evident to me he was a shamed and as I thought feared that I should discover his behaviour or at least throw up some hints while he was present but I said nothing relating to his conduct till after he was gone.

now Bedtime soon arrived; we went to rest and I seemed much fatigued, [and] rested extraordinary well. the next Morning after Breakfast my Uncle took us about the City to shew us its fine Gardens and other curiosities but in our returnd a Strange event happened which I can not pass by in silence and [it] was thus: we happened to pass by the Principal Inn of the City, which bore the Name of the Black Eagle, and almost as soon as we were against it some Body opened a Window in the second Second Story and called my Father by his Name. this struck him with admiration and wondering greatly who could be there that knew him. but he had not [a] long Time to wonder

136. Altona.

for he soon found that it was his Master who lodged there with his Lady. they both were going to a place called Acken,[137] famous on account of a Fountain in its Neighbourhood to which the Gentry flock from a great distance to use the Bath and drink its salutary Water. [53] now so sunden and unexpected [an] event gave my Father such a shock—although his temper might be compared to thunder and hail he now became as gentle as a refreshing shower in May. it put his whole frame in such agitation as I never saw him in and he confessed himself that he never felt so in all his Life for he nearly trembled and a pain seized him in his left side so violent that it almost made him hollow[138] out. he considered a little while not knowing what to do, for he greatly feared the consequence of having so great a Man for his Enemy in a place where he was altogether a stranger and it is not to be wondered [that] he should dread the consequence of so ill a conduct as his. but my Uncle told him that he had nothing to fear for as he was in the principalest Hance Town[139] in the World, he was intirely out of his Master's power and the Law would protect him from all violence. by this Time the Nobleman called again pretty sharp bidding him come up. my Father then gathered up all the remainder of his courage and went. we accompanied him to the Door where we sat in the Porch wainting the issue of the event. and within a Quarter of an Hour my Father returned with a chearful countenance saying all was well and [that] he had fared better than he expected or deserved for his Master had not only promised to restore him again to his employment if he returned within three Months but also had given his Word that he would write to his Steward with a charge to take care that his Family should not suffer. this was fine news for me and I rejoiced at it in heart. the reason why my Father speeded so well I have good reason to believe was that the unexpected shock made him very penitent and hample.[140] for he said the nearer he approached the Room the worse he felt and when he got in the presence of his master he was scarcely able to stand, and when he was asked what ailed him he was incapable of giving an answer. but he soon began to get better and replied he could not tell, to which his master said his disorder appeared very plain and that he could easily tell him it was nothing else but the lashes of an evil conscience which thus chastised him and he hoped it would prove for his good and he should take it as a warning. [54]

We then went home and related to my Aunt what had happened to which she replied "it was strange what admirable things could happen in the World." the next Day being the first of the Week, we went to Altena to see the

137. Aachen.
138. Holler.
139. Hanse Town (a town that had been included in the Hanseatic League).
140. Humble.

curiosities of the City, my Uncle also, to the Roman [Catholic] Chappel where my attentions were closely engaged on inspecting their way of worship and I beg pardon for my freedom of declareing my sincere opinion of one matter, which perhaps may prove insipid to the taste of a Roman, which is that [what] I greatly disapprove is the delivering a Sermon or any spiritual performance whatsoever in a Language not to be understood by the generality of the Congregation but only such as are Men of learning.[141] for it is an undeniable truth that the Soul can not receive any benefit by a sormon except the Ear can hear and the heart comprehend it—which is impossible to do if it is delivered in an unknown tongue. it is not my intention to write by way of railery, for I should be sorry to employ my pen in flinging sarcastic darts at any Man, especially at his religion—if it should occasion any censure, it must certainly light on the head of the Priest. yet not withstanding it is my sincere opinion that all those that are hypocrites, blind leaders and hireling shepherds will have an account at the time or day of reckoning which will appear very gloomy and supicious to their Master, the true Shepherd and owner of the flock, for leading them in so barren, desolate and gloomy [a] wilderness where there is no pasture or herbage except the noctious weeds of Nightshade. which only serves to stupify them so that the shepherd might shear them according to this pleasure which some of them through covetousness do so close that they frequently clip out pieces of skin as well as shearing the wool.

But to turn from this degression, after we left the Chappel we went to see Gardens and others curiosities and returned home. the next Day my Father was for setting off for home but he seemed destitute of mony and knowing I was supplied with cash he made free enough to ask me for to lend him as much as to bear his expences home. but the ill usage I had received from his hands rose so fresh and lively [55] in my mind that I was at a stand for some time whether to assist him or not, being assured in my heart he did not deserve it. but, how ever, I was in hopes of him returning to my Mother and perhaps [to] do better for the future. although it was not in my power to forget him, it was to forgive him, and I gave him thirty two shillings Hamburgh Currency which [he] promised to send back to me in a little[142] after he arrived home but I received neither mony nor little, but as I did not expect it, [it] was no disappointment to me.

Now after nearly a month was expired in which I was unemployed in any sort of business but like a Gentleman walked about with my hands in pockets, rattling what little Mony I had, looking at others who were my equals or rather superior getting their sustenance by the sweat of their brow. but my

141. Protestants conducted services in the vernacular, Roman Catholics in Latin.
142. Letter.

Uncle thought fit to ask me what I was intending to do, to which I replied
that ny[143] intention was to seek my fortune on the Sea. to this unexpected
reply my Uncle seemed to be some what surprized and endeavoured to put
me out of that notion by saying that he greatly wondered at my choice to
expose myself to the dangers of the Sea and [that] the Life of a Sailer was
much [like] the life of [a] Soldier whose Life was not much superior to the Life
of a Dog and in reality not half as good as some. he further said the season
was also to far advanced, for the Ships were manned and gone, and there
were also a great plenty of Sailers so that I who was intirely unexperienced
in the art of sailing would be hard put to get employ. he therefore advised me
to stay with him and learn the trade of a Cabinetmaker assuring me it was
both as good and hendsome employment and that I should meet with the
same usage in every respect as if I was his own Son. hereupon I concluded
to try it and see how I liked [it].

Accordingly I began the first of July and tried at it till February, which
was near seven months and a Week, but to my shame I must confess I was
no further advanced in learning the trade than when I began. but the chief
[thing] I did was breaking of Gimblets,[144] [56] bending of Chysels and Saws,
spoiled boards and planes, so that I did almost as much mischief as my Neck
was worth for which indeed I deserved correction and without doubt would
have had received it had I not been with so good natured an Uncle and I wish
in my heart that it could be in my power to reward him with that Gratitude
which I am assured of being indebted to him. it was not that I was so stupid
and dull of learning but it was as altogether my carelessness and inattention
to that [which] I was doing for my thoughts were continually roving from
place to place gathering as the saying is "flowers in a fady[145] Field". my Uncle
now saw it would be to no purpose to keep me to the trade [and] concluded
to let me try my luck on the Sea. the time was now beginning for ships to
refit for their respective Voyages and my Uncle, willing to assist me as much
as lay in his power, went to some that were Captains of Vessels. but their cry
was they could get more sailers than they needed. this was a sore stroke upon
me and I thought it an ill beginning but I was not so easy discouraged and
flattered myself that an ill beginning often made a good end. and my Uncle,
who was acquainted with one, an Officer at the Beam house,[146] whose business obliged [him] to examine all ships that passed and repassed the beam
which furnished him with an opportunity of knowing the greatest part of
Captains and sailers, my Uncle concluded the best thing he could do for me

143. My.
144. Gimlet, a tool for boring holes in wood.
145. Shady.
146. Perhaps a civil servant at the customs house or at the lighthouse.

was to take me to this Man that so I might hear his opinion. accordingly we went but I met with little encouragement. he seemed to be a Man who regarded not much offending me by saying I did not look fit for a sailer: I had too down cast and effeminate [a] Countenance [and] that I seemed not lively or rather wicked enough. I also appeared to him as if I never had been trained up to any labour and fatigue and in short that I was no ways qualified or calculated for a sailer. he therefore advised me to learn some trade or else endeavour to get my living by my pen. for this my Uncle replied that he had persuaded me as much as lay in his power for to learn a trade but it appeared plain to him that it [57] was to no purpose and nothing would do but the Sea, therefore [he] desired him to pity me as I was a Stranger and a poor Fatherless Boy. upon which he promised his assistance and bid us to come again in two or three Days time. pursuant to his orders I went but met with less encouragement than before. he said a great Number of Jetlanders[147] were arrived who were for the most part experienced sailers and offered their service for low wages and so it was very unlikely that I, who knew nothing of navigation, should get employ while there were so many that had followed it.

I went home with a heavy heart and seemed to be grieved at so great a dissapointment but three Days after this the principal Merchant of the City whose Name was Rose was hireling[148] sailers and fitting off[149] seven of his Vessels for the straits of David, Greenland.[150] this opolent Man, whose riches were almost innumerable for he had no less than thirty odd Vessels capable of bearing from five to eight hundred lasts[151] per Vessel besides a number of Schooners, Brigs, Shallops, &c. so that he had nearly one thousand men employed in his service. and although he was so exceeding rich, he was so great a devotee to mammon that by his appearance one would think he was scarcely worth an hundred pounds. he always offered the lowest wages and whosoever did not make a sure bargain might expect some hook or crook at the Day of payment. this Man as I was saying hired sailers and my Uncle and me also went to see if anything could be done concerning me but I was surprized when we arrived within five or six perches of his house: we scarcely could get further for the crowd. my Uncle then told me I might see with my

---

147. Jutlanders, from Denmark.
148. Hiring.
149. Out.
150. The Davis Strait, between Greenland and Baffin Island, prime fishing grounds.
151. A last was "a dry measure containing 80 bushels of corn, or 12 barrels of cod, or a cargo generally, also a weight of 4,000 lbs." W. H. Smyth, *The Sailor's Word-Book: An Alphabetical Digest of Nautical Terms, including some more Especially Military and Scientific, but Useful to Seamen as well as Archiaisms of Early Voyagers, Etc.* (1867; reprint, London: Conway Maritime Press, 1991), 433.

own Eyes the truth of what I had heard and it appeared very evident I should be hard set to get employ. I then concluded to turn back again and think of something else and in our return we met one that was a Commadore of a large vessel fitted for Greenland. my Uncle made [58] free to speak to him concerning me but his reply was he had already more hands than he needed. we then went home and I seemed greatly mortified to be thus crossed in my intention.

My Uncle now desired me to think of something else, promising to assist me in any lawful and decent [employ] upon which I concluded to try at the Art of refining Sugar or the trade of sugar baking, as they call it, of which there was a great stroke performed in that City and many factortaries erected for that purpose. my Uncle then asked some Masters of the art concerning me but none seemed to fancy me. he then took me to a place where their club met on every seventh Day of the Week. when we arrived there were many, both Masters and journeymen, but it was the same cry: I pleased none of them. they said [I] looked too nice and feeble for that labourious employment and that I could be no service to them except of being a lacky Boy and there was none that wanted such. we then went home again but I was greatly perplexed to think I should be crossed in every thing. my Uncle advised me now to learn the trade and if I once could work so as to make a good joint and fit a Tenon[152] I then might go a while to a Ship carpenter to get some insight [into seafaring] and then there was no danger for me to find employ as a ship carpenter and my Wages would not only [be] three times as much as [I] would get at that time—if by chance I should meet with employ—but also the honour and great distinction there was between Ship carpenter and a Cook's scullion or Ship's swab.

Now this was as good advice as any man could have given me but my stupid inconsiderate mind [could not] comply with this, it could not be confined to so small a place as a shop that was scarce twelve feet diameter, no, it seemed as if the inside world was scarcely sufficient to contain [it.] my Uncle saw that nothing would do [and] gave me his last advice which was for me to return again to my old master. but this was no way suitable to my temper and I absolutely refused to comply with [59] that advice, for my spirit was too great to think of returning to him in so short a time and worst by far than when I left him. and I I told my Uncle this would never do for me and I would rather meet Death in the face than to return to my old master. at this resolution my Uncle seemed somewhat displeased and told me I should yet have time to consider but he would know before long what I intended to do and so went into the shop. two Days after this he entered the room where I was

152. In carpentry, a tenon and a mortise form a type of joint.

and by his countenance I perceived that the time prefixed was expired and I should now quickly hear my doom, in which I was not mistaken, for he presently said he was now come to know my conclusion and was resolved to know before he left the room. I then said I had concluded to seek for a passage to Amsterdam and perhaps sailers might not be so plenty there as in Hamburgh and if I could get no employ on board a merchant [ship] I was most sure I could on board of an East Indiaman. to which my Uncle replied sinced there was nothing that would do for me but to go headlong to destruction he gave me up, telling me further I knew in my heart he had done for me all that lay in his power and still was ready to assist me if I could think of anything in reason. but as for the conclusion I had come to he would have nothing to do with [it] but I must go and look about for myself and if I should [come] to misery and want not to blame him nor my Aunt nor any body but myself. he also desired me to go to one who was his peculiar friend named Minder who was an Apothecary [and] a noted man in the City for to tell him with my own mouth the conclusion I had come to that so he might be a witness in case some malicious neighbour might throw it up to him and say how he had sold his poor Fatherless Cousin which I performed and said Minder also gave me short but good advice and bid me farewell.

The next Day I went to a place called the hill of [60] Hamburgh where I looked about and beheld a sign hanging, whereon was painted the figure of a Ship [with the] inscription "free passage to Amsterdam." I thought then to myself this is the very place I wanted but before I entered the house I took a serious walk to myself in the commons, I think nearly for two hours, deeply pondering within myself what I should do. but at last I concluded "nothing venture, nothing win." upon this I returned again to the house looking a little while at the sign and was soon accosted by the owner of the house who asked me what I wanted, to which I said I scarcely knew myself what I wanted. he then bid me come in and desired me to sit down and drink a Glass of Wine, which I did. he then began to give me a long detail of many people that had come to him on purpose to seek their fortunes in the East Indies and some had returned loaden with wealth and honour and that there [were] nearly forty passengers at that time in a vessel which was nearly ready to set sail. I then asked him how much he demanded for my passage to Holland, to which he said nothing and also he would find me in provision during the Voyage. I then desired him to explain himself what he meant that I had nothing to pay for I was sure in my mind that he could not afford to send so many people as he said to Holland and also find them provision for nothing. to which he replied he was in partnership with a great Innkeeper at Amsterdam to whom he sent all his Men, that they were kept there and provided with all necessaries and conveniences agreeable to Life till the ships

were ready to set sail for Batavia,[153] that the Innkeeper then received satisfaction from the East India company and he looked for his pay from the
Innkeeper. I now thought I had hit the very nail on the head and told him I
was willing to go and venture, to which he smilingly said there was nothing
like it than for a young man to seek his fortune in the wide World. I then [61]
told him the place of my abode and desired him to send me word when the
Vessel was ready to set sail which he promised to do and I went home seemingly with a chearful heart but I may say with this Poet:

> So does the Ox to his own slaughter go
> But little knows of the impending blow[154]

When I acquainted my Uncle with what I had done he was no ways pleased
and my poor Aunt could not forbear shedding tears.[155]

It was on the fifth day of the Week when I agreed with this Emissary and
on the succeeding first Day morning he came to let me know the Vessel was
ready to sail.

Chapter 7: Journey to Amsterdam

Now here was another heart melting farewell to be taken not only from my
friend and native country but also from the whole quarter of the Globe. yet it
was much lighter than the first separation and had it not been for my Aunt

153. Batavia, located on the island of Java, was the capital city of the Dutch East Indies and
the headquarters of the Dutch East India Company, founded in 1620. The city is now Jakarta,
Indonesia. The company had grown wealthy from a monopoly on the spice trade but was over-
extended in the late eighteenth century, facing internal unrest and high administrative costs. By
1799 the company was bankrupt. "Dutch East India Company," in Robert Cribb, ed., *The Historical Dictionary of Indonesia* (Metuchen, N.J.: Scarecrow Press, 1992), 130–31. See also Leonard
Blusse, "One Hundred Weddings and Many More Funerals a Year: Chinese Civil Society in
Batavia at the End of the Eighteenth Century," in *The Archives of the Kong Koan of Batavia*, ed.
Leonard Blusse and Chen Menghong (Leiden: Brill, 2003), 13–18.

154. "The Poet" is Whitehead himself. But see John Dryden: "A soldier half, and half a sac-
rifice; / Falls like an ox, that waits the coming blow, / Old and unprofitable to the plow." "Tenth
Satire of Juvenal," in *Works of John Dryden: Illustrated with Notes, Historical, Critical, and Explana-
tory, and a Life of the Author by Sir Walter Scott* (Edinburgh: Patterson, 1882–93), 13:198, lines
415–17. See also Stephen Duck: "So, to the Plough, the Heifer yet unbroken, / Walks Chearful
on, nor dreads th'impending Yoke; / Till in the Fields, urg'd with the piercing Goad, / She
groans and writhes, reluctant with her Load." "Avaro and Amanda," Canto IV, in *Poems on
Several Occasions*, published in the *Spectator*, vol. 1, no. 6 (1736), no page numbers.

155. Sixty percent of those who sailed in the employ of the VOC died on their first voyage,
making Amsterdam "the grave of Germany," according to Thomas Malthus. Jan Lucassen,
"A Multinational and Its Labor Force: The Dutch East India Company, 1595–1795," *International
Labor and Working-Class History* 66 (fall 2004): 15–16.

who wept bitterly and melted my heart into tears I should not have minded
it so much as might have been expected. my Uncle accompanied me to the
house of the Emissary who treated us with a bottle of wine—which we drank
together for the last [time] without the least expectation of ever seeing one
another again. my Uncle then accompanied me to the Boat which was waiting for me and two more intended companions to take us to the vessel in
which we embarked for the City of Amsterdam near the middle of March
1773. my Uncle stood on shore as long as I could see him—which was but a
short time for both wind and tide seemed in our favour, so that [we] passed
the rid tun[156] the following Day and soon arrived at the cape. but before I go
further I shall insert here a few lines of a Soliloque which I made on leaving
my native country:

Ah must I thus then leave my native Land
Yes yes Alas I am resigned to fate
And this is fates command: rear up the Mast
Spread out the canvas wide to catch the impase[157]
Of the fair western bleeze[158] that gently blows
And let our Bark the rolling Waves divide [62]
But Oh me thinks I hear too well, I hear
Such peircing accents as makes me tremble
And my heart to melt like wax before the Sun
And some Daemon whispers I must go but ah
I never shall return, ah never more
To breathe my natal Air, tremendous thoughts
Assist me, Heaven, tis more than I can bear
But who is there to blame, ah none but me
Myself the cause to be thus banished
For ever from my pleasing native soil
Yet voluntary without compulsion
Fortune except by her great influence
I am thus led to brave the foaming Main
Be prosperous then ye Winds, ye Zephyers blow
And with your impulse fill the swelling Sail
Waft me with speed to fair Batavia's Coast
If fate has so ordained, if not alike
To me is India, Ganges, Nile or Niger
Perhaps some wealthy Ethiopian Dame

156. German *Richtungstonne,* meaning a buoy.
157. Impulse.
158. Breeze.

Chance may throw in my Arms, tho' black as Jet
Yet bright with Shining Gold, fair recompence
Besure for all my toil and piercing Grief
That now encroach upon my troubled Heart
Come then bright Sun of hope, dart forth thy rays
Disperse this gloom that clouds my troubled Breast
And if my lot must be the liquid Tomb
I am resigned to fate and still will hope the best
The worst will come itself no doubt full soon
But that be as it will I do my best
And leaves the rest as highest Heaven thinks fit
Come resignation, come chear up my Heart
And let me bid my Native Land adieu

When I entered the Vessel I was saluted by a jolly company for there were no less than Sixty odd passengers who were all like myself in pursuit of fortune and hoped to meet with her favours in the East Indies. they seemed all to be very jocund [63] but my heart was too sad and it was not in my power to be as chearful as they seemed to be, of which they presently took notice and began to teeze me but I excused myself by saying I had the Tooth ach which in reality I had yet not so bad as I pretended. yet however this had its desired effect and I was freed from their molestations.

There was one thing happened as in this short Voyage which I can not pass over in silence. it was as follows: the Master of the Vessel thought it most suitable to keep near shore for two purposes: first the Vessel being small, he did not choose to launch forth in the wide Ocean and the latter because it was his nearest way. but by so doing he had to pass over a dangerous Shoal called the Watton[159] on the coast of Holland which was of a considerable breadth but what occasioned the disaster most was this: before we were scarcely half over a gust with a smart squall of wind arose which put the Sea in a great commotion and accasioned the waves to roll in upon us to a surprizing degree and sometimes dash against our larboard[160] side with great violence. but the worst of all that threatned our destruction was when we were riding to the top of the waves, they sometimes broke beneath us by which the Vessel fell and received a tremendous shock on the sand. it sometimes crashed to that degree that we expected nothing else but that all its Knee timbers[161] were or must break in pieces if it held on much longer. and

159. Wadden.
160. The port or left side of a vessel.
161. Timber with natural angular bends or "knees," used in the frames of ships.

to all human probability had the vessel not been very strong we should have all perished instantaneously and, as we expected nothing but Death, a great consternation arose amongst us and we might in some degree be compared to the crew of that Vessel wherin the prophet Jonah fled from the presence of the Lord, where everyone prayed to his God: we had a few Jews who directed their supplication to the Father, the Lutherans to the Son, and as for the Romans they prayed to the Mother for intercession and invoked the Saints, [and] also made their assession to any object what so ever [that] first struck their sight or thought. for it seemed a case of indifference to them what or who was priest which at first appeared very odd to me but by due consideration I had to believe that without any doubt it had the same effect (and was as acceptable to the first Parent and Supreme Lord of the universe who holds as it were the boundless Ocean in the hollow of his hand[162] and bids the Stormy winds be still)[163] as if it had [64] been performed in a place of the greatest sanctification or before the Chair of confession. some ran to the Master to enquire his opinion of the matter but he being a low Dutch man they could not make him understand what they meant but by his coun-tenance they precived he also was terrified which hieghtned their agitation and they ran about crying "Lord help us, we are gone, we are gone," and indeed it seemed that Death was looking us in the Face with an uplifted Arm. but it pleased Heaven to direct it otherwise and we got safe over the Shoal with-out receiving any considerable damage, except the ships joints were opened and we had to exert ourselves at the pump pretty constant. but as there were so many of us it proved an easy task and we reflected on the danger we had been in.

Now as for my own part I do not pretend by any means to be more right-eous than the common class of people, nor am I of a stout and bold disposi-tion but rather to the contrary, yet not with standing when there seemed nothing but instant Death, which was as I thought approaching with horrid[164] strides, I appeared unconcerned as if there was but little danger and although I had as much learning and sense as some of the rest for to make a prayer or Lamentation, it was not in my power but I sat silent in my usual place waint-ing[165] the event which was not in my power to govern. yet I deeply pondered in my heart and [in] passtime[166] to see if I was in a state and condition to meet the King of terror[167] and many things appeared in my mind both good and

162. Cf. Isaiah 40:12.
163. Cf. Mark 4:39, Psalms 89:9.
164. Perhaps Whitehead means "hurried."
165. Awaiting.
166. In past time, or memory.
167. I.e., death.

evil and of all the evils I had committed the greatest was as I have mentioned before [was] being dishonest to my trust. this appeared very gloomy to me in this trying juncture till this hope sprung in my Heart as I through Grace had done better after my Conscience had reproved me. I had not rebelled against my Maker but what I had done was performed in a State of Ignorance and therefore I was cleansed from that guilt by the blood of my Redeemer and so I seemed to be perfectly satisfied and resigned to Will of Heaven.

I think we were nearly an hour and a half in this dismal situation but as the time [of] danger seems long it might not have been an hour. it was in the afternoon when this happened and a little past Midnight we were again alarmed with a few shocks. some ran on Deck in great confusion because the Night [65] being very dark and obscured our situation which greatly added to our terror. butt the shocks were light and insignificant to what they were before and after sometime we found ourselves intirely motionless which we greatly admired but as soon as Day appeared we were relieved of our fears for we were lying on dry sand and the water had left us as far as we were capable of pursuing it with the naked Eye. we then laughed to see how we were frightened in the dark lying thus upon dry sand. the greatest number of us went out for to see wonders of Nature which are to be found in the Waters as well as on the land. I greatly admired the many curious little shells and shining sands with which this place abounded so that one may justly say "Great and Marvellous are thy Works O Lord."[168] but while I was thus viewing and contemplating on the works of Nature, some undertook a different task, for they were so frightened at what had happened they concluded to fly from that dangerous Element and set their feet again on a firmed foundation than two Inch plank. but this undertaking had like to have cost them dear. we were as near as I could guess about a league and an half from shore and no water appeared between us and it, therefore they concluded to emplace[169] that opportunity of making their escape. and they saw many WindMills: they proved great temptations to them because they were of that occupation they flattered themselves [that they would meet] with ready employ. but to their great mortification when they arrived, as they said, nearly within a quarter of a Mile of shore, they met a smart current of water, how deep they could not tell but by all appearance it was too deep for them to attempt to go through, for none of them knew any thing of the art of swimming but while they were going to and fro to seek a landing place and a place of safety they had like to [have] perished in pursuit of it. the master now gave the signal for returning, for the tide was approaching and a smart breeze attended it [and] made it

168. Cf. Revelation 15:3.
169. Embrace.

come apace. us that were near the vessel arrived without any difficulty but them that fancied themselves to enjoy the Land were too far to hear our callings or see the signal till the flood came rolling on and told them, as it were, if [they] returned not with the wings of speed they would be overwhelmed. they were now greatly alarmed and they soon forgot the shore and made off as fast as possible for their two Inch plank. the Master saw them [and] appeared concerned about them but having no Boat it was out of [66] his power to lend them any assistance. and had it not been that fear assisted them with wings, they would by all likelyhood have perished. but as they were strong robust fellows capable of pushing forward they arrived to the Vessel and we helped them in. they seemed almost spent with fear and fatigue and they said that when the water got up to their Knees it proved exceeding slavish traveling in the quicksand but as the water increased upon them exceeding fast they concluded there was nothing more certain than Death if they had not pushed on with all their might and they believed that the name of Death, which was to them so terrible, had at that time saved their lives. there were five in Number and some whose Bodily strength was superior arrived first and when the last came to the Vessel they were in water nearly to the waist.

We soon after hoisted Anchor and were in a capacity of setting sail. we arrived without further disasters to the City of Amsterdam on [the] Sixth Day in the Evening and as soon as dusk lay in close to the wharf.

Chapter 8: The Soul Sellers

The Master then went to acquaint his copartners in the traffic with his cargo who came early the next morning to conduct us to our pretended Inn. we were drawn up in a circle and then had to tell the Names of [our] Emissaries, by which our conductors or overseers knew how to separate us so as for them to get each one his own share. the reason why this was performed so early in the morning was, as I afterward learned, for fear of the sailers who sometimes would lie in wait and give those Soulsellers, as they called them, a severe drubbing and rescue their prey which happened not long after when three of the overseers conducted some of their men to the wharves in order to be transported. the sailers fell on them and beat them without mercy and while things were in confusion some of their men deserted and made their escape and some were took up by the Jews who are very officious in this infamous business and so took [them] back again to their Masters. but the greatest number returned of their own accord and instead of being well received and praised for their fidelity in returning, they were looked upon as the main spring of that abuse they[170] received from the sailers and therefore to be revenged they fell on them like wolves on a flock of a Sheep and abused them in a cruel manner which [67] two of them who were pretty far advanced in Years took so hard they went and hanged themselves.

But to return, we were divided into six divisions and then were soon separated by each division following his conductor. it happened that our division was but small being only three men besides myself. we followed our Guide till we arrived to a large house painted on the outside with a pale green colour and looked well but it was indeed their emblem of hypocrisy. it looked well as to the outside but Death and darkness riegned within. as soon as we entered the house we saw a little apartment at the left hand where there stood a Woman which we took to be the Mistress of the house. she called and bid us come there and as soon as [we] entered the first thing was of stripping us of all we had except a few things we had on our backs. this struck me immediately to the heart and I was seized with unusual fear. we were then conducted through an entry into a narrow dark passage which led us into a small Yard nearly twelve feet wide and about eighteen or twenty long, inclosed by other buildings so as to complete a wall no less than forty feet high. I soon perceived a door standing half oven[171] in which I looked and found it to be a sort [of] Ketchen which appeared very gloomy. there [were] nearly a dozen or fifteen men in it who seemed to be of an unpolished behavior, especially one who went by the name of Jack. he was by birth an Englishman and had followed the Seas almost from his youth. what chance had brought him there I can not say but some conjectured he was guilty of some capital crime and fled there for Safety. he was very skilful in fitting our Hamocks in which we lay at Nights, for which each of us was obliged to give him [a] treat of Geneiva[172] or Brandy. the first salutation I recieved from him was "Ha Ha you Dog, have you Gelt?[173] have you Gelt?" to which I replied that I had none for him at which he gave me a sailers blessing[174] and so retired.

I then went into the Yard where I sat down on a stone that lay at the Door and bewailed myself nearly to this effect:

"Alas, alas, am I awake or do I dream? is this the happy place? is this the Inn where I was to be furnished with all the necessaries [for] Life and liberty? if so what mean these mighty walls which hear surround me close? ah me, unhappy [68] what meant that sound which like harsh thunder pierced my heart and ear? ah, was it not the voice of the hinges which, as it were, groaned

170. The overseers.
171. Open.
172. Geneva, or gin.
173. Gold, or money.
174. Sailor's blessing, i.e., a curse.

beneath the weight of heavy Door loaden with plank and Iron and the schieching[175] of the Key declared its labor of turning the polt[176] of a mighty lock? why does yon light break forth with such a melancholy gloom? does it fear? no, it disdains to enlighten this place of horror. the chearful rays of the sorce of light faintly its beam through the massy bars of Iron which like [a] net work placed before yon Window, which keeps the light obscure, and also keeps me here unpitied and forlorn. alas what [am] I now? is this my lot and my unhappy fate to be confined here? am I a thief, am I a munderer[177] or what felony have I committed? ah none so great as to deserve such [an] ignominious Goal[178] yet I am the cause my self, me who did distain the counsels of the wise. ah where is now the wholesome precepts of my worthy Master and the fair instructions of my tender Mother, the many good advices of my dear Uncle and all the persuasions of my near and dear relations? which if they knew my dismal situation they could not forebear shedding tears of pity although I am not in the least deserving it—and why, because I rejected all and followed my own headlong self presumptious will. ah my dear Master, I remember thee because of my affliction but Oh it is now too late! too late alas!"

Here I was interrupted from further reflections by a great tumult and rattling of Keys which [I] heard upstairs, at which I greatly wondered but I soon was relieved by seeing a great number coming down who were all, like my self, depending on the smiles of fortune. there were nearly the number of ninety six at that time. we were divided into three classes according to the rooms we lodged in which were distinguished by the lower, middle and upper room. the lower one contained nearly thirty, the middle thirty six, and the upper thirty. they seemed to take but little notice of me as a new comer nor did they appear to be chearful but to the contrary which proved no ways comfortable to me. their first employment was to wash and comb themselves. and [then they] gathered together in the Yard where an anctient man stood on a stool and read [a] prayer and after it they sang a Hymn [69] which I joined with all my Heart and I believe that I never in all my life sung a Hymn with greater Devotion. we performed every Morning and Evening.

Now as soon as our Devotion was ended the overseers pushed open a Window and handed to us our Breakfast which was no ways luxurious and deserves in particular to be mentioned. the meal consisted of Oats and Rye and sometimes Beans were mixed [in] them and as the Oats of this country contains a thick husk or shell and [were] ground very coarse and no ways boulted,[179]

175. Screeching.
176. Bolt.
177. Murderer.
178. "Gaol," jail.
179. Bolted, i.e., strained through a sieve.

I must confess the Bread often scratched my throat so as to think I had swal-
lowed a Pin. yet this was not the worst, for we had so little of it that the portion of four men was scarcely sufficient for [one man] that is hearty. the paste
was made into loaves nearly a foot in length and four Inches Diameter. of
this loaf we received a slice apiece according to the humour of the overseers
or mistress. the slice was commonly from half an Inch to a full Inch and this
was called a stick. now to this pound cake we had a following tea which was
boiled in a tea kittle that held nearly five gallons. to it was put nearly about as
much tea as a boy of five Years old could [hold] in the hollow of his hand,
without any kind of sweetening or milk. and as there were but few cups for
such a number of men, there was always a great bustle of getting the first the
cups for such would always have the best chance, for they not only received
a cup full but the tea or water [that] was hot whereas the next that came
recieved nearly half a cup full and often the next again recieved none at all.
and so the one that had the good fortune to get the first cup would surely
hand it next to his friend, by which it frequently happened to some: no friend,
no cup, and no cup, no tea. I for my part if I missed the first chance of getting a cup I cared but little afterwards for the warm water which was fitter to
give a man a vomit than for a Breakfast. but on the Sabbath or some holy Day
we recieved a stick with white, as it was called, which is a slice of wheat bread
as [thin as] it could possibly be cut and put on the top of the other and then
we had a delicious Breakfast. and after this repast we had to scour the stairs
and wash out the rooms, sweep the kitchen and yard which would take up
our time nearly till dinner, which we had to prepare thus: a certain measure
of potatoes was [70] handed out to us which we scraped and so put them in a
large kittle which was fastened in a Wall and contained nearly a barrel. those
potatoes [were] sometimes boiled as thick as paste and some times for a
change into a thin pap without either salt, meat or any kind of fat, except
sometimes they got fat from the butcher's. but this was often fitter for soap
grease than for to be put in the dish of a man, except on the Sabbath, we then
received a little meat which [was] carefully divided after the following manner. there were two chosen that were well advanced in Years and were called
our carvers who divided the meat in as many pieces as there were men, each
piece equal in bigness and quality with an other as near as possible. Now then
a man was chosen to turn his back to the table and all of us stand before
him, one of the carvers then laying his knife on a piece and asking him with
his back turned who should be its owner, who then mentioned such a one's
name or else point with his finger who should receive it. the meat being thus
divided [then] one man of every mess, or a bock as they called it, would go with
his dish to the cook and receive the share of bock which were three ladles full
for eight men which was mostly the number belonging to a bock or mess.

NOW him that could eat excessive hot was the happiest man and always got by far the largest share. but the poor, the poor fellow that had to spend much time in blowing it had often [had] to go with an empty belly which proved to be my lot more than once till I found it would never do where one had but little and to be deprived of that little seemed to be too hard a thing. upon this I began to lay in that the skin of my tongue and mouth sometimes stuck to the spoon and I compared it to nothing better than to have one's mouth full of hot sand. I have heard some say since that it would be impossible for them to do so if they even had to perish with hungar but a man does know but little [of] what he can do except [what] experience has taught him and I can assure my reader that I had to undergo [a] severe punishment before my mouth was seasoned to it. but hunger is an exceeding sharp sword and will drive a man to do that which altogether without it would seem altogether impossible. [71] our suppers seemed for the most part shelled barley boiled in water and sometimes mixed with butter milk which was held amongst us as an elegant repast. and sometimes we only recieved a stick with white and so went to our Hamocks.

I have thus given account of our diet and lodging. I shall now proceed with a detail of the ill usage which we recieved from the hands of our merciless overseers and Master. it happened to be my good fortune that there was amongst us a man who by his luck[180] and behaviour seemed to be above the vulgar and he went by the name of a young Merchant. what ill chance had brought him to this state of misery I never could learn. he soon took notice of me and taking me above the common rough sort of people he pitied my being so uncommonly cast down and sorrowful. he therefore took the first opportunity that presented, for no private conversation was allowed, to give me the following short but extraordinary kind instruction. first I must not be thus cast down but I always must appear brisk and Jolly, if even my heart was far from it. secondly I must never say the least thing relating to the business of that place or whatsoever belonged thereunto. but if I could not extoll it to say nothing at all but keep my thoughts to myself and by so doing I should many times escape the severity of the master and overseers which I found all to be too true. for not long after one of our carvers happened to give his tongue a little too much liberty concerning our exceeding poor diet and other inconveniencies of life which soon reached the ears of our cook, who immediately went and acquanted the Boss or Master with it and I make no doubt related the matter to its full and if not beyond its extent, for he was a very crabbed, ill natured man, and there was no other way to obtain his favour but by frequent treats of Geneiva or Brandy upon the Boss, [who] might be

180. Look.

compared to a lion like man—both to his bodily strength and the savageness of his nature—he came thundering in calling us the Children of thunder and lightening, or as [in] the Dutch language "san you dunder un blicksent kint have you nich fratten ganoch."[181] with that he picked up the poor trembling fellow like a child and dashed him down on the pavement and laid on him with a tarred rope, nearly two feet and a half long, in a most inhuman manner till at last one of the overseers named Schliree was moved with compassion towards the poor fellow, went and took hold of the Arm of this fury and begged of him to desist which had its desired effect. he gave all of us who were crept off as far as we possibly could, for fear of falling Victims to his wrath, a few of his blessings and so went off. [72]

A little while after this one poor fellow in the morning when Breakfast was handed out, he reached his hand twice and so got a double share. but the overseer percieved that his pieces did not hold out [and] mistrusted that one or other had taken twice. therefore two of them came at the next time and watched very narrowly to find out who did it. the poor fellow who saw he had sped so well concluded to try it again, little expecting how narrowly he was watched. but nothing was said about [it] till evening after supper when one of the overseers came and seemed to be [in] an uncommon chearful humour and after several antic questions he called this poor fellow and said he looked but a poor ignorant fellow and he believed he was scarcely able to count twenty five and bid him try, upon which the poor fellow began to count untill he had finished the aforesaid number. which he no sooner accomplished but the overseer said it was now his turn to try if he was able of counting and with that drew out his rope, which was concealed under his coat, and gave him twenty five lashes with all his might, telling him further that if he presumed the like again he then would see if he was able to count fifty. but the poor fellow thought it fittest to punish his belly than for to make the back pay for it at so dear a rate.

Not long after this the overseer who had the care of the middle room, which was the place of my lodging, told us that we nead not to roll or hang up our Hamocks after the usual way but have them hang as they were and by so doing they would be ready in the evening to go into them and he would have no need to wait so long on us with a candle as he had to do. hereupon we left our hamocks according to orders but it was only two Days after that he had [met] with some affront or disappointment as was generally believed by us. for he had been abroad and came home in a very ill humour and to give vent to his passion. poor us, as was mostly our lot, suffered on the occasion

181. "You child of thunder and lightning, haven't you eaten/destroyed enough?" Translation from the Dutch courtesy of Klaas Kresse.

for he came and called in a tone of displeasure that all them that lodged in the middle room should appear. I presently smelled a rat, as the saying is, and concluded their was something in agitation not of any great good and [73] so kept behind as much as possible. and as soon as we were drawn up the said overseer, whose name was John, saluted us with a great preamble of curses upbraiding us with our carelessness in not performing his command, telling us further we had [little] or nothing to do and yet were so stinking full of ~~laziness,~~ indolence and slovenly, we did not hang up our hamocks. upon this [the] foremost of us told him they were left so according to his orders which he absolutely denied saying it was a damnable lye and he would learn us better to observe and obey his commands and so fell on the foremost and gave five or six a severe beating. then taking sometime to rest [he] fell to work again and corrected (as he called) it five or six more. then taking the second rest he corrected four or five more but then he seemed to be almost spent with anger and fatigue. he stroked [his] Arm [and] hunched up his shoulders, loading us all the time with curses for neglecting our duty and making him spend all his strength and vigour in correcting our Carcases. but as his strength was spent at that time, and there were nearly one half of us yet that had not received a lash, he would leave it till another time when he had refleshed[182] himself. this he spoke with a countenance truly terrible to us for his Visage looked pale and his Eyes red and firery. he was also a great chawer of tobacco and chalk which together with the froth of [his] mouth, made him appear very formidable. he then went away and left us that had not received our punishment in fear and anxiety, expecting every moment his return, so that the bustle or noise alarmed us greatly and seemed almost more punishment to us then the lash itself. but it happened to be our good fortune to escape, for he got in a better humour or else thought it too much labour and not worth his while to fatigue himself again.

It would be tedious to ennumerate here all the ill usage we received in this infernal place. but to give the reader a more perfect idea of it and to set it forth in its full light, I think I can do no better than acquaint him with the following event. there was one who by indisposition of body was confined to his hamock but every morning they made him come into the yard to exercise himself or to stir his blood, as they called it, with some amusement or other which were mostly beyond his ability to perform for which he recieved correction on pretence of disobeying their command. and at the very last, when the time of his disolution was at hand and [74] Death worked visibly upon him, he was fetch'd into the Yard for to amuse himself with the usual exercise which he was altogether incapable of performing. but after being a laughing

182. Refreshed.

stock for sometime the fidler was led [to] play up a merry tune for him and the aforesaid John seized him by the shoulders and bade him rise and dance or else he would shake the life out of him and with that gave him stroke or two with a tarred rope. the poor creature then by the help of two more to support him rose from his seat and made a faint motion. then turning his eyes to Heaven he gave a groan and expired. his body was thrown into a Cellar till night and what became of him none of us could learn but it [was] supposed by all of us that he was sold to a Doctor for an Anatomy.

There is something which happened in particular to me while I remained in this place and although it is my desire not to prove tedious I can not forebear mentioning the following event. we were for the most part once a week drawn up two and two, except our fidler who was placed single before us and in this arangement we, attended by our guards, marched through [the] city into the commons on purpose to take the air and amuse ourselves at ball [illegible] or some other exercise. and him that proved the greatest mimick and the most expert one [at] antic jesticulations or other in our march was the finest fellow and greatly extolled by the master. but him [that] could not be a merry Andrew[183] was looked upon as a dull awkard thump of a fellow. they also taught us two songs which they commanded us to sing as we marched through the streets. the first song appeared to me very odious and vain and the latter very insignificant and foolish for it had niether sense nor meaning but concisted only of a confused noise more like the hubbub of Hottentots[184] than a song or any articulate sound. if the reader should have any curiosity in knowing them they are as follows:

> How does the brave husar[185] to Heaven up ride   hupsaw
> Upon the gray Mare which he bravely doth stride   hupsaw
> And so up to Heaven he boldly does ride   hupsaw
> Pupsaw Rosaw Mepaw Pulskaw

This was the first song which we mostly sung as we marched out. [75] The latter was thus: Ba be bi bi bo ba bi bi bo bu ba be bi bu.

At this we had strained our lungs to that degree that we were heard a considerable distance over the City and our melodious song frequently drowned intirely the sound of the vial[186] and if any were observed by the overseers to

183. A buffoon or clown.

184. A tribal group of South Africa, but used in the seventeenth and eighteenth centuries to indicate human degradation. The comment reveals contemporary prejudices that many white Europeans and Americans held about Africans.

185. Hussar, a cavalryman.

186. Viol, i.e., a stringed instrument.

be cast down and dejected they soon would find jolly tar, which was the tarred rope, came round their shoulders to inspire them with mirth and jollity.

But the chief [event] I am going to relate is this: as we were thus marching along and I busily engaged at the aforesaid song, a young man, well dressed, stepped out of a fine house and came briskly up to me and said "why John what in the Universe has brought you here?" and I must confess [it was] so sundden and unexpected a blow as this, to be known in a part of the world where I least expected it, and worst of all in so wretched and ignominous a state and condition. it struck me so that I fairly trembled and was for some-time incapable of giving him any answer, till after a few moments of silence, I gave a sly look from under my hat, for I durst not look him in the face, and as soon as I beheld his Visage I knew him to be once my particular friend and Associate. I then asked him if he knew me, to which [he] replied "yes I know you very well," and futher gave me such a straight account that I had no reason to believe the contrary. yet in the heighth of my confusion I flat-tered myself thus: as my dress and appearance was every way far different from what it was when we were associates—especially my hair which I had worn cewed,[187] [with] a high top and wings [over my] ears [which were] well powdered but were not cut off close to my neck, and instead of wings [my hair now] hung in strings About my neck—that if I denied being the person he mentioned I perhaps might baffle him and make him conclude he was mistaken. and so with [a] dejected look that bespoke my shame and confusion, I replied he was mistaken, for I was not the person he imagined. upon this he stepped aside and I did not to look after him [and] saw him no more. he was a young man named Frederick Vansel[188] and had been a Vallet de chamber to one Secretary Slowman, who was a Brother in law to my former Master Vanesson and lived in the city of Stralsund. but he, the said Frederick Vansel, being dissatisfied with that sort of employment, went and agreed with a shopkeeper for three years,[189] which time was no sooner expired then he, like myself, left the place of his nativity and went in quest of his fortune which he found in a far different manner than poor me.

187. Queued, that is, tied behind and braided.
188. This is possibly Friedrich Marcus Montelius (1752–1805) from Stralsund, the illegiti-mate son of Johan Montelius, a Swede. According to family lore he was "enticed" on board a ship by *Neulanders*, labor recruiters. Montelius sailed with Whitehead and Büttner onboard the *Sally*. He was purchased by the Quaker Samuel Garrigues, a shopkeeper, and later sold to his future father-in-law, Peter Bartholome, allowing him to marry Christina Bartholome in Philadelphia in 1777. He fought on the American side during the Revolutionary War and became a shopkeeper and postmaster in Reamstown, Lancaster County. See www.familypangaea.net/ MonteliusMainPage.htm. While the surname is different and Whitehead claims not to have seen him again, the given name, former residence, and occupation of shopkeeper match. Both would have been in Amsterdam at the same time, prior to shipment overseas.
189. I.e., he apprenticed himself to a shopkeeper.

Alas how strange and various is the vibration of that pendulum of [76] fortune which by the least screw or shift is capable of making all the schemes, ingenuity and works of man go at random and come to nothing. we may flatter ourselves to Day to grasp, as it were, an empire and tomorrow be chained in a dungeon. but as it is impossible for a man to stand a considerable time erect on a round ball, so it is also with fortune whose various emotions consists of her impossibility to erect on so tottering a foundation as a round ball.[190] therefore [it] is not to be wondered at that her devotees should be mortified with contraries and disappointments.

NOW this young man before mentioned, who once was no ways my superior, as [he] being only the son of a fore singer[191] of [a] country church in the Village of Stonehagen[192] but now by all appearance seemed to be by his looks and dress to be in a genteel way of business and what was I, alas, not only poor and miserable but reduced to the lowest ebb of fortune so that my flesh and bones which nature collected and operated for my existence before I came forth from [the] womb were not now my own but altogether subservient to the disposal and power of a tyrannical master who indeed chastised us with scorpians instead of rods, and whose little finger was far superior in the weight of cruelty than my former master's whole body.[193] moreover I was without mony and without friends and the worst of all without the benefit or protection of the law so that I was altogether defenceless against assaults of any kind and nothing was left but hope and patience with full resignation to my fate whether I was to be sent to Batavia or Amercia[194] [or] to Algiers at the bay of Vandorus,[195] to Spendo Mastram,[196] or the Grave. but as there was then no time for reflection I, to avoid the embraces of jolly tar whose company appeared to me so formidable, gave a few sighs and so again, though exceedingly against my will, employed my lungs on relating how the hosars[197] rode to Heaven.

But when we arrived at the place of our amusement, I was so dejected and low in spirit that I had not the least taste for any diversion or amusement but what I did was intirely performed by compulsion and fear of the lash. but as a forced work, let it be whatsoever it will, it [is] far different from that which

190. Fate or fortune was considered a feminine force, "Dame Fortune." Fickleness was considered a trait of both women and fortune.

191. One who led church congregations in singing.

192. Steinhagen, a city south of Stralsund.

193. Cf. 1 Kings 12:10–11, 2 Chronicles 10:10–11.

194. America.

195. Perhaps Vandalus, Latin for the Germanic tribe known in English as the Vandals, who controlled Algiers in the fifth and sixth centuries.

196. "Spendo Mastram" has not been identified, although Mastram may be maelstrom, a whirlpool.

197. Hussars.

arises from a voluntary motion. I appeared very careless and awkard [at] whatever I performed for it is the spirit which exhilarates the body and where there is a dejection of spirit there can be no activity or vigour to the body. and by this means [77] it happened that in one our exercises performed by a rope I was thrown to the ground with great violence which not only bruised my flesh to a great degree but also sprained my right knee so that I for sometime seemed in the greatest agony imaginable. but one of the overseers seemed skilful in such accidents—[he] twisted and pulled at my leg and I presently felt relief so that within three hours time I was capable to limp home with the rest of my companions. and I may say in some degree that this Day proved to me a Day of uncommon affliction. I made free to relate my sad story to one who seemed to be well advanced in Years and also a steady demure countenance. but to my unexpected mortification, instead of finding him a father as I hoped, I found him like of one of Job's comforters. upon this I disisted from further mentioning it to anyone and kept it altogether within my own breast but it made so deep [an] impression in my heart that I could have wept bitterly had I been at a house of mourning but as I was at a house of compeled mirth and laughter, singing and dancing, and often performed with a bruised back and empty belly yet there was no room for me or anyone else to be otherwise. for all low mindedness, grief and discontent, murmuring and the least disobedience were severely punished by the merciless hands of our master and overseers.

> But when the night had drawn its sable train
> And silence spread its solitary reign
> When slaves and masters all were fast a sleep
> My heart then melted and my eyes did weep
> Reflection then shone forth divinely bright
> And contemplation beam'd its heavenly light
> Which only could my Death-like bosom fire
> And my sad Soul with future hopes inspire
> Untill sweet slumber closed my weeping eyes
> And fancy's dear deluding Dreams arise
> Which sometimes plac'd me on Batavia's shore
> Where I with pleasure grasp'd the shining Oar[198]
> Loaden with wealth and trophies of my toil
> I back return'd unto my native soil
> With polish'd Gold my silken Vest did shine
> And all my garments extra superfine

198. I.e., ore, gold.

A costly banquet for my friends I make
And all relations of the feast partake [78]
My tender Sister and my Brothers face
But my dear Mother at [my] sid I place
Delicious Wines from Tuskens[199] happy Hills
Or fair Ibaria[200] our Bright goblet fills
They all admire till with great surprize
They see the Master of the feast arise
Embrace his Mother and with Tears of Joy
Declares he is her [al]most forgotten Boy
    Thus in Elisium[201] fancy wraps my Soul
But sad illusion only sums the whole
For in the heighth and ecstacy of Joy
Behold I wake and in my Hamock lie

Now as I said before that the adventure of the Day made a deep impression on my heart. I confess I truly dreaded the time of going again. therefore the next time when we were ordered to prepare ourselves to march, I went to one of the overseers who seemed the most humane and forged, as I may say, the following excuse: which was that my knee had not got perfectly well of the hurt it received and also my shoes were too little and for want of grease were become exceeding hard so that I was thereby disabled in my feet of marching. I therefore desired him that he would be pleased to let me stay at home. this excuse, although in some degree it was a true one, yet in reality was not so bad as to prevent my going had I been so inclined but, however, it had its desired effect and I was left at home at which I rejoiced [only] for a moment or two for who should come but our master to see if [all] was right, the Doors polted[202] and if any had stayed behind. and seeing me I soon recieved his blessing and [had] the sad reflection of falling into his hands and having none to intercede for me except [if] the mistress or his Daughter had took compassion on me. I trembled with fear and added considerably more than was true to my excuse so that thereby I might escape the hands of so furious a master and I had the good fortune to succeed.

Now I may venture to say those few moments of being alone were indeed the happiest time I had enjoyed for a considerable time. it [is] strange and wonderful to me how a man can think it irksome of being sometimes alone since he is endewed by all wise Providence [79] with the excellency of divine

199. Tuscany's.
200. Iberia.
201. Elysium.
202. Bolted.

contemplation, whereby a slave that is chained to the Roegally[203] or in the gloomy habitation of a dungeon may enjoy not only his liberty but also the pomp and respect of a King. he also may transport himself in Idea to whatever part of the world he pleases or wishes to be and grasp in Theory, as it were, imaginary empires. therefore it must be guilt that can make retirement horrible and create perturbations so as to drive the self tormenting soul into any company to avoid [the] agony of remorse but a man that fears not being alone will find the best of company in being so, although on the top of a mountain or in the cavern of a rock without society or books or any exterior means of amusement. it is true, agreeable company sometimes bestows the most elegant pleasure he can taste and yet were we to be confined for a considerable time it would prove insipid and tiresome and I may venture to say it would be as great a mortification never to be alone as to be too much so. I now had time not only to reflect on transactions past but also make my observations on my present state and condition and anticipated my fancy [would] point out what happy events might ensue for the future.

Thus I passed the few happy moments in a state of tranquility till I was interrupted by the returning crowd. after this I composed the following Verses:

> Hail sweet retirement, best companion, hail
> Dear to my soul even in this impious Jail
> O could my Genius climb the Aonian[204] mount
> The sweet recesses of the muse to hunt
> Then should my Verse with pleasing numbers glow
> And thy due praise in beautious order flow
> Retirement then should forth in lustre shine
> And contemplation beam in every Line
> I first would teach our Lords themselves to know
> And how more mercy to their slaves to show
> I'd teach them that they have a Soul to save
> That spark Divine which lives beyond [the] Grave
> A Life of love, sweet harmony and peace
> Or else of torments that will never cease
> That [one] of those as certain is their Doom
> As they are laid into the silent Tomb. [80]
> Reflection next with memory should join
> And with past pleasure thus divert my Mind

203. Row galley, forced laborers on ships powered by oars as well as by sails.
204. Ionian.

And recollection all should, hand in hand,
Traverse the regions of my native land
Bright fancy next, which future things discries
Should with prophetick fire illume my Eyes
Calm my sad Soul with visionary schemes
Or prompt my hopes by fair enchanting Dreams
    But where is all confusion, noise and fears
The muse soft warbling can not reach my Ears
Where lash and curses makes the place to sound
And wretched slaves all trembling stand around
Except that happy, most auspicious Day
When all were gone and I was left to stay
T'was then the muse my Bosom to inspire
Caught one fair ray of dull poetic fire
O blest retirement then, thy praise I sung
Though weak my Genius and my lyre unstrung
But O I scarcely had began my song
Till I was baffled by the coming throng
The crowd return'd, the shouts the muse did scare
And hupsaw and pupslaw fill'd again my Ear

Chapter 9: Finding a Berth

Now what added greatly, as I thought, to my misfortune and Grief, was that
I happened to come at this place nearly two Weeks too late, for the East India
Vessels were all manned and fitted for their Voyages from the city of Amsterdam and I saw no other chance but one Vessel called the Flute which was
yet on the Scaffold but would be ready to set sail at the month of September.
I expected nothing else but I should have to spend the whole Summer in
this Sad and gloomy habitation unfit for the dead and more so for the living.
but it happened not long after that our Boss came and selected eight of us,
of which number I was one, and acquainted us with the joyful news that there
were two Vessels to be fitted out for Batavia from the City of Horn and the
crew [81] would be enlisted the following Day. he therefore had a mind to take
us there to try our luck. accordingly we received a suit consisting of Shirt,
Trowsers and red Jacket. we also recieved two sticks with white, one for our
Breakfast, for it was early in the morning, the other for our Dinner. we then
were conducted to the wharf where we embarked in [a] small vessel for the
city of Horn. the wind being contrary and boistrous, attended with a great
rain, so that we, being in an open vessel, got exceeding wet and cold. and the

greatest number of us thought it a very tedious and disagreeable Day for we did not arrive at the city till late at night. our master then took us to an Inn where we kindled a good turf fire and so spent the remaining part of the night in drying our Clothes and a little sleep. the next morning at nearly eight oClock our master conducted us to the house of the East India company to present and offer our service but it was so crouded with people that it seemed almost impossible to get nearer than within two or three perches of the Door and I then concluded the world was all over crowded and stocked with people. but our master, who seemed to be well acquainted with the house, took us round and by a private way we arrived into the very entry of the house within five or six feet of the room where the company sat—this by way which I think must be on purpose for them to pass and repass at their pleasure in which they could not perform except a guard would open a lane for them through the crowd. but yet this had not quite the desired effect by an unfortunate mistake which was by our Boss saying "push through boys, push through." but this, instead of pushing through to get into the room, which [was] the intent of our master, [we] pushed through the entry by the Door which was shut and [had] a guard placed to only let in three men at a time which were mostly them that were nighest the Door. but as I said we passed the Door in our mistake and wrought with all our might on right contrary so that we [were] in the midst of the croud before we perceived our mistake and there was now no other remedy than for to work back again as fast as we could. five of [us] were stout robush[205] fellows and were able to work back with greater rapidity than the remainder of us and so had the good fortune to have their desires accomplished. but two more and myself who were but weak and small did not get back [82] till the company broke up. it being nearly one oClock it was said they would sit again at three but whether they did or not I can not say, for the wind being fair for home our master gathered us up and we again embarked for Amsterdam where [we] arrived late in the evening.

Now whilst we were at Horn I saw many that had the chance of presenting themselves to the East India company. yet their service was not excepted[206] for when the market is glutted with provision the buyers are mostly warey and so it was here. they had their choice, as it were, of multitudes which made them be very particular and nice in choosing so that all such as they thought too ancient or too young, too unhealthy or any wise deformed or decripid were all turned off as unfit for service. but in case this should have been my lot I prepared myself with the following speech which I was intending to make to them and [it] was nearly thus:

205. Robust.
206. Accepted.

"Most honourable lords and rulers of this illustrious Assembly and East India company of the City of Horn, be graciously pleased to give a moment's attention to the humble petition of one that desires no other happiness in this world than for to be your Servant. behold my limbs are sound and braced by the strength and activity of youth who, shall I solemnly protest, act to the utmost of my power in your service and punctually obey whatsoever your[207] are pleased to command, whether by Sea or land. only [be] pleased to except[208] me, [and] my heart shall then not only rejoice but by your goodness and generosity my spirit shall be animated and glow with emulation so as to dare the most pernicious of your enemys at Batavia."

This speech might perhaps have done something for me and it also might have [been] looked upon as a rash, bold and impertenot action but let that be as it would. I was resolved to bear the consequence of the event but as I said before I had no chance to represent myself nor petition then. I had to conclude that all was best.

Not long after this one of the overseers came [and] culled out six of which number I was one. he then told us to follow him, which we did. he then took us in the front room where our master was sitting in company with two men. he then began to tell us that we had missed our chance at Horn and there were now no more vessels [83] to be fitted out for that year, except the Flute, which would not be ready to set sail till late in the fall. he therefore [thought] it fit to sell us to those aforesaid men who who would send us to a country far superior to that of Batavia. we then desired him to let us know upon what condition, whether we were to remain there during life or if we had liberty to return at a certain period to our native land.

To this one of our new masters replied that we have to serve two or per- haps three years for to discharge our debts which we had contracted in our passage both from Germany to Holland and from thence to America. and after that short period of servitude we were then at full liberty to do as we pleased in respect of our returning to our native land or to stay in the country but [he] was well assured in his mind we would like it so well as to never think of returning. he further said that it was for truth a delight- ful country and might safely be called the new Canaan, flowing with milk and hony: that [the] air was clear and pure and [the] climate like our native country; the seasons regular—spring, summer, autumn and winter—its soil fertile, of capable of bringing forth all the necessaries of life almost sponta- neously by the help of a little agriculture, that it was also furnished by nature with springs and rivelits of excellent water and in short we would [find] that

207. You are.
208. Accept.

his discription would fall infinitely short of the country if we should live to see it.[209]

Now although he spoke this in a tone of gravity and declared it was the truth yet as he was a man that traficed[210] in those Species and, as I thought a copartner with our hard hearted master, I could not help being otherwise than the unbelieving disciple.[211] the story seemed to me too fair to be true and I could not be convinced untill I both saw and felt.

But, however, let it be as it would, I had no choice. it was out of my power to choose or refuse and All I could do was to lean upon my usual Staff which was full resignation to my fate. as we went out of the room my comrades gave a loud "huzza," but my heart was too sad and I could not join them in their rejoicing although I was pleased that I should be relieved out of that disagreeable habitation. yet my future state was unknown to me. whether it would be better or not clouded [84] my mind with a sad and melancholy gloom [so] that I rested but very indifferent all that night which was to be the last for ever in that hamock in which I more than once had fancied myself on the coasts of Batavia.

The following morning after Breakfast we were ordered to be ready to go. we then took leave of our comrades and so went up stairs where each of us received a stick with white. we then left the gloomy habitation of the Soul seller and embarked for the City of Rotterdam in a vessel called a Trackskoot[212] which is small but very commodious and is drawn by a horse which goes on the shore at the rate of three Miles an hour. we arriv'd at Rotterdam the following Day about eleven oClock A.M. and I may say this passage would have proved truly charming to the eye of an unclouded mind. for at first we glided along between the most beautiful Gardens ever my eyes beheld, for it seemed as if both art and nature had contributed to make them elegant and pleasing both to the sight and taste of man. and after this beautiful scene we were entertained with fine enamilet meads[213] and although it was but the latter end of April yet they were covered with abundance of grass and herbage. sometimes we passed fine pasture fields crouded with lowing Oxen and Milch Kine[214] and I may venture to say the largest I ever saw.

---

209. The average terms of service stated here are far too brief, while the language of the sales pitch duplicates that of a typical recruitment tract for colonial settlement. Our thanks to Hermann Wellenreuther for this latter observation.

210. Trafficked.

211. Doubting Thomas. John 20:24–25.

212. *Platschuit*, Dutch for barges.

213. Enameled meadows.

214. That is, mooing oxen and milk cows.

Chapter 10: Crossing the Atlantic

But alas! what are all the beauties of both Nature and Art to a Heart filled with grief and anxiety? all those delightful Scenes served only as so many Mementos to heighten my misfortune, as I thought, than for to asswage them. as soon as we arrived at the City there were two men waiting for us to conduct us to an Inn where we had been but a little while till the merchant came to take a view of us, of whom we received two Dollars per man and so ordered us to be sent on Ship board, the Name of which I never could learn. some thought she was named the Caroline, Captain Osman Master.[215] she was lying nearly within twenty Perches of the Wharves and when we arrived there were near two hundred Servants and Passengers but the accomplished number or Cargo was to be nearly three hundred. [85]

The first thing we received was Provision, of which we had great need, for it being nearly twenty four hours in which we had little or no sustenance but now I may say we fared sumptuously and I had a glorious or elegant feast after so long a Time of Lent, as nearly six weeks, which was the time of my abiding with the Soul sellers. for we had plenty of choice: Beef, Bread and Butter, Cheese, Flower and Rice and Mony in our Pockets so that we fancied ourselves perfectly happy and that melancholy gloom which had clouded my Mind for a considerable Time was now by the bright Sun of chearfulness entirely disbursed for it. I had left the house of sorrow and was entered in the mansions of joy and gladness. every other Day a Woman came who was particularly skilful in striking the Lyre which sounded so harmonious in the Ears of many that they spent the greatest part of that Mony in Dancing which was given them by the Merchant on purpose to lay in a necessary store for so long a Voyage—as Coffee, Tea, Sugar, Rum, Oranges, &c. but what drew my attention most was the nimbleness of a little Girl of about six Years of Age and very small for such a number of Years. she was the only Daughter of the Musician who seemed extremely pleased with the activity of her Daughter and although I am naturally an Enemy to common Dancing yet I could not help being charmed with the activity of this little Creature for every Step seemed to be graceful and all her movements [made] punctually to the stroke of the Lyre so that I may say I never was more delighted with this Diversion in the course of my Life except the Pantomeans[216] which were acted on the

---

215. Whitehead's ship was actually the *Sally.* His signature appears on the ship list as "Johann Fridrich Kukuck," his stepfather's surname. The ship's captain was John Osmand. See Ralph B. Strassburger, *Pennsylvania German Pioneers: A Publication of the Original Lists of Arrivals in the Port of Philadelphia from 1727 to 1808,* vols. 1–3, ed. William John Hinke (Norristown, Pa.: Pennsylvania German Society, 1934), 2:867–68.

216. Pantomimes.

Stage which always drew my attention to a great degree and although I was but a Boy, I had no inconsiderable Ideas of their dumb signs and jesticalations and I remember once in particular when that Vice of Drunkenness was presented it made so great an impression on my Heart that I abhorred a Drunkard above all other Vice. and I may say that if People would frequently visit such places, let them give a Moment's attention to my advice, which is this: not to look upon the Actors as their Dress, their Voice and activity, but let them truly consider the Character which they present and by giving a due attention to them, I may venture to say they may sometimes reap almost as great benefit as if they had heard a Sermon dilivered from the pulpit. but let [86] the Reader by no means think I am persuading him to go [to] the Play house instead of going to Church. for it is to such I am directing my Advice that care but little about going to Church but are highly diverted with the activity of the Actors in the Theatre. to such I say that although I was but a Youth or rather a Child, yet by true consideration of the presented Characters in a Tragedy it made so deep [an] impression that I could not forebear weeping bitterly. but as I have been already too long on this subject I think it best to desist and turn again to relate our Transactions on Shipboard.

Since my Subject has been upon Characters I think I also should acquaint the Reader with ours on board the Ship which I I think can not be set forth in a better light than to compare us to a parcel of poor starved Hogs that are put up by a Farmer to fatten, whose nature is so well known that a description is needless. only this: if care is not taken at first to feed them by degrees they will soon stall and that Provision or Victuals which they once so eagerly longed for will become lothsome; this was the case with us. perhaps some may think this an odd and clownish comparison but since I am an Inhabitant of the Country it may be reasonably expected that I am the most accustomed to rural business and as a customary thing becomes natural, the reader must not expect to find in me the politeness and high complimential Strains of a first rate Courteor[217] or a high bred Citizen. remember, you can not gather Oranges from the Bramble, Citrens[218] from the Thistle, Pomegranets from the Briers or Cucumbers from the Thorns.

Now the first thing we did after having satisfied our Appetites was to clean our lodging place or Coig, as it was called, of the filth and Chamberpotts which had been placed there by the uncleanliness of some of their other Passengers or Servants which had been there before us. the Number of Coigs between Decks were thirtysix, and they consisted of rows distinguished by the lower and upper row. the upper one was mostly taken up by Women and

217. Courtier.
218. Citrons.

the lower by Men but for the greatest part they promiscuously lay thro' one another: Male, Female, the Youth and aged, and there was no [87] apartment for any private business but every thing was performed openly and exposed to the view of all, except some few who had so much modesty in them as to shift themselves or change their clothes in the Night Time. this however created [an] abundance of debauchery for there were some of the Women that were redeemed from the rasp house[219] Jail and Baudhouses or other infamous places so that they may be properly called the very Dregs and Siftings of the Country and so void of Shame and Modesty that they had little or no regard for whatever they acted. and the Men, who were for the most part young and foolish, were easily seduced by those lewd and infamous Women. and as he that is too great a Devotee to Venus, especially when performed to excess in an illegal way, is smitten with her disease—it frequently happened to be the case amongst us so that the Captain was obliged to send some of them to Rotterdam to undergo the operation of the cure, where they remained till the Vessel was ready to set sail. and some of them returned sound and well but others again not half cured and some returned not at all but were hurled off the Stage of Life.

There is one thing I remember which was soon after our arrival a young Man came to us in a friendly manner and gave us, as he thought, the following excellent instruction: that if we thought to live comfortably we could do no better than for to choose one or two pretty Girls to lodge with us and if we pleased them they would be kind to us and do our washing and cooking.

Now to look at this only with the naked Eyes would indeed appear very pleasing and agreeable but for to take the [spy]Glass and make a true Observation it would soon become sullen and gloomy. and I could by no means agree to it till further inspection, in which I was presently joined by two more who seemed to agree with me in my opinion and being but three more, which was the Number our Coig contained, we opposed them till after some Time they began to see we were in the right and it was more profit for both Soul and Body to be thus alone but, however, by so doing we escaped not the keen Invectives of some who were the [88] most inconsiderate who would frequently call us harmless Josephs[220] and poor bashful Fellows hardly worth a Louse.

But as for not being worth a Louse, [that] whould have been indeed a happy thing had it been verified but, alas, we soon found [the ship] not only to be in the possession of one [louse] but thousands. and as for being called harmless Joseph I did not regard it but only laughed at those Sons [of] Babel

219. *Rathaus,* German for town hall.
220. A reference to the biblical Joseph, who married Mary when she was pregnant with a child not his own. He "knew her not till she had brought forth her firstborn son." Matt. 1:25.

who indulged themselves in their Carnal Gratifications to the highest degree
and if ever there was a State of Transmigration in the World it certainly was
on [our] Ship board. it is strange and unaccountable that one who is by his
Maker invested with Power of being lord over all Sublunary Creation and
endewed with the excellency of reason, should debase himself so as to take
upon him the Nature and Quality of a Beast. but alas, when Vice is once
suffered to get a Head, reason is expelled from her Throne which is the only
thing Man can reasonably boast of in being superior and distinguished from
the Brute Creation. and reason, being thus deposed by Vice, soon feels the
Iron Sceptre of that Tyrannical Queen by making her subservient to all her
laciviousness and Crimes and where this is the case:

No wonder who may be called Divine
Should be transform'd into a Noble Swine

But as I am altogether incapable of finding words to express the Crimes
and frauds together with the Lubrisite[221] of the People without putting Modesty to the blush, I think it best to disist. yet pardon my freedom in mentioning this only thing which [was] that even the operation of bringing forth
the Innocent Produce of mutual Embraces[222] (which ought to be performed
with all manner of decency and secrecy imaginable) was not much regarded
amongst us.

I shall now detain the Reader with a short account of our Discipline and
Decorum amongst us. there were (as I have before mentioned) thirty six
apartments or Coigs. each apartment contained six or eight Men who were
called Messmates, and each Mess had wrote its Number on the Side of [89]
their Coig, from Number one to thirty six, which was a great ease to the Steward in handing out the usual allowance of Provision for knowing how many
Men belonged to a Mess he could easily throw in his Scales the Portion of
six or eight at once. and so dividing whatever was handed out as meat, flour,
butter, cheese or biskets into thirty six parcels, he then only had to call the
Number of the Coig or Mess who always sent one of the Mess to receive
the Portion. and so beginning at Number one and ceasing at thirty six he
always was sure he had missed none, as also that none had received a double Portion. and further to frustrate all Animosities and disturbance that
might arise amongst us by thinking some had to do more than their Share
as in receiving the rashings,[223] dress and cooking it, each individual had to
take regularly his turn for a Day both to receive, dress and cook for the whole

221. Lubricity.
222. That is, childbirth.
223. Rations.

Mess he belonged to, except he by indisposition of Body or some other obsticle was incapable of performing it. as for washing our Clothes each one had to do it for himself, except such that had in possession a Female favourite.

Now after we had been riding at Anchor better than a Week we were ordered to prepare ourselves for the Voyage and that the Vessel would be ready in a few Days to set sail. upon this my Messmates and me went to Town to buy ourselves a Chest and Tea Kittle, Spoons and Utensels, and also Sugar, Tea, Coffee &c. and having laid in a Store according to our small Purse, we were ready to put out to Sea and soon after the Pilat[224] arrived and we hoisted Anchor near the eighteenth of May. the River having many turns, it took us nearly a Week before we arrived at [the] Sea called the Mad Dog,[225] where the Pilate gave over his charge to the Captain and recommended us to the Protection of Divine Providence and so bid us Farewell.

The first accident that happened to us was just before we entered this boistrous and Tumultuous Sea, which I thought was rightly named, it was a large West India Vessel which by the mismanagement of the Sailers ran against the Head of us, by which we received a severe Shock. but we had the [90] good fortune to escape with no other damage but breaking the top of our Boltsprit or the jib Boome and the Spritsail Yard. this, however, occasioned a great consternation amongst us and the most superstitious took it as an ill omen and soon began to Prognosticate future events of the same Nature. and I must confess that I also inclined a little that way but not by any Influence of Enthusiasm[226] but I feared the wickedness of People would provoke the Almighty to Anger and I would some Times say to my particular Friend and Asociate named Charles Rose[227] that I greatly feared Eternal Vengeance from on high would overtake us and sink us in the unfathomable deep, which also seemed to be his opinion. but through the goodness and Mercy of God we were preserved from future events of that Nature both in this afore mentioned Sea as well as in the wide Atlantic Ocean.

We arrived safe and in a pretty good State of Health at Portsmouth in in England on the third of June, the following Day being the Birth Day of His Britanic Magesty George the Third which occasioned a great deal of rejoicing

224. Pilot.
225. North Sea.
226. Religious enthusiasm, that is, for followers of established churches, the superstition of the unorthodox.
227. Adolph Gottfried Carl Rose appears on the ship list just above Whitehead's name; see Strassburger, *Pennsylvania German Pioneers*, 2:868. Godfrey Charles Rose was indentured on September 27, 1773 (two days before Whitehead) for six years and six months for a sum of twenty-nine pounds; see *Record of Indentures of Individuals Bound Out as Apprentices, Servants, Etc., and of German and Other Redemptioners in the Office of the Mayor of the City of Philadelphia, October 3, 1771, to October 5, 1773* (Lancaster, Pa.: Pennsylvania German Society, 1907), 306–7. His master resided in Berks County, so it is possible that the men remained in contact.

and Military Ostentation. I counted the Streamers and Broad pendants of forty Vessels of the Line, being chiefly second and third rate,[228] which greatly annoyed my Ears with such thunder as soon after attempted to shake the Foundation of Columbia.[229]

The Captain had but little business at Portsmouth except the taking a Number of Cheese and some Casks of Pisket[230] which [were] received in the afternoon and so [he] hoisted Anchor and lanched our Vessel forth into the wide unfathomable Ocean where we after a long and tedious Voyage of nearly thirteen Weeks arrived at the long wished for Coast of Columbia. but before I proceed any further I shall detain the Reader with an account of our Disasters and affliction which we Suffered in this Voyage. it was not above two Weeks after we left the Coast of England that we were visited by a mortal Disease which soon swept away all such as were any ways infected with the [Disease of Impurity] Venereal Disease. but although it seemed to begin upon them first, it seized likewise such as were known to lead an inoffensive Life. our Doctor seemed to be unacquainted [91] with it; he scarcely knew what to call it, but it was generally believed to by a branch of the Scurvy or Yaws.[231] the first Simtoms of it was a violent itching round the Fundement[232] which soon generated into a Number of Pustels[233] which were small in the beginning but soon grew to the size and shape of a small Pea attended with a constant burning and itching. the Patient also was afflicted with a constant Fever and loss of Senses and exceeding weak and fainty, especially when exposed to the Air. and I have seen some to crawl upon Deck who seemed pretty chearful while they remained beneath but as soon as they came in the Air

228. Ships of the line (ships designed to sail in the line of a battle fleet) were divided by size into different "rates" or ratings, primarily by the number of guns the ships carried. Ships of the first rate generally carried more than a hundred guns and had at least three full decks; ships of the second rate usually carried between ninety and a hundred guns, also with three decks; vessels of the third rate carried between sixty and eighty guns, but the most common warship of this class—and in the Royal Navy in general at the time—was the seventy-four-gun ship of two decks.

229. Columbia, meaning America and the coming of the American Revolution.

230. Biscuit.

231. Scurvy is a disease caused by a deficiency of vitamin C; its symptoms include swollen, bleeding gums. Yaws is a contagious disease of tropical countries, characterized by raspberry-like excrescences or tubercles on the skin. While there may have been cases of syphilis and other diseases on board, the symptoms described here best fit a diagnosis of epidemic typhus. Typhus, caused by a rickettsia, is spread through the bites of lice, which Whitehead notes were flourishing in the unsanitary and crowded conditions on board this ship. Onset of the disease is five to fifteen days from exposure and is abrupt. Headache, fever, chills, nausea, and a rash develop. In fatal cases delirium occurs. Between 5 and 40 percent of those with the disease die when untreated. Children have mild cases, adults have higher mortality. Kenneth F. Kiple, ed., *The Cambridge World History of Human Disease* (New York: Cambridge University Press, 1993), 1080–81. Farley Grubb estimates that as many as 15 to 30 percent of Whitehead's fellow passengers died during the voyage, compared to an average shipboard mortality of around 5 percent.

232. Fundement.

233. Pustules.

they would fall into a swoon, if not expire. the Mariners themselves, from the Captain down to the Shipswab did not escape the Disorder. the Mate and Cabbin Boy, with near half the Sailers, were interred in the Liquid Tomb and our Doctor with nearly forty Passengers and Servants shared the same fate. and I think I may venture to say a Vessel never crossed the Atlantic in a more feeble condition than we, for scarcely ever more than two or three sailers were capable of Duty so that there was frequent occasion for some of the Servants to exert themselves in assisting the Sailers, especially in the Time of a Storm and what is most to be wondered at is that never any were canted overboard. now as for the burial of our Dead, I can assure the Reader that we made as little solemnity as ever any People in the World did that profess themselves Christians, for as the Grave was always ready to recieve the Corpse and we had nothing to do but sew them up in a piece of sail cloth with a Bag that contained nearly two Quarts of Sand across their feet and so plunged them in. but towards the latter part of July they seemed to die apace and there was scarcely a Morning when we arose without finding two and sometimes three dead amongst us. this roused us, as it were, from a State of slumber and not knowing whose turn might be next, we thought it Time to begin a reformation. we choosed our Surgeon, who was pretty far advanced in Years and of a tolerable good Character, as also a Scholar, for to be our Priest and we began not only to interr our Dead [92] decently [with] Prayers and singing Hymns but also met on the Sabbath together on Deck [with those] that were capable of coming in order to worship. this was greatly recommended by our Captain who ordered us further to read Morning and Evening Prayers and sing an Hymn or two which we did and continued it even while we were lying before the City of Philadelphia.

There happened to be one amongst the Number of the Deceased who I rightly call my Countryman because he was born and educated in the same City where I received my being. the fortune of this unhappy Man was particularly singular and I think deserves a place in this History. but to give the Reader a more perfect Idea of him I must go back as far to my German Master Theodorus Fonesson as had two Sisters. the younger was married to an able Vintner[234] who lived [in] the City [of] Statteon.[235] the elder had the ill fortune to bury three of her Husbands, although she was when I knew her but a middle aged Woman. the first of her Husbands was named Seppelien[236] and the second who was a Widower named Miller:[237] these two were Merchants.

234. Wine merchant.
235. Stettin.
236. Carl-Wilhelm Zeplin married Margarethe Barbara von Essen, "single," on December 1, 1751. He died January 10, 1752. Marriage and Death Registers, SHS.
237. In German, Müller, a very common name.

her third Husband was named Remarrous[238] who was a Physician and the fourth with whom she lived when I left the City was a Merchant nam'd Leven Hagon.[239] but her second Husband, as I have already mentioned whose name was Miller and a Widower, he had one Son and that Son was this unfortunate Man who as soon as he came to be acquainted [with] me gave me nearly the following detail of himself which was that his Father had [left] him a handsome Patrimony but to his Shame he demanded it as soon as it was in his power to obtain it and, as he was naturally given to licenciousness he then gave a full swing to it without restraint, by which [he] spent his whole Estate almost sooner than he imagined. and what mortified him most was that his Associates and companions with whom he had spent his Purse in wild flories and Debauchery now scarcely looked at him and if by chance he fell in company with some of them they only proved like Job's comforters.[240] and being destitute of both Mony and Friends as also greatly ashamed for to be seen where he was so well known, he resolved to seek his Fortune somewhere else. accordingly he went to the City of Schweirien[241] in Meclenburgh[242] where he listed in the Army and distinguished himself from many of the rest by uncommon bravery so that he was taken Notice of by Officers of rank and fortune [93] [who] favoured him with the place of a Sergent. but not long after he happened to fall into [a] Quarrel with one of his Fellow Soldiers whereupon they fought a Duel in which he overcame his Antagonist but whether he was slain on the spot or mortally wounded I could not learn. but, however, he had to fly from the Sword of Justice and arrived at Berlin in Prussia where he again listed. and being a tall, well shaped Man and one that had received a liberal Education, he again had the good fortune to be noticed by some of officers so that he was again reenstated to the place of an under officer. which [he] enjoyed but a little Time for he happened in one of [his] drunken Frolics to abuse one of [his] Superiors and fearing the consequence as soon as he was sober he again deserted and arrived at the City Bramin[243] where he fell into [the] hands of an Emissary or a Co-partner of the Soulsellers who sent him on Ship board to be Transported to America. I remember the Evening he departed out of the World: he seemed in great agony and distress of Mind. he also for the most part was very delirious; sometimes he shrieked out and bid us stand off for it seemed as if he thought he was stabbing and some times shooting. his Sentiments were irregular and confused, so that nothing

238. Samuel Freidrich Reimarus married Margaretha Barbara von Essen, widow of Carl Wilhelm Zeplin, a spice trader, on September 18, 1755. Marriage Register, SHS.
239. Levenhagen, another common name.
240. Job 16.
241. Schwerin.
242. Mecklenburg.
243. Bremen.

could be gathered, but towards Midnight he seemed easy and in the Morning he was found dead.

I have inserted this short account on purpose that he who rejoiced in the strength of his Youth and ability may take warning by this unhappy Man, who once was no ways inferior to many, as of a good and honourable Family, endewed both with riches and learning but by dethroning Heaven-born reason and giving Vice its full reign, he at last parted with the World a poor and dejected, unlamented, and perhaps forever miserable object.

There was also one that was my particular Friend and Asociate who went by the Name of the Hamburgher because he was born and educated in that City. it happened one Day that it raind a good deal, attended with frequent squals of Wind, and I being some what indisposed wished our Supper was dressed because it was my turn to cook. upon this my Friend immediately offered his Service, [94] saying as long as he seemed to be in a State of Health he was willing to assist to the utmost of his power all such as were indisposed. and although he was none of our Mess yet he went and made our supper which [was] a Tea Kittle full of dropt Dumplings. but soon after he was seized with a pain in his Head and so went and lay down in his Coig, which was adjacent to ours, and about ten oClock as near as I could guess he cried out "O my Father, my Father." but we thought he [was] dreaming and having no light to see his situation we left him uninterrupted but in the Morning as soon as light appeared we percieved he was dead.

I could detain the Reader with events of this Nature but as I already have spent a good deal of Time in relating the circumstances and Narratives of others I think it Time to desist and begin again with my own. there was one of our Messmates who was pretty far advanced in Years and by profession a stricht Roman [Catholic] and although I was but a Child in comparison to him I could not [help] being offended at his Doctrine, especially that Article [of] their Creed [about] the impossibility of Heretics being saved and further and that [those who] were not baptized with Water were intirely damned. this agravated my Spirit to a great degree and I opposed it as I thought with becoming Zeal for ever since I had any Idea of Religion it always was my opinion that every Man that was born into the World, let him be a Christian, a Jew, a Mahometan or an Indian, all and none excepted, recieved true Grace in Christ, a Guide within them and every Man, none excepted, which truly followed that Guide would always walk in the Path of Virtue which none could deny was the true Path to Heaven.[244] and further, that it would be the most uncharitable thing in the World for to send to Hell all the good and

244. The foregoing sentence suggests that the author had been influenced by the Quaker belief in the "inner light."

Virtuous Heathen Philosophers who even suffered Martyrdom in the [cause of] Virtue, especially Seneca[245] and Socrates.[246] but this could no ways convince my Antagonist and yet all he could say to support his notion was only [an] epicurian[247] answer, which was because it happened to be so ordained. and when I asked him what became of all the Patriarchs from Adam to the royal Prophet[248] [95] who had been a Man after God's own Heart, for both him and me might be sure [that] they never recieved baptism nor the Popes benediction, to which he replied that they all were in Purgatory till that Time when Christ expired on the Cross. his Spirit then descended to Hell and brought from thence all those that had believed and waited for his Redemption. but when I desired him to tell me how he knew it to be so he made the aforementioned answer. but what raised [my ire] the most was that some others who professed themselves Lutherians were of so [   ][249] a Spirit, which like a Weathercock always turned to the strongest party and I being as it were a Child frequently had to give up the Contest.

Now although the Disease raged amongst us to a great degree, I kept in a good State of Health till near the beginning of August and then it seemed as if not only the Disease attacked me with all its Fury but I was also afflicted with, as I called it, an Elephantic[250] Itch, for I never have seen such an Itch to my Memory in my Life. for my Arms and Hands, both within and without, were almost covered with Pustels nearly as big as a Spanish Fivepence, filled with yellow offensive matter. my Thighs and Hams were in the same Condition and the rest of my Body was nearly covered with small red Pustels resembling the Seeds[251] of a Fish. but my Hips and Seat were greatly afflicted with the aforesaid intolerable Disease which spread with such rapidity that in a little Time my whole Seat was in one intire Scab. and although I greatly suffered in those parts, it seemed tolerable[252] easy to what extreme pain I underwent in a part which Modesty forbids me to mention and had I not been well assured I had no reason to think of being infected with the Venereal Disease, I should have concluded I had been in a State of peutrifaction. I many Times [was made] to think on Job and I thought I could truly say with him that I was lothesome to myself.[253] and my Garments did cleave to my Flesh

245. Lucius Annaeus Seneca (the Younger, c. 3 BCE–65 CE), Roman Stoic philosopher.
246. Socrates (469–399 BCE), Greek philosopher. Both Socrates and Seneca, considering criminal charges against them to be unjust, chose to commit suicide.
247. An epicurean accepts the corruption of the world but seeks to maximize personal pleasure through self-control and moderation.
248. The biblical prophet Zephaniah.
249. Intentional blank appears in the manuscript.
250. Elephantine.
251. That is, eggs.
252. Tolerably.
253. Job 7:5.

and its colour changed by the violence of my Disease and what added greatly to my affliction was the inability of cleansing myself by which I became almost covered with filth and Lice. my Head also was full of sores and Scabs full of Lice and Nits till one of my [96] Messmates was moved with compassion towards me and undertook to cleanse me. it was also my ill fortune to be destitute of the help of a Doctor or Surgeon for the first being buried in the deep and [as for] the latter his Salves and Ointments were all spent so there was [no] visible help for me. but the Invisible Lord and Supreme Physician was graciously pleased to delivered me, as it were, out of the Jaws of Death. for whilst I was standing, as it were, on the Brink of the Grave and expecting nothing else every moment than for to be plunged in the abys of Eternity, I was relieved and began to recover beyond all expectation, so as to crall about and I gathered Strength pretty fast so that I was in a State capable of cleansing myself. I often had to think on the vast difference there seemed to be between us poor infirm Mortals on Shipboard and them on Shore: where they [on land] may lie on their Beds of Down and their Friends and Relations administering all the help and relief in their power to make the situation as easy as possible—to turn him with a Sheet from Side to Side and sometimes raise him high or low according as he finds the most ease and if any thing might please his palate he enjoys it as soon as possible. but alas! the hard Oak Plank had to serve us instead of a downy Bed and the violent motion of the Vessel, especially in the Time of a Storm, was the Sheet that shifted us from Side to Side. and as every one had enough to do for himself, the poor, infirm and dying People often rolled in the greatest agony one over another or sometimes till the Side board of their Coig, or perhaps the Pumps, Stairs or Masts stopped them. and the delicacies to please their Palate was hard and sometimes mouldy Pisket soaked in stinking Water with a piece of saltd Rusty Beef. sometimes the Captain would send a little broth or a drink of Water out of his own Store to them who seemed to be at the point of Death but even this was performed so seldom that it was called a Miracle.

Now nothing more remarkable happened except the cleansing of our Vessel between Decks and washing them well with Vinegar once and sometimes twice a Week and one Day [97] we were alarmed by a Vessel that [gave] us chase. the Captain took his Observation through a [spy]Glass and took her to be a Pirate from Algiers. he then ordered every one that was capable of coming on Deck and Stir about as lively as possible. also some of the Cabbin Passengers had a Number of German Rifles which they intended to sell or exchange for Land in America which the Captain thought fit to be exposed to view so that he thereby might perhaps deceive the Pirate. but whether this had its desired effect or whether it was a Pirate at all or not I can not say. but be that as it will, the Vessel tacked about and we lost sight of her soon after this. I was entertained with the pleasing yet awful sight of a Whale which was steering his course from the West to the North East and a Week after I saw a second one within half a League of the Vessel.

Chapter 11: Philadelphia

The Time now of our being at Sea began for to be very long and tedious so that we wished for Land when awake and sighed for it when a Sleep, in which Time [our] busy fancy often deluded us with the charms of a beautiful Country. the Land now seemed to be the subject of our chief Discourse and some were vain enough to frame conjectures as fancying themselves in the great Channel and if the Wind should prove fair we in a little while should arrive in the small Channel and soon after at the Capes of Delaware. but they found their mistake and that all was nothing but the illusion of fancy till the second Day of September in the Afternoon when from the misen Shroud[254] one shouted out with an exclamation of Joy "O Land, Land," and I must confess, although it was uttered in a loud and harsh Voice, it rung more melodious in my Ears than the most harmonious concert I ever heard in my Life. and many that were capable of ascending the Mast ran up to feast their Eyes with the extraordinary sight. I also attempted a few steps up the Shroud but I was seized with such gidiness that I was obliged to return and Content myself with hearing it. them that had been aloft said it looked it looked like a blue Cloud. but the following Morning as soon as light appeared I arose and was truly delighted [98] with the reviving prospect and soon after we received a pilot who took upon him the charge of the Vessel and conducted us safe on the eleventh Day of September within a half a Mile of the City of Philadelphia. the next Day we were visited by two Physicians and some other Gentlemen from the City to examine if any uncommon Disease appeared among us and finding none we had leave to hoist Anchor and lie in close. the following Day we were conducted to a large Stone House where the Oath of Allegence and Supremacy was tendered us which we took and after having sworn to be faithful Subjects to the Church [of England] and King George we again returned on Shipboard.[255]

I might now have had some fun with my old Antagonist, for as I suppose he had been taking the Oath which was chiefly on account of the Roman

254. A sail on the mizzen mast, or the rear-most mast on a ship.
255. The ship list for the *Sally* lists the date that the oath was administered as August 23, 1773, implying that the ship arrived in Philadelphia a few days before; see Strassburger, *Pennsylvania German Pioneers*, 2:867.

conspiring against the Episcopal power.[256] I might have Questioned him if [he] did not fear the papel thunder but as he was an ancient Man and settled on his Lees I thought it fittest to let him alone.

Now whilst we were at Sea we greatly flattered ourselves that if we had once the good fortune to arrive before the City of Philadelphia we there again should fare like we did at Rotterdam but to our mortification we found we were greatly decieved in this, for instead of receiving good Wheat Bread and Beef, Beer and Cyder, as [we] had fancied ourselves, we only received our usual Provision and Allowance, except the Water which was now augmented from two quarts per Man to as much as we pleased to drink and instead of salt rusty Beef we recieved fresh Mutton at the rate of three Pounds a Week per Man but the Biskets were now become very mouldy and full of Worms which rendered them exceeding lothesome to us. and none can imagine but him that by experience his[257] felt the misery of a long and tedious Voyage and can recall the desires and agitation which the Ideas of the Produce of the Land had raised in him; such, I say, can only [99] judge with what eagerness we feasted our Eyes in the Bread and Beer, Tarts and all sorts of Fruit and vegitables with which the Hucksters crouded our Deck. it [was] almost enough to tempt us to raise and so take by force that which [we] could not obtain without Mony, of which the bigest Number of us were destitute. but as this would have been too rash an undertaking, there seemed to be no other way than for to make ourselves Masters of Mony and to obtain this necessary evil there was no other way than for to sell off all [we] possibly could spare, beginning first at our Chest and other Utensels and from that to our Clothes, as Shoes and Stockings, Coats, Hats &c., concluding that if we were only in possession of Breeches and Shirt it would be sufficient. and I can not forebear acquainting the Reader how our compassionate Country People defrauded us in the things they bought or exchanged,[258] for we knew but little the price of Goods in this Country and therefore had to leave it intirely to the buyers as they thought fit. it would be tedious to mention the many things we sold for little or nothing, only this: that I sold a pair of Shoes nearly as good as new for a Quarter of a Dollar and they only cost me two Shillings and Six [pence] Sterling in Europe. I thought I had a tolerable good bargain considering the little wear I had out of them and so every thing went according to this.

The Merchant sent also a few Bushels of Apples to be divided amongst us but they were distributed so unequally that some received double and thrible

256. A reference to contemporary suspicions of Catholics in Protestant Great Britain and her colonies.

257. Has.

258. Here the author is being ironic, mocking the stereotype of American rural folk as simple and honest.

and some none at all, of [which] Number I was one. there came also some Friendly People from the Jerseys and distributed Fruit amongst us, but I, like the rest of Sluggards, happened to be under Deck fast asleep till I awoke by the tumultuous Noise but by the Time I cralled on Deck the Sport was over, at which I first seemed to be greived but I had thus again missed my chance, but when I understood how they were distributed I had more occasion to be glad than sorry for it seemed the Benefactors had intended [100] to have sport instead of pay, which made them cast Anchor by the Vessel's Side and threw the Fruit on Deck, by which means them that were strongest and most active got the bounty and the feeble and Infirm who had the most need for refreshment received none, so by all likelihood had I been there I should have only received a lame Leg or bruised Bone.

The Masters now began to come pretty fast to supply themselves with Servants of all sorts, both Tradesmen and Farmers, but none seemed to fancy me. but I did not expect that any would choose one [such as me,] a poor distressed looking object, whilst they might have their choice out of so many hale looking Men. for the greatest Number, especially them that were first seized with the Disorder, were now pretty well recovered and some as fleshy and ruddy as ever. but as it seized me at the last I was only just beginning to recruit[259] and so it was not to be wondered, as I said before, that none seemed to fancy me. it was no great disappointment to me, yet I could not help exclaiming against my ill fate.

Now as the first Question of the [prospective] Masters were chiefly how much our Passage was, I went to the Captain in order to know how much I was indebted that I might know if I had the good fortune to meet with one that fancied me. and to my astonishment I found my Debts were rapidly increased from the Time I left Rotterdam, which was at first a great Mistery to me how it could be, for I was sure that I never had received the tenth part of it at Sea. but after sometime the Mistery was unfolded and I came to know that the living had to pay for the Dead and as there were so many of our Companions buried in the Deep, we that survived had to defray their Passage which I thought a hard and very wrong case. but what vexed me the most of all was this: while we were at Sea we often recieved Rum, Sugar and Tea at the Cabbin which was not counted among our common Provision but we called it buying all one as out of a Store on trust. [101] now I fancied myself the less I bought, which was the most reasonable, the less I should be in Debt and, as I never was a lover of Rum or any Intoxicating Liquor, I got two Quarts the whole Voyage and that was chiefly on account of the extreme badness of the Water; I also got a Pound of Sugar and [of] Tea none at all. but it

259. That is, recover.

seemed they had mixed frugality with bestiality for one to balance the other, for to my great vexation I found by enquiry that they who had received Rum as it were by wholesale and other Articles amounting to more than ten Times the Value to that of mine and yet their Debts were not a farthing higher or lower than mine but it seemed that all expense and loss were equally divided among us which had augmented my Passage from about Nineteen Pounds to Twenty eight Pounds thirteen Shillings and Sixpence, a round Sum indeed to give for a Servant without knowing whether he would live a Year, a Mounth or a Day, or whether [he] would be [a] dutiful Servant or good for nothing or worse that nothing.[260] but be that as it will, since there is nothing certain to us in this World, the Master must take his chance here like [in] all other things.

But not long after an Inhabitant of the City arrived in order to choose for himself both a Male and Female Servant. he culled the Man but as for the Woman he was too curious in his choice and finding he could not please himself he thought fittest to refer[261] it to the following Day and so bring his Wife to choose for herself which he did accordingly and ~~an~~ his Wife seemed to take a fancy to me after choosing her Girl. this greatly revived my Spirit, as it was the first Time any had taken notice of me, and telling them how much I was indebted we agreed for Six Years Servitude. the Woman who was then to be my Mistress I seemed to fancy tolerable well but as for my intended Master I was far from being satisfied for two reasons. first, that of him not being of my Profession,[262] and secondly he being an intolerable brag. for he gave [102] us a long detain[263] of his Possessions which he had enjoyed in Germany and how magnificent he used to live and when he set off to come to America he sailed down down the River Ryne[264] with all Instruments of Music playing before him. and further how greatly he was mortified when he arrived in this Country to have a fine House in Germany exchanged for a

260. By law, the cost of a deceased passenger's fare could only be assumed by the family, not by all passengers, but it may be that the owner sought to circumvent the law given the high mortality on this voyage. Whitehead is perhaps naïve about the costs of his passage to Philadelphia. He fails to remember that he also owed the recruiters (soul sellers) money for transportation from Hamburg to Amsterdam and for the eleven weeks' worth of food and lodging (however miserable) in Amsterdam while awaiting transport overseas. Our thanks to Farley Grubb for this analysis. Marianne S. Wokeck finds evidence of high interest rates charged on the fares—20 to 25 percent for three months—and other forms of sharp dealing, if not outright fraud, so that Sophia Leonora Heistrigen, who also arrived in 1773, was quoted a fare of £16/10/0 and ended up owing £23/6/0, a markup of 41 percent. Marianne S. Wokeck, *Trade in Strangers: The Beginnings of Mass Migration to North America* (University Park: Pennsylvania State University Press, 1999), 100–102.
261. Defer.
262. That is, religion or faith.
263. That is, the buyer long detained them with details of his possessions.
264. Rhine.

Cottage in America but that he now again lived easy and in [an] extraordinary manner, having but little else to do but to receive Mony and lay it out again and in short by his Story one might think he was the happiest and Wealthiest Man in the City. now although I greatly disliked the disposition of Qualities of this Man, I was too much after the Ladies of Spain or Portugal, who for the most part seldom refuse the first offer for fear they should not meet with the second chance, and I thought that Six Years was no Eternity which made [me] strike a bargain [with them]. they went off and told us they would [come] for us the following Day but as he told us he had little else to do than for to receive Mony and lay it out again, it seemed by all likelihood that his export was greater than his import, for he being incapable of satisfying the Merchant for our Passage and not having Credit enough so as to obtain us on trust, he had to give up his bargain and we were told by the Captain not waint[265] or on him but look again for another Master, of which there came several that enquired of me how much I was in debt but the price was rather too high or else some other obsticles unknown to me and none ventured so much Mony for my redemption till at the Time of the Yearly Meeting held at Philadelphia by the People called Quakers.

it happened that two of the said People, Viz. Mordecai Lee[266] and James Starr,[267] arrived on Ship board to choose a Servant for one John Starr[268] who was Brother in Law to the said Mordecai Lee and an own Brother to James Starr,[269] all three Yeoman residing in Maiden Creek Township, [103] Berks County in Pennsylvania. I happened to be under Deck when they arrived but by receiving Tidings that Masters were come I went up on Deck in order

265. To wait.

266. Mordecai Lee (1733–1812) was married to Deborah Starr. See EMMR. He is listed in the 1790 census for Maidencreek, Berks County, with a male under sixteen years of age and one female; see U.S. Bureau of the Census, *Heads of Families at the First Census of the United States taken in the Year 1790: Pennsylvania* (Washington, D.C.: U.S. Government Printing Office, 1908), 37 (hereafter *HF*). He is also listed as a farmer with significant landholdings in the Maidencreek Township tax roles for 1767, 1768, 1779, 1780, and 1781; see *Pennsylvania Archives*, 3d series, vol. 18 (Harrisburg, Pa.: William Stanley Ray, 1897) (hereafter *PA*), 70, 144, 246, 378, 505.

267. James Starr (1725–1807) is listed as a head of household with a male under sixteen and four females in the 1790 census; James Starr Junior is also listed in a household with two female members; see EMMR and *HF*, 37. James Starr appears in the township tax roles starting in 1780; see *PA*, 379, 506, 641, 766.

268. John Starr (1722/23–1801) appears as a head of household with one older male, three females, and one other free person (either an African American or Native American servant); see EMMR and *HF*, 37. He also appears as a significant landholder in the tax roles through 1785; see *PA* 70, 145, 247, 379, 506, 641, 765.

269. John Starr was the second child of Moses Starr and Deborah King, born January 16, 1722/23; James was their third child, born December 13, 1724 or 1725; Mordecai Lee married their seventh child, Deborah, who was born February 19, 1735. See *Friends' Meeting Records of Berks County* (bound photocopies of originals), comp. John E. Eshelman, Historical Society of Berks County, Reading, Pennsylvania (hereafter *Friends' Records*), 310–11. Until 1751, March 25 began the New Year in Great Britain and her colonies.

to look at them for little I expected. and they soon were inclosed by a ring of Men who offered their Service. some said they could plow and sow and others again could reap and mow, some could drive [a] Team [of horses or oxen] and others were Tradesmen. I for my part thought it not worthwhile to enter the ring or to encroach upon them which made [me] keep off a small distance but it was my good fortune to be eyed by the said Mordecai Lee who beckoned to me to come near him, which I did joyfully. he then, like the rest of [the] Masters, first enquired after my Debt and having acquainted him with it, he replied it was very high and [asked] how long I purposed[270] to serve for it, to which [I] replied I thought six Years were sufficient. the next Question was what was my occupation but alas this baffled me greetly and I was like Aesop[271] of old when the same question was put to him by his Master: he said he knew nothing at all, for his Fellow Servants could do every thing. yet to let them know I was not intirely brought up [with] nothing, I, with a downcast look, replied I was altogether unacquainted with any kind of labour but I had received something of learning. upon [this] they discoursed awhile together, which I could not understand being in the English Tongue, but as I suppose must have been about me. the said Mordecai Lee then replied that if it were for himself he should conclude that, if I was a good Boy, the Number of six Years would be sufficient but as it was not for himself but for his Brother in Law, [he] knew not how to do. yet if I would give in six Months more he would redeem me at a venture, to which I replied that it seemed a long Time to serve, especially if I should have the ill fortune to get an ill natured Master or Mistress. to which he said he could assure me if I was a good Boy I should have no reason to complaint but if I proved to the contrary I might also expect the same from my Master. upon this I concluded that if I once had finished that period [104] of six Years certainly six Months would soon follow after them and as they both appeared to be Men of a sober yet chearful and familiar behaviour, especially the said James Starr who was as I said before [the] own Brother to my intended Master, I agreed to serve the aforesaid Time. they then gave me a piece of Mony which I thankfully received. they then told me that their Team would be in Town by the middle of the following Week, which was to conduct me unto my Master and so they wished me well and went off. and the said Mordecai Lee's Team arrived in Town according to the appointed Time in company with another named James Hutton,[272] Yeoman,

270. Proposed.
271. Aesop, the legendary enslaved Greek author of moral fables.
272. James Hutton married Hannah Lee, a sister of Mordecai Lee; see *Friends' Records*, 144–45, 186–87. Hannah Hutton is listed as living next to Whitehead in the 1790 census; see *HF*, 37. James Hutton appears in the township tax roles prior to 1790; see *PA*, 69, 144, 246, 378, 505, 764.

a Neighbour to my intended Master who [was] also in quest of a Servant with which he was furnished on board our Ship. he then conducted both his own Servant and me to the Mayor of the City named John Gibson,[273] where we received our Indentures on the 29th Day of September, 1773,[274] to serve, that is myself, the period of six Years and six Months from that Day forward as a Dutiful Servant and after the expiration of said Time I was to be free and recieved two compleat Suits of Apparel of which one was to be new. the said James Hutton then conveyed us to an Inn called the Tree[275] where we refreshed ourselves with a little drink and a most elegant Dinner.

Now while we were walking the Streets I must confess I was greatly ashamed at the Figure [I] presented and I could not help reflecting on the difference there was in two Years past and what I was then. for instead of a Gold laced Hat, a Broad Cloth Coat, Sattin Vest and Breeches, Silken Stockings and Cordevan Shoes, I was now without Shoes or Stockings, Coat or Hat, but my whole attire consisted of dirty Linnen Breeches and Jacket of the same and a fulled Cap of a reddish Colour which by reason of being fulled pretty thick together with the fifth,[276] Lice and Nits, it stood nearly a foot perpendicular above my Head and thus like a Grenadier[277] I followed the said James Hutton to the aforesaid Inn.

Now I think it suitable to acquaint my Reader here with the following Ideas which I framed before my arrival [105] into this happy Land. I compared Columbia to a beautiful young Virgin adorned with Innocence and simplicity, as also in a state of immaturity but I must confess I could not but admire to see so beautiful a City as Philadelphia, for when I beheld the regularity of the Streets, together with the Churches and Dwelling Houses, although not of so inormous a size as in Europe, yet neat, elegant and commodious, I thought it no ways inferior to any City I ever saw in my Travels and perhaps not to any in the World. and further, when I got knowledge of that famous invention of the ingenious and celebrated Rittenhouse called the

273. John Gibson served as mayor of Philadelphia from October 1, 1771, to October 4, 1773, having been elected to two consecutive one-year terms. See http://www.seventy.org/stats/mayors.html.

274. Whitehead's indenture (where he is listed as "John Frederick Cuckoo," a translation of his stepfather's surname into English), dated September 29, 1773, says that he was bound to Mordacai Lee and John Starr, of Maidencreek Township in Berks County, for six years and six months for a sum of 28 pounds, 13 shillings, and 6 pence. *Record of Indentures of Individuals Bound Out as Apprentices, Servants, Etc.* The editors thank Farley Grubb for this reference.

275. Philadelphia had more than "a hundred licensed public houses" by 1744; see Robert Earle Graham, "The Taverns of Colonial Philadelphia," *Transactions of the American Philosophical Society* 43, part 1 (1953): 318.

276. Filth.

277. Soldiers in grenadier units wore tall hats.

Orary,[278] I could not forebear saying in my Heart "O Columbia if thou canst perform such wonders in thy Infancy, what great and marvelous Deeds shall issue forth when thou arrivest to a state of maturity?"

Chapter 12: Berks County

But to return, after we had refreshed ourselves at the Inn and [had] the Horses fed, we prepared and fitted ourselves for Home. the said James Hutton's Team was drove by his Son Nehemiah[279] and said Mordicai Lee's by a hired Man named Dennis Lary.[280] nothing remarkable happen'd to us in our Journey except almost as soon as we left the City it began to rain, accompanied with cold Wind, which made our Journey very disagreeable and fatigueing and I being very indifferently dressed I suffered a great deal [with] the cold. it lasted nearly till we arrived at the Borough of Reading by which means the Roads were become exceeding deep and muddy but it cleared up on Seventh Day[281] Morning. from the North the Clouds were dispersed and the Sky appeared again beautifully serene and [we] arrived safe at the House of Mordecai Lee on the second Day of October, bieng the last Day of the Week at nearly two oClock P.M. here I happened to get the first [look] of my new Mistress Eunice Starr[282] who seemed to be no ways delighted or taken with her new comer and Servant and although I could not understand a single Word she said, [106] except the Word "Irish" which she repeated several Times, I could perceive by her Countenance that she seemed a good deal dissatisfied. and I must confess that I at that Time took as great a dislike to her as she did to me for she appeared to me a Woman of an exceeding high

278. Orrery, a mechanical device that simulates the motion of heavenly bodies. David Rittenhouse of Philadelphia built two orreries c. 1769. See M. J. Babb, "The Relation of David Rittenhouse and His Orrery to the University [of Pennsylvania]," at http://www.library.upenn.edu/vanpelt/pennhistory/orrery/orrery.html.

279. Nehemiah was James's first child (of seven), born August 7, 1758, apparently named after his maternal grandfather. See Friends' Records, 144–45, 186–87.

280. No Dennis Lary or Leary appears in the 1790 census for Berks County or the surrounding area, although only heads of households are mentioned by name; there is no listing in the township tax rolls.

281. I.e., Saturday. The usual day names were not used by Quakers, who considered them pagan.

282. Eunice Lord (1732–1810) married John Starr on January 18, 1760. They had six children, Sarah, born 1761; Elizabeth, 1762; Deborah, 1764; Eunice, 1765; Ann, 1767, and Jeremiah, 1770. See Friends' Records, 310–11, and EMMR. She inherited twenty-nine acres of her husband's plantation and all of his household goods after his death in 1801. The son got 189 acres, while Deborah, Eunice, Ann, a grandson, and a son-in-law received sizable legacies. When Eunice Starr died seven years later she left the bulk of her estate to her unmarried daughters, Eunice and Ann, and gave legacies to a few other relatives. Alfred Smith, comp., Abstracts of Bucks County Wills, 1798–1825 (Philadelphia: Genealogical Society of Pennsylvania, 1898), 2:67, 270.

temper [and] a stern Countenance accompanied with a Voice that bespoke authority. but I was inured to hardships and concluded that six Years and six Months was no Eternity and there was now nothing but [to] endure all events with Patience.

After I had received some refreshment the aforesaid Dennis Lary conveyed me on Horse back to the place of my a bode which was nearly a Mile distant from the place of my arrival. my Master happened to be from Home and I saw him not till the next Morning. the Family seemed to be no ways charmed with me but rather to the contrary scared and afraid of such an ugly Fellow and the girls desired the said Dennis Lary to stay as a safeguard till their Mother arrived who come soon after. the first I received was a stout Ditch[283] of Meat and Beans and although I had received refreshment at the House of the said Mordecai Lee, I now again eagerly devoured the aforesaid Mess for it seemed as if I could not be satisfied but capable of eating almost continually and I had the good fortune to enjoy a place where there was plenty, all the necessaries of Life, and I can truly say that I never had the least occasion of complaint, not only by way of victualing but in short of any thing whatsoever.

the first task my Mistress had to perform with her new comer was to see how to cleanse him from the filth and Lice of which I had yet a tolerable store. and although I was nearly recovered of the Disease or Scurvy or whatever it was, I as yet [was] greatly pestered by Elephantic Itch as I called it. upon this my Master went to get a root called Alleber,[284] which was bruised [107] and soaked in Water with which I had to wash myself before a good Fire, but this proved too severe by far for me in my condition and I had no more rest for the greatest part of the Night. then, as the saying is "like a Toad under a Harrow," I shouted, screamed and danced about like one distracted. and as I lodged up in the third Story on the Garret, my Master seemed concerned that in the height of my agitation and agony I might leap off the Window and so put an end to my Life. therefore the Alleber was then looked on as useless and Brimstone[285] chosen as a milder cure. this, bruised fine, mixed with Hogs lard and properly applied had its desired effect so that after a little Time I began to strip off my old tattered European Skin, like the Serpents in the Spring of the Year, and exchanged it for a good sound American Buckskin. I now began to recruit pretty fast and by all appearance seemed to enter into a state of strength and vigour.

283. Dish.

284. Black Hellebore is a toxic European plant whose rhizome was traditionally "beaten to powder, and strewed upon foul ulcers [so that it] consumes the dead flesh, and instantly heals them." Nicholas Culpeper, *Culpeper's Complete Herbal and English Physician* (1653; reprint 1826; reprint, Leicester, UK: Magna Books, 1992), 74. There was also a similar, less toxic, American plant called Hellebore.

285. Brimstone, i.e., sulfur.

but alas, it was not long after till I was seized with a violent pain [in] my Ancles[286] and feet which intirely disabled me, so that I was good for nothing and worse than nothing for any kind of business. my Master then concluded to take me to a Physician who lived in the Borough of Reading named Jonathan Potts.[287] upon this I was conveyed on Horseback to the said Physician who after examining me said to my Master he was confident it was the Dropsy[288] that disordered me, upon which he gave me Drugs which cost my Master 10s. 6d. but if [it] had done me 6d. worth of good my Master might have given him the 10s. for his trouble but I did reap little or no benefit by it to my Knowledge. but it happened not long after that an old German Druggist passed by our way who called in to see if the Family wanted to buy and any Drugs, Cordial or Hungary Water.[289] my Mistress then bid me acquaint this Man with my infirmity that perhaps he could give me some relief. upon this I told him my ailment with which he seemed to be well acquainted for he was not only capable of telling me how I was held but also could shew me the very spot that seemed to be [108] the most affected. he then told me he thought he could help me and so gave me about as much as a large Thimble full of stuff which he called Swissors Balsom of Life,[290] for which my Mistress gave him 1s. 3d. and I think it was the rankest and most disagreeable stuff I ever smelt or tasted in my Life but as desperate disorders require desperate remedies, the ill flavour of Drugs must not be regarded. I had to take Morning and Evening three drops inwardly, as also the same quantity to be applied a little below my Ancle Joint. this had its desired effect and I was restored again to Health and activity, yet not so as to be perfectly cured but often felt the disorder, yet not so as to disable me from my business and I verily believe that had I received a double quantity of that excellent Balsom I should have been intirely healed but since none of us knew where he came from or where he went, it was out of my Power to receive any further benefit.

not long after I again was taken with a great Pain in the small of my Back and between my Shoulders which continued nearly from the beginning of June til August in which Time I for the greatest part was incapable of Business and as it was the throngest[291] Time of the Year with a Farmer, it was a

286. Ankles.
287. Jonathan Potts graduated from the Philadelphia Medical Institute in 1768, according to Morton L. Montgomery, *Historical and Biographical Annals of Berks County, Pennsylvania*, 2 vols. (Chicago: Beers, 1909), 1:99.
288. A collection of fluid in tissues or cavities of the body.
289. Also called the Queen of Hungary's Water, a decoction of rosemary flowers that had many medical uses. William Woys Weaver, ed. and trans., *Sauer's Herbal Cures: America's First Book of Botanic Healing, 1762–1778* (New York: Routledge, 2001), 262–64.
290. The *Pinus alies*, or silver-leafed fir, found mostly in the Black Forest region of the German states, was a balsam whose imported bark and shoots were used to heal injuries. Ibid., 290–91.
291. That is, crowded or busy.

great loss to my Master who was destitute of my assistance in that busy Time but as we are incapable to obstruct diseases and pain, there was nothing but to endure it with patience. the next disaster that befel me was an accident that happened unto me in the fourth Year of my Servitude and was thus: one Evening I was sent to an Neighbours named John Hutton[292] for to borrow an Handsaw. but to make the greater speed I went to the Stable and got a Colt in order to ride but to my misfortune when I arrived at the said John Huttons, there happened to be a [109] covered Waggon, at which the Horse took fright just as I did alight[293] and I being unwilling to be mastered by him had a great struggled but he tore loose from me and lashed out with both heels by which I recieved a violent blow in the Breast which soon ended the dispute and I lay motionless on the Ground. but soon recovering again I staggered towards the House and the People hearing the noise came out to see what had happened and I told them I had recieved a hurt from the Horse but I believed not very bad and I told them my errand [and] so went Home. but it seemed I was not sensible at first of the pain for it now began to be sharp and severe so that I was scarce able to go along and when I arrived near halfway Home I found the Horse entangled in his Bridle and all I wished for then was only to be in a state of ability to correct the Beast for his ill manners and [the] usage I had received but I was glad to get him freed from the Bridle which was as much as ever I could perform, let alone correcting him. upon this he gallopped Home and I went quietly after him. from this hurt I did not recover for a considerable Time and although I went about my Business after a day or two I laboured in a good deal of punishment, for it affected me nearly a twelve Month so as to make me very cautious in lifting Logs, Bags of Grain, or any thing of burden.

but before I got rightly recovered of this I met with another accident of the same nature which happened thus: one of [the] Neighbours named Francis Parvin[294] came about some business to my Master's House and fastened his Horse to the Fence. I then was called from the Barn on purpose [to put] him in the Stable and it happened the youngest daughter of my Master named Ann was at the Barn: she being a little Girl[295] diverted herself with hunting Eggs. we both went together to [the] House [and were] busy talking by which

292. A brother of James Hutton; see *Friends' Records*, 146–47. He also appears in the township tax rolls; see *PA*, 69, 144, 246, 378, 505, 640, 764.

293. That is, dismount.

294. Francis Parvin Jr., who was married to Sarah Lightfoot; see *Friends' Records*, 250–51. He was listed in the 1790 census as the head of a household including three males under sixteen years of age, two older males, and four females; see *HF*, 36. He was listed as both a farmer and a tanner in the tax rolls; see *PA*, 70, 144, 246, 378, 505, 640 764.

295. Ann Starr was born in 1767, so that if this incident took place after four years' service, she was about ten years old.

means I neglected speaking to the Horse but went and put my Hand on him at which he took fright and I recieved a blow in the pit of the Stomach and, as the Ground was of a little descent, I staggered back for near ten feet and so fell. but soon recovering again I went to lean my Head against the Fence to support myself, for I got exceeding faint and sick, but I remained so but a little while till I sunk to [110] motionless to the Ground and when I recovered again I found myself stretched on the Floor of my Masters House and my careful Mistress washed my Temples and Breast with Vinegar. I regained my Senses a considerable Time before I had any occasion of breathing so that I lay stretched on the Floor to all appearance as gone to my long Home. I felt no Pain or any Thing else whatsoever nor could I think of any thing yet I was capable of understanding what they said. and I remember that my Master gave me intirely up but my Mistress seemed not so quick discouraged but [she] replied she hoped I would be worth two Dead Men. yet now after I had lain a considerable Time as in a Trance, the breath of Life returned and I again by giving a great sigh began to breathe and by the care of my Mistress, who ordered Teas of Cumphry[296] and other healing Herbs for me, I recovered beyond expectation and although at the first it seemed a sad accident yet I was in a few Days restored so as to go about my Business. but before a Twelvemonth was elapsed it happened I was sent in company with one of my Master's Cousins named Pearson Starr[297] to one of our Neighbours, Joseph Lightfoot,[298] with a parcel of Barley, my Master having a large roan Horse[299] which I took in order to carry the Barley to the said Neighbours who followed the Business of Malting. I arrived safe and discharged my Business but in my return Home I happened to ride on the descent of a Hill. the Horse slipped and fell with all his weight on my left Leg and Foot and as the Ground was very rough and frozen hard, being in the Winter season, I received a violent bruise which confined me near two Weaks to the Room and nearly five Weeks before I was capable of any business.

Now although that period of Six Years and six Months makes a great sound and seems a tedious while to spend in Servitude for a Debt of nearly thirty Pounds, yet I think that a Master would not enrich himself very fast in

296. Comfrey; a decoction of the roots was used to heal wounds and stop bleeding. Weaver, *Sauer's Herbal Cures*, 114–15.

297. Pearson Starr (1754–82) was a nephew of John Starr, listed as a single freeman with no property in the township tax rolls for 1779, 1780, and 1781; see EMMR and *Friends' Records*, 310–12, and *PA*, 248, 380, 506.

298. A brother of Sarah Lightfoot, the wife of Francis Parvin Jr., Joseph Lightfoot appears in the township tax rolls for 1768, 1779, 1780, 1781, 1784, and 1785; see *Friends' Records*, 208–9, and *PA*, 144, 246, 378, 505, 640, and 765 (he was listed as a blacksmith with no landholdings in 1768 but acquired land later).

299. A brown horse flecked with white.

such bargains as me, considering what abundance of Time I lost by infirmities and disasters. for whether in Bed or in the Field, all counts in the Time
of a Servant. yet notwithstanding I flatter myself that if my Master was no
[111] great gainer he was no loser by the following calculation: reckon the
first six Months to call me good for nothing and six Months more to call me
worse than nothing, which makes a full Year. then again take six Months and
call me what you please, a bad or an Idle Boy, and put six Months to that to
satisfy my Master for his expence and trouble. this will reduce the Time of
my Indenture to four Years and a half, and as the Wages of a hired Man was
at that Time [was] from 18£. to 22£. per Annum, it would at that rate [be]
nearly another Year and a half to pay for my Passage which would reduce the
Time of my Indenture to three Years. now subtract again from the three
Years a Twelvemonth for my clothing, in which I may say I was uncommonly
saving so that three pair of Shoes lasted me nearly two Twelvemonths, and
the rest of my clothing according to this. now to this Twelvemonth must be
added six Months more for my Freedom Apparel,[300] which I may say to both
the praise of my Master and Mistress were very good and serviceable. there
will then remain a Year and a half to be called profit for the venture which
my Master had to run in gaining it or losing all so that by this calculation it
will appear that my Master, including all my infirmities, just doubled his
Money, except we reckon the Interest of my Passage. if so, this will take
another six Months and then the total remainder of profit will be a Twelvemonths Wages which will be sufficient provided I was a good Servant which
I flatter myself I was. for although this [is] not for me to say [and] must be
left to my Master, yet I may venture to say this far, that [we] seperated in
Friendship which has continued even unto this Day and I hope may continue
so untill our dissolution.

Having now given an account of my disasters and infirmities I shall detain
the reader next with the greatest difficulty I had to encounter which was my
ignorance of the English Tongue. this let in a disposition[301] and jealousy
between me and the Family, who I always thought were making thier fun of
me, especially when there happened to be a little merriment among themselves so as to occasion laughter or even a smile if I happened to be present,
[it] would kindle a fire [in me],[302] although it often was nothing concerning
me and [it] also occasioned many mistakes [112] in my business so that I often
did first what should have been last and sometimes was nothing at all relating

300. The two sets of clothing, one to be new, that were due him at the completion of his
servitude.
301. Dissension.
302. That is, make him angry.

to what I was ordered to do. for it happened to be my ill fortune that the chief [part] of the Family were as ignorant of the German Language as I was of the English, except my Master and a Boy. and as for my Master I could just make out to understand him for he spoke exceeding broken but the Boy both understood and spoke it well by which means [he] served as an Interpreter between me and the Family. and as he was one that seemed to be a good deal edicted[303] to verify the old saying that "it is not easy to work hard," he frequently would interpret matters so as to answer his purpose and in his favour. this however served him for awhile but after I became a little acquainted with the English it proved a source of great Animosity, not only between the said Boy and me but also between some of the Family and me. for as he was the greatest favourite and knew how to explain his story to them, they frequently took his part and the ugly Fellow—that I was stiled by some of the youngsters—had to go and perform the Task whatever it was. yet [it was] not without great vexation of Mind to think that I who had seen so much of the World should thus be led by the Nose like they do the Bears in Europe and that by a young Beardless Boy who had scarcely seen any thing in the World but his Mothers Chimney. but, however, there was nothing for me but patience and hope for Better Times. yet our contention grew sometimes to very high words and would have frequently ended in blows had I not feared my Master's displeasure who expressly forbid me striking him. and as for our duty in point of business when both of us were together, I must confess to my shame that both him and me were exceeding careless. and as for my own part I knew little or nothing about work and to tell the truth, as I had lived always an easy and indolent Life, I cared but little about it whether I sped in my business or not. and as for the Boy's part he was one that was endewed by nature with a taste of speculation, by which we could spend a great deal of Time in admiring the flight of a large Bird and the activity of a Squirrel or ajelity[304] of the Serpent and calling me frequently to take [a] share of the sight. our Time, which should [113] [have been spent in] Labour, fled away almost unknown to us so that they often would sound the Shell to come to our Breakfast before we had began to work and for our Dinner when we had rightly got to work and the Sun would [set] before half our work was performed. for which I must confess we deserved correction and without doubt would have recieved it had it not been our good fortune to have so indulgent a Master. for I can truly say I never in the whole course of my Servitude received more than a single Stroke which was so light that the shame was far superior to the smart. and as the occasion of it seems but a simple thing

303. Addicted.
304. Agility.

to detain the reader with yet as it was the only stroke I recieved I shall take the liberty to relate in short the occasion which was thus: I happened to be in particular very unfortunate in the business of the Plough which I for the most part drove Jehu like,[305] which was furiously. and by so doing, especially amongst Rocks and Stumps, I frequently would not only break Chains and swingletrees[306] but also the Plough beam itself if [it was in] any ways inclined to decay. and there happened to be a hired Man named George M'Kenny[307] who was at plow and I making [a] Fence in an adjacent Field. and as I went Home to my Dinner I found the plough coulter[308] leaning against a Tree which I took up and found that its point was cracked. upon which this foolish notion rose in my Head and I said to my[self] "ha! I will now break that point quite off and then tell my Master George can break things as well as me." and so I bent it under a root of the same Tree till I accomplished my design and as soon as I saw my Master I acquainted him with it, saying that George had broke it, to which he replied he knew it was cracked. now if I had considered the least I might easily have known that he was acquainted with the whole circumstance but I without any consideration replied that it was not only cracked but broke smack off. to which he said that if it was broken smack off it was [me] that had done it, for he not only happened to be present when it was done but also assisted the said George in putting in another Coulter. I now was fairly catched in the Trap, both as to the mischief and untruth, and being ashamed of my self I received a stroke without the least thought of resentment or murmuring, being well assured I deserved more than a stroke or two, and perhaps a dozen would not [have] excused me had I been in the power of some Masters. I could [114] mention several events of this nature and how I knocked over the Hens and Gun and almost breaking the Backs of Teat pigs[309] and other petty Crimes which I committed, especially in the first and second Year of my Servitude. but for fear of being tedious I think fittest to omit them, only this: I may say I had the good fortune never to abuse any thing so as to perish except [illegible] an anctient Hen.

Now in the third Year of my Servitude it happened the aforesaid Boy went to learn a Trade and I was left by myself which soon convinced my Master the Truth of that saying that "a Boy is a Boy, but two Boys are only half a one and three none at all." for I now began to work diligent when by myself and when in company it was [with] my Master or some hired Man that knew

305. The biblical Jehu, King of Israel, known for his speed when driving a chariot; see Kings 9–10.
306. I.e., singletrees or whiffletrees, the pivoting crossbar on a plow to which the harnesses are attached.
307. Not listed in the 1790 census or in township tax rolls.
308. The blade or wheel attached to the beam of a plow that makes vertical cuts in the soil.
309. Nursing piglets.

how work should be performed which not only taught me how to do it myself but also inspired me with ambition, so as to think [what] a shame it was and would be in Time to come for to be out done by every Body and that my Master could nor would [not] give me the Name of a good Servant at the expiration of my Time and without a recommendation none would choose to employ me. in [and] by due consideration I came to see what was and must be the duty of a Servant which is diligence and obedience punctually to whatever he is bid, provided it be reasonable and Lawful by his Master, by his Master and Mistress and further if any one of the Family should ask his assistance as in bringing in wood or Water [or] any thing of such like Nature, to due it chearfully without murmuring or as much as a hard thought. this will make his state—or at least did mine—perfectly happy. it created not only a regard between me and my Master and Mistress but also the whole Family so that I was almost looked upon as one of the Family as much as a Servant.

It being now a Time of Trouble and distress for as the Quakers could not for Conscience sake join the Military Power in a War which was then commenced between Great Britain and America,[310] my Master, who as I have said was one of said People, he greatly suffered in having his Cattle and Grain taken by the greatly domineering Collectors which [he] bore with all patience imaginable. they also boarded two Lighthorse [115] men upon him the greatest part of the Winter who were exceeding troublesome and boistrous, especially when intoxicated with Liquor. and as they drew their Rashings[311] on every Seventh Day of the Week [we] mostly had a very disagreeable Sabbath which we had to endure till my Master's Hay was nearly spent and having no provender for their Horses they were by orders of Col. Morgan and Cap. Vanhair[312] quartered at another place and I may say that all of us were truly glad to get rid of so disagreeable [a] company. and as it was still in the height of War and Hostilisties, many Battles were fought and People slain on both Sides which occasioned my being greatly pestered not only by recriuting Officers but also by some of our German Neighbours whose Names I forbear mentioning[313] but they certainly did not wish the wellfare of my Master,

310. American Revolutionary War (1775–83).

311. Rations.

312. According to Montgomery, *Historical and Biographical Annals*, 1:115, in the summer of 1778, "16 men were enlisted at Reading to make up the company of Capt. Bartholomew Von Heer, for the purpose of performing provost [police] duty. They were mounted and accoutered as Light Dragoons, to apprehend deserters, rioters and stragglers. Col. Jacob Morgan reported in August that he had forwarded 180 men to Sunbury, and 123 men to Easton to render frontier service against Indians."

313. There was very little Tory sentiment in Berks County during the Revolution. About three-quarters of the eligible men served in the war, and the rest were pacifists—Quakers,

else they never would have presumed to persuade a Servant to run away and join the Army. I was offered from ten hard Dollars to thirty Pounds by way of Bounty but their Money nor all their powerful harangues they used in extalling the glorious Life of a Gentleman Soldier was not capable of making an impression on me for three reasons which I thought very plausible and just. the first was that I had already seen and felt so much of miseries of Life that I did not choose to throw myself voluntarily again [to] the fatigues and turbulent Life of a Soldier. and secondly I knew I had a Master and Mistress that were both endewed with reason [and] humanity and as a Gentleman Soldier, as they called it, had not one but many Masters, it could certainly be no other ways but that some, especially the upstarts and petty Officers, should be proud and ill natured. and thirdly if I listed I should thereby defraud my Master of his property which in reality I was untill I had fully satisfied him not only what he gave for my redemption but also the expense and trouble together with the Interest and profits which he reasonably might demand on the venture to redeem so poor and despicable an Object as I appeared at that Time when I entered in his Service, which I shall now conclude as finished.

for nothing more remarkable happened unto me in the Service of this [116] worthy Master, whom I may venture to call so without flattery although his natural faculties were rather too much inclined to perturbation which created a sort of disquiettude to himself if matters went contrary to his expectation. yet notwithstanding he was a kind hearted Man not only to his Friends and Neighbours but extended to all even as far as to his Enemies; an affectionate Husband and an indulgent Father to his Children and as for a Master no ways severe. and as for my Mistress I have to say although [her] natural faculties were high and full of ~~fire~~ Spirit which sometimes, by not keeping strictly on her guard, led her astray so as to not escape censure yet notwithstanding this she was endewed with the excellency of sound reason which enables her for the most part to govern her mental faculties so as to deserve the Name of a worthy Woman and I have no reason otherwise than for to sum up her Character in the following Terms: an extraordinary kind Friend and Neighbour, willing and able to reach forth her helping Hands, whether by Day or Night, to all that were truly afflicted, whether by poverty or Disease or any accident incident to human Life. an affectionate Wife, as far as ever I have seen, [to] her Husband, my Master, and a tender Mother to her Children and not only an excellent Mistress to me but also a Mother to me and may I honour and revere her so as long as I draw the Breath of Life.

Mennonites, Schwenkfelders, and Amish. Karen Guenther, "Berks County," in *Beyond Philadelphia: The American Revolution in the Pennsylvania Hinterland*, ed. John B. Frantz and William Pencak (University Park: Pennsylvania State University Press, 1998), 67–84.

Chapter 13: Freedom

Now after the Time of my Indenture was expired I again hired with my Master for six Months after which Time a[314] wrought about amongst the Neighbours by the Day having my Home at my old Masters and assisting him when ever he had any occasion. but I soon perceived that by the many hardships and miseries which I had endured at Sea, together with the accidents on the Land, I was reduced to a state of inability to stand the fatigues of a Day Labourer who always are put to the most Laborious work there. I therefore concluded it would be best for me to learn some Trade and I agreed with one named Hugh Hughes[315] who was a Mason, the bargain I thought [117] was pretty good on my side, being two Months work without Wages and then [wages] according as I improved in the business. this was in the Winter when I agreed and the Work was to begin early in the Spring. but it seemed that my old disappointments had not yet forsaken me for when I thought to begin to work the owner of the Building, named John Reaser,[316] absolutely refused of having any but such as were learned Masons by which means I was disappointed. I then concluded to learn the Shoe maker Trade in the City of Philadelphia but as I was altogether a stranger in that City, I thought it best to get a recommendation to shew that I was no runaway or an Idle spendthrift of a Fellow. upon this I went to one of our Neighbours named Thomas Lightfoot[317] who wrote me a recommendation directed to Arthur Howel[318] who was a Tanner and an Inhabitant of said City. I then took my leave of my Neighbours and Friends and set off in company with one named Penrose Wily[319] who went with his Teams to the City where we arrived safe without any misfortune. but I was greatly mortified and crossed in my expectation, for instead of being metamorphosed or rather refined from a Country Pumpkin[320]

314. I.
315. Listed in the 1790 census for Northumberland County as head of a household with three males under sixteen years and five females. See *HF*, 188.
316. John Reeser Sr. is listed in the 1790 census as head of a household with one other male aged sixteen years or more; John Reezer Jr. is listed in the 1790 census as head of a household with two females and two "other free persons." See *HF*, 37. The elder Reeser appears in the township tax rolls as a large landholder as of 1768, and his son (with no or unlisted landholdings) as of 1784; see *PA*, 145, 247, 379, 505, 641, 764.
317. A brother of Sarah and Joseph Lightfoot; see *Friends' Records*, 208. Listed in the 1790 census for Berks County as head of a household with three males under sixteen, two older males, and six females. See *HF*, 37. Appears in tax rolls throughout the period, in earlier years with no landholdings; see *PA*, 71, 145, 246, 378, 505, 640, 765.
318. Arthur Howell appears in the 1790 census living on Chestnut Street, Philadelphia, with four males under the age of sixteen, one other male, and five females. See *HF*, 225.
319. Penrose Weily is listed in the 1790 census as head of a household with two other males aged sixteen or more, two males under sixteen, and five females. He appears on the township tax rolls from 1780; see *PA*, 379, 506, 641, 766.
320. Bumpkin.

into a Citizen, I was glad to return with the Wings of speed unto the place from whence I came. and I thought I had great occasion to be thankful for to have the good fortune [to] escape the Hands of the Citizens who seemed in great confusion and uproar, it being a little after the surrender of lord Cornwallis,[321] which occasioned a deal of Ostentatious rejoicings as also a great deal of mischief which was performed by a foolish inconsiderate mob whereby many that were worthy and peaceable Citizens greatly suffered, of which I make no doubt but there were many great benefactors, even to such as were the most active in mischief. witness that kind and truly Christian Matron Margaret Haines[322] whose noble Character is so well known by popular applause that a description seems unnecessary, yet notwithstanding all her bounties and far extended Charity [these] would have availed but little had it not been for Rueben's Beer which they did Quaff so eagerly that it satisfied their thirst of doing them mischief and so extinguished that pernicious fire of malice and [illegible] envy. but alas, he that had no Beer to quench the fire, [118] had to burn and suffer no inconsiderable loss, especially the People called Quakers. although there is nothing more certain and reasonable than for him that can or will not sow, [he] can not expect to reap, and so if any Man who can not for Conscience sake or any thing else whatever lend assistance to obtain a Victory, [he] can not rejoice with the Conquerors nor ought he to have a share in the Triumph. but, however, the City being thus in an uproar frighted me so that I was at a stand whether to go to my Counsellor or not but I concluded at last to go and see what Advice I should recive from the said Arthur. and I went but soon perceived I might have spared my going thither for he advised me not to think of learning a Trade in Town, especially at so a critical Time,[323] and he could assure me that it would cost more than I could imagine. this advice, as it was what I expected, proved no disappointment to me, and I returned again to Maiden Creek where I, instead of the awl, laboured awhile longer with the Flale and Pitching Ax.

but not long after I had knowledge that our Neighbouring Shoemaker named George Worrall[324] had a great stroke of work. he was one in general esteemed as both a good and neat workman and I thought the best thing was

321. Lieutenant General Charles, Lord Cornwallis, surrendered his army to Major General George Washington at Yorktown, Virginia, on October 19, 1781, in the last major engagement of the American Revolutionary War.

322. Margaret Wistar Haines was a Quaker elder in the Philadelphia monthly meeting. See Elizabeth Drinker, *The Diary of Elizabeth Drinker*, ed. Elaine F. Crane, 3 vols. (Boston: Northeastern University Press, 1991), 3:2232.

323. The prospect of the war's end would have raised concerns about the economy.

324. George Worrall (1748–1832) married a niece of John Starr's, Deborah Starr, on May 12, 1779; see *Friends' Records*, 313, 386–87, and EMMR. He appears as George Worra in the 1790 census for Berks County as head of a household with six females; see *HF*, 37.

for me to agree with this Man for a certain Time which was to work a Twelve-month without Wages and to find my washing and Idle[325] Diet myself and at the expiration of said period [I would] deliver him ten Bushels of Wheat. upon which I began to work with the Awl in full expectation that at the end of the Year I should be capable of fitting the Foot of a Country Man with a good strong pair of Neats Leather[326] Shoes with a thick soal and high heel well filled with pegs driven up plumb to the head and after I [became] capable of performing this as to fit well, sew and pare well, and drive the peg with a single blow, I then might venture at Cordevan Boots, Morocco Slippers and stuff Shoes with white ramshart[327] toes and a cork heel of a Citizen. but all this proved only like thinking to erect a Castle in the Air for after I had been excercising myself at the Trade for near two Weeks, Work began to be Slack and I had to desist so that I was forced again to exchange the Shoe making Impliments for the Flax Break and Theshing Flale which [119] I swung the chiefest part of the Winter

and in the Spring some of my Friends persuaded me to learn the Weaving Trade to which I seemed no ways inclined but always took it to be the most perplexing business that a Man could go to. yet by the persuasion of my Friends, together with the dislike I had against the fatigues of a Day Labourer, I concluded that perhaps it might be better than I imagined and it was certainly to be preferred to having no Trade at all. upon this I went to one named James Embrice[328] who lived at Tulpehocking where he followed that business. I soon acquainted him with my intention of learning his Trade, also telling him what I designed to give, which was the same agreement before mentioned with the said George Worrall, except all my Diet and washing to be in the bargain but I received no satisfactory reply although he knew both [my] old Master and me very well. yet he could not forebear giving some hums about it and to give me a History of his Apprenticeship, how long and how faithful he had served together with his diligence in his Masters absence by which I quickly percieved that he seemed not to have the good opinion of me which I flatter myself to be my due. but to the contrary he took me [to] be rather slothful, which I could not stomach, although I once had been of that disposition yet it was now become so detestable to me that they could put no greater affront upon me than to think I was a sluggard. but, however, I said but little and return'd again to Maiden Creek leaving him to the said

325. I'd or I would.
326. Leather from cattle.
327. This is one possible reading of a difficult word, perhaps the membrane from the heart of a male sheep, which would be white.
328. James Imbrey is listed in the 1790 census as living in Tulpehocking, Washington County, with four males under the age of sixteen and four females. See *HF*, 256. He married Phebe Starr in 1771; see EMMR.

James Embrice to consider of it. but I made no farther enquiry after his conclusion, for soon after [I heard from] one of our Neighbours named Thomas
Pearson,[329] who drove on the Weaving business and was not only an Artist at
plain Work but also well acquainted with that truly curious Art of weaving
figured Work. I received intelligence from him by his Daughter of Esther
Coles[330] that he had been acquainted with my intention of learning the Weaving Trade. therefore, as the Time of his Apprentice was expired if [I] chose
[120] to try at it I might come as soon as I pleased. upon this I abandoned the
Impliments of Agriculture and went [to] exert myself at flinging the Shuttle
which I performed [and] formed with so much dexterity that my first Webb,
which contained thirty five Yards of tow Linnen,[331] was accomplished in a little better than a Week which led my Master and others in a belief that I would
be an expert workman. but as I ran up the Hill with uncomon alacrity I
thereby arrived soon on the top, where I did and shall remain untill Age and
infirmity will oblige me to crawl back again by degrees till at last I shall be
covered by obscurity and sunk into Oblivion.

Now while I was fulfiling the agreement contracted between my new Master and me I became so truly charmed with his company and agreeable temper, which consisted of innocent chearfulness mixed with a familiar affibility
and tenderness, that after the said Time was expired I saw no place more
suitable for my abode than with him. he asked of me 16£ Per Annum, which
I thought reasonable for my Board and Washing, together with the Loom
and Impliment of Weaving. and after the expiration of the first Year I agreed
for an other at the rate of the 12£ because I had some Reeds and Geers[332] of
my own but towards Fall the work began to come in slack which obliged me
to leave the Shop and go at journey work with one Jesse Penrose,[333] but as
soon as work began to be strong at Home I returned and so between the
two places I was furnished with nearly constant employ till the said Thomas
Pearson, who was an Ancient Man and a Widower, broke up Housekeeping
and moved to his Brother in Law John Parvins[334] and from thence to the New

329. This Thomas Pearson is not the same person as the schoolmaster but is his uncle. He
is listed in the 1790 census for Berks County as living with another male under sixteen years
of age (*HF*, 37), and is listed as a weaver in the township tax rolls for 1767 and 1768. See *PA*,
70, 144.
330. Thomas Pearson's second child, born December 8, 1747. See *Friends' Records*, 258.
331. Tow linen is the roughest and cheapest grade, used for bags, work clothing, and similar
items. Adrienne D. Hood, *The Weaver's Craft: Cloth, Commerce, and Industry in Early Pennsylvania*
(Philadelphia: University of Pennsylvania Press, 2003), 162.
332. Reeds are devices that set the density of the cloth; gears could refer to many of the complex devices required in weaving, but perhaps here to a spoolwinder and spools. Ibid., 91.
333. Penrose married a niece of John Starr's, Sarah Starr, on May 7, 1780; see *Friends'
Records*, 270–71, 310–11. Listed as a weaver in the township tax list for 1780; see *PA*, 378.
334. Pearson's youngest sister was married to John Parvin, a brother of Francis Parvin Jr.;
Friends' Records, 250–51, 258–59. John Parvin is listed in the 1790 census for Berks County as

Purchase in Roaring Creek Vally.[335] I then wrought altogether with the said Jesse Penrose, except the Work was too slack for us both to be employed, [and] I exercised myself a little at Farming business.

Now while I lived with the said Thomas Pearson in the third Year, I became acquainted with a Young Woman [121] named Ann Tomson with whom I, with the approbation of her Parents, joined in Marriage on the 11th Day of May 1786[336] but I was no sooner entered into Wedlock than I found by experience the Truth of a saying, which is that "a young Man is always uneasy and dissatisfied till he enjoys the odd Rib, which is his dear Companion, his second self and Co Partner of all his joy and prosperity, [but who] is also his adversity and Grief."[337] yet notwithstanding after he is arrived to the height [of] happines in that point, he soon finds that as he first only wanted a Bosom Friend and Companion, he now is in need of almost everything else which I may truly say was the Case with me. for as my Companion was of but low circumstance in the World, it drained my little Purse amazingly[338] which I had laid up as a saying is for a rainy Day. but being favoured by Heaven with Health and activity so as to exert myself in labour and having furnished myself with necessary Household Stuff and Utensils, I stood as it were on a poise till I had rested myself from the career I [had been] taking down Hill and so began to regain again as fast as I was capable my former

living with two females; see *HF*, 37. Appears in many township tax rolls; see *PA* 144, 247, 378, 505, 640, 765. He married Mary Pearson in 1768; EMMR.

335. The New Purchase refers to land acquired by treaty in 1764. Violence, including the Wyoming Massacre, troubled the early history of the region. At the end of the Revolutionary War, "after the frontier settlements in Northumberland County became once more a peaceful land in which to dwell, many of the Friends returned to the Catawissa region in or about the year 1785." John E. Eshelman, "The Journal of Moses Roberts—A Minister of Oley," *Historical Review of Berks County* 8 (April 1943): 74. Friends' Meetings were established at Roaring Creek and at Catawissa, neighboring townships in what is now in Columbia County, near Bellefonte.

336. Frederick Whitehead married Ann Thomson, daughter of Michael Thompson, at her father's home in Maidencreek Township. The Rev. C. F. Wildbahn of Trinity Evangelical Lutheran Church in Reading performed the ceremony on May 11, 1786; see the Records of the Trinity Evangelical Lutheran Church, 1751–1812: Baptisms, Marriages, Burials, Confirmations, and Communions (bound photocopies of originals, n.p., n.d.), Historical Society of Berks County, Reading, Pennsylvania, 16. See also the copy of the Records of the Trinity Evangelical Lutheran Church at the HSP. This was the only time Whitehead had a recorded contact with the church. None of his children was baptized here or elsewhere in the county. If Ann Thomson Whitehead was forty-one at her last child's birth, then she was five years younger than her husband, married at age twenty-four, and lived to be fifty-seven.

337. Compare "But in Marriage do thou be wise; prefer the Person before Money; Vertue before Beauty, the Mind before the Body: Then thou hast a Wife, a Friend, a Companion, a Second Self; one that bears an equal Share with thee in all thy Toyls and Troubles." William Penn, *Some Fruits of Solitude in Reflections and Maxims*, in *The Harvard Classics*, ed. Charles W. Elliot (1682; reprint, New York: Collier, 1909), 348.

338. It appears that Ann Thomson did not bring a dowry and that the couple had to acquire the household goods—pots and pans and bedding—that other brides brought with them to a marriage.

Station and although it was exceeding slow yet it is better for a Man if he only enjoys a Groat[339] clear at the end of the Year than to be threepence behind hand.

the greatest difficulty which attended me after joining in a Marriage state was to have a convenient Dwelling House, for there happened to be but few or next to none that were to be let or rent, and such as were to be rented [had] so many inconveniencies attended them that nothing but necessity would entice a Man to choose any for his Abode. the one I rented was a Cottage belonging to one Jacob Maura,[340] Yeoman in Maiden Creek Township, but it had no Window Glass nor as much as a Chimny in it but the worst of all was an exceeding bad Roof so at any Time when it rained we might almost as well be out of Doors and there was little or no good property except the two Elements, which is Fire and Water. this made our stay but short and at the expiration of a Year we left it and moved to a House belonging to one John Hutton, Yeoman in the said Township. here we dwelt for the space of two Years in perfect harmony with the Family of the aforesaid George Worrall and after the [122] expiration of the said period we moved again to a House of John Parvins, Yeoman in said Township. and at the end of the Year we moved again [to] a House of Thomas Lightfoots, Yeoman in said Township,[341] where we again dwelt the space of two Years and from thence removed back again to the House of the aforesaid John Parvin where I now reside through the blessings of Heaven in a pretty good State of Health but nearly two Months before my [last] removal, being the latter end of February, I was seized with a Rheumatic disorder which continued nearly till the month of June before I was capable of exercising myself at any kind of labour which alarmed me greatly so that I began to fear the consequence which certainly would have been poverty and distress had I remained so. but it pleased Heaven to restore my Limbs again to a good degree of strength and activity so that I, contrary to my expectation, am in a capacity of exerting them to the sustenance of myself and Family and although I am but of low circumstance in the World, yet thanks be to Heaven I am not pestered by poverty so as to

339. A coin worth four pence.

340. Jacob Maurer was not a Quaker but an ethnic German. He is listed in the 1790 census as living in Montgomery County with one male under sixteen years of age and one female; see *HF*, 166. He appears in Maidencreek Township tax rolls throughout the period. In 1794, for example, he was among the richest taxpayers, owning 280 acres and operating a tannery; see *PA* 70, 144, 246, 378, 505, 640, 765. This was apparently the only time that Whitehead chose to live with Germans.

341. Whitehead is listed as living next to Thomas Lightfoot in the 1790 census; see *HF*, 37. Whitehead's household included one male under sixteen years of age and two females, which is one more female than accounted for in the listing of his children; see Appendix C to his memoir. Perhaps a sister-in-law or other relative of his wife was in residence.

fear the Bailiffs to enter my dwelling and seize myself or the little effects I possess for Debt. my Table also, though not covered with Dainties, yet for the most part contains a good brown Loaf with a piece of meat and if destitute of Meat something else to supply its place as Milk, Butter or Cheese. and as my Companion has a share of pride in keeping her Garden clean, we are supplied with plenty of Truck as Cabbage, Potatoes, Beans, Peas &c. provided the Season be favourable.

> For without it we may both plant and sow
> But O we plant, we sow and toil in vain
> For little we shall have to reap or mow
> If Heaven is pleas'd for to withhold the Rain
> Or if too long the Sun's proliphic Beam
> Veil'd in a Cloud obscurely flies it's way
> Each tender plant turns to a fading Green
> And all things languish for the Lord of Day [123]
> But Rain or Sun alternately may come
> And drooping Nature with fresh Life suply
> Yet there is nothing sure beneath the Sun
> For Flies and Worms may still the plant destroy

And although my Tenement is not attended with every conveniency of Life, it yet in some degree is charming as to its situation. for when I turn myself to the left I behold a beautiful Orchard laden with a variety of excellent Fruit, of which by the generosity of my Landlord I am at liberty to partake as my own.

And when I turn to the Right I am charmed on beholding a fine enamolet Mead decked with a Carpet of vivid green, intermixed with little Flowers curiously decorated by the Pencil of Nature which together with other solutory[342] Herbage not only provides this sustenance of my Landlords Cattle[343] but also distill its juicy sustenance in the Udder of my Cow and furnishes her with Provender. and fierce Acquarius[344] shakes the Air with Storms and open the Northern Magazine to send forth Hail, Ice and Snow.

And again when I look before me I am entertained with a Fountain of transparent Water as also a soft murmuring Rivelet which for the greatest part

342. Salutary.
343. John Parvin owned four cows, according to the 1794 Maidencreek Township tax list.
344. The constellation Aquarius, the Water Carrier, visible in the night sky from late spring to early winter. Its association with water may stem from the fact that the sun passes through this constellation during the rainy season or late winter, in February and March. See Adrian Room, *Dictionary of Astronomical Names* (London: Routledge, 1988), 59.

of the Year [runs] Serpentine through the Mud till through many Meanders
it joins the fair Streams of Maiden Creek and from thence in curling Edies
flows into the River Schuylkill which are then all three so united [as to] discharge themselves with many more into the Delaware where they roll on in
Waves Majestic untill they arrive to the Source from whence they came.

[It is] A true Emblem of the Soul of Man, who after many windings while
in this Tabernacle of Clay, at last arrives from the precipices and cataracks of
affliction to that great and everlasting Source from which it may reasonably
boast to have its being.

And lastly when I turn back my Eyes are entertained with the sight of a
Barn glowing with the bounties of Autumn, as also the Mountains whose
lofty Summits often entertains my ravished Eyes with a truly delightful prospect of a diversified [124] Landscape: Farms and Plantations, little Hillocks
and levelit plains intermixed with Woodland and crystal Streams, so that I
frequently have to say within myself:

> Here let the Limners curious Pencil try
> If all its Art can with Dame Nature vie

And although none of those things are my own, yet I rejoice and am truly
delighted to see them and by being content to live in that Sphere which
Heaven is pleased to place me, I not only enjoy a tranquility of Mind but all
the sweets and delights of a rural Life.

Having thus detained the Reader with the History of my Life for nearly
the space of thirty eight Years, I shall here conclude as nearly finished, for I
make no doubt that it already consists of too many matters too simple and
insignificant to afford the Reader any amusement. yet I flatter myself that if
they are destitute of diversion they may perhaps prove a Lesson of Instruction, especially if it should come to the perrusal of a Youth who like myself
might reject the Counsels of the aged and follow his own presumptuous will,
for I can truly say that from the Moment I resolved to abandon my Friends
and Native Land I was hurled, as it were, from a state of tranquility into
the Vicisitude of continual vexation and disappoints, which remain'd while I,
with a predominant eagerness, pursued the Phantom of Fortune. by whose
whispers I was deluded so as to fancy myself to accumulate Wealth by heaps
and not to be subservient to the caprice of a Master who was in reality no
ways capricious or hard and had I remain'd in his service to the Age of maturity I, without the least doubt, would have been placed in a state of Genteel
business whereby I might have gained my sustenance with ease and I would
have been unacquainted with the tenth part of that misery which I experienced. but the best remedy that now can be procured is to conclude that all

has wrought for the best. so [I] close here my History [125] with the following Prayer of the engenious Abraham Cowley:[345]

> For the few Hours of Life allotted me
> Give me great God but Bread and Liberty
> I'll beg no more if more thou'rt pleas'd to give
> I'll thankfully that overplus receive
> But if beyond this no more be freely sent
> I'll thank for this and go away content[346]

Chapter 14: "Verses On Severel Occasions"

Their is know need to Detain the reeder with an appoligy concerning the following work Since I Already have Said Sufficiant In the preface of my History, only this: that I Composed it Chief In my head when Buisy at work And So noted it down at So[me times] in the Dusk of Evening, till I could meet with achance [to have it] Coppyed off for my own amusement.

And as I only Possess avery faint Spark of Poetick Fire, it would Be but vanity to think myself A Poet. But yet I hope Since their is Nothing to give modisty ablush, that Simplicity will pardon its Defects and perhaps together here and there for her Amusement. and if so I Care but little for the learned and the men of taste, who I make no doubt will Behold it with an Eye of Deresion and with A Sarcastic Look throw itby. [126]

Pastral[347]

> Upon a toomb Beneath a shady thorn
> Reclind Sad Deman his ill fate to mourn
> Pensive and Sad he leand upon his Crook
> Till Chearfull Dafness, thus the Silence Broke
>   What ails my friend, what molencoly gloam
> hangs on thy Brow befiting but the Toomb
> has Some fierce beast thy tender flock destroyd

---

345. Abraham Cowley (1618–67), English poet.

346. This prayer concludes Cowley's essay "On Liberty"; see Abraham Cowley, *The Complete Works in Verse and Prose of Abraham Cowley*, 2 vols. (Edinburgh: T. and A. Constable, 1881), 2:311–14, quotation on 314.

347. Pastoral poetry has its roots in classical conventions. Whitehead writes in the form of an eclogue, a dialogue between two shepherds, and employs common pastoral themes of bucolic rural life, loss, and mourning. Damon and Daphnis were first used as characters by Virgil in "The Eclogues," written in 37 BCE. Later poets, including Andrew Marvell, also used these names to identify shepherds in pastoral poems.

Or thy Sad Soul with horrid yells Anoid
Or hast thou lost By Death's all conkering hand
Some tender brother or aspecial Friend
Or has the charming mira[348] provd unkind
Atell thy friend what Clouds thy anctious mind
    Deaman
No Ravenous Beast has my Fair flock Destroid
Nor my Sad Soul with horrid yells Anoid
Nor have I lost abrother nor afriend
If So I Should Submit to heavens Command
Nor will the Lovely mira Slight her Swain
While Rain and Sun Alternate Cheers the Plane
But Pomerania Oh for her I mourn
And I Shoose[349] my toomb Beneath this Shady thorn
    Dafness
Oh Pomerania, Name forever Dear
It well Deserves aSithe, agroan, atear
Yet Shall her Son then thus forever Mourn
An Heir to him, a Cheerful Day beborn
Shall grief and Sorrow all his Bliss Destroy
And wail each Day from Every Ray of Joy
Shall he that in Mays Vernel Beauty Bloom,d[350]
For Dark December Seek to be intomb,d
Tis true Each herb Each tender plant and Flowr
That Springs Spontanious at Mays Genial Show,r
In Dark December are Nomore be Seen
Nor all the Smiling Beautys of the Green [127]
[missing] Man Not So whose Soul By heaven Refind
[missing] yet Bare misfortune with a will Refin,d
[missing] as arock in Every Shock Remain
No once to Murmer or at heaven Exclame
    Deaman
Tis True we are by grecous heaven Refind
And ought to Suffer with A heart Resignd
Yet man is weak and Shrinks Beneath the Blow
Like yon Sweet flower Beneath A Storm of Snow
Oh Pomerania I Shall Neir forget

---

348. Myrrha was the mother of Adonis in Greek mythology and supposedly held an "incestuous love for her own father." See *Brewer's Dictionary of Phrase and Fable* (London: Cassell & Co., 1957), 803.

349. Choose.

350. The comma before the "d" in this and following words is in place of an apostrophe.

Thy Sweet Enjoyments But the Loss Regret
   Dafness
  Tis Sad Reflection And a stroke Severe
To be Such Distance from aland So Dear
Where miles Count thousands and the Roaring of [Seas?]
Extends her bellows in awild Commotion
Yet Shepard Sease, oh Sease thy Plaintive Strane
Fair Pennslyvania Shall assuage thy Pains
  A Provance charming and aland So fair
Can without Doubt my Deamons Loss Repare
   Deamons
A Provance Charming and aland So fair
Can Neaver Neaver thus my loss Repair
Whilst Crimes and frauds of Anarky Doth Rain
And human Blood lies Clodded on the Plain
Thou well Remembrest how with Ease we fed
Our flocks Secure Closeby afountain head
Whilst whiterobe Peace Sat on Adulphas[351] Throne
And Sweedish Sheppards Call,d their Flocks their own
On Strelas[352] plains our Shady tents we spread
And without fear the tender lanbkins led
As Soon as Phosphar wak,d the Silver Dawn
And Pearly due Drops glitter,d ore the Lawn
[End]

[This page, the reverse of the one above, is quite ragged from age, and most of the margins are missing. It is a rhymed draft of an advertisement presented in two columns, first in English and then in German. The German is not given here. The words in parentheses are approximations of the missing material.]

       [illegible line]
      Ten Shilling Reward[353]
Only honest hearts of men giv ear
For naught but honesty will care
To listen to my loss so great
Which I here unto you relate
A little flock of eight fine Sheep

351. Gustavus II Adolphus, Swedish king, reigned 1611–32.
352. Stralsund.
353. Thanks to Emily Rush, Guilford College, for help in this transcription. A search through surviving Berks County newspapers indicates that this was never published. Handwritten copies may have been posted in public places.

All Through the last cold winter keep
(now tha)t all of them are gone a Stray
(at least) not now just till the day.
in the latter part of June
twas on a thuseday noon
(that) they all disapeard
(just) two weeks after they were sheard
(their) marks I nearly have forgot
(some) were mark'd and some were not
(one had) a stump tail and Lopd ear
(brought about) by frost severe
(the others) I have not forgot
(one) to ear has a black spot
[missing] one other and five years
[missing] now who knows
(how many) of them doth remain
(man)y perhaps are cheifly Slain
(sa)fe I sought them fare and near
nothing of them I can hear
Such makes me fear, and think, they are
(taken) from me I know not where
These some graceless picaroon[354]
(hides) and kills them as his own
(I) hope men would disdain
(their) conscience with Sheeps blood to Stain
(and any) women child or man
(that) helps me to my Sheep again
(I prom)is him up on my word
will have in full th'above reward
as far the charge there be
So shall be paid by me
[illegible] a needfull h[int?] to tell
[illegible] for township dwell
[illegible] (no)t a mile from Carters Town
the place at Hamburg known
near . . . I give
[one line missing and illegible]
Windsor Township Berks County
Fred:ck Whitehead 9th mo. 15th 17[missing]

354. Rogue, thief, pirate.

Appendix A: Will and Estate Sale

In the name of God Amen.

I, Frederick Whitehead of Colerain township, Hamilton county in the State of Ohio,[355] being weak in body but of sound mind, memory and understanding, do make and ordain this my last will and Testament in manner and form following (towit): It is my will and desire that my wife Ann should have, so long as she remains my widow, all my estate of what kind soever the same be. but at my widow's decease or marriage, as the case may be, I will and desire that the residue and remainder of my estate be equally divided among my seven children (viz) John, Michael, William, Jesse, Maria, Esther and Sarah, except my son John who is to have forty dollars more than any of the rest. I also will and devise that my son William be placed out to some trade as soon as convenient and that Jesse remain two years with his brother John and then be put out to some trade. And lastly, I nominate and Appoint my Brother in law Michael Thompson And my Son John Whitehead to be the Executors of this my will, hereby revoking all other wills, legacies and bequests by me heretofore made and declaring this and no other to be my last Will and Testament.

In witness whereof I have hereunto set my hand and seal this twenty fifth day of April in the year of our *Lord one thousand eight hundred and fifteen

Frederick Whitehead [illegible]

[page end, continued on other side of the paper]
*Signed, sealed, published, pronounced and declared by the testator as his last will and testament in the presence of us who in his presence and at his request have subscribed as witnesses:

Abner K. Starr[356]

John Brick[357]

---

355. Whitehead may have been in Ohio only a few years. He lived in Maidencreek at least through 1794, appearing on tax roles for 1789, 1791, 1793, and 1794; he is listed as living in Windsor Township, Berks County, Pennsylvania, in 1800; and "Frederick Whitehall" appears as a farmer in Catawissa Township in Northumberland County, Pennsylvania, in the 1810 census. The listing of household members for "Whitehall" corresponds roughly with the number and ages of Whitehead's children as listed in Appendix C (although two children who would have been seventeen and eighteen years old in 1810 appear to be listed in the sixteen-or-under category of the census). See reels 52–53 of Berks County Tax Lists (microfilm of originals, HSP); *Pennsylvania in 1800: A Computerized Index to the 1800 Federal Population Schedules of the State of Pennsylvania*, ed. John "D" Stemmons (Salt Lake City: Stemmons, 1972), 655, and *Population Schedules of the Third Census of the United States 1810*, roll 53, Pennsylvania (Washington, D.C.: National Archives, 1953), 245.

356. Abner Starr was a nephew of John Starr. In 1790 he and his father, Moses Starr Jr., received certificates of removal to Roaring Creek Valley Meeting. In April 1807 Abner Starr requested a certificate of removal from the Exeter Monthly Meeting of Friends in Berks County to join the Miami Monthly Meeting in Ohio, which was apparently granted in May of the following

[the following is written between two folds of this page, on what would be the outside face of the paper after folding]

Frederick Whitehead's last will and testament presented, proved, allowed and filed by the two subscribing witnesses. Abner K. Starr and John Brick in open court August 7, 1815, Executors Sworn by John S. Gano[358]
[new page]
State of Ohio   sct[359]
Hamilton county

       Be it remembered that in the Term of August in the year of our Lord one thousand eight hundred and fifteen of the court of common pleas held at the court house in the Town of Cincinnati in said county, Personally appeared in open court Abner K. Starr and John Brick, the two subscribing Witnesses to the alow last Will and Testament of Frederick Whitehead, deceased, who being duly sworn according to law depose and that they were personally present when the Testator singned, sealed, published and declared the within instrument of writing to be his last will and Testament, and these Deponents further say that they believed the said Frederick Whitehead dec'd to be of sound mind, memory, and Judgement, and that they subscribed their names as Witnesses thereto in the presence of the said Testator,
Sworn and subscribed
Before me in open court
August 16: 1815
    John S. Gano clerk

---

year. He was received by the Miami Meeting in June 1809. Abner "R." Starr is listed as residing in Colerain Township, Hamilton County, Ohio, in the 1820 census; Abner "K." Starr appears in the same location in the 1830 census. Frederick Whitehead would follow, moving to nearby Catawissa Township before 1810 and to Ohio by 1815. See *Friends' Records,* 312–13; John E. Eshelman, "Descendants of Moses and Deborah Starr—Early Quaker Settlers of Maiden Creek Valley," *Historical Review of Berks County* 12 (1947): 74; Kenneth L. Cook, "Glimpses of Life in a Frontier Friends Meeting," *Historical Review of Berks County* 60 (summer 1995): 142; William Wade Hinshaw, *Encyclopedia of American Quaker Genealogy,* vol. 5 (Ann Arbor, 1940; reprint, Baltimore: Genealogical Publishing Company, 1973, 1974), 125; *Ohio 1820 Census, Index A-Z* (Bountiful, Utah: Heritage Quest, 1999), 494; and *1830 Federal Population Census, Ohio: Index,* 2 vols. (Columbus: Ohio Library Foundation, 1964), 2:1172.

    357. John Brick is listed as residing in Colerain Township, Hamilton County, Ohio, in 1820; see *Ohio 1820 Census Index.*

    358. A son of the chaplain John Gano who served with the American army in the Revolutionary War, John S. Gano was an early settler of Cincinnati and one of the founders of Covington, Kentucky, in 1818. See Devereux Lake, *A Personal Narrative of Some Branches of the Lake Family in America* (Lorain, Ohio: Lorain Printing Co., 1937), 127.

    359. Abbreviation for the Latin *scripsit,* meaning "he wrote this."

State of Ohio   sct
Hamilton county
        Whereas in the Term of August in the year of our Lord one thou-
sand and eight hundred and fifteen the last Will and testament of Frederick
Whitehead dec'd a true copy whereof is hereunto annexed was proven and
allowed by the Judges of the Court of Common Pleas for the County aforesaid. And the said deceased having [page end—copy of other side of page is
missing]

The Conditions of the present Vendue held the 16th day of September 1819[360]
are such that the highest bidder shall be the buyer, any person purchasing
to the amount of two Dollars and upwards shall have six Months credit by
giving their notes with approved security, and all under that sum to be cash,
any person bidding off any article and not complying with the Conditions of
this sale shall return the article with 25 per cent to be sold at a second sale
and if not sold as high at the second sale as at the first, the former purchaser
to make good the deficiency.

> Michael Thompson
> John Whitehead
> Executors of the last will of
> Frederick Whitehead.
> Deceased

$, Cts
162, 62

Names	articles sold	
Abraham Augustus	1 chair	0.34½
John Whitehead	1 do[361]	0.31¼
William Tomlinson	1 do	0.50
John Whitehead	1 ax	1.50
Abner K. Starr	1 spade	0.93¾
John Whitehead	1 log chain	3-00
John Whitehead	1 pair steelyard	2-37½
Henry Wilsey	1 pair pincers	0-18¾
Abner K. Starr	shovel and Tongs	1-06¼

360. This sale is in accordance with the terms of Whitehead's will that the estate be distributed among the children after his wife's death. Note that there is little farming equipment and
no weaving equipment. Other items we would expect to find in his possession—e.g., tables,
clothing, etc.—are absent. These had either been sold or had been distributed among the children at an earlier date, so that these remaining items only hint at the material wealth accumu-
lated by the Whiteheads during their lives. They had acquired some luxury items: silver spoons,
a tea service, books, and a looking glass.
    361. Do., abbreviation for "ditto."

Michael Thompson	1 basket	0-62½
John Brick	1 barn shovel	0-84½
David Dubbenhire	1 tin horn	0-50
John Thompson	smoothing irons	1-62½
Abner K. Starr	1 spining Wheel[362]	2-43¾
Abner K. Starr	2 Ladles	1-56¼
John Whitehead	1 brass kettle	0-50
Abner K. Starr	1 tea kettle	2-90
Joseph Gross	1 iron teakettle	2-06¼
John Thompson	1 dinner pot	2-75
Abner K. Starr	1 do do	1-31¼
John Thompson	1 spider[363]	1-00
do do	1 bake kettle	2.31¼
William Wilkinson	1 iron kettle	6.25
Michael Thompson	1 do do	3.75
Henry Sedam	1 grid iron	0.81¼
Michael Thompson	tramel chain	2-25
Henry Wilsey	1 iron kettle	3-00
Abner K. Starr	sarver & bread basket	1-00
do do do	Tea cups and saucers	0.50
John Whitehead	2 bowls	0.34½
		[page end]

amount brought forward—

Abner K. Starr	tea pots	1-25
Abraham Augustus	pewter bason and moulds	0-45
John Brick	1 pewter dish	1,37½
Abraham Augustus	1 pewter dish	1,25
do do	1 do - do	0,68¾
Henry Wilsey	knife box knives & forks	2,50
Henry Sedam	5 pewter plates	2,00
Francis Hedges	6 do do	3,18¾
Joseph Gross	1 straner	0,25
do do	pepper box and plates	0,18¾
Abraham Augustus	1 coffee pot	0,32
Joseph Gross	1 coffee mill	0,45
William Tomlinson	Grater & candlestick	0,39
John Whitehead	sausage stuffer	0,62½

362. The only sign of cloth production. A spinning wheel could spin both linen and wool thread, but one wheel was insufficient to supply yarn to a full-time weaver; six to twelve spinners were required to supply thread for each weaver. Hood, *Weaver's Craft*, 72, 74.
363. A spider is a frying pan with legs that hold it above the hot coals of the fireplace.

Michael Thompson	spons (Tea silver)	4,50
William Whitehead	1 slate	0,50
Michael Thompson	1 sifter & lantern	0,50
William Buckhanon	hammer and brush	0,12½
John Whitehead	1 sifter	1.18¾
Abner K. Starr	fire pan	2,56¼
William Whitehead	1 bible	6,00
Saml. Shannon	do do	1,18¾
John Whitehead	spelling book & testament	0,56¼
David Dubbenhire	3 books	0,50
Abner K. Starr	1 looking glass	0,50
do do do	beadsteads bead & beding	20,00
John Whitehead	1 bead	3,45
Michael Whitehead	1 chest	0,62½
Mr Tomlinson	1 cow	18,50
William Wilkinson	1 do	19,25
John Whitehead	1 bell and collar	2,12¼
John Thompson	bread trey	0,56½
Samuel Shannon	1 keg	0,25
Henry Wilsey	1 Tub	0,75
John Whitehead	vinegar keg	0.45
do, do	1 barrel	0,06¼
Jacob Chambers	1 Fryingpan	0,31¼
John Whitehead	1 Keeler[364]	0,43¾
James Chambers	funel and cream cup	0,25
Benjamin Mckewen	case drawers	8,00
William Wilkinson	1 bead stead	0,56¼
John Thompson	1 tin Kettle	0,25
Michael Thompson	pot chain	2,25
Wm Whitehead	Thos. Chalkleys Journal[365]	0,50
John Whitehead	iron wedg	1,12

[page end]

364. A keeler is a shallow tub.

365. Thomas Chalkley (1675–1741), *The Journal of the Life, Travels, and Christian Experiences of that Antient, Faithful Servant of Jesus Christ, Thomas Chalkley, Written by Himself*, first published in 1747. He was a Quaker mariner and traveling minister along the Atlantic seaboard and in Great Britain. His journal, frequently republished, often with other documents, was widely read in the Quaker community.

Appendix B

A ~
PROPHECY OF THE ∞
REVOLUTIONS AND COMOTIONS
OF
THE ∞ WORLD ~

in 1794 there will be few or no forms of Religion observed in France.
    1795 a destructive disunion will ensue amongst the Powers of Europe
    1796 there will be a great sheding of Human blood by sea and Land
    1797 Gog and Magog[366] shall rise to make war with the Nations.
    1798 A great distraction will thin the inhabitants of the East
    1799 A descendent of David[367] shall rise to perform such acts of grace
        derived from the power of Almighty as to destroy Gog and Magog,
        and cause all Nations in the year Eighteen hundred to be not only
        of one Religion but of one Heart and Mind united forever in the
        bonds of Love and true felicity.
    Happy the Man that lives to see it[368]

[Appendix C: List of the Births of John Frederick and Ann Thomson Whitehead's Children]

Sarah Whitehead was born the 13th of March 1807. 4 o'clock at night.[369]

                             [page end, continued on other side]

John Whitehead was born on the 8th day of the 6th Mo 1788 at 10 a clock in the morning under the sign of Leo ~[370]

Jesse Whitehead was born the 23d of the 12th m[o] 1789 nearly at 5 a clock in the Morning under the Signs Pisces and Aris. Died on the 11th of the first Mo the Same Year.

∞

366. Gog is chief prince of Meshech and Tubal, who will fail to conquer Israel at the end of the world, and, according to Ezekiel 38:2, Magog is his country. In the Book of Revelation, 20:8, the leaders are Gog and Magog, as heads of the nations of the world pitted against God.

367. A possible reference to the second coming of Christ.

368. This apocalyptic vision, apparently composed c. 1793, indicates the profound impact of the early stages of the French Revolution on the working poor.

369. This entry appears to have been added much later, when the writer ran out of room on the other side of this page.

370. There is no indication that the children were ever baptized. Whitehead may have followed Quaker precepts or may have been influenced by revolutionary anticlericalism. As Adrienne Hood notes, "because weavers carried out most stages of cloth production within their own households, a large family was a real asset." Hood, *Weaver's Craft*, 28.

Lydia Whitehead was born the 14th 11th Mo. 179[2] at 4 a clock in the morning under Aris, and Tauris.

∞

Michael Whitehead was born the 7th of the 3 Mo 1793 nearly at 4 a clock P.M. under Capricorn.

∞

William Whitehead was born the 18th of the 7th [Mo] 1795 at 2 a clock in the morning, under Capricorn.

∞

Anna Whitehead was born the 4th of the 4th Mo 1797 under Cancer and Leo ~

∞

Jesse Whitehead was born the 5th of the 7th mo 179[?] at near nine o clock P.M. under the sign Leo.

∞

Maria Whitehead was born the 17th of May 1801 at one oclock at night under the signs Cancer and Leo.

∞

Esther Whitehead was born the 10th of the 10th mo 1803 Nearly 9 oclock morning.

Part II: Johann Carl Büttner

Introduction
On the Trail of Johann Carl Büttner

At first glance, the story of Johann Carl Büttner seems beyond belief. The narrative reads more like the plot for a miniseries with a colorful historical setting than an accurate accounting of an immigrant servant's experiences in the American colonies. Yet the narrative stands up to scrutiny and most of the seemingly far-fetched tales can be authenticated.

Born in 1754 in Senftenberg, Saxony, Büttner was the third son of a minister who, with his wife, eventually had eleven children. After receiving schooling in preparation for the university, Büttner decided not to attend and instead was apprenticed to a surgeon in Camenz,[1] where he learned the trade of barber-surgeon. After completing his apprenticeship he resisted his father's desire that he complete his studies at Dresden's medical school, instead choosing to travel in search of his fortune. In the winter of 1772, having traveled and practiced his trade without becoming wealthy, he found himself in Hamburg. There Büttner met up with VOC (Dutch East India Company) recruiters who promised to get him an interview for a position as ship's surgeon with the VOC if he would sign up and go to Amsterdam with them. He did so but failed to get the position. With his debt to the recruiting agents mounting, he agreed to sail for the American colonies as a redemptioner immigrant. After an unusually difficult voyage he arrived in Philadelphia, where he was sold as a servant to a Quaker farmer in New Jersey. He ran away but was captured and returned to his owner. Some time later Büttner

1. Now Kamenz, located about fifteen miles northeast of Dresden.

broke a plow, and his master struck him. Büttner complained to a neighboring magistrate, who ordered Büttner's master to sell him. He did so; Büttner was sold to a New Jersey tavern keeper. With his new master's permission, Büttner joined an American regiment of German servants formed shortly after the start of the War of Independence. He deserted his regiment during its first engagement and joined a troop of Hessians with whom he remained until the battle of Red Bank. At Red Bank he was wounded and gave himself up to the Americans. He was befriended by the surgeon at the American hospital and became the surgeon's serving man and assistant. The surgeon asked that Büttner be exempted from prisoner exchanges and arranged safe passage for him to Philadelphia, where Büttner hoped to find a way back to Germany. Unable to find passage, he signed on with an American privateer headed to the French West Indies, but when the privateer captured a British ship, Büttner was put on board as one of the crew who would sail the prize back to Philadelphia. On board the prize ship, Büttner befriended the British captives and, joining to the British side, he aided them in retaking the ship in return for a promise that he would be sent to Germany when the Hessian troops returned. The ship, now under the orders of the British captain, was diverted to New York and, once arrived, Büttner was reassigned to his former Hessian regiment. He was given a position as barber-surgeon and spent the rest of the war with them near New York City, returning to Germany with them in 1783. There he married, settled down, and finished his certification to become a surgeon. At the age of seventy, he wrote his memoirs.

The VOC

The Verinigde Oostindische Compagnie (VOC or United East India Company) was the result of a veritable free-for-all, among companies in Holland and Zeeland, in the importation of pepper and spices from the Spice Islands and Java.[2] Fierce competition and unregulated trade had created broad and unpredictable market fluctuations both in the islands and in Europe, and created a sharp drop in the prices commanded by these goods on the European market. In order to forestall complete disaster, the companies involved requested that the state step in to organize and regulate the Dutch trade in the East Indies. Formed in 1602, the VOC comprised six chambers, Amsterdam, Zeeland, Hoorn, Enkhuizen, Delft, and Rotterdam. Each chamber operated independently of the others, but all were subject to governance by a federated

2. Jonathan Israel, *The Dutch Republic: Its Rise, Greatness, and Fall* (New York: Oxford University Press, 1995), 320–22.

board of directors. These companies held exclusive Dutch rights to shipping and trade east of the Cape of Good Hope or through the Straits of Magellan.[3]

Between its formation in 1602 and its dissolution in 1798, the VOC embarked nearly half a million soldiers and sailors in its ships to the East Indies.[4] Hiring took place irregularly, prior to voyages, rather than steadily. Because of the huge and irregular demand for personnel, the Netherlands alone could not provide enough able-bodied men willing to undertake the long and often risky tour of duty with the VOC. This gave rise to a system of recruitment run by private brokers, called *volkhouders,* in which agents traveled throughout Europe searching for recruits.[5] These agents provided transportation to the chamber cities, food, and shelter to the potential recruits, as well as trying to place them with the VOC. Each potential recruit signed a contract, called a *ceel,* guaranteeing repayment to the agent of the debt incurred by the *volkhouder* on the customer's behalf. The VOC worked in concert with *volkhouders,* providing an advance that would cover a portion of the recruit's debt and deducting the rest in installments from his regular pay until the debt was satisfied.

Between other kinds of migration and that sponsored by *volkhouders,* the VOC was able to compensate for the shortfall in Dutch recruits with foreign hires. Overall, nearly half of those who embarked as employees of the VOC were foreigners.[6] In the eighteenth century, approximately 283,000 recruits embarked, of which more than half—about 155,000—were foreign. In the decade during which Büttner and Whitehead were recruited, 1765 to 1775, a total of 82,000 embarked, of whom 51,800—nearly two-thirds—were foreign. Most of these foreign recruits were German.[7]

Volkhouders focused their efforts intensively on port cities, where the likelihood of finding experienced seamen to enlist was greater. As well, port cities were a gathering point for large groups of immigrants newly arrived and still without employment. Thus it is not surprising that Büttner encountered *volkhouders* shortly after his arrival in Hamburg. We know from his own account that stories of travel to the East Indies had enticed him to leave school and had informed his choice of career. After a long period of working as a peripatetic barber-surgeon's assistant, the opportunity to become a barber-surgeon

3. J. R. Bruijn, F. S. Gaastra, and I. Schöffer, *Dutch-Asiatic Shipping in the Seventeenth and Eighteenth Centuries,* vols. 1 and 2 (The Hague: Nijhoff, 1979, 1987), 6.

4. Extrapolated from ibid., 156.

5. Ibid., 149–50.

6. Ibid., 155–57.

7. Ibid., 157; Israel, *Dutch Republic,* 942–43; Jan Lucassen, "The Netherlands, the Dutch, and Long-Distance Migration in the Late Sixteenth to Early Nineteenth Centuries," in *Europeans on the Move: Studies on European Migration, 1500–1800,* ed. Nicholas Canny (New York: Oxford University Press, 1994), 172.

on board a VOC ship would have been welcome. The position not only paid well but also bestowed on Büttner the rank of junior officer, which would have exempted him from the more onerous conditions faced by ordinary seamen.[8] He would have had his own cabin and would have eaten and had other intercourse with officers and upper-class passengers. In addition, Büttner would probably have been familiar with stories of those who, after arrival in the East Indies, had become successful medical men in their own right.

Verifying Büttner's Tale

Verifying the early portion of Büttner's story is difficult. He is unlikely to have made up much about his family life and schooling, however, since he published his autobiography in Camenz (Kamenz), not far from Lauta, where he was born, and refers to people and incidents that must have been known to many people still alive at the time of printing and who must have had children, siblings, nephews, and nieces still alive at that time. His comment that his father wanted him to attend medical school in Dresden is certainly within the realm of possibility; Dresden's Collegium medico-chirurgicum was founded in 1748 and was the precursor of the medical school that still exists today as part of the Technical University of Dresden.[9] The early travels described in his narrative follow a fairly logical route; there is no reason to disbelieve the broad strokes Büttner paints, although the details cannot be confirmed.

Verifying Büttner's tale of being recruited for the VOC, of the difficulty of finding a position, of becoming a redemptioner, and of the long and difficult voyage would also be problematic were it not for the closely matching tale told by Whitehead of his own experience. While the two had not met prior to their recruitment, and while it is not clear at what point they came together, Whitehead's story closely parallels that told by Büttner in almost every particular. While Whitehead regards his experience far differently than does Büttner, in almost every instance the differences are those of personality rather than of fact. Whitehead's account of meeting recruiters closely resembles Büttner's. His account of the trip to Amsterdam and the circumstances of his stay there matches Büttner's. And while Büttner may have had an inflated idea of his chances of being hired as a ship's surgeon, Whitehead confirms that they arrived in Amsterdam at a time when the VOC was not doing much hiring. Both narratives indicate that the men were incurring debt that would have to

8. Bruijn, Gaastra, and Schöffer, *Dutch-Asiatic Shipping*, 161, 166–67.
9. Zweigbibliothek Medizin, http://www.tu-dresden.de/slub/standorte/zweigBibo/zb_32_med.htm, and Institute of Medical History, http://www.tu-dresden.de/medigm/englischo1-05.htm (both accessed June 19, 2005).

be cleared in some way, and that taking passage as a redemptioner immigrant to America was presented as a viable alternative. The long and traumatic voyage that Büttner recounts is verified by Whitehead's recollection of the conditions, the illnesses, and the delays. Whitehead's tale confirms the presence and nature of the illness on board, the deaths of many of the passengers, and the paucity and poor condition of the provisions that had to be stretched to last far longer than anyone had anticipated.

Büttner's memoir does not provide dates for the voyage, and Whitehead's recollection of dates is sometimes incorrect. But it seems certain that the ship left Rotterdam in April 1773.[10] Even being conservative and using early May as the start of the voyage, the journey would have been unusually long. At a time when the voyage from Rotterdam to Philadelphia normally took between eight and ten weeks, this journey took at least seventeen weeks—more than four months.[11] The date of the ship's arrival in Philadelphia is easily confirmed. The *Pennsylvania Gazette* published news of ships arriving at Philadelphia's port. The issue of August 25, 1773, includes the following sentence: "Saturday last the Ship Sally, Captain Osman, arrived here from Rotterdam, but last from Cowes, with Germans." This places the ship's arrival on Saturday, August 21.

There is no reason to doubt the *Pennsylvania Gazette*, but a second document supports this arrival date. Far more important than confirming a date about which there is little doubt, this document proves that Büttner and Whitehead were both on board. A shipper's main concern was to sell his cargo, including redemptioner passengers, as quickly as possible. Redemptioners could not be sold until the able adult males (all males over age sixteen were considered adult) took an oath abjuring all other sovereigns and swearing allegiance to the English king. Those who took the oath also signed a register. By 1773, swearing to and signing this oath seems frequently to have taken place at shops where shippers had established trading connections. Arriving on the twenty-first, the ship's captain and crew would have been occupied by the business of putting into port. The oath could not have been administered on the twenty-second, a Sunday, when shops were closed. On Monday, August 23, the first day possible after the ship's arrival, the able adult male passengers of the *Sally* under the command of Captain John Osmand were presented at Willing and Morris's store in Philadelphia, where they swore the usual oath and signed their names.[12] Among the signatures was that of

10. Anne M. Pfaelzer de Ortiz, "German Redemptioners of the Lower Sort: Apolitical Soldiers in the American Revolution?" *Journal of American Studies* 33 (August 1999): 280–81.
11. Ibid.; Marianna S. Wokeck, *Trade in Strangers: The Beginnings of Mass Migration to North America* (University Park: Pennsylvania State University Press, 1999), 115–16.
12. Ralph B. Strassburger, *Pennsylvania German Pioneers: A Publication of the Original Lists of Arrivals in the Port of Philadelphia from 1727 to 1808* (Norristown, Pa.: Pennsylvania German

Johann Carl Büttner. Whitehead, who at the time used his stepfather's surname, signed as Johan Fridrich Kukuck (German for cuckoo), although his K looks like an R. A facsimile of their signatures on this oath follows:

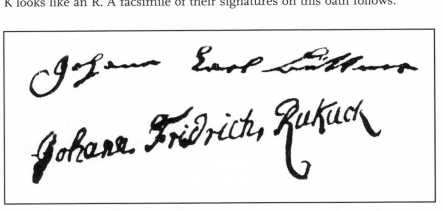

Fig. 4 Signatures of Johann Carl Büttner and Johan Friedrich Kukuck (John Frederick Whitehead), from the oath they signed upon arriving in Philadelphia on August 23, 1773.

After swearing the oath, the men would have been escorted back to the ship, where they would stay until their passage debt was redeemed. Büttner says he was among the last six boys sold, and that their sale was so delayed because they refused to consent to a long servant contract. He explains that they capitulated only when the captain threatened to take them to Barbados to work in the cane fields alongside slave laborers. Büttner reports that his debt was thirty pounds sterling and that he had to agree to a contract of six years to pay this debt. His memoir states that the contract, equal to nearly 150 dollars, was purchased by a Quaker who owned a plantation in New Jersey.

Documents exist that prove portions of this tale to be flawed. More than fifty years intervened between the events surrounding Büttner's sale as an indentured servant and the publication of his memoir. We will never know whether Büttner simply did not recall events correctly or whether he was embroidering the tale. There is no doubt that Büttner had a flair for the dramatic. He also acknowledges that his is a cautionary tale in many respects. He could have intentionally embellished details of his story when it suited his purpose or fancy.

Record of Indentures of Individuals Bound Out as Apprentices, Servants, Etc. and of German and Other Redemptioners in the Office of the Mayor of the City of Philadelphia, October 3, 1771, to October 5, 1773 is a register that includes

Society, 1934), 1:748; 2:867–69. Osmand's name has been variously recorded as Osman, Osmand, Osmon, and Osmen.

information valuable to both historians and genealogists.[13] Recorded are the date of each contract, the name of the apprentice or servant and his or her point of origin, the name of the master and where the master resided, the kind of work the apprentice or servant would be doing, any stipulations to the contract, the length of the contract, and the monetary value of the contract. This register was probably only one of many for the port of Philadelphia, but it is the only one currently known to have survived intact between 1746 and 1784.[14] Luckily, the date on which Büttner was contracted into servitude falls during the period covered by this register. The entry in the *Record of Indentures* belies Büttner's story of being among the last six to be sold. Büttner agreed to a contract within four days of signing the oath of allegiance, and was approximately thirtieth out of at least a hundred contract sales for adult male redemptioners from the *Sally*.[15]

But Büttner was certainly telling the truth about not wanting to work a long contract. He had not come from the servant class, although he, like most young men who had served an apprenticeship, had experience serving a master. He had not set out to find employment as a servant or laborer but as a barber-surgeon. In addition, he and his companions had been told in Amsterdam that redemptioners had to work for only a couple of years to pay for their passage. While this was not quite a lie—the average contract for redemptioners was about four years, and two-year contracts did occur—this was not the case for those in Büttner's group. They had accrued a significantly larger debt than most redemptioners. Büttner's debt was almost a third more than the average for a German redemptioner. On top of the larger debt, Büttner

---

13. *Record of Indentures of Individuals Bound Out as Apprentices, Servants, Etc. and of German and Other Redemptioners in the Office of the Mayor of the City of Philadelphia, October 3, 1771, to October 5, 1773* (Lancaster, Pa.: Pennsylvania German Society, 1907).

14. Farley Grubb, "Servant Auction Records and Immigration into the Delaware Valley, 1745–1831: The Proportion of Females Among Immigrant Servants," *Proceedings of the American Philosophical Society* 133 (June 1989): 154–69. As previously noted, spelling—even of names— was not standardized. This created difficulty in matching the names of those who signed the oaths of abjuration and allegiance to those listed in the servant register. It is likely that whoever kept the servant register either copied handwritten names from contracts or wrote names that the parties to the contract dictated to him. This process certainly engendered further errors, as did the transcription of the handwritten records to typed lists. Büttner confidently scrawled his name on the list of those who took the oath; his writing is hard to read. In the servant register, he appears as John Charles Bittner. We know from Whitehead's narrative that his stepfather's name was Kukuck. When signing the list of those who took the oath, Whitehead signed the name Johan Fridrich Kukuck in a clear hand, although the K looks like an R. He appears in the servant register as John Frederick Cuckoo, the English translation of the surname.

15. Only contracts that could be matched to a name on the list of those who took the oath were counted. The number is approximate because some adult males may have been too ill to sign the register but still sold before Büttner was, and some youths may have been husky enough to sell for an adult price although they were not yet sixteen, when the oath became mandatory. Women and children did not take the oath or sign the register.

and many of his companions had been seriously ill during the long and difficult voyage. In addition to having recently been ill, Büttner was rather short. He probably did not look like he could do the sort of vigorous work that would merit a short contract term. In any event, the register confirms that the contract to which he agreed, which would pay a debt of thirty Pennsylvania pounds, was six years in length. Büttner's contract was not unusual for the group with which he traveled. For instance, Whitehead's contract was even longer—he had to agree to serve six years and six months to pay a debt of twenty-eight pounds, thirteen shillings and sixpence (Pennsylvania pounds). Indeed, for the redemptioners of the *Sally*, the average debt was 28.4 Pennsylvania pounds and the average length of contract was five and a quarter years.[16] Given that the typical redemptioner's debt was approximately twenty-three Pennsylvania pounds, paid for by a work contract of about four years, it is easy to understand why Büttner and his fellow redemptioners were disgruntled over the length of the contracts they were obliged to sign.[17]

Büttner's tale of the captain's threat to take laggard redemptioners to Barbados is less credible. Destination was one of the terms included in the written contract between shipper and redemptioner. Shippers could not change their minds, nor could they take redemptioners to another port if they did not sell at the port of arrival.[18] In 1765 Pennsylvania passed a law giving an immigrant thirty days in which to redeem the price of his or her passage. Almost all redemptioners found a contract or arranged another method of payment within this time period. To the best of our knowledge, if a redemptioner did not redeem his passage within thirty days, the captain could arrange a contract without the person's consent, but he was not allowed to transport the redemptioner to another port.[19] To give Büttner the benefit of the doubt, it is not clear that all redemptioners understood this. Büttner and other redemptioners gathered by VOC agents in particular would have had no reason to

16. The average is that of contract prices and lengths for the ninety-nine adult male indentured servants who could be identified as being from Büttner's ship. (A previous calculation in Pfaelzer de Ortiz, "German Redemptioners of the Lower Sort," 281, was based on the average for eighty-nine servants.)

17. Farley Grubb, "The Auction of Redemptioner Servants, Philadelphia, 1771–1804: An Economic Analysis," *Journal of Economic History* 48 (September 1988): 588, 590; Farley Grubb, "The Long-Run Trend in the Value of European Immigrant Servants, 1654–1831: New Measurements and Interpretations," *Research in Economic History* 14 (1992): 171.

18. Karl Frederick Geiser, *Redemptioners and Indentured Servants in the Colony and Commonwealth of Pennsylvania* (New Haven: Tuttle, Morehouse & Taylor, 1901), 64–68; Wokeck, *Trade in Strangers*, 133–34.

19. Farley Grubb, "The Disappearance of Organized Markets for European Indentured Servants in the United States: Five Popular Explanations Reexamined," *Social Science History* 18 (spring 1994): 5–9; Frederic Trautmann, "Pennsylvania Through a German's Eyes: The Travels of Ludwig Gall, 1819–1820," *Pennsylvania Magazine of History and Biography* 105 (January 1981): 40–41; Wokeck, *Trade in Strangers*, 101, 153.

investigate the process of redeeming their passage fare; they had anticipated a voyage to the East as employees of the VOC, not immigration to the American colonies as redemptioners. It is possible, then, although unlikely, that the captain may have threatened to take malingerers to Barbados. Barbados was known to be a cruel and often deadly destination. The heat, disease, and poor treatment of laborers were no secret, and to be put to work in such an atmosphere, and with slaves, certainly would have motivated the young men to sign contracts in Philadelphia, regardless of their length.

Nonetheless, Captain Osmand was not likely to have made this threat, or Büttner to have believed it even if it had been made. Philadelphia had an active German Society that sent representatives to each ship carrying redemptioners.[20] One of the chief roles of these representatives was to ensure that the redemptioners understood their rights and to mediate in cases where redemptioners had complaints about treatment. To prevent abuses, a member of the society boarded each redemptioner ship upon arrival in Philadelphia and informed passengers in German of their rights and of the laws regulating the redemption and contracting process. Osmand was no stranger to the redemptioner trade—he had certainly carried redemptioners to Philadelphia on previous voyages.[21] He would have been aware of the German Society, a representative of which would certainly have visited this group of redemptioners, and Büttner would have known his rights.

Other known facts suggest that it is unlikely Osmand threatened his passengers with Barbados. Rather than being in a rush to unload this group of redemptioners, Osmand gave them more than the normal amount of time to fix contracts and redeem their debts to him. A number of items in the *Pennsylvania Gazette*, added to the constraints involved in transatlantic voyages, certify that Osmand allowed his passengers nearly two months to make their arrangements. The *Pennsylvania Gazette* announced the ship's August 21 arrival and on September 1 carried the first advertisement of the availability of Germans whose passage needed to be paid:

> GERMAN PASSENGERS. Philadelphia, August 23, 1773. THE Ship SALLY, Captain OSMAN, is just arrived from ROTTERDAM with Two Hundred

20. See, for example, Frank R. Diffenderffer, "The German Immigration into Pennsylvania Through the Port of Philadelphia from 1700 to 1775. Part II. The Redemptioners" (part 7 of "The Narrative and Critical History"), *Publications of the Pennsylvania German Society* 10 (1899): 1–328; Geiser, *Redemptioners and Indentured Servants*, 64–68; Whitehead's narrative.

21. Information indicating that Osmand had carried at least two other groups of redemptioners from Rotterdam to Philadelphia can be found in the *Pennsylvania Gazette*, November 1, 1770, and December 9, 1772. The former is an advertisement announcing the availability of redemptioners for sale; the latter is a runaway ad stating that the servant who absconded arrived recently with Captain Osmand on the *Sally*. Strassburger, *Pennsylvania German Pioneers*, 3:212, lists Osmand as captain for five previous voyages.

fine young GERMAN Passengers, whose Passage is to be paid to SAMUEL HOWELL, in Water street, or the Captain, on board said Ship, near Chestnut street Wharff.

More than a month later, on October 6, a second advertisement appeared:

GERMAN PASSENGERS. THERE is on board the Ship SALLY, Captain OSMAN, from ROTTERDAM, young healthy GERMAN Passengers, that are willing to serve a reasonable Time for their Passage money. For Terms, apply to SAMUEL HOWELL, in Water street, or the Captain, on board the Ship, near Chestnut street Wharff. Philadelphia, October 5, 1773.

How do we know that this advertisement was for the same group of redemptioners? First, the eight- to ten-week time period, on average, needed for the trip between Europe and Philadelphia means that Osmand could not possibly have made the round trip to Rotterdam and back to Philadelphia with another group of redemptioners. Next, in the *Record of Indentures,* we see that in early October a number of contracts were registered for people who had traveled with Büttner.[22] Redemptioners were housed on board the ship on which they arrived until they were sold.[23] So Captain Osmand and his ship must still have been in port; the ship would not be free for a new voyage until all redemptioners from Büttner's group were contracted out. Finally, and most conclusively, ship departures, like arrivals, were recorded in the *Pennsylvania Gazette.* Captain Osmand and the *Sally* do not appear in the list of outbound ships until October 20, 1773, and not until November 10 do they appear in the paper's list of ships that have cleared the bay (the former date would be the day the ship left port and the latter would be the day the ship entered open ocean). While we cannot know why Osmand allowed this group of redemptioners so much extra time, it is possible that he was sympathetic to passengers who had suffered both debilitating illness and an inordinately long and rough passage. After such a voyage, many of them must have been sickly and might have been unable to negotiate a favorable contract unless they had some time to recuperate. Allowing them extra time may have been his way of compensating them for the unforeseen hardships. Or the ship may have required some repairs before it was again seaworthy.

22. Strassburger, *Pennsylvania German Pioneers; Record of Indentures of Individuals Bound Out as Apprentices, Servants, Etc.*

23. Not only was this part of the contract, but advertisements for redemptioners usually stated that they were on board a certain ship.

Büttner reports that his contract was for thirty pounds sterling. He is correct about the number but errs in stating that the denomination is pounds sterling. Transactions in the *Record of Indentures* were recorded in the denomination commonly used in Philadelphia—Pennsylvania pounds. Büttner may not have understood the distinction between Pennsylvania and British pounds sterling and might have assumed that the transaction was being recorded in pounds sterling, or he may simply have remembered incorrectly by the time he wrote his narrative.[24] More difficult to understand is an error in the English translation of Büttner's original German publication. The text, in German, mentions the sum of thirty pounds sterling being worth almost two hundred thalers.[25] In creating the English version of Büttner's story, the translator correctly translated "30 Pfund Sterling" as thirty pounds sterling but turned the sum of two hundred thalers into 150 dollars.[26] The mistranslation of "dollars" for "thalers" is easy to understand, but the substitution of 150 for 200 is not. The original text is unmistakable—one does not even need to know German, as the number is written in arabic numerals: "gégen 200 Thaler."[27] Why the translator would have provided a different number is baffling. The U.S. dollar did not exist in 1773. To colonial Americans a dollar was the Spanish dollar, more commonly known as a piece of eight. But the translator could not be referring to Spanish dollars; at the exchange rate for 1773, he would have had to report that thirty pounds sterling was equal to about 135 dollars.[28] The U.S. dollar did not come into existence until the early 1790s—nearly twenty years after Büttner sold his labor to pay his debt—and the initial exchange rate was roughly the same as that of the 1773 Spanish dollar to pounds sterling.[29] The only explanation that suggests itself is rather complex. If the translator knew that Büttner's contract price had been recorded in Pennsylvania pounds rather than British pounds sterling, he might have worked out the value of the actual contract. Thirty Pennsylvania pounds, in 1773, would have been worth 149.4 thalers.[30] But why the translator would

24. His debt in pounds sterling would have been about 18.04. See John J. McCusker, *Money and Exchange in Europe and America, 1600–1775: A Handbook* (Chapel Hill: University of North Carolina Press, 1978), 174–88.

25. Büttner here understates the value of thirty pounds sterling by about 25 percent. In 1773 thirty pounds sterling would have amounted to about 249 thalers. See ibid., 9.

26. Johann Carl Büttner, *Büttner, der Amerikaner. Eine Selbstbiographie Johann Carl Büttners, jeßigen Amts-Chirurgus in Senftenberg und ehemaligen nord-amerikanischen Kriegers, Mit dem Bildniffe des Versaffers* (Camenz: E. S. Krausche, 1828), 60.

27. Ibid.

28. McCusker, *Money and Exchange,* 10.

29. Lawrence J. Officer, *Between the Dollar-Sterling Gold Points: Exchange Rates, Parity, and Market Behavior* (New York: Cambridge University Press, 1996), 54.

30. A direct exchange rate is not available. The sum was derived by converting the amount in Pennsylvania pounds (30) to pounds sterling (18), and the sum in sterling to Spanish dollars. Eighteen pounds sterling was also equal to eighty-one Spanish dollars.

have made the correction in calculating the sum but then mistakenly changed thalers to dollars is a puzzle. Whatever the reasons for the error, Büttner was correct in reporting the amount in thalers rather than dollars. The thaler was a common German currency of the time. Had he gotten his exchange rates correct, the number Büttner reported would have matched the figure the translator used.[31]

To New Jersey

The *Record of Indentures* for August 26, 1773, indicates that Büttner's contract was purchased by Charles Smith of Eversham Township, Burlington County, New Jersey. Eversham (also called Evesham) Township was an agricultural area settled by Welsh and British Quakers in the last decades of the seventeenth century.[32] Incorporated in 1692, Eversham Township originally covered an area later divided into other townships: Mt. Laurel, Medford, Lumberton, Hainesport, Shamong, and Washington. Eversham was defined by a branch of the Rancocas River to the east and Cropwell Creek to the west. It was one of thirteen townships in Burlington County and lay across the river, about fifteen miles east of Philadelphia. One hundred years after incorporating, Eversham Township was still largely agricultural. A large number of redemptioners found work as agricultural laborers, and many Eversham Township landholders had redemptioner and indentured servants. For example, the October 1771 to October 1773 *Record of Indentures* indicates that in those two years alone one hundred indentured and redemptioner servants were purchased by residents of Burlington County, of whom fifty-one were German.[33]

Verifying this portion of Büttner's story is difficult because no surviving records indicate that a Charles Smith lived in Eversham Township. Smith must have been a person of some wealth in that he had enough money to purchase a servant. Such a man would have left traces of his existence. Even if he did not appear in court records as a result of lawsuits undertaken by or against him, or in tax records or records of land rents, he ought to have been in the birth, marriage, or death records that have been preserved and

31. To give readers an idea of the value the debt, Büttner owed the equivalent, in 2002 U.S. dollars, of about $2,044. See John J. McCusker, "Comparing the Purchasing Power of Money in Great Britain from 1264 to Any Other Year Including the Present," Economic History Services, 2001, http://www.eh.net/hmit/ppowerbp/ (accessed August 25, 2003); "U.S. Dollar: Historical Exchange Rates," http://www.triacom.com/archive/exchange.en.html (accessed August 25, 2003).

32. See http://www.twp.evesham.nj.us/about_evesham.htm (accessed June 19, 2005).

33. Farley Grubb, "Immigrant Servant Labor: Their Occupational and Geographic Distribution in the Late Eighteenth-Century Mid-Atlantic Economy," *Social Science History* 9 (summer 1985): 258, 260.

are widely available to researchers. Yet no such record exists. References can be found to an Eversham Township family with the surname Smith in *Documents Relating to the Colonial, Revolutionary, and Post-Revolutionary History of the State of New Jersey.*[34] But this is the Thomas Smith family, not the Charles Smith family. No amount of searching reveals a Charles Smith in Eversham Township, Burlington County, New Jersey, during the correct period of time.

Not until a document verifying another portion of Büttner's tale came to light was the mystery surrounding Charles Smith solved. The master's name was incorrectly written. The source of the error is not certain—it could be that the clerk recording Büttner's indenture made a mistake or that the person transcribing the records for publication misread the clerk's writing. But an advertisement in the *Pennsylvania Journal and the Weekly Advertiser* of June 14, 1773, reports that "a certain John Charles Botner, a Dutch servant man, belonging to Thomas Smith of Eversham" had run away.[35] The Smith who purchased Büttner was not named Charles. His name was Thomas.

Once Smith's first name was known, information about the man who purchased Büttner's contract became easily accessible. Thomas Smith did indeed own a farm in Eversham Township. In an assessment made in September 1773 Thomas Smith is listed as having 431 acres of land, thirty-two cattle and horses, and one servant.[36] Seven years later Thomas Smith Sr. passed away, leaving an estate inventory valued at just over 590 pounds, presumably in New Jersey currency.[37] He made provisions in his will for his wife, Elizabeth, his seven surviving daughters, two surviving sons, and one "boy," probably an indentured servant. In 2002 U.S. dollars, the inventory of Smith's estate would be approximately $85,000.

This information confirms much of Büttner's description of the Smith family's residence, farm, and living conditions. He describes the house as large, having a six-foot-wide fireplace, and several outbuildings. He says Smith owned "ten to fifteen head of horses, fifty to sixty cows and oxen, and more than a hundred hogs," and that in the winter it could take him up to half an hour to trudge through the snow to reach the place where the cattle were feeding. The 1773 assessment shows that the month after he purchased Büttner's contract, Smith had a farm large enough to allow such a walk. If Büttner's reckoning of the livestock holdings does not match the assessment's,

---

34. *Documents Relating to the Colonial and Revolutionary, and Post-Revolutionary History of the State of New Jersey,* 1st series, vol. 34, *Calendar of New Jersey Wills, Administrators, Etc.,* vol. 5, 1771–1780, ed. A. Van Doren Honeyman (Trenton: MacCrellish and Quigley, 1931), 481.

35. Germans were frequently referred to as Dutch, a corruption of the word "deutsche."

36. Kenn Stryker-Rodda, "New Jersey Rateables, 1773–1774," *Genealogical Magazine of New Jersey* 36 (1961): 128. The servant was probably Büttner.

37. Honeyman, *Documents Relating to the Colonial and Revolutionary, and Post-Revolutionary History,* 481.

this does not mean that he lied. During the course of Büttner's tenure with Smith, the livestock holdings may have fluctuated. It is possible that not all of Smith's livestock were taxable. Then again, to someone like Büttner, unused to farm labor, thirty-two horses and cows may have seemed like many more, particularly when he had to care for them. Büttner's descriptions contain many other clues of the family's prosperity. The farm's production of cheese and butter was sufficient not only for the family and servants but for sale. He indicates that meals were generous and that he was served meat at least twice each day. Equally indicative is that Büttner was set to plowing uncultivated land, indicating that the plantation was large enough that some of it had not been farmed previously. A less well-to-do family probably could not have afforded to purchase a servant's labor, would not have had such a large and comfortable house or such generous meals, and probably would have used every available scrap of land to make ends meet.

On the Run

Büttner's experiences living and working for the Smiths cannot be substantiated directly. He mentions no name or incident that can be verified between his purchase on August 27, 1773, and May 14, 1775. But what happened on May 14 does verify portions of his story. Büttner indicates that he frequently attended the Quaker meeting on Sundays and that he was given the use of a horse to reach the meetinghouse. He must have impressed his master as both responsible and trustworthy, because on at least one Sunday he was given the freedom to go alone to Philadelphia to visit the Protestant church there. In Philadelphia he met some other German servants. They wanted to run away, and persuaded him to join them. They arranged a time, place, and date to meet, and on Sunday, May 14, 1775, Büttner ran away with two other German servants.[38] The runaway ad placed by the two masters indirectly confirms that Büttner could leave the farm on a Sunday without raising suspicion. In addition to providing his master's real name, the ad gives evidence that Büttner must have had some sort of social life, one he did not hide from the Smiths, for Smith and the master of the other runaways were able to figure out that the three had run away together. Büttner's desertion would seem to cast doubt on his story of sharing the family's abundant meals and enjoying good treatment. On the other hand, Smith's ability to guess that Büttner had accomplices speaks of the easy sort of relationship developed when one lives and shares activities and meals with a family.

38. *Pennsylvania Journal and Weekly Advertiser,* June 14, 1775.

The advertisement provides a detailed physical description of Büttner.

> He is about 5 feet 2 inches high, a chunkey thick set man, dark complexion, light eyes, black hair; he is very talkative and speaks the best English of the three; had on when he went away, a reddish brown upper jacket with wooden buttons, a kind of yellowish snuff coloured under one, an old Oznaburg shirt, a pair of buckskin breeches with brass buttons, black gray stockings, a pair of calf-skin shoes with white metal buckles, a yellow silk handkerchief, and a middling good hat.

It is from this ad that we know Büttner was short, which is important in understanding the length of his contract. We also discover that he was gregarious, and—courtesy of the yellow silk handkerchief—a bit of a dandy.

Büttner writes that he and his companions, living in the rough and traveling at night, got as far as Virginia before they were captured and imprisoned. He says that a reward of five pounds, or more than thirty thalers, had been offered for him.[39] The runaway ad indicates that he inflated the value of the reward a bit; Smith actually offered three pounds and expenses to anyone who captured and jailed Büttner. An ad dated July 5, 1775, placed by one Thomas Young, the jailer of Prince William County in Virginia, in the July 12, 1775, edition of the *Pennsylvania Gazette* tells us that:

> There is in Prince-William County gaol, three runaway servants, vis. Matres Brown, and Catherine, his wife, who say they belong to the Widow Lippencott in one of the Jerseys. Also a servant man, who says his name is John Charles Bitten, and belongs to Thomas Smith in the Jerseys. The owners are desired to take them away, and pay the fees due.

At first, Büttner also appears to have exaggerated the distance they traveled—he says they had gone almost three hundred miles and had just crossed the border of Virginia. The distance, on modern roads, is about 150 miles. Büttner probably was not stretching the truth here, however, or at least not stretching it very far. The three runaways were traveling across fields and through forests, and would probably have stayed away from any well-traveled roads. Büttner and his two companions walked for nearly eight weeks from Eversham Township to reach Virginia. Had they been able to follow modern roadways

39. Again, his calculation of pounds to thalers is off. If he means pounds sterling, the amount in thalers would have been about forty-two; if he means Pennsylvania pounds, the amount would have been twenty-six thalers.

this would represent a movement of about three miles a night. Even going on foot and foraging for food as they went, and being unable to travel very far some nights because of poor weather, they ought to have reached the Virginia border much sooner if one figures the distance of the trip using a calculation based on the fairly direct routes made available by modern highways. Büttner's estimate of three hundred miles is credible, both in terms of distance they would have had to cover by not following a direct route and in terms of the distance they might have been able to cover on an average night. If they covered three hundred miles, their forward movement would have been, on average, 5.5 miles a night. On sidewalks or other paved surfaces, walking at a fairly brisk pace, the average person needs fifteen minutes to walk a mile. Given the constraints—traveling in the dark, over rough ground, perhaps hungry or thirsty, in good weather and bad, having no fixed destination, certainly pausing to hide at the least hint that someone might be passing by or looking for them—it is not hard to imagine that they both traveled twice the distance of a more direct route and far more slowly than fifteen minutes per mile.

After being returned to the Smiths, Büttner was pleased, though somewhat taken aback, to receive few recriminations. This is less surprising than one might think, for two reasons. First of all, the May 14 date of desertion indicates that Büttner may have been present for at least some if not most of the spring tilling and planting. The bulk of his absence fell during the growing season. In colonial America, large farms had no irrigation system to maintain and no pesticides or fungicides to spread, and the animals needed far less care in summer than they did in the winter, since they could be left in the pasture. Although there would have been plenty of work, Büttner's absence might not have caused his master undue hardship. According to the timing of the ad announcing his capture, Büttner was probably returned to the Smiths in plenty of time for the harvest and fall plowing. The second reason involves laws that discouraged running away. Most colonies had some set scale of punishment for runaway servants and apprentices. In New Jersey the established penalty was that the runaway owed his master two days for every day of absence. In addition, the price of the reward and any expenses related to the person's capture and return were converted to time (probably using the same rate established at the time of the contract purchase) and added to the contract length. When Büttner ran away, he was gone somewhere between eleven and sixteen weeks, or between 77 and 112 days, meaning that Büttner's penalty would be somewhere between 154 and 224 days. On top of that, between the reward, capture, and return, say that the expenses involved were the five pounds that Büttner mentioned. If he had to reimburse Smith for five pounds at the rate established by his contract purchase and length, he would have owed another year's servitude in addition to the runaway penalty. In total, by running away, Büttner managed to tack another seventeen to twenty months onto his original six-year contract. Thus, while Smith was certainly inconvenienced by Büttner's absence, he would be recovering his expenses and receiving a premium in repayment, which could explain why he was not angrier and did not punish Büttner more severely.

A New Master

The next portion of Büttner's time in America is easier to trace thanks to his mention of names and places. Büttner's second master was Abraham Eldrige, who owned an inn not far from the Smith farm.[40] Büttner's contract was sold to Eldrige, who paid for it with a pair of oxen. No documents exist to show that Büttner ever belonged to Eldrige, but records indicate that an Abraham Eldrige did live at that time in Eversham Township. In the same 1773 assessment listing Thomas Smith, Abraham Eldreg [sic] is listed as having two hundred acres, twenty-nine cattle and horses, and two servants. In 1774 he had 220 acres, twenty-eight cattle and horses, and one servant. At the same time, he is listed in the Nottingham Township (also in Burlington County) survey as being a householder.[41] By the time of his death in 1788, Eldrige appears to have moved to Nottingham, for this is where his will was proved. The will mentions his wife, three surviving sons who are not yet adults, three more who are adults, and four surviving daughters. Whether he still owned the tavern cannot be said, but in his will he parceled out 350 acres to two of his sons, and he indicated that he owned at least one other house, which was rented out. The inventory of his estate is valued at 684 pounds (presumably New Jersey pounds).

Büttner first says he worked two more years for Smith before the incident that caused his sale to Eldrige. This cannot be correct. We know he was returned to Smith in the summer of 1775. By April 1777 not only had he broken the plow and been sold to Eldrige but he had joined a regiment in the American War of Independence. A few sentences after stating that he worked two more years for Smith, Büttner indicates that he had been in America for about three years before being sold to Eldrige, which is a far more reasonable estimate. This means he would have worked another four to nine months for Smith post running away. He could have worked for Eldrige no longer than a year before running away again, this time to enlist. Fortunately for Büttner,

---

40. Eldrige's name is also recorded as Eldridge, Eldredge, and Eldreg.
41. Stryker-Rodda, "New Jersey Rateables," 77.

his new master was a member of the militia and must have been sympathetic to the American cause. Instead of charging Büttner with running away, which would have been his right, he agreed to his service as a private in a German regiment fighting for the Americans.[42]

Büttner indicates that a condition of his enlistment was that he had to pay Eldrige one pound per month out of his pay for twenty months, a sum he complains is far too high. Once again Büttner says the sum is in pounds sterling, but this is unlikely. The colonies issued bills of credit denominated in pounds, shillings, and pence.[43] His pay would have been in Pennsylvania or New Jersey pounds. Büttner is also wrong about the sum being far too high. At the time of his sale to Eldrige, he had worked for Smith for about three years. That meant he owed at least another four and a half to five years, as the cost of his running away would have been included in the price. He worked for Eldrige for six months to a year, leaving anywhere from three and a half to four and a half years still owed. At the originally contracted rate of five pounds a year, the twenty pounds would just have covered the value of the unserved portion of his contract if he owed four years, which is likely.

Military Service

As a soldier, Büttner continued to be something of an adventurer. We can document some of his escapades as a soldier for the Americans and the British. Büttner claims he joined the corps of Ortendorff [sic] and served for about six months. Nicholas Dietrich, Baron von Ottendorf, was commissioned late in 1776 by George Washington to form an all-German regiment to fight in the War of Independence.[44] Büttner's name appears on the muster role of Count Ottendorf's companies for January through April 1777. "Charles Butner" was a private in the fourth company, commanded by Captain Jacob Bauer.[45] Büttner's appearance on this list not only verifies his story but also

42. The master's permission was needed before servants could be enlisted. See *American Archives: Consisting of a Collection of Authentick Records, State Papers, Debates, Letters and Other Notices of Publick Affairs, the Whole Forming a Documentary History of the Origin and Progress of the North American Colonies; of the Causes and Accomplishment of the American Revolution; and of the Constitution of the Government for the United States, to the Final Ratification Thereof. In Six Series.* 5th series, vol. 3, comp. Peter Force (Washington, D.C., 1853), 164.

43. Louis Jordan, *Colonial Currency: A Project of the Robert H. Gore, Jr. Numismatic Endowment.* University of Notre Dame, Department of Special Collections, http.//www.coins.nd.edu/ColCurrency (accessed August 31, 2003).

44. *American Archives,* 1034; "The Corps of Count von Ottendorf, 1776–1780," in *Pennsylvania in the War of the Revolution, Battalions and Line, 1775–1783,* ed. John B. Lind and William H. Egle, *Pennsylvania Archives,* 2d ser., 2 (1891): 89–99; W. T. R. Saffell, *Records of the Revolutionary War* (Philadelphia: G. G. Evans, 1860), 219–21.

45. "Corps of Count von Ottendorf," 98–99; Saffell, *Records of the Revolutionary War,* 221.

Joh. Carl Büttner

Fig. 5 Johann Carl Büttner, approximately age twenty-three, in his Hessian grenadier uniform. Frontispiece of the English translation of Büttner's memoir, *Narrative of Johann Carl Buettner in the American Revolution,* trans. Charles Frederick Heartman (New York: Heartman, 1915). Courtesy of the Pennsylvania State University Libraries, University Park.

helps us reckon the length of the remainder of his service to Smith, to Eldrige, and in the German regiment.

Ottendorf's regiment first saw action at Short Hills, New Jersey, in late June 1777. It was during this battle that Büttner says he deserted. Büttner's description of his first engagement with enemy forces matches that of the battle of Short Hills so closely that there can be little doubt that he saw action in the battle. Büttner indicates that after desertion he was sent to join Kyphausen's Hessian regiment, fighting for the British, and that he was with them through the battle of Red Bank. Kyphausen's regiment was involved at Red Bank, and again the action of the battle agrees with Büttner's description.

Approximately thirteen thousand Hessians were employed by King George to fight against the rebelling American colonists in 1776, though the name Hessians is somewhat misleading.[46] Called Hessians because of the large number of Germans from the Hesse-Kassel area of Germany, the so-called Hessian regiments also came from the Brunswick, Hesse-Hanau, Anspach-Bayreuth, Waldeck, and Anhalt-Zerbst areas of Germany. By the end of the war about thirty thousand Hessians in field, garrison, and grenadier battalions had been called into service, making up approximately one-third of Britain's total fighting force.[47] Hessian regiments were instrumental in many of the major battles of the war, including the battles of Long Island, Fort Washington, Trenton, the Brandywine, Red Bank, and Yorktown. Elite forces, such as the grenadiers—attack forces who got the name through their use of grenades—and the Jaegars, a force of light infantry including sharpshooters, were considered well-disciplined fighters and were much respected for their prowess.

Büttner reports being wounded during the battle of Red Bank. He was sent to the hospital at Princeton with the rest of the wounded. Once there, he encountered a member of his first regiment, who recognized him. At this point, fearing prosecution as a deserter, Büttner was compelled to make up a story about how he had been captured and forced to join the Hessians on the British side. He says this conversation took place in English and was overheard by the physician in charge at Princeton, named Tilton, and that when Tilton discovered that Büttner was a surgeon, he decided to take him into service. In effect, Büttner had deserted again, switching back to the American side.

46. Rodney Atwood, *The Hessians: Mercenaries from Hessen-Kassel in the American Revolution* (New York: Cambridge University Press, 1980), 52. More contemporary sources cite the number first arrived in the colonies as eighteen thousand. See, for example, http://www.nationmaster.com/encyclopedia/Hessians (accessed June 19 2005).

47. See http://www.nationmaster.com/encyclopedia/Hessians; see also Edward J. Lowell, *The Hessians and other German Auxiliaries of Great Britain in the Revolutionary War* (New York: Harper, 1884), appendices B and D, http://www.americanrevolution.org/hessahtml (accessed June 19, 2005); and J. G. Rosengarten, *The German Allied Troops in the North American War of Independence 1776–1783*, trans. Max Von Eelking (Albany, N.Y.: Joel Munsell's Sons, 1893).

We know that Büttner's Hessian regiment fought at Red Bank. Another document confirms Büttner's presence there beyond doubt and also allows us to verify other details. James Tilton's papers are held in the Hall of Records in Dover, Delaware. A letter written by Tilton in February 1778 gives an account of the Hessian prisoners from Red Bank. In this letter he confirms the bulk of Büttner's story:

> Dear Sir,
>   Before I leave this place, it may be proper for me to give some account of the Hessian prisoners that were under my care. . . .
>   The German Lad, you were kind enough to let me keep in my service, remains with me still and having behaved himself very faithfully, I must beg the favour of you, not to forget the peculiar circumstances of his case. He is a Saxon born, came oversea young, enlisted in our army, was taken by the Hessians at Short-hill— among them was a Corporal of his own countriman, who persuaded him much to enlist in their service, he however resisted all Importunity, until his Countriman took him to the gaols of New York, and convinced him he would soon lose his life there if he did not enlist. As soon as he could afterwards (at Red-bank) he made his escape, by falling down among the dead until the Hessians were gone[,] then running into our fort. This is his own story, which he closes by assuring me he had rather be sent to purgatory (being a Catholic) rather than returned to the Hessians. I flatter myself, these several circumstances will excuse the poor fellow from the rigor of the late resolution of Congress and even excuse him from any exchange.[48]

Tilton could mean no one but Büttner. The letter confirms that his former companions believed his tale of capture and the threat of jail and that he served Tilton, and it indicates that he was excused from the prisoner exchanges between the British and American sides. It is unclear whether Büttner was wounded or whether he just pretended to be wounded in order to escape the worst of the battle or to avoid retreating and rejoining the Hessians. Tilton's words could easily mean that the injury was entirely feigned. The letter also reveals another falsehood. The son of a Lutheran minister and a Lutheran minister's daughter, Büttner was no Catholic. This illustrates Büttner's facility for stretching a tale to fit his needs.

48. James Tilton, "Dear Sir," letter from Princeton, February 17, 1778, Papers of Dr. James Tilton, Bureau of Archives and Record Management, Hall of Records, Dover, Delaware.

After Princeton

Most of the rest of Büttner's story cannot be authenticated. His description of working at an inn in Philadelphia, being hired as a hand on a ship bound for the Indies, the capture of a British ship, and the retaking of that ship and its return to New York may be accurate, but he mentions no significant names and thus we cannot search records that might authenticate his account. Certainly such things happened, and since many of Büttner's seemingly fabulous stories *can* be authenticated, there is no reason to discount this portion simply because documents cannot be found to back them up. His presence in New York with Kyphausen's regiment is certain, as is his return to Germany with the Hessians.

All the same, that we have been able to verify a large part of Büttner's story does not mean that the entire work is accurate. In addition to previously mentioned inaccuracies (or falsehoods), his chronology of the war is sometimes incorrect. For instance, he places himself and his Hessian regiment at the siege and fall of Charleston. He correctly recites the name of the ship on which the regiment traveled (*The Two Sisters*), the time of year (winter into spring), and the events involved, but then places them in time prior to the battle of the Brandywine. That battle took place in September 1777, but his regiment did not leave for Charleston, and the siege of Charleston did not occur, until the winter and spring of 1779–80. This misdating is curious, given the accuracy of most of his story. Büttner's description of the battle of the Brandywine is accurate down to the minutest details. He recites correctly the sequence of battles in which his regiment was involved—Brandywine, Germantown, and then Red Bank, all of which took place in September and October 1777. His error in chronology is even more puzzling given that he very probably had access to letters he had written home during the war. In a letter to his parents in the late spring of 1782, Büttner mentions having written to them about the siege in his previous letter, which he believes might have been lost, since they do not refer to it in their most recent letter to him.[49] This reference ought to have helped him date the siege and surrender accurately.

---

49. Wilhelm Zeithe, "Mein Lehr und Wanderjahre," http://www.dewarim.de/de/texte/z1.html (accessed June 18, 2005); and Henry Retzer, personal communication with Anne Pfaelzer de Ortiz, June 18, 2005. This letter also confirms Büttner's place in von Knyphausen's regiment of von Borck's company, stationed in New York City, and is dated May 3, 1782. This is the address he tells his parents to use when they reply to his letter, and the letter also verifies that he is employed in the regiment as a barber-surgeon, since he requests that his parents enclose some blood-letting blades in their next letter to him and remarks on the difficulty of getting other instruments he needs for his practice.

Insights Provided by the Narrative

Büttner's memoirs are no less important for not being completely verifiable. The portions that have been authenticated provide valuable information, dispelling commonly held ideas about the conditions under which redemptioners and other indentured servants traveled and then lived once in the colonies.

Büttner and Whitehead tell contrasting stories of their stay in Amsterdam in VOC recruitment houses. While Büttner, like Whitehead, deplores his loss of freedom after signing up with VOC recruiters, it is clear in both men's tales that the recruiters make good on their promises to help their charges obtain interviews with the VOC. And while the recruits are indeed kept under lock and key, they are not mistreated, according to Büttner. Unlike Whitehead, Büttner does not feel that he is malnourished. Contrary to Whitehead's description of thin gruel and meager slices of tough bread, Büttner describes three meals a day that, while perhaps not generous, were certainly substantial enough to content him. While Whitehead describes being forced to scrub down the quarters where he is housed and to perform other arduous labor from mealtime until dusk, Büttner describes being led daily to an area where he and his fellow inmates were free to pass their time in recreation. When Whitehead mentions the same thing, he says they were marched along to the recreation grounds once a week, and he focuses on his dislike of songs they sang on their way and on the recriminations suffered by those who appeared glum. Whether the two young men were taken to different houses is unclear, though their wildly different descriptions would seem to indicate that they were. But it is also possible that the difference in their temperaments and in how each man dealt with adversity may account for the discrepancy. Whitehead's glass is always half-empty; Büttner's is usually half-full.

Whitehead's tale is somewhat improbable, actually. It would not be in the interest of either the recruiting agents or the VOC to subject potential recruits to miserable conditions that might damage their health. Certainly recruitment agents may have housed some of their clients in harsh conditions, but this would have been the exception rather than the rule. The imprisonment of potential recruits by *volkhouders* is understandable given the sizable debt recruiting agents incurred for their assistance as well as for food and housing; only by restricting the freedom of the debtors could the recruiters guarantee that they would receive payment. Both Whitehead and Büttner portray themselves as willing and eager to go with the *volkhouders,* whom they later condemn as soul sellers. But this in itself shows that, far from being the kidnappers, soul vendors, and white slavers of the tales told by more well-to-do immigrants, these agents were involved in the redemptioner trade only incidentally. Their efforts were wholly on the behalf of the VOC.

A casual examination of indenture records during the period around Büttner's arrival in Philadelphia indicates that, while few or no other ships had redemptioner groups composed largely of those who failed to secure work with the VOC, many ships had some individuals who may have been in that situation. There are a number of redemptioners whose debts are larger than normal and whose contracts are accordingly longer. Their debts and contract lengths fall in the range established by Büttner's group, indicating that these individuals may, like Büttner and Whitehead, have hoped for employment by the VOC but failed to secure a position. With no other way to pay their debt, these men and women probably jumped at the opportunity to travel to the colonies as redemptioners, thus forming a class of accidental emigrants to the American colonies.

Inevitably, these immigrants would have sent letters home describing their dashed hopes and unexpected new status as redemptioners bound for servitude in America. Perhaps it is through these letters that ship captains carrying redemptioner passengers became confused with the VOC agents. Regardless of how the myth of the callous, evil soul seller and kidnapper arose, VOC agents and captains of ships carrying redemptioners were not commonly guilty of such nefarious activities.[50] While such characters must have existed, the bulk of VOC agents and ship captains seem to have honored and been ruled by the contracts they made with their recruits and passengers. These accidental emigrants may have been bitter about the ill fortune that defeated their hopes of bringing home riches from the East, and they may have vented their bitterness in letters home. The letters may have discussed the freedom they lost through their deep financial indebtedness to the agents and/or shippers. But few of these people seem to have actually been kidnapped, nor were they forced to sign contracts against their will. If Büttner and Whitehead are typical, some of these accidental emigrants to the American colonies stayed to live out their lives in the new land, while others returned to their native land whenever and however possible.

The conditions under which redemptioners made the voyage to America were undoubtedly harsh. Meals, while providing adequate sustenance, were by necessity repetitious and far from luxurious. In instances when the voyage took much longer than the average, food would have been rationed less generously once it became apparent that it would need to last longer, and the more perishable provisions would certainly have spoiled and been, at best,

50. Georg Fertig, "Transatlantic Migration from German-Speaking Parts of Central Europe, 1600–1800: Proportions, Structures, and Explanations," in Canny, Europeans on the Move, 229–31; Guenter Moltmann, "The Migration of German Redemptioners to North America," in Colonialism and Migration: Indentured Labour Before and After Slavery, ed. P. C. Emmer (Boston: Martinus Nijhoff, 1986), 116; Wokeck, Trade in Strangers, 33–34.

unappealing. The passengers shared cramped quarters and had no privacy. Not even washing or relieving oneself could have been done in private. But the redemptioners did not expect private cabins. Neither did they seem to feel that the provisions for their passage were niggardly, although they expressed displeasure over the repetitious meals and the staleness of provisions. Redemptioners were cautioned to bring along extra provisions, but it is clear from the contracts they signed that they could survive the passage quite well even if they did not bring along extra food. The one condition that seemed as unexpected to the redemptioners as it did to the wealthier passengers was the lack of separate quarters for the single women. These young women were mingled with the rest of the redemptioners, single men and families alike, which both Büttner and Whitehead noted with surprise and regret.

Büttner's account also dispels the idea that the lot of an indentured servant was a joyless life of harsh treatment. The liberties allowed by the families for whom he worked and his living conditions with those families indicate that servants were treated well. Büttner was given a fair amount of personal freedom both while working and during his free time. He also was allowed to keep tips he was given. Clearly, most servants shared a master's bounty as well as the hard labor. Note the pleasure with which Büttner describes the provision of meat at two or more meals a day, and the huge cheese from which anyone could take as much as was wanted. He thinks nothing of being allowed the use of a horse or of being allowed to attend church in Philadelphia on his own. That he takes these things for granted strongly suggests that other servants would have been allowed such freedoms. Indeed, most servants must have been treated so. Had they been treated harshly, their letters home would have discouraged further emigration. Far from depicting ill treatment as an accepted norm, Büttner's account shows that servants even had recourse to justice when they were mistreated. He knew that he could go—and thought it worth going—to the local magistrate when his master struck him. He would not have been likely to do so without being fairly sure the magistrate would take his part, as this action would certainly have enraged his master further and perhaps resulted in an even worse beating. Magistrates, instead of siding with the far wealthier and more influential masters, frequently took the side of penniless servants against their masters. Servants, then, must have expected justice and must have known they could improve their condition if they had a legitimate complaint.

Büttner's story is no less entertaining for being in large part verifiable. By his own admission he is an opportunist, a teller of tall tales, one who gets into scrapes and depends on his wits and his luck to slide out of them. He is both a rascal and a romantic of the first order who in old age looks back fondly upon his youthful exploits even while recommending prudence to his

Johan Carl Büttner

Amtschirurgus in Senftenberg.

geb. 1754 zu Lauta b. Senftenberg.

Fig. 6 Johann Carl Büttner in his later years. Frontispiece of the German edition of Büttner's memoir, published in 1828 as *Büttner der Amerikaner*.

readers. It is not difficult to imagine that if he were writing today he would try to turn his story into a screenplay. To enlighten while entertaining is a worthwhile endeavor; thankfully, it is an endeavor in which Büttner succeeds.

To improve clarity, the editors have inserted information in brackets into the text, occasionally altered paragraph breaks, supplied chapter titles, and changed the spelling of Buettner to Büttner. All numbered footnotes are the editors'. Otherwise the text is as it appears in the original 1915 translation.

Narrative of Johann Carl Büttner
in the American Revolution

[Introduction by the translator, 1915] The following Narrative*[1] is a translation from the German. The original German edition is a very scarce Book.
The translation is abridged in so far as the greater part of his adventures
in other countries is left out, being of little interest for the American reader.
The part produced here is an interesting medley of serious incidents and accidental exploits, and strews side lights on the American revolution not to be
undervalued. The German literature is still full of unpublished interesting
material relating to important events of American History. If this little attempt
finds support, other books may follow.

BÜTTNER, THE AMERICAN: THE AUTOBIOGRAPHY

THE ADVENTURES OF
JOHANN CARL BÜTTNER

Chapter 1—Childhood and Education

The place where I, Johann Carl Büttner, the American,*[2] first saw the light in the year 1754, is Lauta, a village situated in the district of the royal province of Senftenberg.[3] My father, Johann Ehregott Büttner, a regularly ordained minister, preached there the best of all religions.[4] My mother's name was Johanne Christiane, and she was the daughter of a clergyman named Pittius of Nussdorf, near Forste, situated in Niederlaussitz.[5] I was the third child of my parents, who were blest with eleven children, four of whom are alive at present.

Nature endowed all my brothers and sisters with a lively temperament, and in this respect was not less generous to me. Love of excitement and adventure, that I have not lost even in my seventieth year, became noticeable in my earliest youth. By the time I had the full use of my legs, there was no piece of daring that I would refuse. The higher the tree, the happier I was to climb to the top. Naturally on account of this, I sometimes suffered mischance. Thus it happened that in my fifth year I climbed a tree in the garden of the Rectory at Lauta, and had reached the very top, when the limb to which I was holding suddenly broke. I fell to the ground, and lay there like one dead. Summoned from the house by the terrified cries of my playmates, my mother rushed to my side. But instead of sympathizing with me, she restored me to consciousness with several smart cuffs on the ear.

---

1. Asterisk denotes note by the translator appearing in the 1915 edition, Anon., trans., *Narrative of Johann Carl Büttner in the American Revolution*, Three hundred and twenty Copies printed for CHAS. FRED. HEARTMAN, New York City, two pages prior to p. 1. The note reads, "*Büttner, der Amerikaner. Eine Selbstbiographie Johann Carl Büttner's, ehemaligen nordamerikanischen Kriegers.* XIX, 137 pp. Camenz 1828." The actual full German title of Büttner's memoir was *Büttner, der Amerikaner. Eine Selbstbiographie Johann Carl Büttner's, jeßigen Amts-Chirurgus in Senftenberg und ehemaligen nordamerikanischen Kriegers, Mit dem Bildniße des Versaffers* (Camenz: E. S. Krausche, 1828).

2. Asterisk denotes Büttner's note, which reads, "That I added to my family name the title 'American' might strike many as uncalled for and arrogant; but I did this not without sufficient reason. Although I no longer live in America, I spent, however, my best years in that part of the world, fought in the significant, decisive North American struggle for independence, and moistened with my blood the soil of the great North American republic."

3. These places were in the Electorate of Saxony in the eastern German states. Saxony, formerly a powerhouse among the Germanic states, had been invaded by Prussia at the beginning of the Seven Years' War (1756–63). The subsequent political and economic decline of the state may have been one factor in Büttner's decision to try his fortune elsewhere. Senftenberg is about thirty-five miles northeast of Dresden, and Lauta is five to ten miles southeast of Senftenberg.

4. Büttner and his family were Lutherans. Conflict between Lutherans, Calvinists, and Roman Catholics had contributed to turmoil in the German states for two centuries.

5. Niederlausitz was in the Margravate of Brandenberg, north of Saxony.

I did not quarrel with the fate that very early in my life gave me opportunities to exercise and develop my bodily powers. Had I been coddled by my
parents as many children are, the burden of physical trials and tribulations
that the future had in store for me would have been harder to endure. Therefore I counsel parents in the higher walks of life to take thought not only
of the training of the spiritual powers of their children, but also to concern
themselves with the development of their physical fitness. The exercise and
development of the bodily powers are indeed requisite to the complete education of men and women, for parents can never tell into what circumstances
their children may sometime be placed, where perhaps just the lack of early
training of their physical powers having left them timid and lacking in
courage, might render them incapable of doing that which they are required
to do. Doubtless in after years I would have borne less easily my lot as apprentice to a surgeon and as volunteer in America, had I been weakened physically by indulgence. Accordingly, the development and strengthening of my
body was provided for; or rather, I saw to that myself; and very little did any
one concern oneself with my spiritual education, for that matter.

My father was otherwise engaged with his ministerial offices, or with his
farming, or with the instruction of my older brothers. The incumbent schoolmaster to whose mercies I was intrusted was little fitted to handle so wild a
boy as I. My father and my mother came to realize this, and finally the latter
took some pains to arouse in me an interest in the doctrines of religion (for
which I am now not unthankful); they also sent me to Senftenberg, to the
school at that time taught by Kretschmar, the rector who has since become
widely known because of his tragic end. This man was indeed an excellent
schoolmaster, but was suffering even at that time from hypochondria.[6]

In the school at Senftenberg I laid the foundations for a knowledge of the
teachings of Christianity, of the Latin language, and of other useful branches
of learning, and was thus prepared for one of the higher institutions of learning. Notwithstanding the fact that it is unpleasant to remember that I caused
my teachers at Senftenberg a great deal of trouble, more on account of my
lively disposition than because I was impelled by any bad intentions, yet I like
to think often of my sojourn in this town. Much of this pleasure is caused by
recalling the intellectual enjoyments that appeal to a boy, and that I experienced here. Gladly do I remember the times when I chartered a canoe, in
company with playmates no less lively than myself, to explore the Elster River
and to land with them near a place where stood the old castle which was
demolished by the Hussites in the year 1431, and of which a few ruins are still
to be seen. Here it was that in the Middle Ages, predatory and belligerent

6. I.e., mental depression.

knights fell upon itinerant merchants. And here at the approach of danger those robbers fled to their Sumpfenberg[7] through stone-walled secret passages, known only to themselves, deep under the Elster River. And here it was that we, spirited young knights, also usually started our rambles. Not for profit-seeking merchants were we on the search; but for wild geese, innocent ducks, and other water-loving birds whose eggs we wanted to find.

I visited each year the vineyards on the hills that surrounded Senftenberg like an amphitheatre; not only to enjoy the wonderful view that revealed to us far-away Bautzen and Dresden,[8] but also on account of the cherries, the grapes, and all the other fruit of the fall. I was especially delighted with the joyous activity in the vineyards in the wine season, and with the feasts and the festivals that were constantly being celebrated. I paid very little attention at that time to the earthworks in the vicinity of the vineyard; these doubtless had been thrown up by Slaves and Wends[9] when they tried to resist their German victors in the woods and marshy places near Senftenberg.

After I had prepared myself in Senftenberg for a higher school, I followed the advice of my parents and matriculated at the lyceum at Camenz [Kamenz],[10] where in those days taught Vogt, Praetorius,[11] Schultze and others whose memories will always be dear to me. My father had a few friends in Camenz who very soon proved useful to me in many ways. After a short time, I ate my noonday meal with hospitable families; such families were never scarce in Camenz. The archdeacon Julich, a university friend of my father, gave me shelter in this friendly Camenz. Naturally all the teachers, and also my reverend host, influenced me in no small degree. This last named patron was a kindhearted, humor-loving man whose pleasure it was to entertain the son of his old friend in the most interesting manner, especially during the long winter evenings. He not only related to me tales of the natural curiosities of our own country, but he also drew my attention to the features of other parts of the world. Especially he talked about the beauties of the East Indies, and of the silver and gold mines of America, and not infrequently gave me to read descriptions of travel written by men who had seen these parts of the world and in many cases had grown very rich there. The good man did not suspect in those days how these stories of his, and the interesting contents

7. A reference to a castle.
8. Dresden, about a hundred miles south of Berlin, is the capital and principal city of Saxony. Between 1750 and 1800 it had a population between 52,000 and 55,000. See Jan de Vries, *European Urbanization, 1500–1800* (Cambridge: Harvard University Press, 1984), 142, 272–73.
9. By "Slaves" Büttner means Slavs, who, with the Wends, were Slavonic-speaking peoples defeated by Germanic-speaking tribes by the twelfth century.
10. Kamenz is about halfway between Senftenberg and Dresden. By 1800 both Kamenz and Senftenberg still had populations of fewer than 10,000. Vries, *European Urbanization*, 272–73.
11. Perhaps Michael Praetorius, baroque composer and writer.

of the books he had given me, would influence my future life. But it was at precisely that time that I began to consider seriously the possibility of visiting those celebrated regions of the world, after I had completed my studies; and with these thoughts I combined the hope that perhaps I too might succeed in returning from the East Indian and American paradises a rich man. How I was deceived in my hopes!

Partly because I was urged and partly because of my own inclinations, I entered the school-choir at Camenz. This choir had to sing not only in front of the houses of the citizens in the city but in the suburbs as well. On an occasion of this sort, one very hard winter, I had the misfortune to freeze my feet. It became necessary for me to seek the advice of a surgeon. During one of the visits of the surgeon's assistant, a young physician, it was mentioned that surgery is the one profession that could take one through the world, because it is necessary everywhere. This remark drove me to the decision to adopt this profession myself. My mother gave her consent immediately, because as she said, it was pretty hard on my father to give me an opportunity to study, since my brothers had studied away all his money; my father objected at first, saying he would have liked to see me study theology also; but after a while he complied with my wish and gave his consent.

I became the apprentice of Kirsten, the surgeon at Camenz; and I laid many a plan to go out, after my apprenticeship was finished, into the wide world, perhaps to America, or to the far-away beautiful East Indies. And now I learned not only how to trim beards and the other accomplishments of surgical skill, but was obliged also, as an apprentice, to polish the shoes of my master, and to attend to other domestic duties. In those days I did not have the slightest suspicion that in time to come, on the other side of the Atlantic Ocean, I should have to perform more menial and much more difficult tasks with my hands. But meantime I was contented with the lot I had chosen for myself; I was obedient and did all that my master and his wife expected me to do; and altogether, I did not have a very bad time of it during my apprenticeship.

During this period nothing happened to cause a memorable change in my life. On the twenty-first of February, during the last year of my apprenticeship, I witnessed the grewsome execution of a man who had murdered his mother, his father and his brother, in the village of Goeda, two miles outside of Camenz. This three-fold murderer, named Jacob Ritter, was twenty-four years of age. He had murdered his father and his mother out of disgust that they had lived so long and had disappointed him in his inheritance; afterwards killing his brother for fear he might make known to the world his devilish deed. But he received his much-deserved punishment. He was dragged on a cow-hide to the place of execution; after being pinched with red-hot tweezers, he was broken on the wheel.

Chapter 2—Wanderlust

After I had completed my apprenticeship, I returned to the home of my parents. Had I followed the wishes of my father, I would have gone to Dresden, to complete my studies in that city's anatomical institution,[12] under the supervision of another of his university friends, D. Demiani. If only I had taken the advice of my excellent father, I doubtless would have had a more fortunate career. But I had no inclination whatever to go to Dresden, and I longed for the wide world. Finally my father consented; and after I had said goodbye to all my relations I left the place of my birth, with the firm decision not to return until Dame Fortune had put me in a position to come back in a coach and four. How vainly did I wait on her favor! Perhaps she considered me unworthy of her gifts. The start of my years of pilgrimage was quite pleasant. My father gave me enough money to take a stage to Dresden, and my two older brothers accompanied me thus far. I had plenty of money, since my grandfather, whom shortly before my departure I had shaved for the first time, had given me a ducat. Moreover my father handed me, just as I was leaving, the entire contents of my savings bank. A merry trio of brothers, we reached the hotel in Dresden called Kammerdieners and took a room, deciding to spend a few days there, in order to have a good time. And we carried out our intentions. All day long we bowled; and we played cards all night.

But since all good things finally pass, this merry life had to come to an end. After a few days, my fortune had been squandered and my brothers had to return home. With empty pockets and a heavy heart, I bade farewell to my kinsmen, and went towards Prague [Praha].[13] During this journey I had plenty of time to reflect on my recent foolish and profligate carryings-on, and especially to realize the harmfulness of immoderate card-playing.

I had the good fortune to find shelter in Prague. I liked very much this curious capital of Bohemia, where more than four centuries ago Johann Huss[14] kindled anew the light of Christian truth. But as the people here tried to persuade me to embrace the Catholic faith, I took my departure; and still indignant over their attempts to proselyte me, I wandered towards Vienna [Wien].[15] Here I arrived one evening and took lodgings in an inn called

12. The Colegium medico-chirurgicum, founded in 1748.

13. Prague (Praha) is the capital and principal city of Bohemia and is located about seventy miles south-southeast of Dresden. Between 1750 and 1800 it had a population between 59,000 and 77,000. See Vries, *European Urbanization*, 278.

14. The Czech dissenter who was put to death for heresy in 1415. He is considered a precursor to the Protestant movements of the sixteenth century.

15. Vienna (Wien) was the capital and principal city of the Austrian Hapsburg Empire. It is located on the Danube River about 145 miles southeast of Prague. Between 1750 and 1800 it had a population between 175,000 and 231,000. See Vries, *European Urbanization*, 278.

Posthoernchen in Leopold City, a section of Vienna. Worn out, I threw upon a bench my gripsack, through the straps of which I had thrust my sword, ordered a half bottle of wine, and sat down to await my supper. Notwithstanding the fact that during my journey from Prague to Vienna I had been disgusted with myself over my card-playing, I could not resist the temptation of watching the game of two journeymen apprentices. While I was looking on, a petty officer and six men came hurriedly into the room and accosted the persons at the table with: "Well, Well! And this is where we find you!"

The soldiers quickly arrested one after the other of us three. Without listening to the explanation that I had only an hour ago arrived from Prague, and did not even know the other two fellows, they searched my pockets, confiscated my portfolio, my diploma, and my razor, and escorted me over the bridge of the Danube inside the city of Vienna. Here in a little house which was situated near an insignificant marketplace, I was asked the following questions: Where had I come from, what was my business, who were my parents, how many brothers and sisters had I, and what were their first names. After this examination, still one more question was put to me, and that was if I were one of "those that eat meat."[16]

And then the soldiers took me to the so-called Rumor House high up on the fourth floor. I was horrified to find that some of those who were detained there, were in chains. I thereupon sat down on a bench, and notwithstanding the fact that I knew I was innocent of misdeed, fell to weeping. "Oh, do not cry," the others called out, trying to comfort me. "Neither are we thieves nor murderers, but honest men. We are farmers whom they brought to this place because we refused the increased vassalage that was demanded of us. But everything will come out right in the end." Quietness and even a degree of cheerfulness were restored to me by these consolations. And later on, it occurred to me that this undeserved punishment in Vienna was justly meted out to me by God's providence for my passion for card-playing, and to prevent me even from looking at others playing cards. With these thoughts I fell asleep.

In the morning I received one cent's worth of bread; at noon a little bowl of fish soup which had been collected in the monasteries and in the evening again a little soup. Every day came a petty officer to ascertain the state of our health. After enduring these conditions eleven days, I was finally led by a Rumor soldier down two flights of stairs for an examination. Here in a room sat a man clothed all in black. He put to me again the questions that I had answered at the time of my arrest. I explained to him how everything

16. Presumably, if he ate meat on Fridays and during Lent, he was not a Roman Catholic but a Protestant.

happened, and drew his attention to the fact that if he would only consider what I had told him about my part in the affair, my innocence must be established. The gentleman in the black clothes thereupon gave me three shillings, and dismissed me with the consoling assurance that I would be set free very soon.

But eight days passed before a petty officer appeared who ordered me to follow him. He led me down one flight of stairs, where I was given back my portfolio, my razor, and all my belongings, and was ordered to limit my stay in Vienna to five days; also not to go around to the members of my profession with requests for money. I was told to report to the commander of the city each evening, and to make a request for a pass that would enable me to remain in the city the following day.

Glad to have regained my freedom, I went down to the Leopold City to get my gripsack from the Posthoernchen Inn. All my inquiries seemed to be in vain. Every one professed not to know me, and no one seemed to have seen the gripsack I had left behind. Finally the waiter remembered that he had found a gripsack several weeks ago, early in the morning, on one of the benches in the dining room, and that he had taken charge of it. He brought it, and after I had shown him the key to convince him that it really belonged to me, he handed it over, but without the sword, which had gone astray. Now he demanded a gratuity. I would have been happy to satisfy him, but this was impossible because I did not have a cent in my pocket. This happened on a Saturday, and as the waiter surmised I might be a Protestant, he advised me to attend on Sunday forenoon the services in the chapel of the Danish ambassador, but first to state my condition to the pastor and announce my intention to quit the city. The waiter said this Protestant minister would provide me my traveling expenses. I followed his advice, and received from the pastor two dollars, enough to pay my passage to Hermansstadtim Siebenbuergen. After I had received in addition to this a viaticum of sixteen groschen[17] from the master of the guild of surgeons, I started the next day on my journey from Vienna to Pressburg.[18]

This fortified place is situated at the mouth of the Waag [River] where she pours her waters into the Danube, and is inhabited by Hungarians, Slavs and Germans. Mentioning this village, I cannot refrain from pointing out a theory of mine regarding the name of my present residence, Senftenberg. Senftenberg means in the Wendish language Kommorow, a name which is

17. A viaticum was money to aid journeymen in their travels. Groschen possibly refers to Grots, a German monetary unit—in which case sixteen groschen, in the early 1770s, would equal about 0.04 pounds sterling. See John J. McCusker, *Money and Exchange in Europe and America, 1600–1775: A Handbook* (Chapel Hill: University of North Carolina Press, 1978), 63, 79.
18. Present-day Bratislava, on the Danube River about thirty-five miles east of Vienna.

similar to Kommorn.[19] But not only the names but the topographical situation of these two cities are very similar. Both are situated on a level, marshy
plain, crossed often by rivers. Kommorn is still a fortified place and Senftenberg used to be one, although on a much smaller scale. All this would not
be sufficient evidence to cause me to think—which I do—that Senftenberg
received its first and original name from Kommorn, if history did not con-
firm my belief. History states that the slaves[,] of which the serfs are a part[,][20]
started their operations in this place against the Greek Empire.[21] That was
in the sixth century, at the time that the Avars under Chan Bajan[22] forced
the servs [Serbs] to leave their homes in the Kommorn, Slavonia, Croatia,
Bosnia and Servia [Serbia]. They wandered through Jschechia [Czech lands]
or Bohemia towards Meissen and into the Lausitz, bringing with them not
only the culture which they had acquired during their wars with the Greeks,
but also gave to the cities and villages that they founded, the names of those
which they had inhabited near the Danube. In our times the British, Span-
iards and Germans who emigrated to America did the same. They called the
places which they founded in the new world by the names of the cities and
towns where they were born, or that were similar in respect to topography.

From Kommorn I wandered towards Ofen,[23] the old capital of the kingdom of Hungary. After I had looked at everything worth seeing in Ofen and
had wandered over the plains of Rakosch near the city of Pesth opposite Ofen,
I took passage on a vessel bound for the fortress Peterwardein.[24] Very interesting was the voyage down the Danube from Ofen to Peterwardein. From
here I started toward Carlowitz, two hours away, which is a very well-built
place and gives a beautiful view of Peterwardein. At this place I accepted a
position as assistant to a Slavonic surgeon and barber. But I did not enjoy
my duties, because in this part of the world the business of a barber is quite
different from what it is in our northern countries. I had to travel with my
master from one market to the other. He always occupied a stand of his own.
We set up a big kettle of hot water and on request from each man, shaved
his beard, washed his head, cleaned his ears and anointed his chin whiskers

19. This is present-day Komorno, on the Danube River about fifty-five miles southeast of
Bratislava.

20. Büttner here conflates ethnicity (Slav) and systems of bound labor (slave and serf), or
perhaps he meant Serbs, not serfs.

21. I.e., Byzantium.

22. Khan Baian led the Avars, originally a Mongolian people, who settled in Dacia, now in
Romania.

23. Ofen is present-day Buda of Budapest, on the Danube River about fifty miles east-
southeast of Kommorn.

24. Peterwardein is present-day Petrovaradin, just a few miles downstream on the Danube
River from present-day Novi-Sad in northern Serbia, about 180 miles south of Budapest. Carlowitz
is present-day Sr. Karlovci, a few miles downstream from Petrovaradin.

until they shone. For this they had to pay three pennies. Among the common people in these regions it is not the custom to shave each week; never more frequently than four weeks, and often not until eight have passed.

Fourteen days later I said good-by to Carlowitz, and traveled through a mountain region to a little market town called Ruma.[25] Here I immediately found work as assistant to a district surgeon. I liked this place much better, because my duties consisted not only of trimming beards, washing heads and cleaning the ears of farmers, but because I also had an opportunity to perform various surgical operations. My master was superintendent of a hospital in which daily operations, amputations and trepannings were performed. Johannes Leben—that was the name of this district surgeon—was a Catholic, but his wife was Lutheran and a native of the province of Brandenburg. In this situation I decided to remain a long time, partly because I had a chance to gain more experience in my profession, and also because winter was approaching and knowing how hard I was to please, I hesitated to push on farther.

The New Year presents that I received from my regular customers among those whom I shaved, amounted to almost twenty gulden. During my sojourn in this place my master died. The village judge, who was a native of Leipzig and a countryman of mine, tried to persuade me to marry the widow. The proposition was not a bad one. I really liked the little woman. She had no children, a comfortable home, a respectable pharmacy and all the surgical instruments necessary to open a practice. Very tempting were the conditions under which I could settle in this place; but I felt that my knowledge of medicine was not sufficient, and my skill in surgery too slight to perform honorably the duties of a surgeon; and chiefly again my restless spirit induced me not to remain there, but to hurry on out into the wide world. Well did I remember the proverb my father used to recite so often: "Fronte capilata post haec occasio calva." (If you make a habit of seizing fortune by the forelock, there will come a time when she will be bald.) But the voice of my inclination counseled me differently. Obedient to it, I said goodbye at the first appearance of spring and hurried with a light heart to Semlin, a big, well-built market town at the junction of the Sau with the Danube.

This place also lies opposite the well known Turkish fortress, Belgrade.[26] I had a great desire to travel from Semlin through Turkey to Constantinople but they persuaded me not to enter Turkey, since traveling in that country, inhabited by barbarians,[27] could not be very safe. And just at that time a

25. Ruma is about twenty miles due south of Novi-Sad in present-day Serbia.

26. This is present-day Beograd, capital of Serbia, and is on the Danube River about thirty-five miles southeast of Ruma. Semlin is present-day Zemun.

27. I.e., Muslims, sometimes called Mohammedans, whom Christians of the era considered barbarians.

plague was sweeping through those parts. Much as I desired to travel to Constantinople, Damascus, Jerusalem and other places, I felt little inclined to have my young life cut short by a plague or a raving Mohammedan. I stamped my feet in rage on the Turkish border, because Asiatic barbarians were in possession of beautiful lands in which the tree of European culture first blossomed so wonderfully, where the human mind first unfolded its powers, where Rome, the mistress of the world, enforced her laws, and to which for many centuries scientists and artists made pilgrimages as to a holy land.

At Semlin the world seemed to be nailed up; for no one was allowed to cross the Turkish boundary unless he were willing to run the risk of being held on his return, often as long as seven weeks in quarantine. All the Greek and Turkish merchants crossing the border from Turkey were liable to this inconvenience. In Semlin there were Turkish merchants besides Christian and Jewish. So it happened that in each week, three Sundays were celebrated: Friday, the holy day of the Turks, Saturday, the Sabbath of the Jews, and the following day was observed as Sunday by the Christians. Decidedly against my inclinations, I had to take backward steps from Semlin. Near Belgrade, I crossed the Danube, and after seeing the Janitschar[28] parading around the fortifications, I went on to Banzowa[29] a small town with good, solidly-built houses and very well protected by walls and sentry boxes.

I took lodgings in an inn, to have my noonday meal and to pick up a traveling companion, since it was very dangerous to travel alone in these regions. But aside from the people who kept the inn, I saw no one but a man reading a book. I was very curious to know what the book might be that he was perusing so diligently, and after he had left the room, I picked it up and saw at a glance that it was the New Testament. Before I could lay the volume back on the table the man entered the room again, and asked me in Slavic if I knew what book that was. Since I had been an assistant to a Slavic surgeon and had had a chance to learn the language, which is somewhat similar to Wendish, I answered, "yes." So I was obliged to read a chapter of the New Testament to this man, who was a Greek merchant. He was greatly pleased, and started a conversation with me. After I had disclosed to him my intention to travel to Siebenbuergen, he said that his residence lay in the same direction and offered me a seat in his carriage and also to pay my expenses, which courtesy I accepted with many thanks. Furthermore he promised to do his best to get me a position in his home city, saying that there was a German district surgeon in charge of the big hospital. This gentleman lived up to his promise. I secured a position in his native city. After I had remained there for half

28. Soldiers, Janissaries.
29. This is possibly present-day Pancevo, located just a few miles north of Belgrade.

a year, had witnessed many surgical operations and gained much experience on the medical side of my profession, I resigned and continued my way to Siebenbuergen.

During this journey, I passed at one time a village inhabited by Wallachs.[30] The houses were the shape of sugar loaves and were built of turf and clay. Instead of windows, these dwellings had openings over which oiled paper was pasted. In the middle of these habitations burned a fire around which the inhabitants were grouped. I entered one of these places and asked for refreshment. They gave me a longhandled gourd filled with very strong brandy made of unripe plums and other fruits. I took a big drink from the vessel and very soon felt a burning in my stomach. I complained of the pain, and they gave me half a watermelon to extinguish the fire in my vitals. The watermelon, which was blood-red inside, was very cooling and I found it more palatable than the sugar melon common with us in Germany.

Finally I arrived at the fortress Temeswar,[31] surrounded by wastes and swamps, and at least for the Germans that emigrated to this part of the country, not very salubrious. I found that out myself. Not long after my arrival I came down with an intermittent fever from which I suffered four weeks. At this place I decided not to go on to Siebenbuergen, and following the advice of the surgeon who looked after me during my illness, returned to Ofen and to Vienna, passing through the German Empire towards the cities on the North Sea where surgeons are always in demand, especially for boats bound for the East Indies and America. My passage to Ofen did not cost me a cent. I fell in with a military transport and marched with the soldiers to Ofen. I felt as it I were coming home on my arrival in this city. Although Ofen is thirty-six miles away from Vienna, the splendid King's Highway starts here. The villages are not so far apart and the Hungarians are much more civilized than the Wallachs.

I stayed only one day in Vienna, afraid that the same misfortune that marked my first visit in the city might happen to me again. Through the lovely, romantic regions of Lower Austria I hurried to Regensburg,[32] where I received some assistance and where I remained only four weeks. Here I was, however, put to the necessity of selling all my books containing the medical and surgical notes that I had collected during my practice. I traveled from Regensburg to Stuttgard[33] and Ludwigslust in Wuertenberg [Württemberg]. Here I met a relative of mine who was a wigmaker and who wanted

30. Wallachia was an independent principality that later became part of Romania.

31. This is present-day Timisoara in Romania, about eighty miles north-northeast of Belgrade.

32. Regensberg, in Bavaria, is about 210 miles up the Danube River from Vienna. In 1800 its population was about 23,000. See Vries, *European Urbanization*, 273.

33. This is present-day Stuttgart in Baden-Württemberg, about 135 miles west of Regensberg. Between 1750 and 1800 its population was between 17,000 and 20,000. Ibid.

to teach me his noble art. I refused his offer, left him after a few days, and
went to Rastadt,[34] which is now the German fortress Landau. From thence I
went to Mannheim,[35] beautifully laid out and consistently built. After I had
visited Frankfort-on-Main [Frankfurt am Main], I traveled through Hessia, to
Hildesheim, to Hanover [Hannover] and Bremen.[36] I could not get a position
in any one of these cities.

Chapter 3—Hamburg and Amsterdam

Therefore I decided to go seafaring. With this determination I started for
Stade and Buxtehude, where I passed over the river to Hamburg.[37] I remained in Hamburg several days. On one occasion I took a walk outside
the walls and ascended the so-called Hamburger Mountain. At the foot of this
mountain I saw nearby a beautiful city. This Danish Hamburg was Altona.
During this walk I met some men who must have remarked that I was a
stranger. They asked me where I came from and what profession I followed.
When I told them I was from Saxony, they exclaimed, seeming greatly
pleased: "From Saxony! What city is your home? Not Dresden or Leipzig?
We too are from Saxony and are therefore your countrymen!" They listened
attentively to the story of my life, and when they heard that I was tired of my
wanderings on land, and that I had been unable to find a position for some
time, their faces seemed to mirror some secret joy. After they had become
acquainted with the facts of my history, they cut me off in the middle of a
sentence and said: "But why do you run around blindly? You will find that
you will hardly be able to get a position in Hamburg or in Altona. Come with
us to Altona. We will drink a bottle of wine there, have some breakfast and
talk matters over."

34. Rastadt is about forty-five miles due west of Stuttgart.
35. Mannheim lies at the confluence of the Neckar and Rhine rivers about forty-five miles
north of Rastadt. Between 1750 and 1800 Mannheim's population was between 20,000 and
22,000. Ibid.
36. Frankfurt am Main is about forty miles north of Mannheim. Hildesheim is about 160
miles north-northeast of Frankfurt am Main. Hannover is about twenty miles northwest of
Hildesheim. Bremen, on the Weser River with access to the North Sea via Bremerhaven, is about
sixty miles northwest of Hannover. Between 1750 and 1800 the population of Frankfurt am Main
was 32,000–35,000; of Hildesheim, 10,000–12,000; of Hannover, around 17,000; and of Bremen, between 28,000 and 36,000. Ibid., 272–73.
37. Hamburg is on the Elbe River with easy access to the North Sea. It is the largest city in
what was the Hanseatic League of city-states—a trading group consisting of ports on the south
side of the Baltic and North seas, including Bremen, Hamburg, Lübeck, Danzig, and Stettin. It
is about sixty miles northeast of Bremen. Between 1750 and 1800 Hamburg's population was
between 75,000 and 100,000. Ibid., 273.

The pretended countrymen assured me that they were overjoyed to have met a Saxon and without my solicitation promised to look after my interests. After we had reached the wine cellar, they ordered bread, butter and cold roast and turned the conversation to the East and West Indies. When they heard that I had desired for a long time to visit these happy places, and that it was one of my cherished wishes to obtain a position as ship's surgeon, they promised immediately to give me a recommendation to their good friend, a ship's captain in Amsterdam, who surely would be able to procure me the desired position. They also promised to pay my passage to Amsterdam and my board. The same day I received from my alleged countrymen all that was necessary. They gave me a good dinner of roast veal and brought me aboard the ship that was to sail to Amsterdam.[38]

There were on the deck of this ship about fifty young men and women who, influenced by pretended friendly countrymen, had decided to go to the East and West Indies; and all of whom had been recommended to their good friend just as I had been. It was then that I understood that I had been lured on board this ship by notorious slavers and so-called soul-venders, and why they had rejoiced as soon as they knew that I desired to go to the East Indies or to America. It was quite necessary in those days to keep on the lookout for such men in the Hansa cities.[39] Many young men and young women were persuaded by them to go on a search in foreign parts of the world for a fortune that they could have found just as well or even better at home. Although I now knew that my pretended countrymen had no honest intentions towards me, and that while showing me affection and love, they had been working only for the money they received from the shippers of human freight or dealers in human flesh to be delivered in Amsterdam, I felt no decided rancor against them, because I desired so much to seek my fortune in another part of the world, and because it was through these people that I had secured my promise to be made surgeon of the ship. The next morning the vessel put out to sea. I thought of my parents and my brothers and sisters, calling farewell to them in spirit. With a favorable wind, after three days, we reached Amsterdam.

Chapter 4—The Soul Venders and Finding a Berth

When the ship landed, the dealers in humankind came forward. One took in charge ten, another twenty and another thirty. Myself with many others, they led along several streets to a house in which we were placed in company with

38. Between 1750 and 1800 the population of Amsterdam, the commercial and financial center of Holland, was between 210,000 and 217,000. Ibid., 271.

39. These men were most probably recruiters for the Dutch East India Company or VOC.

perhaps one hundred apprentices. They welcomed us joyfully with the question: "Were we, too, going to East India?" In this lock-up we had everything we wanted. We received in the morning buttermilk soup, at noonday meat with vegetables, and in the evening soup again. At night we slept in hammocks in which we could rock like a child in a cradle. These hammocks were given to us by the slavers with a purpose. The swaying of the hammocks was intended to accustom us to the rocking of the boat. It can be easily understood that this dormitory resounded with lively talk, since all of us were young, healthy men expecting to acquire riches and treasure on the other side of the ocean. One fell out of his hammock, because the old rope with which it was fastened, broke. Another ascended without suspicion his pendulous bed, but fell to the floor very soon because a mischievous neighbor had cut the cords which held it up.

Nothing else was wanted here by the young people but golden liberty, and even of this we were not robbed altogether. Every day we were led, by two and two, from the city to the neighborhood of the windmills, where we could play ball under the supervision of our guards, or could pass the time according to our liking. At sunset, however, we had to march back in the prescribed order, and were locked up in the big room. As little as I believed in the high-mindedness of the slavers, I must confess to their credit that they did all in their power to place us each according to our liking. Thus they tried very hard to have me appointed as ship's surgeon. They registered me at the East Indian House as a surgeon. Immediately I received beautiful clothes to wear, and a silver time-piece, and was ordered to report for examination. But I am sorry to say, I came too late. Another had already been accepted. The boats bound for the East Indies had all sailed for this season. I was advised there would be no more call this year for surgeons on the East Indian ships. I returned sadly to my lock-up, took off my nice uniform and my silver watch, and at the orders of the master, donned again my old clothes.

A few days later the master entered our room and exclaimed: "Boys, there is one ship more leaving port, bound for America. It is a wonderful country, where gold grows and pearl fisheries abound. And moreover, it is not as far as the East Indies. My son was there only three years, and made so much money that after his return he bought a house for himself here in Amsterdam. Of course you will have to work one or two years without receiving any salary, in order to pay for your board and transportation; but after that you will be free. You may go wherever you please and earn daily two or three dollars, doing quite easy tasks, such as loading and unloading ships. And naturally if you have a profession you can practise it just as you please." Shortly after this discourse of our master, we all, weary of this life without liberty, decided to emigrate to America.

We were shipped immediately in big boats to Rotterdam,[40] where we received an excellent noonday meal and as much wine as we wanted; perhaps to give us courage. Then we were taken to a great three-masted schooner that lay at anchor in the river Meuve.[41] On board this boat, there had already been gathered about three hundred persons, mostly handcraftsmen and young women clothed in blue striped linen dresses. We too were provided on the spot with jackets, shirts and trousers of the same color.

Chapter 5—Crossing the Atlantic

The following day our ship started with a favoring wind towards England. In a few days we reached the channel that divides England from France and unites the North or German Sea with the Atlantic Ocean. We anchored near Dover, which is an unimportant city and has a fortress in which there are generally Crown prisoners incarcerated. This city is noteworthy chiefly because of the short passage thence to Calais in France. Ships were constantly coming and going. We remained here only one night, and sailed on the following day to Portsmouth,[42] which is a fortified city with an excellent harbor in which were to be seen several English war vessels. Our ship rode at anchor here for a few days, and took in fresh meat and fresh beer. The vessel was also visited by commissioners who examined everything and registered the entire ship's crew. The sails were repaired and everything examined and put in condition necessary for a trip across the Atlantic Ocean.

40. Rotterdam was the second-largest city in the Netherlands, after Amsterdam, and was the principal port for traffic between the North Sea and the Rhine River. Between 1750 and 1800 its population was between 44,000 and 57,000. See Vries, *European Urbanization*, 271.

41. This is the *Sally*, registered in Philadelphia on October 22, 1766, as being 150 registered tons, built in Philadelphia, captained by John Osmand, and owned by Samuel Howell. This voyage listed 193 freights on board (number of adult-equivalent passengers) and is estimated to have landed 210 passengers in Philadelphia. See "Ships Registered for the Port of Philadelphia, 1727–1775," *Pennsylvania Magazine of History and Biography* 26 (1903): 487; Ralph B. Strassburger, *Pennsylvania German Pioneers: A Publication of the Original Lists of Arrivals in the Port of Philadelphia from 1727 to 1808* (Norristown, Pa.: Pennsylvania German Society, 1934), 2:867; Marianna S. Wokeck, *Trade in Strangers: The Beginnings of Mass Migration to North America* (University Park: Pennsylvania State University Press, 1999), 248.

42. Portsmouth is on the English coast in Hampshire County near the Sussex County border, just across from the east end of the Isle of Wight and centrally located for accommodating shipping in the English Channel. It was the second-most-frequent port used to clear English customs and take on extra provisions on the way to British America for ships with German passengers from Rotterdam. See Strassburger, *Pennsylvania German Pioneers*, vol. 1. Between 1750 and 1800 Portsmouth's population was between 10,000 and 32,000. See Vries, *European Urbanization*, 271. The heading written above the oath that Büttner took upon landing in Philadelphia indicates that his ship cleared English customs, its last port before Philadelphia, at Portsmouth, thus confirming this part of Büttner's narrative. See Strassburger, *Pennsylvania German Pioneers*, 2:867.

One evening after everything was in readiness, we set sail for America. But we had proceeded only a few days westward when there sprang up an unfavorable wind that drove our ship now this way and now that. As a result the greater part of the ship's crew became violently ill; even the captain himself vomited constantly like the rest of us, and almost threw up his intestines. This sickness, caused by the constant rolling of the ship, lasted with some for eight days. After we had recovered, food began to taste all the better, we were merry; we sang and whistled. This care-free life was interrupted by a little storm that broke over us, and was so severe that it tore away the railing of the deck and the private chambers fastened to it. The loss of these was hard on all of us; especially on the women. For they, while performing the duties of nature, had to forego all sense of shame. Each one, when one wished to relieve oneself, must hold to the ship's rope with one hand, while with the other, hold one's clothes over one's head and let oneself be splashed by the brine whenever the waves ran high enough.

Mentioning this indecency forced upon us by necessity, I wish to speak about a far more serious and deplorable custom which was permitted on this transportation boat. Men and women did not sleep in separate cabins; the sixty girls were distributed among the three hundred men in their quarters. It can be easily understood how wide, under these circumstances, the doors of immorality were opened. I see tears in the eyes of the angel of innocence and he covers his face. Perhaps such reprehensible practices are no longer in force on transport ships, and should they be, I wish that the philanthropic statesman of Holland, the noble-minded Baron of Gagern, might succeed in ending them.

I would advise unmarried women who have not the means to take quarters in the Captain's cabin, not even to enter a ship. Their innocence is much more in danger than on land. Some one may bring up the question: Why did the captain permit persons of different sexes to spend the night together on his ship? Oh! If I did not have to answer that a pernicious, unpardonable love of money, the root of all evil, was at the bottom of this! Of course, the ship's captain could expect to receive for a woman who was with child a greater amount of money upon landing in America.

Many of the girls on board died a frightful death before the ship landed. Once they contracted the loathsome disease, by some called the "gallant" one,[43] they usually met their cruel end. This will surprise no one who knows the character of this terrible disease and the conditions necessary for its cure.

43. I.e., syphilis or gonorrhea. While Büttner may have believed that one of these diseases was responsible for the deaths of these women, neither disease causes death so rapidly (and often not at all); it is likely that the culprit here was epidemic typhus. See note 231 to Whitehead's memoir.

The treatment of this disease calls specifically for fresh nourishing food, pure air and good nursing. All of these are lacking on board a ship. The women worst infected were taken into a separate cabin under the capstan,[44] where they died in unutterable misery. No one came near this spot unless obliged to, because of the horrible odor that prevailed there. The deceased were sewed up in a piece of sail cloth, a bag filled with sand was tied to the feet, and they were buried in the waves of the sea. Usually the bodies thrown into the water were immediately claimed as prey by the big fish. The captain found that if a number of these fish were swimming near the ship in the morning, he might conclude that corpses had been thrown overboard in the night.

After some time, I had a very violent fever that, as my companions told me, brought me very near death. I suffered utter delirium, and the surgeon was obliged to let blood from both my arms of which I knew nothing. Of this attack I remember naught save the torture like the suffering of the damned that I saw constantly in my dreams. After I had recovered my mental balance, I often prayed with all my soul for the forgiveness of my trespasses and sins. I was quite aware that I had not respected the commands of our holy God. By the help of God I soon recovered fully.

Our progress was very slow as we had most of the time winds from the wrong direction. Since our departure from the English coast, fifteen weeks had passed, while we were on the high seas and without sight of any land. Then our ship's captain, determining the longitude at noon in bright sunlight with his instruments, announced that we would sight the dry land of America within twenty-four hours. His prediction was fulfilled on the following day. Every one shouted with joy at the sight of the American coast. Already we saw coming towards us from shore, pilots and tugs to guide us past the shoals. It was a windless, murky August day. The sea shone like a great clear mirror framed in the coast of America; hardly a breath of air rippled the water's surface but a countless multitude of fishes could be seen playing around the boat. Even the monsters of the deep raised their huge awkward bodies close to the surface with an undulating motion, and then sank again to the black depths where they belonged, and then the captain said to us: "Children, pray, we are going to have a storm."

Soon we heard a distant rumbling; the sun began to darken; everything on the boat was in the greatest commotion in which many human voices mingled; with all possible speed the seamen furled the sails and bound them fast. The American pilots turned and hurried with their little boats coastward. The hatches were closed and over them were nailed pieces of strong canvas

44. A vertical cylinder rotated manually to hoist weights, such as a ship's anchor, by winding a cable or chain.

soaked in tar. Ever stronger and more terrifying became the roaring of the hurricane. Like black, forbidding chains of mountains we saw the waves piled up by the storm bearing down upon us. The lightning tore through the frightfully black heavens and the thunder roared. Suddenly the ship flew like a ball, now among the clouds, and now as swift as an arrow, into the trough of the sea. All around powerful bolts of lightning fell into a fearfully raging sea, and the thunder exploded with terrific report. In inexpressible rage the waves beat against the ship, or coming from opposite directions collided with each other above the decks. Every minute was as if we were suffering the most terrific bombardment. Every one was praying, and even the nefarious and the God-forsaken, of which there were plenty on board the ship, folded their hands as the Lord of the worlds spoke to them through the heart-crushing voice of the elements. As the sun on the following day scattered his rays over a quiet sea, I, with many others, in prayer and song, thanked the Lord who helps, and even in the mercy of His judgment, saves from death.

Oh, how unworthy of His grace were the most of us on board that ship! Our eyes could no longer see the coast of America, so longed for and so joyfully hailed. The drinking water became scarce, and for this reason we did not receive more than half a measure of water daily. Besides, this had a very unpleasant smell and tasted like ink. Notwithstanding, they fed us day after day with salted meat that increased our thirst. We received cheese on certain days. In need of more fluid, I gladly exchanged as did many others, my portion of cheese for half a measure of water. To prevent myself from drinking more water than absolutely necessary to quench the thirst from which I constantly suffered, I stuck a quill through the cork of the water bottle and drew in the fluid slowly. Not only did this portion of water that we received not suffice to quench our thirst, but it was also needed to soften the ship's biscuit, to cook the peas, the oatmeal, and the meat. The bread that we received was so hard that an axe was required to break it, and it looked green and yellow inside. The peas were only half cooked and were very difficult to digest. We liked best the oatmeal rations. It can easily be seen why we desired even more than ever to reach dry land, and why we were more than happy when we sighted it for the second time, after a lapse of three long weeks.

Chapter 6—Philadelphia

Again the pilots that we had seen once before came toward us in their little boats, and this time guided us successfully into the great arm of the sea leading to Philadelphia, called Delaware Bay, which is eighty miles long and three miles wide. But yet eight days passed before we reached Philadelphia, because the ship could proceed only very slowly on account of the current of the Delaware. We anchored amid stream in the river and took delight in gazing at the great beautiful city of Philadelphia.[45] On the following day, we were led to a building in the city,[46] where we took the oath of allegiance to King George III of England,[47] under whose control at that time the North American territory was. As we put our feet on land, on coming from the ship, the earth seemed to sway beneath us and we staggered like drunken men. But this condition lasted for only a quarter of an hour.

Philadelphia is very beautiful and built with nearly the same regularity as Mannheim; but is much larger. The number of houses at that time in the city was estimated at six thousand and it was said that forty thousand people lived in them. Now [1828] the city is said to have fourteen thousand houses and more than ninety thousand inhabitants. It is situated at the confluence of the Schuylkill and the Delaware rivers. The streets run in straight lines from the water front and are called by numbers, as First, Second, Third, Fourth, Fifth, Sixth, Seventh Street. These streets intersect King's and Market Streets. The latter is broad and has fine, massive arcades under which the merchants offer their wares. This street is similar to the Muehlendamm in Berlin. On both sides of this thoroughfare carriages can be driven without hitting each other, and during rainy weather it is possible to walk past the houses on dry cobble stones, under balconies.

There are more than twenty churches here, in which the inhabitants belonging to different religious sects worship in their own way the unseen, perfect Creator of all things whom we call God. Whoever sees in this place the churches of many different religious sects, among which even Anabaptists and Universalists, and who listens to services here in English, there in German, here in Swedish, there in French, must confess that this city has been rightly called the City of Brotherly Love.

Among other things worth seeing are the well-equipped workhouse and reformatory, with which are connected a lying-in hospital, an orphans' asylum and an infirmary. This house is massively built and has in the center a paved court where the prisoners can take exercise. The prisons are paved, kept clean and furnished with the necessary windows. Beautiful boulevards are laid out around the city, and not very far away little groves of chestnut and other nut trees afford refreshing shade. Near Philadelphia is situated Germantown,

45. Urban Philadelphia's population in 1772 was between 27,000 and 31,000. See Billy G. Smith, "Death and Life in a Colonial Immigrant City: A Demographic Analysis of Philadelphia," *Journal of Economic History* 37 (December 1977): 865.

46. Willing and Morris's store.

47. See Figure 4 for a reproduction of Büttner's actual signature on this oath. See Strassburger, *Pennsylvania German Pioneers*, 1:xxvi–xxvii, for transcripts of the actual oaths taken by German immigrants.

a little city mostly inhabited by Germans, who make their living mainly by building carriages and weaving linen. Many Germans also live in Lancaster, where they engage in manufacture, principally of woolen and cotton cloth.

After we had taken the oath of allegiance to the king of England, we were obliged to return to the boat. Shortly after, an announcement could have been read not only on the street corners of Philadelphia, but also in the American newspapers: "That a boat at present lying in the harbor of Philadelphia had arrived from Europe carrying a load of male and female persons, and that whoever might wish to purchase some of them, was invited to visit the boat."[48] Shortly afterwards, professional men arrived from the cities and owners of plantations from the country, who bargained with the ship's captain for our persons. We had to strip naked, so that the prospective purchasers could see that we had perfectly developed and healthy bodies. After the purchaser had made a selection, he asked: "How much is this boy or this girl?" Many strong and healthy young men, and especially the pregnant women brought as much as sixty pounds sterling ($300.00).[49] Some of my companions had to serve ten, twelve, or even more years without receiving anything more than their board and clothes.[50] This amount of money was received by the captain in payment for our transportation to America and for our board.

The length of service was according to the price. After these aliens had worked for the time required, they received a certificate of freedom. Then they had to decide whether they would hire themselves out or start in business on their own account. These servants were not given wholly over to the discretion of their masters, but were still to some extent under the protection of the law; and the only difference between them and free citizens was that for the specified time, they could not work for themselves. So it is easily seen that the conditions under which we had to labor after our arrival in North America were in no way a formal and life-long slavery, and that we could have gone immediately about our own business, had we been in the position to pay the ship's captain what we owed him. Even now, as I am informed, the poor European arrivals in North America have to work out the cost of their

48. See the preceding introduction to Büttner's memoir for the transcription of the actual newspaper ads placed.

49. In 1773 £60, if sterling and not colonial currency, would be equivalent to £4,347.47 in 2002. See John J. McCusker, "Comparing the Purchasing Power of Money in Great Britain from 1264 to Any Other Year Including the Present" Economic History Services, 2001, http://www. eh.net/hmit/ppowerbp/. However, no one from Büttner's ship was sold for anything approaching this amount, and the prices were recorded in colonial currency, not pounds sterling. See *Record of Indentures of Individuals Bound Out as Apprentices, Servants, Etc. and of German and Other Redemptioners in the Office of the Mayor of the City of Philadelphia, October 3, 1771, to October 5, 1773* (Lancaster, Pa.: Pennsylvania German Society, 1907).

50. Only one person from Büttner's ship could be identified in the *Record of Indentures* as being sold for ten years or more.

transportation after they land there; but they are no longer exposed to the whims and avarice of ship's captains, as previously. In latter times, the Baron of Gagern,[51] known as a wise and philanthropic man, did very much to ameliorate the conditions of immigrants, and in Philadelphia there exists at this time a humanitarian society for their assistance.

Soon the persons that composed the load of our ship were all sold except six boys, among whom was myself.[52] They, like myself, were unwilling to consent to a long term of service. This made the ship's captain wild with anger and he threatened, if we refused again to take service in America under his conditions, to carry us to the Antilles, especially to Barbadoes, where the heat is unbearable and where we would have to work with negroes. We realized that we would gain nothing by a trip to the West Indies, where our miserable fate would become even more intolerable, and that there was no salvation from the power of the ship's captain; so we resolved to work out the cost of transportation in the climate of Philadelphia. The captain asked for me thirty pounds sterling and I had to bind myself for the term of six years to the master or overseer that paid this amount of money. The master who paid this money for me—*about one hundred and fifty dollars*—was [Thomas Smith] the owner of a plantation in the province of New Jersey, and a member of the religious sect of the Quakers.[53]

Chapter 7—New Jersey and Servitude

I dined excellently with my new master in Philadelphia, and we drank a bowl of punch. Later we crossed the Delaware in a skiff and stopped at an inn. He had left his horse here, and as he expected to leave shortly, he directed me to proceed through a beautiful oak forest, promising to overtake me a little later, on horseback. I kept to the direction he had given me, and arrived at a fruit orchard where mainly apple trees were growing. I sprang over the fence of the orchard and gathered up a number of the apples lying there and which tasted very good; then continued on my way. In the meantime it had grown dark and my master was nowhere in sight. Shortly after, I espied a light in a

51. Hans Christoph Ernst, Baron von Gagern, an opponent of Metternich.
52. In fact, Büttner was sold within four days of taking the oath of allegiance. He was the thirtieth sold out of the hundred adult male indentures sold from the *Sally*.
53. Thomas Smith lived in Eversham Township, Burlington County, New Jersey about fifteen miles due west of Philadelphia. Büttner gets his raw numbers right—six years for thirty pounds—but gets his currency denominations and exchange rates wrong. He was sold for thirty pounds in Pennsylvania currency, not sterling (£30 Pennsylvania currency equaled £18 sterling in 1773 and is equivalent to £1,314.24 in 2002 pounds sterling). See McCusker, "Comparing the Purchasing Power of Money."

little house which I approached. The family sat around the table eating their evening meal. They soon discovered that I came from the boat and opened up a conversation with me; but as they spoke English, I was unable to understand them. They urged me to take a place with them at the table, and gave me a little bowl of Turkish wheat meal with milk and bread; on the table lay a big cheese, from which I was permitted to cut a little piece for myself. After half an hour had passed, some one knocked at the window. This was my master, who though somewhat far gone in liquor, was glad to catch up with me here.

I was immediately ordered to get up on the saddle behind him, and in this fashion he galloped with me to his plantation. As we pulled up in front of his house, there appeared promptly a boy who took the horse from him and led it to a stall. I entered the living room with him, where his wife [Elizabeth Smith] and children[54] were sitting in front of a big fireplace. They have no stoves in this part of America, but content themselves with great open fires in chimneyplaces, over which are suspended big iron kettles. In these they cook their food, throwing in great pieces of beef, sometimes weighing six and eight pounds. In another kettle they cook in this fashion entire heads of cabbage and whole turnips, and later bring them to the table, where each may take from any of the kinds of food whatever he desires. Also each one is invited to take as much as he wishes from an enormous cheese, often weighing as much as thirty pounds. At breakfast and supper they eat usually a mush made of Turkish wheat meal which is also cooked in a kettle suspended in the fireplace. Each receives with this a little bowl of milk, and there is always a great piece of meat or the cheese on the table, of which one may eat to his satisfaction. I drank only a little water, but a good deal of cider or apple wine.

Each plantation has on it an orchard that sometimes requires half an hour to walk around, and that bears an immense amount of fruit, a part of which is used to make this delicious, healthful apple wine. In these orchards the trees are usually planted twenty steps apart and grow magnificently. In the open spaces between the fruit trees, they grow all kinds of grain that flourishes just as well as if the trees were not there. It is unbelievable what profits the growing of fruit trees brings in America. And when I see here in our own country large gardens and wide pastures without even a single fruit tree, I always regret that fruit culture is not more carefully followed. The farmers here who generally have plenty of land could do a great deal for the improvement of their farms if they would devote even half an acre to the growing of fruit trees. I know a very sensible farmer who, from a comparatively small

54. The Smiths had seven daughters and two sons in 1780.

piece of land on which twenty years ago he planted fruit trees that demand no care, now receives the amount of his taxes and all the fruit that he can use for himself from this orchard. The objection that if each farmer owned his own orchard, the fruit would not sell so advantageously as at the present time, is valid. Of course this cannot be denied; but notwithstanding, fruit growing will become sometime a very important and most useful part of the farming industry, if it is managed properly. Fruit is not only a pleasant and healthful food when cooked, but it also sells well as the base of the manufacture of good wine, vinegar, syrup and brandy; and besides the cuttings can be used for feeding cattle. And that the ground around the trees can be utilized for the growing of other products, I have seen proved in America.

During the harvests, the owners of neighboring plantations assist each other in cutting the grain, so that usually in a single day an entire crop of some sort is gathered. After the grain is cut it is bound immediately into little bundles and stacked up in shocks just as is done with hemp in our country. There they leave it until it dries. Even in rainy weather I never saw the grain sprout because it is so placed in these shocks that the heads are exposed to the air. After the harvesters are through with the gathering of the grain they eat and drink mightily, and after that have dances.

Before I begin to relate my own affairs and the duties of my service and what happened to me during this time, I would like to make a few observations about the provinces of Pennsylvania and New Jersey, so that the reader can have some idea about the places where I spent the first years of my sojourn in America. Pennsylvania, which was named by the Englishman, William Penn, who with a few of his sect made a settlement in its forests, is a great stretch of land larger than one half the Prussian empire and in about the same latitude as Spain. But the climate is similar to that of our country, because the land is not entirely under cultivation; but it is gradually growing warmer as the clearing of the forests and the cultivation of the fields progress.

This province is drained by three big rivers, the Delaware, on which is situated the capital, Philadelphia; the Susquehanna, and the Ohio.[55] It produces a quantity of grain, flax, hemp, and wax and breeds cattle extensively. There are large oak and nut forests. The nuts are not so large as our walnuts and have a thinner shell, so that they can be cracked easily with strong teeth. There is also a stony kind of nut. This serves as food for the pigs that are running wild in the forests. These pigs, after being marked on the ears, are allowed to run wild in the summer time and in the fall are captured again. Each proprietor can recognize his own stock from the brand on their ears.

55. In 1773 the eastern origins of the Ohio River were not clearly or officially part of Pennsylvania. They were by the 1820s, when Büttner was writing.

Vines grow wild here and climb up the trees; especially the sassafras, which grows in great abundance.

The province of New Jersey is much smaller than Pennsylvania, but is still larger than the kingdom of Saxony at present. This province also is under very good cultivation. They grow here much grain, flax, fruits, and potatoes. They have many cattle, and timber is in abundance. Among the different kinds of wood the cedar especially drew my attention. These cedars are over a hundred feet high; they grow only from the tops, where spring the new branches, looking in shape and size like great brooms on which are hanging red berries. These trees stand so close to each other that it is very hard to pass between them. The timber is beautiful and so very light that it is possible to carry on one's shoulder a log ten yards long and half a yard in circumference. This wood is used for building purposes and for the manufacture of shingles, with which most of the houses in this province are covered.

Both provinces, Pennsylvania and New Jersey, have a very mild and pleasant climate. The work that I had to perform on the New Jersey plantation near the Pennsylvania border, was as follows: I had to get up at daybreak, and carry a great log of wood four to five feet long to the fireplace, which measured six feet. Then I placed small split wood under the log and kindled a flame by means of which the log was ignited. Soon the room was warm. Later I proceeded to feed the cattle, consisting of ten to fifteen head of horses, fifty to sixty cows and oxen, and more than a hundred hogs. The latter were mostly fattened on Turkish wheat. After they were sufficiently heavy, they were slaughtered, sometimes ten in one day. After being stuck, they were allowed to run about the yard until they were fully bled and fell dead. After a number had been slaughtered in this way, the carcasses were scalded, hung up and the intestines removed and buried. Sausages were not made. On the following day, we took the dressed hogs to Philadelphia, where we sold them to the meat dealers, who salt the meat and send shiploads of pork and flour to the West Indian islands, receiving in exchange West Indian products such as coffee, sugar and indigo.

The horned cattle remain in summer and winter in the fields and pastures. In the winter I often had to go for half an hour in the deep snow to feed the cattle. Here and there were to be found immense haystacks around which high fences were built against which leaned a ladder that I had to ascend in order to cut the fodder with my long curved knife. I took from the haystacks each time only as much as I needed to feed at that time, throwing it over the fence to the beasts that were waiting outside. If a cow was with calf she was driven home with the other cows that were to be milked. All the milk was put into big copper kettles; and the butter and cheese made from it were sold. In the outhouse of the home of my master was a cheese press which always contained two big cheeses of thirty to forty pounds each in a cylinder which was perforated with holes and had two iron clamps. After the cattle were fed, I went to breakfast, to which we were called about eight o'clock by the blowing of a big conch. Each of the servants received a can of milk, mush of Turkish wheat flour and a piece of salted veal. At noon we had warm meat with whole turnips or cabbage heads, of which each could eat as much as he chose; or we had peas, lentils or other vegetables. The supper was like the breakfast.

When I was not occupied with the cattle, I had to do other kinds of work. Principally I had to plow the fields to make the uncultivated land arable. My master was a Quaker and on Sundays I frequently attended the religious meetings of the Quakers with him and his family. This Christian religious sect originated in the seventeenth century in England, deriving its name from "to quake," which means to tremble, and has many members at present in America. The Quakers or Tremblers have no pastors; but the old and experienced of both sexes deliver lectures during their religious meetings, when they feel incited by inner promptings of the soul. In their meeting-houses they never sing, but pray silently until an old man or woman, led by the spirit, rises and delivers a sermon on some passage of the Old Testament. These declamations are often very pathetic and are listened to reverently, since Quakers in their places of worship are generally very devout. After the services, having been without any ceremonies and lasting two hours, are finished, the men and the women shake hands and leave the place of assembly. The Quakers here, men and women, ride on horseback to their meeting-house, tie the horses in front of the church, which is situated in a little forest, and after their common worship of God return immediately to their homes. I had a horse at my disposal each Sunday in order to reach the church. Besides other distinguishing marks of the Quakers, it must be remembered that they call every one "thou," that they never remove their hats, not even in the presence of the king, and that they, according to Matthew 5:35–37, never take an oath.[56] They ought not to swear, either, but my master, who was a very violent man and spoke a little German, swore not infrequently, especially when he was drunk. Only too often, if he were not satisfied with his servants, did he utter the resounding and terrible English curse: "God damn your soul!"

---

56. "But I say to you, Do not swear at all, either by heaven, for it is the throne of God, or by the earth, for it is his footstool, or by Jerusalem, for it is the city of the great King. And do not swear by your head, for you cannot make one hair white or black. Let what you say be simply 'Yes' or 'No'; anything more than this comes from evil." Matthew 5:34–37.

Chapter 8—Runaway

Although I wanted for nothing in the employ of my master, as can be seen by my narrative, I still longed for freedom and for my fatherland. One Sunday I received permission to visit the Protestant church in Philadelphia.[57] There I met a group of German servants who were having a very bad time at the hands of their masters. They tried to persuade me to run away with them to find a European boat that would take us back to Europe. At first I hesitated at carrying out the plans they had confided to me, but finally I promised to participate in the undertaking. To this conclusion I was brought mainly by a negress who encountered us by chance and who offered to read my future life in the lines of my palm. I held my hand out to her, and learned from the black woman that I should be a soldier and should be wounded. Not [willing] to hear more of what lay in store for me, I tore my hand away from the fortune-teller, and decided on the spot to escape the fate of the prophecy by flight and the longed-for return to Europe. I conferred with my companions as to the time chosen for running away, and went home.

At the appointed day I left my master, just as they did and met them by moonlight at the place we had agreed upon. Immediately we started on our way; but after a march of about two hours we came to a river that was so wide and deep that we could not ford it. Thereupon we walked along the river bank, hoping to find a skiff. We actually did find boats tied near a plantation and unloosing them, we crossed the river. We were very glad to have the river behind us, and went on as fast as we could. At daybreak we lay down in a forest and now sleeping and now awake, awaited the fall of night in which we could continue our journey. We satisfied our hunger with food found here and there in the fields, and which we cooked in the middle of the forest.

In this manner, we had traveled about three hundred English miles, and had just arrived in the province of Virginia, when we were discovered by bloodhounds, captured, and immediately put under custody. Our masters had advertised our flight in the newspapers, and had offered considerable rewards for our recovery. For my capture a reward of five pounds (more than thirty dollars) was offered. Those who found us immediately informed our masters of our arrest, but three weeks elapsed before instructions for our return arrived. During this time we had to sit in the prison.[58]

---

57. Most of the churches in Philadelphia were Protestant. He undoubtedly means St. Michael's Lutheran Church.

58. He was imprisoned in the Prince-William County jail in Virginia. Thirty dollars in 1775 is the equivalent of $711.60 in 2003 dollars. See the preceding introduction to Büttner's memoir for further analysis and transcriptions of the actual newspaper ads concerning his flight and recovery.

One morning I was summoned and immediately led to another house where some gentlemen were convened. One of them approached me and asked if I would like to return to New Jersey to my master. He said he had orders to pay everything, and to bring me back to him again. I was glad that my master desired to have me return, because I did not like it in Virginia, where the servants had to work with negroes, and had only two meals a day. I would doubtless have been sold to a Virginia plantation owner, had I refused to go back to New Jersey. But under the circumstances this never entered my head and I promised immediately to accompany the emissary of my master. He, a ship's captain, paid my expenses and I followed him to his vessel lying in the Potomac River.

With a favoring wind we set sail. We came to Chesapeake Bay and thence through Delaware Bay to Philadelphia, where my master was waiting for me. I was afraid he would afflict me with a load of curses; but he received me very kindly, and told me that he knew I was persuaded by the others to run away, but that I should not have yielded to the temptations of these companions, but should have waited until my term of service had expired; that later he would have given me a certificate of freedom which would have opened for me the doors of all America. After I had promised him that I would never run away again, and would serve him sincerely in the future, he ordered me to mount behind him and we arrived home astride the same horse's back.

Here I had a very friendly reception from the wife and the daughters of my master; they seemed confident that I had not run away because of ill treatment on their part, but had yielded to the persuasion of my partners in wrong-doing. After serving my master two years longer, diligently and honorably, and not being badly treated by him, I brought upon myself quite innocently his ill will. One morning I was plowing a piece of unbroken land with another servant, a Swiss boy of about fourteen years, who was driving the oxen for me. I had the misfortune to run the plow against a large root of a tree, breaking the implement, which was a new one. We placed the broken plow on a wagon and drove home. My master who had observed from a distance what had happened to the new plow, met me with the frightful curse: "God damn your soul and your brain!," ordered me to unyoke the oxen, and to come to breakfast. When we were seated at the table, my master began to curse again, and looked at me with angry eyes. His gestures and his curses, which I fully understood, since I had learned the English language fairly well during my three years' stay in America, seemed to me ridiculous, and I could not keep from showing amusement at his expressions of rage. No sooner did my master become aware of this than he gave me such a box on the ear that the blood sprang from my nose and mouth as if from a fountain.

Instantly I sprang up from the table to the door, and said that I would go immediately to the judge and complain of him, knowing well that the loss he had suffered did not permit such treatment of servants. I had hardly finished saying this when my master leaped from his seat and made an attempt to catch hold of me. I succeeded in escaping, but turning around after a few steps, I saw that he had a gun in his hands and was aiming at me; but his wife and the children seized him to prevent his committing a crime. A few leaps took me beyond the range of his rifle and into the security of the forest.

As soon as I knew myself to be in safety, I hurried to a German cooper who was living about a mile from the plantation of my master. To him I related what had happened, and asked him to show me the way to the judge, which he accordingly did. I had to tell the judge, whom I approached with a bloody and swollen face, all that had occurred in detail. Having done so, I expressed the desire to be sold to another planter as I could no longer repose confidence in or feel affection for my old master. Thereupon the judge took a seat at his writing desk and wrote a letter to my master; sealed it and gave it to me with the order that I should go home again and deliver the letter in person. And he assured me that my master would never again raise his hand against me.

It was Saturday and very late when I came home. My master, who had ridden in pursuit of me, came home after midnight and on his arrival asked the young Swiss, who looked after his horse, if I had come back. Upon this question being answered in the affirmative, he retired. I knew by his voice that he was intoxicated. On the following day after I had fed the cattle and had entered the house, my master, who was sitting near the fireplace, asked me to shave him. He also asked me very gravely if he could trust himself to me. I replied that he must not be afraid, as I had never in my life done evil to any one, and he would be the last person that I would want to harm. I shaved him, and when I had finished, I handed him the letter of the judge. After he had read it through, he was terribly angry, swore terrifically and went into another room; but came back soon with a threat that he would provide me with another master who would let me know what a servant was much better than he had done; and gave me the order to saddle his horse and bring it around.

After I had carried out his orders, he galloped away and did not come home until long after midnight, very drunk. On the following morning I arose as usual very early and fed the cattle. After I came to breakfast, he asked me if I wished to remain in his service. I gave a negative answer, and expressed the wish to be sold to another master. He then said that I would often think of him when I had fallen into the hands of a man worse than he. After a while a gentleman arrived on horseback, and a boy with a yoke of oxen followed him. I knew instantly that the stranger was to be my future master and the oxen were the price for my person. And as a matter of fact, I was given over to the stranger in exchange for the pair of oxen.

Chapter 9—A New Master

Little did those who hung in solicitude over my cradle dream of the fate that awaited me on the other side of the Atlantic! But I could not remonstrate against the trading of the two gentlemen. My new master was proprietor of an inn situated about a mile from the plantation of the gentleman I had served until now. He also was a lieutenant of the militia. His name was Abraham Eldrige. After I had thanked my former master for all the good that I had enjoyed at his hands, I followed my new keeper to his home.

According to the prophecy of my former master, I was to have a much worse time here than with him; but I had every reason to be satisfied with my present situation. Notwithstanding the fact that my master was a very violent-tempered man, he was not a victim of the disgraceful drinking habit as was the man I first served. I filled the position of a porter in his inn, a sort of roadhouse on the way to Philadelphia. This position, which was not a congenial one to me, was nevertheless at this time particularly remunerative for the North American struggle for independence had broken out, and troops of soldiers and their officers traveled along this highway. The latter gave me for the care of their horses, sometimes small, sometimes large sums of money, sometimes as much as a dollar, and in a short time I was able to save a rather respectable amount of money.

At that time there was current in Pennsylvania a good deal of paper money. Each piece bore on one side the name of the United States and the value of the bill; on the other the notice that the penalty for counterfeiting this bill was loss of life.[59] Also there were whole and half coins of Spanish silver money, which were often chopped into four and sometimes into eight pieces. These pieces were used as change and business currency.

It is well known that with the English army which fought the American insurgents there were connected Hessian auxiliary troops, many of whom

59. Continental currency was first issued by the Continental Congress on May 10, 1775, in the amount of $3 million. These initial paper bills had "United Colonies," not "United States," printed on their face. Not until the issue of May 20, 1777, was "United States" printed on the face of currency. In addition, this currency did not say anything about the penalty for counterfeiting on its reverse side. However, the bills of credit (paper money) routinely issued by Pennsylvania and New Jersey legislatures from the 1750s into the 1780s typically said "to counterfeit is death" on their reverse side. See Eric P. Newman, *The Early Paper Money of America*, 4th ed. (Iola, Wisc.: Krause Publications, 1997), 45, 49–50, 58–68, 247–60, 332–55.

deserted.[60] From these deserters I gained much information as to how far away the English and Hessian forces were from the place where I was staying, and how great were their numbers. I learned this with the end in view, if the occasion arose, to join the army and to return with it, after the war was over, to my fatherland, for which I grew constantly more homesick. But when I considered the danger which threatened me should I be captured by the Americans after I had gone over to the English and the Hessians, I gave up each time my secretly cherished plans, and decided at least to wait a little longer before trying to realize my desires.

Chapter 10—A Soldier on the American Side

About this time, I received on request, permission from my master to go to Philadelphia to attend the Lutheran church. At this period in Philadelphia, Major von Ortendorff,[61] who had fought in the armies of Frederick the Great during the Seven Years' War in Germany, was forming under the direction of the commander-in-chief [General George Washington] of the American [Continental] army, a corps of volunteers. Moreover in his proclamation, which was sanctioned by the United States, German servants were invited to join the corps, but on the condition that these servants should make an agreement with their masters that these masters should receive during their servants' term of service a part of the pay. The United States promised the German servants who were willing to bear arms in the cause of the liberation of America, thirteen acres of government land free of charge, to be taken possession of as soon as peace was declared. I was persuaded to enter this volunteer corps, and although I was less concerned about the freedom of North America than about my own, and though I longed for my fatherland, still when I saw the great enthusiasm for the cause of freedom manifested in Philadelphia, I straightway forgot Germany and the plans for my own freedom, took service in Major Ortendorff's corps and received my twenty dollars earnest money.[62]

60. See the preceding introduction to Büttner's memoir for more information on the Hessians.

61. "Saxon adventurer Major Nikolaus Dietrich Baron von Ottendorf commanded a German independent corps of eventually five companies recruited in Pennsylvania in December 1776. When Ottendorf deserted to the British, his corps was broken up in June 1778 into independent companies." Robert A. Selig, "Germans and German-Americans in the Continental Army, 1775–1783," *German Life* (November 2001), at http://www.germanlife.com/Archives/2001/0110-01.html.

62. Twenty dollars in 1776 is the equivalent of $419.17 in 2003.

While I remained in Philadelphia, one of the men of the corps was sent with a letter to my master requesting him to come to headquarters in order to make arrangements with the commander of the corps for my enlistment. My master, who, as I have mentioned before, was a lieutenant of the militia, was very happy on the following day when he saw me in the blue uniform with the green collar and cuffs, and wished me good luck in my new profession. However, he demanded that I pay him every month for twenty months one pound sterling out of my wages, and although I appreciated that he was asking far too much, I consented.

As the corps of Ortendorff had reached the number of three hundred, we marched to join the great North American army which was under the command of General Washington. The service of this corps was very hard. As we received no tents, we were obliged to build huts for ourselves out of boughs. We had to serve as outposts for the main army, and were obliged to patrol all night long. We also had to forage for cattle to be slaughtered for the use of the soldiers. As a rule we took the cattle from the planters who remained loyal to the king. Although the United States were trying as hard as they could to free themselves from English rule, yet there were a few that did not favor the insurrection, and worked against the cause of liberty partly because they were born Englishmen, and partly on grounds of conscience. But they suffered often very keenly for their loyalty to the English government. To discover their attitude in this matter, usually six men went into the houses, pretended to be Hessians and asked questions about Washington's army: how strong it was, where it was located at the present time, and such details. If these people seemed to be glad to see us, and gave us information about the North American army, soon the entire detachment entered and took possession of the plantation, drove away the cattle and often stripped the house. The duped people then sincerely regretted their frankness, gazed with tears in their eyes after their cattle that we were driving away, and seeing the "U. S." on our powder pouches, realized too late that we were soldiers of the United States. Such matters occupied almost every night. The English, who very soon received word of our doings, never forgave us.

After I had served about six months in the corps of Ortendorff, I with six other men decided to desert to the English and Hessians, whose tents we could see in daytime not far from our camp. It was a dark, desolate night when we stole out of our bivouac; but we had gone only about fifty steps into the forest when a picket whom we were not expecting to find at this place called out: "Who goes?" and as we did not answer, fired immediately. Instantly we scattered in all directions and I decided to return as fast as I could to the camp, where I arrived before the commotion caused by the firing of the gun had become general. I joined in the alarm, but my anxiety knew no bounds, for I realized that if any of the deserters were captured and saw fit to betray me, the limb of a tree would furnish my punishment.[63] We had to answer roll-call immediately, and I was mighty glad that the six deserters were still missing and that the patrols sent out to search could not find them.

A few days after this unsuccessful attempt to desert to the combined armies, we received orders to break camp. At daybreak we reached a mountain which was occupied by some thousand regular soldiers of the North American troops, who had with them a few cannon. Here we had command of the road that led around the mountain, which we saw covered with a multitude of soldiers, and the newly risen sun glittered on thousands of bayonets. This was a regiment of the English army with a vanguard formed of Hessian grenadiers. As soon as they came within range we fired our cannon at them. All at once, the endless marching line stood still, separated into divisions and, then disregarding our fire, charged down the mountain with fixed bayonets. When we saw that we were outnumbered and that resistance was hopeless, we abandoned our cannon and baggage and fled down the other side of the mountain. Many threw away their rifles and knapsacks, and ran like hares into the forest. I fell into a ditch and my comrades, leaving me there for dead, jumped over me. As the cannon balls and rifle bullets were falling all around me, and I was afraid of being run through by the enemy that were pursuing us, I crawled on my hands and knees to some thick undergrowth nearby, and lay there until I could no longer hear any firing.[64]

Chapter 11—Switching Sides

After this I arose and went up to the place on the mountain where the skirmish had started. Here I found the Hessian grenadiers in possession of the camp. When I was still twenty feet distant from them, the Colonel called to a petty officer: "There comes a rebel!" The petty officer approached me and led me to the Colonel, who addressed me with stern and threatening words:

63. That is, he would be hanged.

64. This is an accurate description of the battle of Short Hills, in northern New Jersey, a minor engagement that took place on June 26, 1777, when Ottendorf's regiment met Lieutenant Colonel Friedrich Ludwig von Minnegerode's Loyalist Hessian Grenadier regiment, which was acting as the vanguard for a section of the British army. When Ottendorf's regiment fired on Minnegerode, the Hessians maintained strict order, separated into prearranged divisions, and charged. Badly outnumbered, Ottendorf's regiment fled, abandoning their baggage, cannons, rifles, and knapsacks. Anne M. Pfaelzer de Ortiz, "German Redemptioners of the Lower Sort: Apolitical Soldiers in the American Revolution?" *Journal of American Studies* 33 (August 1999): 291, 302. See also Vincent J. Esposito, *The West Point Atlas of American Wars*, vol. 1, *1689–1900* (New York: Henry Holt and Co., 1995), map 7. Short Hills is about eighteen miles due west of the lower tip of Manhattan, and about eleven miles southeast of Morristown, New Jersey.

"Well, you urchin, where do you come from? You were not able to make your escape, were you?" I answered that I had for a long time cherished the wish to be associated with my countrymen, and then I told him briefly all that had happened to me since my arrival in America. My story made a favorable impression on the Colonel and he ordered one of his orderlies to give me a glass of rum and some bread. At the same time he ordered me to remain in his battalion until it should go into winter quarters; also he promised that later on he would make some provision for my future.

After the troops had rested for a few hours, they again took up their march. But we had not marched longer than an hour when we met the entire corps of Ortendorff's men being led along under arrest, captured by an English company. I recognized among the prisoners my own comrades and I called to them: "See! Had you followed my example you also could have been at liberty now!" This exclamation of mine was not the result of reflection and it might easily be fatal for me in the future. And even if this indiscretion did not bring me misfortune in this particular case, I would advise all persons to keep in mind the changeable fortunes of war, and to be more cautious and thoughtful that I showed myself to be on that occasion.

An hour before sunset we arrived at the camp of the main division of the English army. I was led promptly to the tent of Lord Cornwallis,[65] who put many questions to me, but especially how strong the rebels were, where Washington was camped, how defensible the fortifications were, and how well they were manned. After I had given information on all these points, I had to swear allegiance to King George the Third, I received a rifle, and was enrolled in the grenadier battalion of the Knipphausen regiment.[66] Now we marched toward Staten Island, laying opposite New York, where we remained in camp a few weeks. Then we passed over the North River towards the city of New York. We were unable to enter the city, but we dug caves in the ground and covered them with sod in which we had to pass the winter. But the English obtained quarters in the city. Not only were the Hessian soldiers discriminated against in this way, but they were obliged daily to do hard labor, throwing up earthworks about Fort Washington, a fortified place three miles above the city on the other side of the river. We also had to stand a very dangerous watch on an island in the river. A narrow dam which led to this

65. Charles, Lord Cornwallis, British commander, was Major General Sir William Howe's principal field general in the northern and mid-Atlantic land campaigns of 1776–78, of which Howe was in charge. Cornwallis is perhaps best known for his command of the British land campaign in the South in 1780–81. He surrendered his army to the Americans under General George Washington at Yorktown on October 19, 1781.
66. Baron Wilhelm von Knyphausen, Hessian commander. He was the principal Hessian commander serving under the British command of Major General Sir William Howe and later of Major General Sir Henry Clinton.

island, on which was a fortification called Paulus Haak, was the main outpost of our army.

New York, which is situated north of Philadelphia, is the capital of the State of New York. This state is larger than the German kingdoms of Bavaria, Saxonia [Saxony] and Wirtemberg [Württemberg] together. During the Seven Years' War, it suffered severely from conflagration. The port of this city is situated nearer the sea than the one at Philadelphia, and therefore commerce and navigation are more highly developed here than in the latter place. In the suburbs, there is only one spring that has sweet water; all the others are brackish, even containing particles of salt. Along the water front by the docks were many taverns, where dwelt the priestesses of the heathen goddess Venus.[67] It would be very unfitting to call this region "holy ground." Directly opposite the landing place is a lighthouse whose rays can be seen at night very far out on the sea. Not far from the city, in the middle of the Hudson [River] there is an eddy called Hellgate. Ships passing this place had to be very careful not to come too near lest they be drawn in and hurled to destruction. I listened with horror to the roaring of Hellgate when I had to go by it.

After we had camped one or two months near New York, we received orders to be prepared to take ship. It was the nineteenth of December when we boarded the vessel called "The Two Sisters." As our regiment consisted of about eight hundred men besides the fifty seamen, we had to live in rather close quarters. The entire fleet that left New York at this time amounted to almost two hundred ships. The weather was very stormy and the farther we sailed from the coast, the more violent the wind became. In a few days we saw only a few ships near us and finally none at all. Our ship constantly grew more unseaworthy, and the water poured into the hull until the barrels began to swim about. Of course we fired signals, but in vain. No ship was within hailing distance. There was nothing left for us to do but to delay the inevitable sinking of our leaking vessel. We had to lash ourselves with ropes to the pump that was on the upper deck, to prevent our being washed overboard. And we had to pump day and night in order if possible to discharge from the boat the water that kept pouring in from below.

Since we had not been in communication with the rest of the fleet for eight days, our captain opened his sealed orders, and found that our assembly point was South Carolina. Each captain of a transport receives sealed martial orders which he, under penalty of death, may not open until twenty-four hours shall have passed without his having seen any boat. Otherwise he has to follow the orders of the war vessels that always accompany the transports,

67. I.e., prostitutes.

which orders are communicated to him by the firing of guns and by other signals that are understood by him.

Our ship directed its course south. After some time, we sighted dry land. This was the coast of the great State of Georgia that contains over 59,000 square miles. We cast anchor near Savannah, the capital of this state, and made a landing in a convenient place.[68] The soldiers were unshipped, the provisions and other contents of the boat put ashore, and the vessel itself raised. The great leaks from which the old ship had suffered during the storm, were caulked with tow and sealed over with pitch. After eight days we took ship again and in due time arrived at the port of Charleston, the capital of South Carolina, where we were greeted by the other vessels of the fleet that had been scattered far and wide by the storm.

The American fleet lay under the guns of the fort of Charleston, which was guarded with more than a hundred cannon, commanding the canal leading to the city. Besides, all along the canal, there had been sunk small vessels to which iron spikes had been fastened in order to discourage the approach of any unfriendly vessel. But in spite of this, the English fleet, after waiting six weeks for favoring winds, ran past the fortress, through the cannon fire of the Americans, right up to the city Charleston, where it was impossible for them to be shot at. During this venture some of the ships were damaged, and we also had a few killed and others wounded. But before the English sea forces had passed the fortress, the Hessian troops on land had begun to lay siege to the city. It required altogether seven weeks to compel the city to capitulate [on May 7, 1780] to the Hessian-English army.[69] The fortress, that could have held out much longer, capitulated also when the city surrendered. There was also in Charleston a body of troops from France, very strong, estimated at about twelve thousand men, sent over to assist the Americans. This corps was given leave to depart after the city and the fort had surrendered to the English.

During the siege of Charleston, I had an opportunity to see a chief of the free Indians that live in the interior of the North American States but who are gradually being crowded out by the civilized Europeans and the North

68. The British captured Savannah, Georgia, in December 1778. Charleston, South Carolina, would not be captured until early 1780 in a separate action. Clinton and Cornwallis's campaign to capture Charleston in 1780 began with their sailing from New York to Savannah, arriving in January 1780 and then sailing on to land on the outskirts of Charleston in February 1780. See Esposito, *West Point Atlas*, map 8.

69. Büttner gets his sequence of battles confused. His participation in the siege of Charleston (1780) must have occurred after his participation in the battles of the Brandywine, Germantown, and Red Bank (1777), and after he had switched sides to the Americans at Princeton and then back to the British soon thereafter. See Esposito, *West Point Atlas*, maps 4–9; and the discussion in the preceding introduction to Büttner's memoir.

American settlers. He came to examine our earthworks, and to offer our General Clinton a few thousand men as auxiliary troops.[70] But the General refused this offer, perhaps chiefly for the reason that the Indians are savage; and generally are as harmful to their friends as to their enemies. This chief was clothed in a mantle of cloth bordered with bright gold. Instead of shoes, he wore sandals that were bound to his feet with strings. In his nose was suspended a big silver ring that hung to his under lip, and he wore a head-dress from which great wing feathers dangled.

Shortly after the surrender of Charleston all of our men, except those needed to hold the city, were ordered to take ship again, and we sailed north-ward in order to take Philadelphia, then in the hands of the Americans; but our first object was to give a decisive battle to the enemy, whose main army was on the other side of the Brandywine Creek [September 11, 1777].[71] It is said that the North American army was one hundred thousand men strong. We had no more than ten thousand English, Scotch and Hessian soldiers, with some troops from Brunswick. A few days after we had left our ships, we found ourselves only two hours' distant from the enemy. Here we made a camp, not only for the purpose of reconnoitering the position, in order to determine its strength, but also to find out something about the Brandywine Creek over which we hoped to carry, if necessary, our light cannon. After our general's staff had obtained the desired information, we started at mid-night, separated into three divisions. We dragged the great cannon along the highway, and arrived at daybreak within cannon range of the hostile camp. General Washington, who commanded here in person must have thought that this was our entire army, and, that we intended to make an attempt at once to cross the river; for this reason he must have brought there the flower of his troops. I was with the third division that marched the greater part of the way through forests and had to listen to the faraway roar of the cannon.

70. Major General Sir Henry Clinton replaced Howe as senior British commander in America in 1778.

71. At the battle of the Brandywine, September 11, 1777, Washington's troop strength was 11,000 Americans and Howe's troop strength was 15,000—5,000 Hessians under the command of Knyphausen and 10,000 British regulars under the command of Cornwallis. Knyphausen faced the American center commanded by Generals Sullivan, Wayne, and Green, who were positioned just across Brandywine Creek at Chadd's Ford. While Knyphausen held the American center in check, Howe had Cornwallis, with the main British force, engage in a flanking maneuver that smashed the Americans' right side. Knyphausen's Hessians then charged across Brandywine Creek, routing the American center as they tried to turn to meet Cornwallis's attack on their flank. Washington almost lost his army, and perhaps could have lost the war, in this action. Only by successful rear-guard coverage of his retreat and Howe's failure to pursue was Washington's army saved to fight another day. See Esposito, *West Point Atlas*, map 7. The battle of the Brandywine took place near Chadd's Ford, in Chester County, Pennsylvania, on the Brandywine Creek, about twenty-eight miles southwest of Philadelphia and about nine miles north of Wilmington, Delaware.

It lacked half an hour of sunset when we made a halt, threw our knapsacks into a pile and put on our grenadier caps. This meant an immediate
attack. An adjutant approached our general from the right wing, and we were
ordered to march in double file. And now we advanced with fife and drum,
charging with bayonets through the shallow Brandywine, storming the earthworks of the enemy with a rush and causing them to abandon everything and
take to their heels. We pursued the enemy with shot and shell until late in
the night. From the left wing alone we took twenty two cannon of the enemy.
At the center and from the right wing a few more had been captured. Also
a great many men were taken, the exact number of whom I was unable to
ascertain. The field of battle was strewn with rifles and powder pouches.

We remained in camp here eight days. Every day new captures were made
of those who tried to find refuge in the forests. The abandoned rifles and
powder pouches were picked up, piled in wagons, and driven after the army.
Before the battle we had had to contend ourselves with ship's provisions;
but now we received again fresh bread and meat. The owners of plantations
had returned with their cattle to their homes. After that, the Hessian army
marched to Philadelphia without being molested. But since the English were
in possession of that city, the Hessians encamped at a little hill covered with
chestnut trees, about half an hour away.[72] One morning a few days later
we were attacked by a very strong troop of American soldiers [on October 4,
1777].[73] The enemy did not find us unprepared however. We seized our
weapons with all haste and rushed out to meet the enemy, whose cannon
shot began to fall into our camp, and we not only held our positions but also
put our foes to flight and followed them over the Schuylkill River.

After this bloody business was finished, we again withdrew to camp. However, since Philadelphia was in possession of the Americans,[74] our vessels
of war and transports had to fight their way into port with difficulty, for the
enemy had not only sunk in the Delaware River old hulls of vessels to which
iron spikes had been attached, but the river itself was so shallow in places
that our boats were in danger of running aground on the shoals. Besides

72. Chestnut Hill, now part of Philadelphia, is just north of Germantown, now also a part of
Philadelphia.
73. This action is most probably the battle of Germantown, October 4, 1777. Washington's
troop strength was 11,000 and was pitted against a portion of Howe's army—about 9,000 men
at Germantown, including a small Hessian outpost along the Schuylkill River—in what was a
complicated and supposedly a surprise attack at dawn. Büttner indicates that the Americans did
not surprise them, contrary to the standard story of the battle. The coordination in the American attack fell apart and great confusion ensued, perhaps owing to the complicated nature of the
attack plan. After heavy fighting, the British repelled Washington's attack. See Esposito, *West
Point Atlas*, map 7.
74. The British took Philadelphia on September 25, 1777. Thus Büttner is probably referring
to the American blockade of the Delaware River just downstream from Philadelphia.

this, the enemy had thrown up opposite the fort on a tongue of land called Redbank, jutting out from the shore of New Jersey, immense earthworks that had to be taken before the English fleet could hope to proceed into port.

The Hessian army division under the command of Lieutenant General von Knipphausen received orders to take the above-mentioned earthworks from the land side. In the following out of this order, we crossed the Delaware one night in skiffs and barges. After we had crossed over the river mentioned above, we marched through dense forests where I met one of my old acquaintances living in the province of New Jersey, and I said to him jestingly that I was going to visit my old master. This remark was an incautious one, and could easily have had damaging consequences for me in case our expedition miscarried, since I was, as I have shown, a deserter from the American army. After we had marched all day we found ourselves still an hour's journey from the earthworks we were supposed to take. We finally arrived at a forest that was only half an hour's march from the fortress that we meant to capture. The earthworks had been thrown up on an elevated piece of ground, and from where we were, we would see the soldiers there, hanging out their wash to dry. We had to set to work in the forest to get together as quickly as possible material for breastworks, to assist us if necessary in taking the earthworks.

In the meantime, Colonel von Dunopp,[75] who commanded our troop, sent a bugler to the Americans, demanding their surrender. On their refusal, the signal to advance was given, and we went forward to the sound of fife and drum [on October 22, 1777]. Meantime the enemy made all possible preparation for defense and were kept informed of our movements by the American war vessels that lay anchored near the earthworks, and to which they communicated by means of speaking tubes. They opened fire on us before we were well out of the forest, and did us considerable damage. Nevertheless we advanced courageously and reached the first palisade before a few faint-hearted ones showed signs of wishing to run away. This angered me, and as I found that I was unable to climb the palisade, I called to a few of them to help me up, making them believe that Colonel Dunopp was already inside the earthworks and that those were as good as taken. They complied with my request; but as I pressed forward with the invaders, we came to a palisade made of fruit trees, the branches of which had been sharpened. Now we were so near the very heart of the fortification that we could see the enemy in their blockhouses, taking sight of us, but we had to relinquish all hope of the success of our undertaking. A hail of rifle bullets and cannon balls fell around us; warriors dropped on every side. We essayed another attack and Colonel

75. Colonel Count von Dunop.

von Dunopp was among the first to charge. But he was struck down, both his lower limbs being shattered by an exploding cartridge. This accident only increased the helplessness of his men; all started to retreat. Just at the moment when I was trying to pass between the stakes of the palisade, I was struck by a rifle bullet that entered under one of my shoulder blades, passed over my spinal column and out through the other shoulder blade. And so I dropped to the ground, as the others started to retreat.[76]

Racked with agony, listening to the screams of pain from my comrades, I lay there unattended, through the chill October night. Not being able to see my wound I did not know myself how seriously I had been hurt. And even before nightfall I saw the jubilant Americans come down to the palisade in their glittering uniforms and heard them call to us: "Oh, you Hessian scoundrels! Now we are going to put an end to all of you!" Soon after this they came down to the battle-field, and took away from some of the wounded Hessian officers their purses and their watches. American officers seeing this ran out and drove the plunderers back within the fortification, in fear, I think lest the attack by the Hessians be renewed. But this did not happen; and on the following morning all the wounded soldiers were carried on stretchers inside the earthworks.

Messengers were then dispatched to the Hessian army division for surgeons to take care of us. A few of these surgeons arrived that same day, and were able to help at least a few of us. Some of us were promptly bandaged, and on others amputations of legs or of arms were performed. I was among the first to be taken care of by the doctors, because I made the statement that I was a surgeon myself. After I had been cared for properly, I attended the funeral of our commander, Colonel von Dunopp, which took place with all military honors. All the others that had fallen were buried in one big trench. A few days later all the wounded Hessians were taken in closed carriages to the main hospital in Princeton, where they were cared for.

Chapter 12—Switching Sides Again

In this hospital at Princeton I was recognized by one of the nurses who had served with me in the volunteer corps of the Americans, and he asked me how it was that I was with the Hessians. I was not overjoyed at being recognized.

76. James Tilton's description of Büttner's behavior in this action at Red Bank is slightly different and depicts him as less heroic. See Pfaelzer de Ortiz, "German Redemptioners of the Lower Sort," 294–96; and James Tilton, "Dear Sir," letter from Princeton, February 17, 1778, Papers of Dr. James Tilton, Bureau of Archives and Record Management, Hall of Records, Dover, Delaware.

I answered, being afraid of the consequences did I confess my desertion, that I had been captured during the skirmish at the mountain in Pennsylvania when the volunteer corps had been overwhelmed, and that I had been kept a prisoner since that day. As our conversation was carried on in English, it was overheard by these standing near, among whom was the physician on duty at that time. I had to tell him all that had happened to me, and when he learned that I was a physician, he offered immediately to take me into his service. His name was [James] Tilton and he intended having me work in the hospital, as my wound was not giving me any considerable trouble.[77] I accepted his invitation without hesitation, and went straightway to his house. He was not married and had no servant. So I had not only to feed his saddle horse, but to perform domestic duties as well.

In a short time my wound was completely healed, and I was able to take up my hospital duties. Aside from my food I received no compensation except when I shaved some one, let blood or performed some other surgical operation. But soon I was in the position where I could save a small amount of money. Mr. Tilton was a well-meaning and learned gentleman. Often in hours of leisure he would converse with me not only on subjects relating to his profession but also about the American war that progressed with changing fortunes. Although I myself had participated in the opening events of the war, I had to ask him the causes, since he knew more about it than I.

And this is what he said about the North American war: "Of course, England in the year 1765 had won Canada from the French,[78] thus ridding herself of a disagreeable neighbor, but she also heaped upon herself the burden of a debt of forty million pounds. The military and civil government of the American provinces cost America an immense amount of money. All this caused the English parliament to attempt to place some of the responsibility of payment of this debt on the American colonies, so direct taxes were imposed. Especially the North American colonists objected to paying the tax on the consignments of tea that the East India Company were allowed to bring to their ports. All the merchants refused to accept the tea that was sent to them, and if any one failed to reject it, he was adjudged lacking in honor. In Boston a cousin of Governor [Thomas] Hutchinson[79] accepted a consignment of tea, but the people in open revolt seized the three hundred and forty boxes and threw them into the sea. This refusal brought severe punishment

77. James Tilton subsequently became the first surgeon general of the United States. See the letter Tilton wrote about this encounter and their following discussions in the preceding introduction to Büttner's memoir and in Pfaelzer de Ortiz, "German Redemptioners of the Lower Sort," 295–99, and Tilton, "Dear Sir."
78. In fact Canada was captured in 1760 and then acquired by peace treaty in 1763.
79. It was Hutchinson's sons who were among the consignees.

down on the Americans and the British closed the port of Boston. This embargo quickly fanned to a blaze the hidden smouldering fire of rebellion, which is flaming fiercely now on the banks of the Delaware, the Susquehanna, the Hudson, the Potomac, the Savannah, the Ohio and the Mississippi. Since 1774 the provinces of New Hampshire, Massachusetts, Connecticut, Rhode Island, New Jersey, Pennsylvania, Delaware, Maryland, Virginia, New York, North Carolina, South Carolina and Georgia had confederated, formed of their representatives a Congress headed by a President whom the senators elected for a term of six years. The most excellent General Washington leads the defenders of the country, who are determined not to lay down their weapons until the colonies are free. The thoughtful and sincere Franklin is the chief counselor of the commander-in-chief.[80] Even if the English have more experienced soldiers and officers, I am not afraid for the welfare of the American nation. Our commanders and soldiers will shortly learn the trade of war from our enemies, just as the Russians did from the Swedes some time ago.[81] And even if the army of the enemy is courageous, ours is none the less brave, and we have the advantage of greater numbers and knowledge of the territory. The English have to bring reinforcements at great expense from Europe. Our hosts of freedom spring up everywhere. I am living in the happy and confident hope that the struggle for freedom puts forth such strong and deep roots under the protection of the genius of human rights that neither Hessians nor English will be able to destroy. The dawn of better times and of a higher political and moral life breaks for you, 'for your mistreated Fatherland,'" said Mr. Tilton, with a beaming countenance. "The fame of our remarkable uprising is heard from the coast of Labrador to the Gulf of Mexico, from the Orinoco [River] to the Plata [River], from the shores of the ancient kingdoms of the Incas to the West Indian archipelago. Everywhere will arise the consciousness of latent power and the longing for better political conditions. Just as once Asiatic and Egyptian culture, transplanted to the woody shores of Italy and Greece, put forth new blossoms, in the same manner European culture will burst into flower in the forests of America, and the well developed youth will cease to fear the rod of the father but will dwell here, independent and strong for himself. Maybe," concluded my prophetic superior, "our new life in freedom will beneficially influence Europe and the other parts of the world."

This and other remarks of Mr. Tilton, which I did not wholly understand, seemed to me in those days incredible, and I often felt like laughing outright

80. Benjamin Franklin actually spent the war years doing diplomatic duty in France.
81. During the Great Northern War, 1700–1721, Russians ultimately defeated Swedish invaders through a combination of military skill and harsh winters.

in his face.[82] But since in the year 1783, England was forced to recognize the independence of the North American States, I saw clearly that physician Tilton of Princeton had not badly prophesied the political occurrences of the future. I came to this conclusion later, after the eruption of the French Revolution [in 1789]. The army corps that had been sent from France (which was still suffering from the loss of Canada) and who had [been] taken prisoners by the English at the battle of Charleston [in 1780] was doubtless an important factor in the rising of the French Revolution. Also it is a well-known fact that those Frenchmen, who gained their military experience in the North American struggle for freedom, did not only give themselves immediately over to the cause of liberty in their own country, but acted also as mouthpieces for the teachings of Rousseau, Montesquieu, and d'Alembert,[83] and in this way made proselytes for the cause so dear to them. And did not the sight of North American Freedom and its attractive fruits inspire very recently other countries of America to make the attempt to bring about a similar condition of affairs? A new life blossoms on the Orinoco,[84] on the Plata,[85] in Peru and in Hayti; and [North and South] America, which consisted until recently only of European provinces and a few independent states, stands there demanding loudly to be received into the family of the countries of the world, and has already been partly welcomed. Greater and more far-reaching are the consequences of the North American struggle than Mr. Tilton could ever have suspected.

Chapter 13—Switching Sides Yet Again

Although I got on very well with my philanthropic and learned principal, I did not desire to remain in America, but wanted to return to my fatherland. So I made my feelings known to my chief and asked him to procure me a pass to go to Philadelphia, if he thought that I would not be prevented from leaving America. I desired to take passage on a ship that carried French troops or to sail to the West Indies and await there an opportunity to go to Europe. Although Mr. Tilton was not very pleased at my going, he gave me a pass, because, as he said, he was unable to refuse my urgent demand. Moved to tears, I said good-by to this honorable gentleman, and went to Philadephia.

82. The influences that Tilton spoke of would have been more apparent in the 1820s, when Büttner was writing, than in 1777–78, when he listened to Tilton's discourse on the causes of the American Revolution.

83. French proponents of civil rights and republican forms of government.

84. Now in Venezuela.

85. Now in Argentina.

After my arrival I took quarters at an inn, and started immediately to investigate when a ship might be sailing for France or for the West Indies. But to my great disappointment, I learned that owing to the state of war, quite a time must elapse before a boat would sail.

I met here a proprietor of an inn situated one hour outside of Philadelphia, and he offered to take me into his service. I accepted immediately as I wanted to stay near Philadelphia, and await a chance to go to Europe. Again I was a porter, and received as pay my lodging, my board and tips. Among my duties was the care of my master's saddle horse, an English racer called The Redbird. It was an extremely fine animal, and I had to exercise him every now and then. In the feeding and caring for the animal, this was the program: I had to give it food five or six times a day, but I could never give him more than half a measure of very pure oats and some clean clover hay. Every evening, I had to wrap his legs with cow-dung, after I had washed them with soapy water and dried them carefully. I also prepared for him a thick bed of straw. In the morning the cowdung was taken off his legs and the straw removed, so that he stood all day on the bare boards. In the afternoon I had to trot him. During my stay with my present master, a race was arranged between his animal and another one called The Grave House. My master had bet a few thousand pounds sterling that his racer would arrive at the goal first. I had a similar bet with an acquaintance of my entire fortune consisting of five pounds. On the day appointed for the horse race a heavy snow fell and I had to clear the race track. After all the preparations for the race had been made, a few hundred more bets had been closed besides those of the men who owned the horses. Then the races began. Unfortunately the Red Bird passed the goal two seconds after the other horse, and my master and myself lost our money. It was the custom also to place bets on cock fights. The cocks were armed with little iron spurs.

After I had lost all my money on this horse race, I gave up hope of being able to reach Europe very soon, so I took my leave. I went to Philadelphia, having heard that boats would sail in the near future for the West Indies. I went to sea as an ordinary sailor on one of these boats. It was a merchant ship on which I had taken service, bound for the French West Indian colonies, escorted by an American frigate. We put to sea without delay. A few days after we had lost sight of the mainland of America, we saw a ship coming toward us that carried no flag. To learn whether this were an American or an English vessel—that is, if it were friendly or belonging to the enemy, we fired our guns so that we would be answered by the running up of some standard. Our demand was satisfied without delay; not the American but an English flag swayed on its mast. It was a hostile vessel. As soon as we were sure of this, our commandant decided to capture the vessel. Both our ships came alongside and demanded its surrender. As this was refused, we started to fire at the English, and kept it up until they took in their sails and gave themselves up to us.

Our ship's captain decided to send the captured vessel and the crew back to Philadelphia.[86] For this purpose a number of men were chosen by lot who should serve as escort, and I was among those chosen. All the English prisoners were manacled with handcuffs found on the captured vessel; only the English captain, Dauny, was allowed to walk about free. Very soon this captain and I became friendly, especially when he heard that I was a German and longed to return to my fatherland. After he had gathered the impression from our several conversations that I was by no means an enthusiastic republican he confided to me the plan he had formed to gain liberty for himself and his fellow prisoners by causing mutiny among the seamen. He tried to induce me to assist him in carrying out his plans, and promised, that if everything turned out as he wished, to take care of my future and to bring me back to the English army at all events.

This was the plan he proposed to carry out: He himself, a strong daring man, proposed to attack the two American officers at a given time with an old sword that he had secreted in the boat. At the same time I was to free, as quickly as possible, the hands not only of the English officers, but also of he ordinary seamen. It all depended on me, he said, and if I were quick enough, the plan had to succeed. Any one can realize that I suffered a great temptation. I shrank at first from the gravely dangerous business that it was proposed I should take upon myself. But since Dauny spared no effort to persuade me, I finally consented. I realized that by being implicated in this business, I wronged the North Americans; but the arguments of Captain Dauny quieted all that my conscience said against it. The promise of a return to Europe on an English ship in the near future did much to influence me in my decision.

Not without misgiving did I watch the approach of the hour that was appointed by the English Captain for the carrying out of his plan. It meant sure death to me if the project miscarried. The hour arrived. Armed with the old sword that he had secreted, Dauny, without hesitation, fell upon the two American officers, who, not being in the least prepared, were easily overcome. In the meantime I had not only freed all the English officers but had, with hammers, broken off the handcuffs on a part of the men. They fell with

---

86. Privateering and the capture of enemy vessels as prizes for sale were commonplace. For example, in 1779, the year in which this incident took place, the state of Pennsylvania issued fifty-five Letters of Marque and commissions to forty-eight privateering vessels, which in turn brought in forty-two captured enemy ships to Philadelphia that year. See Richard Buel Jr., *In Irons: British Naval Supremacy and the American Revolutionary Economy* (New Haven: Yale University Press, 1998), 175–77. Letters of Marque were documents issued by a government allowing its private citizens to seize citizens or goods of another nation.

terrible shrieks upon the Americans and disarmed them. The sailors that
were high up in the masts did not understand for a moment or two what had
happened, and suspected that a fire had broken out. But when they learned
of the mutiny, they asked for pardon. I was overjoyed at the happy outcome
of this daring deed, of which I cannot even yet think without emotion,
because it saved me from certain death. Also I rejoiced over the fact that there
was no loss of life.

After this event, conditions on shipboard changed. The English took possession of the vessel, and the Americans had to occupy the position that the
English had had before. Captain Dauny took over the command. He knew
exactly where we were, and turned our course towards New York, where the
English fleet lay; and with a favorable wind we arrived there in due time. Immediately on landing, I endeavored to find the regiment of von Knipphausen,
in which I had before enlisted. In New York I was able to find only a recruiting station for this regiment, since the regiment itself was besieging Fort
Washington.[87] The officer who was in charge of this station and who gave
me the information, told me that the regiment was expected very soon in
New York. I made up my mind to wait for it. As a portion of the men, after
the taking of this fort, returned to New York, I applied of Dr. Michaelis for
the position of staff physician of the Hessians. He advised me first to attend
his medical lectures which he was about to give in New York and promised
to give me a position if possible in the regiment of von Knipphausen. I followed the advice of the good Dr. Michaelis, enrolled in his class, and helped
him as well as I could in his hospital duties. After I had attended his lectures
for half a year, the Knipphausen regiment came back to New York, and as
there was a vacancy in the company commanded by Colonel von Burg,[88] I was
made field surgeon.

Here I will mention the tragic fate that overtook a certain Major [John]
Andre during the siege of Fort Washington. This major was ordered by General [Benedict] Arnold, who had gone over from the Americans to the English,
to reconnoitre the fort.[89] Disguised, he had advanced to the last post of the
enemy, when he was recognized and arrested as a spy [in September 1780].
Although Majors Clinton[90] and Arnold did their best to induce Washington,

87. The siege of Fort Washington took place in November 1776.
88. This is Colonel von Borck. See Büttner's letter of May 3, 1782, in Wilhelm Zeithe, "Mein
Lehr und Wanderjahre," http://www.dewarim.de/de/texte/z1.html (accessed June 18, 2005), and
translation by Henry Retzer via personal communication with Anne Pfaelzer de Ortiz, June 18,
2005, in the possession of Anne Pfaelzer de Ortiz.
89. It was West Point, not Fort Washington, that was of interest to General Arnold and the
British in 1780.
90. Major General Sir Henry Clinton was supreme British commander in America at this
time.

the Commander-in-Chief, to release Andre, no attention was paid to these requests and he was hanged as a spy.

Shortly after I had received my position as surgeon, the regiment Knipphausen was transferred to Long Island on the other side of New York. We camped near a little city in which only the officers received quarters. All the men had to build sod-houses for themselves. The surgeons of this regiment erected for themselves a large house of sod, so that they could be easily found. Soon we became known in the little city near which we camped and had a few patients there. Regarding these patients we made an oral agreement, to wit: one after the other should attend the patients and the pay should be distributed equally among us all. Since I spoke fluent English I was more often called upon by the inhabitants of my little city than were my colleagues who did not speak English. This induced me not to respect the agreement, so that I need not divide my very considerable remuneration with the others. That caused considerable excitement among them; and especially a certain Franke did his best to draw me into a quarrel. He said, "You are a rebel." I answered, "I am a German as well as you, and a surgeon as good as you, but you are besides this a scoundrel. If you do not like this statement of mine, then we will fight." The angry man immediately challenged me to a duel, and both of us chose our seconds. We went to a garden where the duel was to take place. When we had taken our positions, my opponent said: "Do we fight to draw blood or to kill?" I answered immediately, "I fight for nothing less than for life and for death." My opponent, who was a very good fencer, had not expected this answer from me. He dropped his sword and cried: "Brother I see that your heart is in the right place and that you are a brave man. I have all the satisfaction I wanted. Come and give me your hand as a sign of reconciliation." And so it happened. We became again the best of friends, and cheered our spirits with a bowl of punch.

In the little city I have referred to, I made the acquaintance of a young Irish girl, called Betsy, the daughter of a merchant. She was a sweet, modest woman, very much attracted to me. But she never permitted any intimacies and resisted all my opportunities in a way that inspired in me a great respect for her. Oh, would that all young girls would act towards men as the lovable Betsy conducted herself with me, and never would permit the closest relationship before the priest has consecrated the bond of their love! Those who do not act as Betsy did are not only regarded without respect by all moral people, but they also are despised by those to whom they have given themselves so easily. Surely I would not be able to think so respectfully of the lovely Betsy had she been less firmly grounded in virtue. After six months had passed, our regiment had orders to march back to New York. I had therefore to collect with all possible dispatch the money owed me by my patients.

Among my debtors were two girls who drove a dishonorable business with their bodies and whom I had cured. They, knowing the orders that we had received, hesitated to pay their debt, as the departure of our regiment was imminent. This angered me, and accompanied by two grenadiers, I paid them a visit at their home and demanded to be paid immediately. They replied that they had no money, and besides used very impolite language. This excited my wrath in a most terrible manner and I took out my sword and with it destroyed the mirrors and windows. The noise I made was heard by a Hessian colonel who was living opposite and he immediately sent the watch to arrest me. After I stated that I belonged to the Knipphausen regiment, I was taken back to camp, and when brought before Colonel von Burg,[91] released on the condition that I repair all the damage if the women should ask it. This I promised.

At midnight the regiment broke up and marched towards New York. On the preceding day, I paid a visit to my beautiful, beloved Betsy to bid her good-by. She seemed very broken up over my departure, but could not decide to follow me to Germany. She asked if I would remain in America she would promise to be mine. I could not make up my mind to do that and with tears in my eyes I left this magnificently virtuous girl who was worthy to be a pattern to all other maidens.

Our regiment went into camp near New York where it remained until peace was concluded. At this time I witnessed a terrible execution. An English ship's captain who had made the attempt to go over with his frigate to the enemy and had been prevented from doing so by an English war vessel, was hanged on a gallows erected near the banks of the North River. Seven accomplices were executed at the same time on a war vessel lying in the New York port.

I could not believe at first that England and the colonies would make peace; but well-informed persons declared that the end of the war was undoubtedly in sight. The English and Hessian army had suffered terribly during the last months. Generals [John] Burgoyne and Cornwallis, who with their troops had occupied the northern provinces, had been forced by hunger to surrender to the Americans. A similar fate had befallen the army division under the command of the Hessian General Rahl.[92] Besides this, the English government realized that it could not rule over the thirteen American states and was inclined to make peace. Lord North and Secretary of State Fox[93] gave the English generals orders to stop all hostilities in the last days of March in

91. In the letter written to his parents from New York City on May 3, 1782, Büttner indicated that his return address should be marked as "Füsilier-Regiment of Lt. Gen. V. Knyphausen and to Colonel v. Borck's Company." Zeithe, "Mein Lehr und Wanderjahre."

92. Colonel Johann Gottlieb Rall died at the battle of Trenton, December 26, 1776.

93. Frederick, Lord North, and Charles James Fox had come to power in 1783, replacing the Shelburne ministry.

1782.[94] I was reminded of the prophesies of Tilton, the physician, in Princeton. Later, in the year 1783, peace was declared through the mediation of France, the English and Hessian army was placed aboard transports and war vessels to the number of two hundred, and shipped off to Europe.

A single ship was commissioned to receive our entire regiment and was therefore very heavily loaded. The fleet sailed in the following order: The transports were surrounded on all sides by war vessels. The admiral's ship, in advance of all others, was in command. The orders were given partly by cannon shots, partly by signaling with differently colored flags; and at night by three big lanterns which could be seen far and wide. No captain was allowed to leave the fleet with his ship unless he wished to invite the severest penalty. Notwithstanding this, our captain one night set all sails and deliberately left the fleet. We sailed with a good wind quickly forward, and landed nearly one month before the other vessels, arriving at the little market town, Bremerlehe, on the River Weser.

Before I proceed to set down a few facts about my later history, I will make some remarks about the conditions at present in the American free states, in which so much happened to me and in which I for my part did not find happiness. These free states have grown very greatly since the year 1783. It has at present an area of more than 197,000 square miles. There could be formed from it eight countries as large as the Austrian Empire. Prussia could find place inside its boundaries twenty-four times. Notwithstanding its extension, the population of the United States does not even equal that of the much smaller state of Prussia. But it increases from year to year. The States consist now of nineteen closely related republics, and a few territories and dependencies. The forests are being rapidly cut away and without doubt, there can be seen plantations and even cities at this time where I, in my day, saw dense woods. How many inhabitants would this great country have were it as closely populated as the Prussian dukedom of Saxony!

Chapter 14—Back Home

After the Knipphausen regiment had landed and had taken a few days' rest, it started its march towards Hessea. Everywhere we went, especially when we passed through the little towns, the people thronged to look at us, attracted especially by the negroes who were employed in the regiment bands. The regiment occupied barracks in and near Grebenstein, not far from Cassel

---

94. Compare this to what Büttner says in the letter to his parents of May 3, 1782. He wrote that they "are in high hopes of soon receiving long-awaited news of peace." Zeithe, "Mein Lehr und Wanderjahre." An armistice was not actually declared until January 1783.

[Kassel].[95] All its foreigners were soon afterwards dismissed. I also received my discharge and my back pay, which amounted to twenty dollars. I started for home immediately. After a few days I stepped on Saxon ground, and shouted with joy. Accompanied by a confectioner who had agreed for a certain price to carry my gripsack, I went to Leipzig,[96] Torgau and from there to Senftenberg. Passing through the village Cletewitz I stopped at the Totzig Mills, half an hour from Senftenberg, in the hopes of seeing some people from that place, but no one recognized me here, not even the proprietor of the mills, who had been my schoolmate in Senftenberg. After I had disclosed my identity and inquired after the welfare of my family, I learned that my mother had died a few years ago and that my father lay very sick. After he had told me of a few other things that had happened in these parts during my absence, I hurried to Senftenberg. Here I was received with great evidences of pleasure by the electoral tax commissioner Roesser, a brother-in-law of my deceased mother.

As I desired to see my father that same day, the son of the tax commissioner was dispatched to Lauta, to prepare him for my arrival. Soon after, I started for the place of my birth. Near Koschenberg I was met by young Roesser accompanied by my younger sisters, who did not know me at all, since they were little children when I went out into the world, and it seemed strange to me to see them as growing maidens. Although we were happy over our reunion, our rejoicing soon gave place to sorrow, when they told me that our father was very sick and could live perhaps only a few more days. With sincere thankfulness on entering my native town again, I praised Providence that had saved me so graciously from so many dangers and so many terrible situations. And although I had to walk on my feet and could not drive in my coach and four, I rejoiced from the bottom of my heart that I was walking on the soil of Lauta.

I entered my father's house with tears in my eyes, and they that were there wept also. Disregarding his great weakness, my father sat up in bed and said in a failing voice: "My son, the light of my eyes has left me. I cannot see you, but your voice tells me that you are my son." I fell into his emaciated arms and we wept. He then told me that during my absence many misfortunes had overtaken him; that after the death of my mother and my brother Friedrich, who had been pastor in Hohenbocka, he had been seized with an epidemic disease and that he was for a long time unable to exercise his duties. Then he

95. This is the capital of Hesse-Kassel in the central German highlands and is about halfway between Frankfurt am Main and Hannover. Between 1750 and 1800 Kassel's population was about 10,000. See Vries, *European Urbanization*, 282.

96. Leipzig was second to Dresden in importance in Saxony and is about forty-five miles northwest of Dresden. Between 1750 and 1800 Leipzig's population was about 20,000. Ibid.

informed me that he had afterwards married the sister of Pastor Zierenberg in Petershain, a woman of his own age, who had taken excellent care of his little children. My stepmother seemed to be very glad to have me at home again, especially, I think, because she believed that in case of my father's death, I would provide for my half-grown brothers and sisters. Only two more days did I see my father among the living. On the third, his soul departed from the worn-out body and went to a higher, better life.

After my father's death I took over the management of the affairs of my family and had to go to the courthouse in Senftenberg, to adjust these matters very often. On these occasions I usually paid a visit to my uncle and my aunt and to the tax commissioner in this city. They all advised me to settle in this place, and to marry, drawing my attention to the daughter of the official surgeon, Alberti. I tried to get acquainted with this girl, and finally won her hand. After our marriage we lived in the house of my father-in-law, and I helped the latter in the discharge of his professional duties. But since there was not enough for both of us to do, I decided to take up the culture of silk, which was officially encouraged in those times, and with which I had acquainted myself during my travels. Since there were already a few mulberry trees in this place, my attempts were crowned with success, as I produced the first year three pounds of silk. Taking the result of my labor with me to Dresden, I applied to the electoral commissioner of industry for a subsidy on which to continue my business. After I had shown the silk which I had produced myself, I not only received a reward of twenty dollars, but also four hundred young mulberry trees, with the directions for planting them. I planted these trees partly near the city, partly in the cemetery and the rest on the streets. But the mulberry trees that had been so well started were destroyed either by stupid persons or by those that wanted to take revenge on me. When I finally saw that I reaped no reward from my efforts, I grew discouraged and gave up the project of silk-culture.

During my errand in Dresden, in connection with the silk-culture, I took the necessary steps at the sanitary department for admission to the examination of surgeons. I passed my examination and was appointed assistant to my ageing father-in-law.

Bibliography

Akerlof, George. "The Market for Lemons." *Quarterly Journal of Economics* 84 (August 1970): 488–500.

American Archives: Consisting of a Collection of Authentick Records, State Papers, Debates, Letters and Other Notices of Publick Affairs, the Whole Forming a Documentary History of the Origin and Progress of the North American Colonies; of the Causes and Accomplishment of the American Revolution; and of the Constitution of the Government for the United States, to the Final Ratification Thereof. In Six Series. 5th series, vol. 3. Compiled by Peter Force. Washington, D.C., 1853.

Annesley, James. *Memoirs of an Unfortunate Young Nobleman, Returned from Thirteen Years' Slavery in America: A Story Founded on Truth and Addressed Equally to the Head and the Heart.* London: Freeman, 1763.

Anon., ed. "George Erion, The Ragman." *Der Raggeboge: The Rainbow* 11, nos. 3–4 (1977): 3–17.

Appleby, Joyce. *Inheriting the Revolution: The First Generation of Americans.* Cambridge: Harvard University Press, 2000.

Arch, Stephen Carl. *After Franklin: The Emergence of Autobiography in Post-Revolutionary America, 1780–1830.* Hanover: University of New Hampshire Press, 2001.

Ashbridge, Elizabeth. "Some Account of the Fore Part of the Life of Elizabeth Ashbridge." In *Journeys in New Worlds: Early American Women's Narratives,* ed. William L. Andrews, Sargent Bush Jr., Annette Kolodny, Amy Schrager Lang, and Daniel B. Shea, 117–80. Madison: University of Wisconsin Press, 1990.

Atwood, Rodney. *The Hessians: Mercenaries from Hessen-Kassel in the American Revolution.* New York: Cambridge University Press, 1980.

Babb, M. J. "The Relation of David Rittenhouse and His Orrery to the University [of Pennsylvania]." Available at http://www.library.upenn.edu/vanpelt/pennhistory/orrery/orrery.html.

Bach, Jeff. *Voices of the Turtledoves: The Sacred World of Ephrata.* University Park: Pennsylvania State University Press, 2003.

Bailyn, Bernard. *Voyagers to the West: A Passage in the Peopling of America on the Eve of the Revolution.* New York: Knopf, 1986.

Bain, Robert Nisbet. *Charles XII and the Collapse of the Swedish Empire, 1682–1719.* New York: G. P. Putnam's Sons, 1914.

Barker-Benfield, G. J. *The Culture of Sensibility: Sex and Society in Eighteenth-Century Britain.* Chicago: University of Chicago Press, 1992.

Becker, Laura L. "The American Revolution as a Community Experience: A Case Study of Reading, Pennsylvania." Paper delivered at the Conference on the Founding of Pennsylvania, University of Pennsylvania, Philadelphia, October 16, 1982.

Bedell, John, Ingrid Wuebber, Meta Janowitz, Marie-Lorraine Pipes, and Charles H. LeeDecker. *The Ordinary and the Poor in Eighteenth-Century Delaware: Excavations at the Augustine Creek North and South Sites (7NC-G-144 and 7NC -G-145).* Delaware Department of Transportation Series no. 159. Dover, Del.: Delaware Department of Transportation, 2001. Chapter 6 at http:www.deldot.net/static/projects/archaeology/augustine_creek/chapter_6.html.

Beiler, Rosalind J. "The Transatlantic World of Caspar Wistar: From Germany to America in the Eighteenth Century." Ph.D. diss., University of Pennsylvania, 1994.

———. "Distributing Aid to Believers in Need: The Religious Foundations of Transatlantic Migration." *Pennsylvania History: A Journal of Mid-Atlantic Studies* (summer 1997): 73–87.

———. "Caspar Wistar: German-American Entrepreneur and Cultural Broker." In *The Human Tradition in Colonial America*, ed. Ian K. Steele and Nancy L. Rhoden, 161–79. Wilmington, Del.: Scholarly Resources, 1999.

———. "From the Rhine to the Delaware Valley: The Eighteenth-Century Transatlantic Trading Channels of Caspar Wistar." In *In Search of Peace and Prosperity: New German Settlements in Eighteenth-Century Europe and America*, ed. Hartmut T. Lehmann, Hermann Wellenreuther, and Renate Wilson, 172–88. University Park: Pennsylvania State University Press, 2000.

———, trans. "Ein Kortzer Bericht von Caspar Wistar." Typescript in possession of Susan E. Klepp.

Benz, Ernest. "Population Change and the Economy." In *Germany: A New Social and Economic History*. Vol. 2, *1630–1800*, ed. Sheilagh Ogilvie, 39–62. New York: Arnold, 1996.

Berkner, Lutz K. "Inheritance, Land Tenure, and Peasant Family Structure: A German Regional Comparison." In *Family and Inheritance: Rural Society in Western Europe, 1200–1800*, ed. Jack Goody, Joan Thirsk, and E. P. Thompson, 71–95. New York: Cambridge University Press, 1976.

Berks County Tax Lists. Available on microfilm at the Historical Society of Pennsylvania, Philadelphia.

Blusse, Leonard. "One Hundred Weddings and Many More Funerals a Year: Chinese Civil Society in Batavia at the End of the Eighteenth Century." In *The Archives of the Kong Koan of Batavia*, ed. Leonard Blusse and Chen Menghong, 8–28. Leiden: Brill, 2003.

Branson, Susan. *These Fiery Frenchified Dames: Women and Political Culture in Early National Philadelphia*. Philadelphia: University of Pennsylvania Press, 2001.

Brewer, E. C. *Brewer's Dictionary of Phrase and Fable*. London: Cassell & Co., 1957.

Bruijn, J. R., F. S. Gaastra, and I. Schöffer. *Dutch-Asiatic Shipping in the Seventeenth and Eighteenth Centuries*. Vols. 1 and 2. The Hague: Nijhoff, 1979, 1987.

Buck, William J., and Gilbert Cope, comps. "Exeter Monthly Meeting Records." Philadelphia: Genealogical Society of Pennsylvania/Historical Society of Pennsylvania, n.d.

Buel, Richard Jr. *In Irons: British Naval Supremacy and the American Revolutionary Economy*. New Haven: Yale University Press, 1998.

Büttner, Johann Carl. *Büttner, der Amerikaner. Eine Selbstbiographie Johann Carl Büttners, jeßigen Amts-Chirurgus in Senftenberg und ehemaligen nord-amerikanischen Kriegers, Mit dem Bildniße des Versaffers*. Camenz: E. S. Krausche, 1828.

Campe, Joachim Heinrich. *The New Robinson Crusoe; An Instructive and Entertaining History, for the Use of Children of Both Sexes*. London: John Stockdale, 1788. Reprint, New York: Garland, 1976.

Canny, Nicholas, ed. *Europeans on the Move: Studies on European Migration, 1500–1800.* New York: Oxford University Press, 1994.

Chalkley, Thomas. *The Journal of the Life, Travels, and Christian Experiences of that Antient, Faithful Servant of Jesus Christ, Thomas Chalkley, Written by Himself.* 1747. Reprint, New York: Wood, 1808.

Clemens, Paul G. E., and Lucy Simler. "Rural Labor and the Farm Household in Chester County, Pennsylvania, 1750–1820." In *Work and Labor in Early America,* ed. Stephen Innes, 106–43. Chapel Hill: University of North Carolina Press, 1988.

Connor, P. S. "Medical." In *The History of Cincinnati and Hamilton County,* ed. S. B. Nelson and J. M. Runk, 221–39. Cincinnati: Nelson and Company, 1894.

Cook, Kenneth L. "Glimpses of Life in a Frontier Friends Meeting." *Historical Review of Berks County* 60 (summer 1995): 122–23, 126–27, 138–42.

"The Corps of Count von Ottendorf, 1776–1780." In *Pennsylvania in the War of the Revolution, Battalions and Line, 1775–1783,* ed. John B. Lind and William H. Egle. *Pennsylvania Archives,* 2d ser., 2 (1891): 89–99.

Cowley, Abraham. *The Complete Works in Verse and Prose of Abraham Cowley.* 2 vols. Edinburgh: T. and A. Constable, 1881.

Cox, J. Stevens, ed. *The Felon's Account of His Transportation at Virginia in America, by John Lauson.* St. Peters Port, Guernsey: Toucan Press, 1969.

Cribb, Robert. *The Historical Dictionary of Indonesia.* Metuchen, N.J.: Scarecrow Press, 1992.

Culpeper, Nicholas. *Culpeper's Complete Herbal and English Physician.* 1653. Reprint, 1826. Reprint, Leicester, UK: Magna Books, 1992.

Curnock, Nehemiah, ed. *The Journal of the Rev. John Wesley, A.M., Sometime Fellow of Lincoln College, Oxford, Enlarged from Original Mss., with Notes from Unpublished Diaries, Annotations, Maps, and Illustrations.* Vol. 1. London: Robert Culley, 1833.

Davidson, Cathy N. *Revolution and the Word: The Rise of the Novel in America.* New York: Oxford University Press, 1986.

Defoe, Daniel. *Robinson Crusoe.* 1719. Reprint, New York: W. W. Norton, 1975.

Diffenderffer, Frank R. "The German Immigration into Pennsylvania Through the Port of Philadelphia from 1700 to 1775. Part II. The Redemptioners." *Publications of the Pennsylvania German Society* 10 (1899): 1–328.

Documents Relating to the Colonial and Revolutionary History of the State of New Jersey, first series, vol. XXXIV, Calendar of New Jersey Wills, Administrators, Etc., vol. V— 1771–1780. Edited by A. van Doren Honeyman. Trenton: MacCrellish and Quigley, 1931.

Dollinger, Philippe. *The German Hansa.* Stanford: Stanford University Press, 1970.

Drinker, Elizabeth. *The Diary of Elizabeth Drinker.* Edited by Elaine F. Crane. 3 vols. Boston: Northeastern University Press, 1991.

Duck, Stephen. *Poems on Several Occasions.* London: [S. Richardson], 1736.

Durnbaugh, Donald F. "Two Early Letters from Germantown." *Pennsylvania Magazine of History and Biography* 84 (April 1959): 219–33.

Eatwell, John, Murray Milgate, and Peter Newman, eds. *The New Palgrave: A Dictionary of Economics.* Vol. 1. New York: Stockman Press, 1987.

1830 Federal Population Census, Ohio: Index. 2 vols. Columbus: Ohio Library Foundation, 1964.

Eltis, David. "Introduction." In *Coerced and Free Migration: Global Perspectives,* ed. David Eltis, 1–31. Stanford: Stanford University Press, 2002.

Emmer, P. C., ed. *Colonialism and Migration: Indentured Labour Before and After Slavery*. Boston: Martinus Nijhoff, 1986.

Equiano, Olaudah. *The Interesting Narrative and Other Writings*. Edited by Vincent Carretta. New York: Penguin, 1995.

Eshelman, John E. "The Journal of Moses Roberts—A Minister of Oley." *Historical Review of Berks County* 8 (April 1943): 70–74.

———. "Descendants of Moses and Deborah Starr—Early Quaker Settlers of Maiden Creek Valley." *Historical Review of Berks County* 12 (April 1947): 67–74.

Esposito, Vincent J. *The West Point Atlas of American Wars*. Vol. 1, 1689–1900. New York: Henry Holt and Co., 1995.

Fabian, Ann. *The Unvarnished Truth: Personal Narratives in Nineteenth-Century America*. Berkeley and Los Angeles: University of California Press, 2000.

"Family Group Data Sheet: Friedrich Marcus Montelius I (1752–1805)." www.family pangaea.net /MonteliusMainPage.htm.

Fertig, Georg. "Transatlantic Migration from German-Speaking Parts of Central Europe, 1600–1800: Proportions, Structures, and Explanations." In *Europeans on the Move: Studies on European Migration, 1500–1800*, ed. Nicholas Canny, 192–235. New York: Oxford University Press, 1994.

Fogelman, Aaron S. *Hopeful Journeys: German Immigration, Settlement, and Political Culture in Colonial America, 1717–1775*. Philadelphia: University of Pennsylvania Press, 1996.

———. "From Slaves, Convicts, and Servants to Free Passengers: The Transformation of Immigration in the Era of the American Revolution." *Journal of American History* 85 (June 1998): 43–74.

Franklin, Benjamin. *Memoirs*. Edited by Max Farrand. Berkeley and Los Angeles: University of California Press, 1949.

Friends' Meeting Records of Berks County. Compiled from the original by John E. Eshelman. Bound volume of photocopied originals. Historical Society of Berks County, Reading, Pennsylvania.

Frost, J. William. *The Quaker Family in Colonial America*. New York: St. Martin's Press, 1973.

Galenson, David W. *White Servitude in Colonial America*. New York: Cambridge University Press, 1981.

Geiser, Karl Frederick. *Redemptioners and Indentured Servants in the Colony and Commonwealth of Pennsylvania*. New Haven: Tuttle, Morehouse & Taylor, 1901.

Gestrich, Andreas. "German Religious Emigration to Russia in the Eighteenth and Early Nineteenth Centuries." In *In Search of Peace and Prosperity: New German Settlements in Eighteenth-Century Europe and America*, ed. Hartmut T. Lehmann, Hermann Wellenreuther, and Renate Wilson, 77–98. University Park: Pennsylvania State University Press, 2000.

Goethe, Johann Wolfgang von. *Memoirs of Goethe: Written by Himself (Aus Meinem Leben, Dichtung und Wahrheit)*. London: Henry Colburn, 1824.

Grabbe, Hans-Jurgen. "European Immigration to the United States in the Early National Period, 1783–1820." *Proceedings of the American Philosophical Society* 133 (June 1989): 190–214.

Graham, Robert Earle. "The Taverns of Colonial Philadelphia." *Transactions of the American Philosophical Society* 43, part 1 (1953): 318–25.

Grubb, Farley. "Immigrant Servant Labor: Their Occupational and Geographic Distribution in the Late Eighteenth-Century Mid-Atlantic Economy." *Social Science History* 9 (summer 1985): 249–75.

———. "The Incidence of Servitude in Trans-Atlantic Migration, 1771–1804." *Explorations in Economic History* 22 (July 1985): 316–39.

———. "Redemptioner Immigration to Pennsylvania: Evidence on Contract Choice and Profitability." *Journal of Economic History* 46 (June 1986): 407–18.

———. "Colonial Immigrant Literacy: An Economic Analysis of Pennsylvania-German Evidence, 1727–1775." *Explorations in Economic History* 24 (January 1987): 63–76.

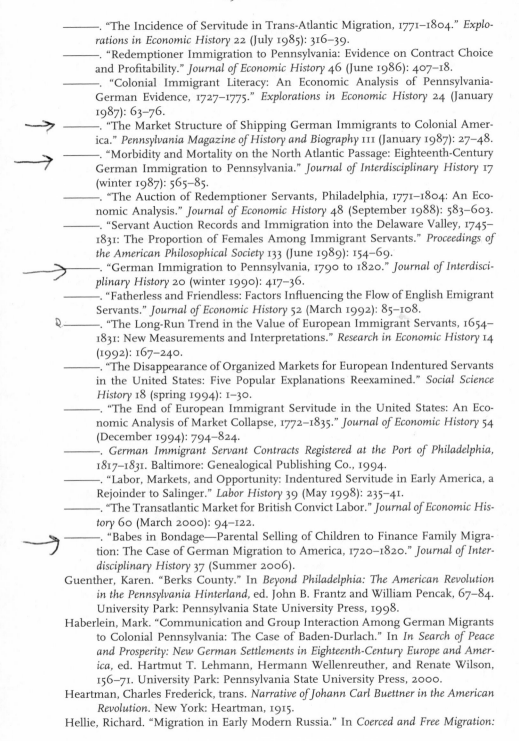———. "The Market Structure of Shipping German Immigrants to Colonial America." *Pennsylvania Magazine of History and Biography* 111 (January 1987): 27–48.

———. "Morbidity and Mortality on the North Atlantic Passage: Eighteenth-Century German Immigration to Pennsylvania." *Journal of Interdisciplinary History* 17 (winter 1987): 565–85.

———. "The Auction of Redemptioner Servants, Philadelphia, 1771–1804: An Economic Analysis." *Journal of Economic History* 48 (September 1988): 583–603.

———. "Servant Auction Records and Immigration into the Delaware Valley, 1745–1831: The Proportion of Females Among Immigrant Servants." *Proceedings of the American Philosophical Society* 133 (June 1989): 154–69.

———. "German Immigration to Pennsylvania, 1790 to 1820." *Journal of Interdisciplinary History* 20 (winter 1990): 417–36.

———. "Fatherless and Friendless: Factors Influencing the Flow of English Emigrant Servants." *Journal of Economic History* 52 (March 1992): 85–108.

———. "The Long-Run Trend in the Value of European Immigrant Servants, 1654–1831: New Measurements and Interpretations." *Research in Economic History* 14 (1992): 167–240.

———. "The Disappearance of Organized Markets for European Indentured Servants in the United States: Five Popular Explanations Reexamined." *Social Science History* 18 (spring 1994): 1–30.

———. "The End of European Immigrant Servitude in the United States: An Economic Analysis of Market Collapse, 1772–1835." *Journal of Economic History* 54 (December 1994): 794–824.

———. *German Immigrant Servant Contracts Registered at the Port of Philadelphia, 1817–1831.* Baltimore: Genealogical Publishing Co., 1994.

———. "Labor, Markets, and Opportunity: Indentured Servitude in Early America, a Rejoinder to Salinger." *Labor History* 39 (May 1998): 235–41.

———. "The Transatlantic Market for British Convict Labor." *Journal of Economic History* 60 (March 2000): 94–122.

———. "Babes in Bondage—Parental Selling of Children to Finance Family Migration: The Case of German Migration to America, 1720–1820." *Journal of Interdisciplinary History* 37 (Summer 2006).

Guenther, Karen. "Berks County." In *Beyond Philadelphia: The American Revolution in the Pennsylvania Hinterland,* ed. John B. Frantz and William Pencak, 67–84. University Park: Pennsylvania State University Press, 1998.

Haberlein, Mark. "Communication and Group Interaction Among German Migrants to Colonial Pennsylvania: The Case of Baden-Durlach." In *In Search of Peace and Prosperity: New German Settlements in Eighteenth-Century Europe and America,* ed. Hartmut T. Lehmann, Hermann Wellenreuther, and Renate Wilson, 156–71. University Park: Pennsylvania State University Press, 2000.

Heartman, Charles Frederick, trans. *Narrative of Johann Carl Buettner in the American Revolution.* New York: Heartman, 1915.

Hellie, Richard. "Migration in Early Modern Russia." In *Coerced and Free Migration:*

Global Perspectives, ed. David Eltis, 292–323. Stanford: Stanford University Press, 2002.

Hinshaw, William Wade. *Encyclopedia of American Quaker Genealogy*. Vol. 5. Ann Arbor, 1940. Reprint, Baltimore: Genealogical Publishing Company, 1973, 1974.

Hinz, Johannes. *Pommern: Wegweiser Durch ein Unvergessenes Land*. Augsburg: Bechtermuenz Verlag, 1997.

Historical Statistics of the United States: Colonial Times to 1970. Washington D.C.: U.S. Bureau of the Census, 1975.

Hood, Adrienne D. *The Weaver's Craft: Cloth, Commerce, and Industry in Early Pennsylvania*. Philadelphia: University of Pennsylvania Press, 2003.

Ireland, Owen. *Religion, Ethnicity, and Politics: Ratifying the Constitution in Pennsylvania*. University Park: Pennsylvania State University Press, 1995.

Israel, Jonathan. *The Dutch Republic: Its Rise, Greatness, and Fall*. New York: Oxford University Press, 1995.

Jordan, Louis. *Colonial Currency: A Project of the Robert H. Gore, Jr. Numismatic Endowment*. University of Notre Dame, Department of Special Collections. http.//www.coins.nd.edu/ColCurrency (accessed August 31, 2003).

Jütte, Robert. "Poor and Poverty Relief." In *Germany: A New Social and Economic History*. Vol. 2, *1630–1800*, ed. Sheilagh Ogilvie, 377–404. New York: Arnold, 1996.

Kelsey, R. W. "An Early Description of Pennsylvania. Letter of Christopher Sower, Written in 1724, Describing Conditions in Philadelphia and Vicinity, and the Sea Voyage from Europe." *Pennsylvania Magazine of History and Biography* 45 (1921): 243–54.

Kent, Daniel. *Letters and Other Papers of Daniel Kent, Emigrant and Redemptioner, to which have been added a few interesting Hawley and Spackman Papers*. Compiled by Ella K. Barnard. Baltimore, 1904.

Kiple, Kenneth F., ed. *The Cambridge World History of Human Disease*. New York: Cambridge University Press, 1993.

Kleiner, John W., and Helmut T. Lehmann, eds. and trans. *The Correspondence of Heinrich Melchior Muhlenberg*. Vol. 1, *1740–1747*. Vol. 2, *1748–1752*. Camden, Maine: Picton Press, 1993, 1997.

Klepp, Susan E. *Philadelphia in Transition: A Demographic History of the City and Its Occupational Groups, 1720–1830*. New York: Garland, 1989.

———. "Encounter and Experiment: The Colonial Period." In *Pennsylvania: A History of the Commonwealth*, ed. Randall M. Miller and William Pencak, 47–100. University Park: Pennsylvania State University Press, 2002.

———, ed. *The Demographic History of the Philadelphia Region, 1600–1860*. Philadelphia: American Philosophical Society, 1989. Also published in *Proceedings of the American Philosophical Society* 133 (June 1989): 81–338.

Klepp, Susan E., and Billy G. Smith, eds. *The Infortunate: The Voyage and Adventures of William Moraley, an Indentured Servant*. University Park: Pennsylvania State University Press, 1992. Rev. ed. 2005.

Klepp, Susan E., and Karin A. Wulf. *A Novel Life: The Diary of Hannah Callender Sansom, 1757–1787*. Pennsylvania State University Press, forthcoming.

Lagerlof, Selma. "Die Stadt auf dem Meeresgrunde." In *Pommersche Erzaehler: Heiteres und Besinnliches*, ed. Lagerlot, 65–73. Tübingen: Horst Erdmann Verlag, 1973.

Lake, Devereux. *A Personal Narrative of Some Branches of the Lake Family in America*. Lorain, Ohio: Lorain Printing Co., 1937.

Langguth, Otto. "Pennsylvania German Pioneers from the County of Wertheim."

Edited and translated by Don Yoder. *Pennsylvania German Folklore Society* 12 (1947): 149–289.

Lehmann, Hartmut T. "Transatlantic Migration, Transatlantic Networks, Transatlantic Transfer." In *In Search of Peace and Prosperity: New German Settlements in Eighteenth-Century Europe and America*, ed. Hartmut T. Lehmann, Hermann Wellenreuther, and Renate Wilson, 307–30. University Park: Pennsylvania State University Press, 2000.

Lehmann, Hartmut T., Hermann Wellenreuther, and Renate Wilson, eds. *In Search of Peace and Prosperity: New German Settlements in Eighteenth-Century Europe and America*. University Park: Pennsylvania State University Press, 2000.

Lemon, James T. *"The Best Poor Man's Country": A Geographical Study of Early Southeastern Pennsylvania*. Baltimore: Johns Hopkins University Press, 1972.

Levy, Barry. *Quakers and the American Family: British Settlement in the Delaware Valley*. New York: Oxford University Press, 1988.

Lewis, Jan. "The Republican Wife: Virtue and Seduction in the Early Republic." *William and Mary Quarterly*, 3d ser., 44 (October 1987): 689–721.

Lowell, Edward J. *The Hessians and Other German Auxiliaries of Great Britain in the Revolutionary War*. New York: Harper, 1884.

Lucassen, Jan. "The Netherlands, the Dutch, and Long-Distance Migration in the Late Sixteenth to Early Nineteenth Centuries." In *Europeans on the Move: Studies on European Migration, 1500–1800*, ed. Nicholas Canny, 153–91. New York: Oxford University Press, 1994.

———. "A Multinational and Its Labor Force: The Dutch East India Company, 1595–1795." *International Labor and Working-Class History* 66 (fall 2004): 12–39.

MacManus, George S., ed. *Memoirs of Charles N. Buck: Interspersed with Private Anecdotes and Events of the Times from 1791 to 1841*. Philadelphia: Walnut House, 1941.

Maidencreek Tax Lists. Microfilm of the originals. Historical Society of Pennsylvania, Philadelphia.

Manuscript Census Returns. Catawissa Township, Pennsylvania, under Whitehall.

McCusker, John J. *Money and Exchange in Europe and America, 1600–1775: A Handbook*. Chapel Hill: University of North Carolina Press, 1978.

———. "Comparing the Purchasing Power of Money in Great Britain from 1264 to Any Other Year Including the Present." Economic History Services, 2001. http://www.eh.net/hmit/ppowerbp/ (accessed August 25, 2003).

McCusker, John J., and Russell R. Menard. *The Economy of British America, 1607–1789*. Chapel Hill: University of North Carolina Press, 1985.

Merrill, Michael, and Sean Wilentz. *The Key of Liberty: The Life and Democratic Writings of William Manning, "A Laborer," 1747–1814*. Cambridge: Harvard University Press, 1993.

Miscellaneous Collection, Box 9c, White Servitude Folder f. 1. Historical Society of Pennsylvania, Philadelphia.

Mittelberger, Gottlieb. *Journey to Pennsylvania in the Year 1750 and Return to Germany in the Year 1754*. Translated by Carl Theo. Eben. Philadelphia: Joseph Y. Jeanes, 1898.

———. *Journey to Pennsylvania*. Edited and translated by Oscar Handlin and John Clive. Cambridge: Harvard University Press, 1960.

Mitterauer, Michael, and Reinhard Sieder. *The European Family: Patriarchy to Partnership from the Middle Ages to the Present*. Oxford: Basil Blackwell, 1982.

Moltmann, Guenter. "Three Hundred Years of German Emigration to North America."

In *Germans to America: Three Hundred Years of Immigration, 1683–1983*, ed. Guenter Moltmann, 8–15. Stuttgart: Foreign Cultural Relations, in cooperation with Inter Nations, Bonn-Bad Godesberg, 1982.

———. "The Migration of German Redemptioners to North America." In *Colonialism and Migration: Indentured Labour Before and After Slavery*, ed. P. C. Emmer, 105–22. Boston: Martinus Nijhoff, 1986.

Montgomery, Morton L. *Political Hand Book of Berks County*. Reading, Pa.: B. F. Owen, 1883.

———. *The History of Berks County, in Pennsylvania*. Philadelphia: Everts, Peck and Richards, 1886.

———. *Historical and Biographical Annals of Berks County, Pennsylvania*. 2 vols. Chicago: Beers, 1909.

Muhlenberg, Henry Melchior. *The Journals of Henry Melchior Muhlenberg*. 3 vols. Translated by Theodore G. Tappert and John W. Doberstein. Philadelphia: Muhlenberg Press, 1942.

"Munstering [Mustering] Book for the *Britannia* Capt. James Peters from Rotterdam 3rd July 1773." Manuscript, AM 209. Historical Society of Pennsylvania, Philadelphia.

Nash, Gary B. "Poverty and Politics in Early American History." In *Down and Out in Early America*, ed. Billy G. Smith, 1–37. University Park: Pennsylvania State University Press, 2004.

Newman, Eric P. *The Early Paper Money of America*. 4th ed. Iola, Wisc.: Krause Publications, 1997.

Newman, Simon P. *Parades and the Politics of the Street: Festive Culture in the Early American Republic*. Philadelphia: University of Pennsylvania Press, 1997.

Nolt, Steven M. *Foreigners in Their Own Land: Pennsylvania Germans in the Early Republic*. University Park: Pennsylvania State University Press, 2002.

Nussbaum, Felicity. *The Autobiographical Subject: Gender and Ideology in Eighteenth-Century England*. Baltimore: Johns Hopkins University Press, 1989.

Ohio 1820 Census, Index A-Z. Bountiful, Utah: Heritage Quest, 1999.

Officer, Lawrence J. *Between the Dollar-Sterling Gold Points: Exchange Rates, Parity, and Market Behavior*. New York: Cambridge University Press, 1996.

O'Reilly, William. "To the East or to the West? German Migration in the Eighteenth Century: A Comparative Perspective." Paper delivered at the Philadelphia [now McNeil] Center for Early American Studies, March 21, 1997.

———. "Conceptualizing America in Early Modern Central Europe." *Explorations in Early American Culture*, supplement to *Pennsylvania History: A Journal of Mid-Atlantic Studies* 65 (1998): 101–21.

Ozment, Steven. *The Bürgermeister's Daughter: Scandal in a Sixteenth-Century German Town*. New York: St. Martin's Press, 1996.

Penn, William. *Some Fruits of Solitude in Reflections and Maxims*. In *The Harvard Classics*, ed. Charles W. Elliot. 1682. Reprint, New York: Collier, 1909.

Pennsylvania Archives, 2d Series, vol. 11. Harrisburg, Pa.: E. K. Meyers 1890.

Pennsylvania Archives, 3d Series, vol. 18. Harrisburg, Pa.: William Stanley Ray, 1897.

Pennsylvania Gazette, August 27, September 1, October 6, October 20, and November 10, 1773, and July 12, 1775.

Pennsylvania in 1800: A Computerized Index to the 1800 Federal Population Schedules of the State of Pennsylvania. Edited by John "D" Stemmons. Salt Lake City: Stemmons, 1972.

Pennsylvania Journal and Weekly Advertiser, June 14, 1775.

Pesch, Dieter, ed. *Brave New World: Rhinelanders Conquer America; The Journal of Johannes Herbergs*. Kommern: Martina Galunder-Verlag, 2001.

Pfaelzer de Ortiz, Anne M. "German Redemptioners of the Lower Sort: Apolitical Soldiers in the American Revolution?" *Journal of American Studies* 33 (August 1999): 267–306.

Pollak, Otto. "German Immigrant Problems in Eighteenth-Century Pennsylvania as Reflected in Trouble Advertisements." *American Sociological Review* 8 (December 1943): 674–84.

Pommerschen Zeitung no. 342, December 11, 1940. Reprint of article of December 12, 1770. Stadtarchiv der Hansestadt Stralsund.

Population Schedules of the Third Census of the United States, 1810, Roll 53, Pennsylvania. Washington, D.C.: National Archives, 1953.

Record of Indentures of Individuals Bound Out as Apprentices, Servants, Etc. and of German and Other Redemptioners in the Office of the Mayor of the City of Philadelphia, October 3, 1771, to October 5, 1773. Lancaster, Pa.: Pennsylvania German Society, 1907.

Records of the Trinity Evangelical Lutheran Church, 1751–1812: Baptisms, Marriages, Burials, Confirmations, and Communions. Bound photocopies of originals (n.p., n.d.). Historical Society of Berks County, Reading, Pennsylvania.

Richardson, Samuel. *Pamela, or Virtue Rewarded*. 1741.

———. *Clarissa; or, The History of a Young Lady; Comprehending the Most Important Concerns of Private Life*. 1747–48.

Riedesel, Friederike Charlotte Louise von. *Baroness von Riedesel and the American Revolution: Journal and Correspondence of a Tour of Duty, 1776–1783*. Edited and translated by Marvin L. Brown, with Martha Huth. Chapel Hill: University of North Carolina Press, 1965.

Rigal, Laura. *The American Manufactory: Art, Labor, and the World of Things in the Early Republic*. Princeton: Princeton University Press, 1998.

Riley, Edward M., ed. *The Journal of John Harrower, an Indentured Servant in the Colony of Virginia, 1773 to 1776*. New York: Holt, Rinehart & Winston, 1963.

Roberts, Michael. *The Age of Liberty: Sweden, 1719–1772*. New York: Cambridge University Press, 1986.

Roeber, A. G. *Palatines, Liberty, and Property: German Lutherans in Colonial British America*. Baltimore: Johns Hopkins University Press, 1993.

Rogers, Pat. *Robinson Crusoe*. London: Allen & Unwin, 1979.

Room, Adrian. *Dictionary of Astronomical Names*. London: Routledge, 1988.

Rosengarten, J. G. *The German Allied Troops in the North American War of Independence, 1776–1783*. Translated by Max Von Eelking. Albany, N.Y.: Joel Munsell's Sons, 1893.

Rothermund, Dietmar. *The Layman's Progress: Religious and Political Experience in Colonial Pennsylvania, 1740–1770*. Philadelphia: University of Pennsylvania Press, 1961.

Sabean, David. "Aspects of Kinship Behavior and Property in Rural Western Europe Before 1800." In *Family and Inheritance: Rural Society in Western Europe, 1200–1800*, ed. Jack Goody, Joan Thirsk, and E. P. Thompson, 96–111. New York: Cambridge University Press, 1976.

———. *Property, Production, and Family in Neckarhausen, 1700–1870*. New York: Cambridge University Press, 1990.

Sachse, Julius F. "A Missive from Pennsylvania in the Year of Grace 1728." *Publications of the Pennsylvania German Society* 28 (1909): 5–25.

Saffell, W. T. R. *Records of the Revolutionary War*. Philadelphia: G. G. Evans, 1860.

Schoepf, Johann David. *Travels in the Confederation, 1783–1784*. New York: Arno, 1968.

Scott, Franklin D. *Sweden: The Nation's History*. Carbondale: Southern Illinois University Press, 1988.

Sebba, Gregor. "Introduction: Goethe's Autobiography, Truth or Fiction?" In *The Autobiography of Johann Wolfgang Von Goethe*, trans. John Oxenford. New York: Horizon Press, 1969.

Selig, Robert A. "Germans and German-Americans in the Continental Army, 1775–1783." *German Life* (November 2001), available at http://www.germanlife.com/ Archives/2001/0110-01.html.

"Ships Registered for the Port of Philadelphia, 1727–1775." *Pennsylvania Magazine of History and Biography* 26 (1903): 482–98.

Simler, Lucy. "She Came to Work: The Female Labor Force in Chester County." Paper given at the Seminar of the Transformation of Philadelphia and the Delaware Valley Project, Philadelphia, May 11, 1987.

———. "The Landless Worker: An Index of Economic and Social Change in Chester County, Pennsylvania, 1750–1820." *Pennsylvania Magazine of History and Biography* 114 (April 1990): 163–99.

Smaby, Beverly Prior. *The Transformation of Moravian Bethlehem: From Communal Mission to Family Economy*. Philadelphia: University of Pennsylvania Press, 1988.

Smith, Abbot Emerson. *Colonists in Bondage*. New York: W. W. Norton, 1947.

Smith, Alfred, comp. *Abstracts of Bucks County Wills, 1798–1825*. Vol. 2. Philadelphia: Genealogical Society of Pennsylvania, 1898.

Smith, Billy G. "Death and Life in a Colonial Immigrant City: A Demographic Analysis of Philadelphia." *Journal of Economic History* 37 (December 1977): 863–89.

———. "Introduction: 'The Best Poor Man's Country'?" In *Down and Out in Early America*, ed. Billy G. Smith, xi–xx. University Park: Pennsylvania State University Press, 2004.

Smits, Jan. "Mathematical Data for Bibliographic Descriptions of Cartographic Materials and Spatial Data." Available at the Koninklijke Bibliotheek website, http:// www.kb.nl/ kb/resources/frameset_kb.html?/ kb/skd/skd/mathemat.html.

Smyth, W. H. *The Sailor's Word-Book: An Alphabetical Digest of Nautical Terms, including some more Especially Military and Scientific, but Useful to Seamen as well as Archiaisms of Early Voyagers, Etc.* 1867. Reprint, London: Conway Maritime Press, 1991.

Soltow, Lee, and Kenneth W. Keller. "Rural Pennsylvania in 1800: A Portrait from the Septennial Census." *Pennsylvania History* 49 (January 1982): 25–47.

Spacks, Patricia Meyer. *Imagining a Self: Autobiography and Novel in Eighteenth-Century England*. Cambridge: Harvard University Press, 1976.

Starr, Jeremiah. *A California Adventure and Vision: Prose and Poetry*. Cincinnati, 1864.

Stauffer, W.T., trans. "Hans Stauffer Note-Books." *Perkiomen Region* 10, no. 3 (1932): 95–114.

Stivers, Camilla. "Reflections on the Role of Personal Narrative in Social Science." *Signs: Journal of Women in Culture and Society* 18 (winter 1993): 408–25.

Stone, Lawrence. *The Family, Sex, and Marriage in England, 1500–1800*. New York: Harper, 1977.

Strassburger, Ralph B. *Pennsylvania German Pioneers: A Publication of the Original Lists of Arrivals in the Port of Philadelphia from 1727 to 1808*. Vols. 1–3. Edited by William J. Hinke. Norristown, Pa.: Pennsylvania German Society, 1934.

Stryker-Rodda, Kenn. "New Jersey Rateables, 1773–1774." *Genealogical Magazine of New Jersey* 36 (1961): 49–55, 121–30; 37 (1962): 24–32, 71–79, 114–21; 38 (1963): 8–12, 56–64, 129–37; 39 (1964): 8–16, 90–96, 136–44; 40 (1965): 34–46, 87–96, 127–44.

Tepper, Michael, ed. *Emigrants to Pennsylvania, 1641–1819*. Baltimore: Genealogical Publishing Co., 1978.

Tilton, James. "Dear Sir." Letter from Princeton, February 17, 1778. Papers of Dr. James Tilton, Bureau of Archives and Record Management, Hall of Records, Dover, Delaware.

Trautmann, Frederic. "Pennsylvania Through a German's Eyes: The Travels of Ludwig Gall, 1819–1820." *Pennsylvania Magazine of History and Biography* 105 (January 1981): 35–65.

U.S. Bureau of the Census. *Heads of Families at the First Census of the United States taken in the Year 1790: Pennsylvania*. Washington, D.C.: U.S. Government Printing Office, 1908.

"U.S. Dollar: Historical Exchange Rates." http://www.triacom.com/archive/exchange.en.html (accessed August 25, 2003).

Vries, Jan de. *European Urbanization, 1500–1800*. Cambridge: Harvard University Press, 1984.

Wainwright, Nicholas B. "The Diary of Samuel Breck, 1814–1822." *Pennsylvania Magazine of History and Biography* 102 (October 1978): 469–508.

Waldstreicher, David. *In the Midst of Perpetual Fetes: The Making of American Nationalism, 1776–1820*. Chapel Hill: University of North Carolina Press, 1997.

———. *Runaway America: Benjamin Franklin, Slavery, and the American Revolution*. New York: Hill and Wang, 2004.

Weaver, William Woys, ed. and trans. *Sauer's Herbal Cures: America's First Book of Botanic Healing, 1762–1778*. New York: Routledge, 2001.

Wellenreuther, Hermann. "Contexts for Migration in the Early Modern World: Public Policy, European Migrating Experiences, Transatlantic Migration, and the Genesis of American Culture." In *In Search of Peace and Prosperity: New German Settlements in Eighteenth-Century Europe and America*, ed. Hartmut T. Lehmann, Hermann Wellenreuther, and Renate Wilson, 3–35. University Park: Pennsylvania State University Press, 2000.

———. "Recent Research on Migration." In *In Search of Peace and Prosperity: New German Settlements in Eighteenth-Century Europe and America*, ed Hartmut T. Lehmann, Hermann Wellenreuther, and Renate Wilson, 265–306. University Park: Pennsylvania State University Press, 2000.

Wellenreuther, Hermann, and Kurt Alands, eds. *Die Korrespondenz Heinrich Melchior Muhlenbergs: Aus der Anfangszeit des Deutschen Luthertums in Nordamerika, 1777–1787*. Berlin: Walter De Gruyter, 2003.

Williamson, Peter. *The Life and Curious Adventures of Peter Williamson, Who Was Carried Off from Aberdeen and Sold for a Slave*. Aberdeen, 1804.

Wilson, Renate. *Pious Traders in Medicine: A German Pharmaceutical Network in Eighteenth-Century North America*. University Park: Pennsylvania State University Press, 2000.

Wokeck, Marianna S. *Trade in Strangers: The Beginnings of Mass Migration to North America*. University Park: Pennsylvania State University Press, 1999.

———. "German Settlements in the British North American Colonies: A Patchwork of Cultural Assimilation and Persistence." In *In Search of Peace and Prosperity: New German Settlements in Eighteenth-Century Europe and America*, ed. Hartmut

T. Lehmann, Hermann Wellenreuther, and Renate Wilson, 191–216. University Park: Pennsylvania State University Press, 2000.

Wolf, Stephanie Grauman. *Urban Village: Population, Community, and Family Structure in Germantown, Pennsylvania, 1683–1800.* Princeton: Princeton University Press, 1976.

Zeithe, Wilhelm. "Mein Lehr und Wanderjahre." Available at http://www.dewarim.de/de/texte/z1.html (accessed June 18, 2005).

Zimmern, Helen. *The Hansa Towns.* London: T. Fisher Unwin, 1889.

Index

Ottendorf, Nicholas Dietrich, Baron von, 190–92, 231–33

Parvin, Francis, Jr., 144
Parvin, John, 39, 154, 156
Pearson, Thomas (schoolmaster), 39, 45, 48, 52, 52 n. 1
Pearson, Thomas (weaver), 154–55
penmanship, 48, 66–67, 178
Penn, William, 224
Pennsylvania, 224–25
Pennsylvania Gazette, 177, 181–82
Penrose, Jesse, 154–55
Philadelphia
    Büttner in, 177–84, 219–22, 231–32, 243–44
    description of, 220–21
    Whitehead in, 134–41, 151–52, 177–78
physical fitness, 203
Pittius of Nussdorf (grandfather of Büttner), 202
poetry (of Whitehead). *See also* literacy
    on farming, 157, 159–62
    on God, 67
    on ignorance, 101
    on nature, 158
    on Pomerania, 92–93, 102–3, 116–17, 160–61
    on solitude, 118–19
    on virtue, 126
Pomerania, 28–30, 92–93, 102–3, 116–17, 160–61. *See also* Stralsund
Portsmouth, 127–28, 216
postservitude period, xiv, 38–43, 151–59, 190–94, 231–51
Potts, Jonathan, 143
Praetorius (teacher), 204
Prague, 206
prefaces, 52–55, 201
privateering, 194, 244–46

Quakers, 226

Rall, Johann Gottlieb, 248
Ray, Nathaniel, 11–13
Record of Indentures, 178–79, 182, 183, 184
recreation
    Büttner and, 195, 206, 207, 215, 244
    with recruiters, 113–19, 195, 215
    Whitehead and, 54–55, 66, 75–76, 113–19, 123–24, 195
recruitment
    by agents, xiv, 100–101, 106–22, 173, 175–77, 195–96, 213–16
    of Büttner, 175–77, 195–96, 213–16

contracts for, 175, 196
    by Dutch East India Company, 101, 214–15
    kidnapping and, xiv, 196
    for migration, xiv, 23, 100–101, 106–22
    by United Netherlands Chartered East India Company (VOC), xiv, 8–9, 19, 175–77, 195–96, 214–15
    of Whitehead, 100–101, 121–22, 176–77, 195
Red Bank, battle of, 192–93, 236 n. 69, 238–40
redemption system. *See also* indentured servitude
    Büttner in, 176–84, 221–22
    destination under, 180–82
    indentured servitude compared, 16–19
    kidnapping and, xiv, 196
    length of service under, 178–80, 196, 221–22
    migration and, 195–96
    oaths and, 177
    process of, 13–20, 195–97, 221–22
    Whitehead in, 136–40
Reeser, John, Jr., 151 n. 316
Reeser, John, Sr., 151
religion
    in Berks County, 36–37
    Büttner and, 193, 202, 203, 206, 210–11, 218, 219, 220, 226
    marriage and, 32
    migration and, 6
    Whitehead and, 39, 84–85, 92, 96, 104–5, 108, 127, 129, 131–32, 134–35, 168 n. 370
Richardson, Samuel, 45, 59 n. 29
Rittenhouse, David, 140–41
Ritter, Jacob, 205
Robinson Crusoe, 22
Roesser, 250
romance
    in autobiographies, 22–23
    of Büttner, 247, 248, 251
    of Flinton, Mary, 45, 70–75
    Whitehead on, 59, 80–83
Rose (merchant), 98
Rose, Gottfried Carl, 127
Ruma, 210
runaways, 106–7, 186–90, 227–30
Russia, 8

Sally
    accident on, 127
    Büttner on, xiii, 1, 4, 5, 177, 216–19
    food on, 123, 126–27, 131, 133, 177, 196–97, 219